Italian and Italian American Studies

Series Editor
Stanislao G. Pugliese
Hofstra University
Hempstead, NY, USA

This series brings the latest scholarship in Italian and Italian American history, literature, cinema, and cultural studies to a large audience of specialists, general readers, and students. Featuring works on modern Italy (Renaissance to the present) and Italian American culture and society by established scholars as well as new voices, it has been a longstanding force in shaping the evolving fields of Italian and Italian American Studies by re-emphasizing their connection to one another.

Editorial Board
Rebecca West, University of Chicago, USA
Josephine Gattuso Hendin, New York University, USA
Fred Gardaphé, Queens College, CUNY, USA
Phillip V. Cannistraro†, Queens College and the Graduate School, CUNY, USA
Alessandro Portelli, Università di Roma "La Sapienza", Italy
William J. Connell, Seton Hall University, USA

More information about this series at
http://www.palgrave.com/gp/series/14835

Gianluca Fantoni

Italy through the Red Lens

Italian Politics and Society in Communist Propaganda Films (1946–79)

Gianluca Fantoni
Nottingham Trent University
Nottingham, UK

ISSN 2635-2931   ISSN 2635-294X   (electronic)
Italian and Italian American Studies
ISBN 978-3-030-69196-7   ISBN 978-3-030-69197-4   (eBook)
https://doi.org/10.1007/978-3-030-69197-4

© The Editor(s) (if applicable) and The Author(s), under exclusive licence to Springer Nature Switzerland AG 2021
This work is subject to copyright. All rights are solely and exclusively licensed by the Publisher, whether the whole or part of the material is concerned, specifically the rights of translation, reprinting, reuse of illustrations, recitation, broadcasting, reproduction on microfilms or in any other physical way, and transmission or information storage and retrieval, electronic adaptation, computer software, or by similar or dissimilar methodology now known or hereafter developed.
The use of general descriptive names, registered names, trademarks, service marks, etc. in this publication does not imply, even in the absence of a specific statement, that such names are exempt from the relevant protective laws and regulations and therefore free for general use.
The publisher, the authors and the editors are safe to assume that the advice and information in this book are believed to be true and accurate at the date of publication. Neither the publisher nor the authors or the editors give a warranty, expressed or implied, with respect to the material contained herein or for any errors or omissions that may have been made. The publisher remains neutral with regard to jurisdictional claims in published maps and institutional affiliations.

Cover illustration: PieroAnnoni

This Palgrave Macmillan imprint is published by the registered company Springer Nature Switzerland AG.
The registered company address is: Gewerbestrasse 11, 6330 Cham, Switzerland

Acknowledgements

Writing a book has a lot to do with who we are. Our initial decision to investigate a particular topic, the way we approach it, and our assumptions about the thing we want to understand are all determined by our biography. I imagine, for example, that the fact that my parents were Communists and my older brother a professional photographer will in some way have influenced my decision to study the visual propaganda of the Italian Communist Party. There are therefore probably many people whom I should thank for their contributions to this book, however small or distant in time, and I hope they will forgive me if I do not attempt to name them all. Fortunately, the help and support I received from some people is still very fresh in my memory.

Most of the research for this book was undertaken while I was at the University of Strathclyde. I want to thank all my colleagues there, especially in Modern Languages and History, and those in Italian Studies above all: what a fantastic team! I would like to emphasize my particular debt of thanks to Professor Philip Cooke. My gratitude also goes to my colleagues at Nottingham Trent University, where this book found its final shape, and especially to Sophie Fuggle and Samuel Barclay. I should also thank Professor Stephen Gundle (University of Warwick).

Many individuals and organizations provided me with access to crucial information. These include the Archivio Audiovisivo del Movimento Operaio e Democratico in Rome (and its staff, in particular Letizia Cortini, Claudio Olivieri, Milena Fiore, and Antonio Mannocchi) and the Fondazione Istituto Gramsci in Rome (and its staff, especially Giovanna Bosman, Cristina Pipitone, and Dario Massimi). Special gratitude goes to the head librarian of the Biblioteca del Cinema Umberto Barbaro in Rome, Angelo Salvatori. I am also indebted to the people who allowed me to interview them: Carlo Lizzani, Mino Argentieri, Ansano Giannarelli, Paola Scarnati, and Luciano Vanni. Marzia Maccaferri and Rosario Forlenza read the first draft of the book and offered valuable advice. Stuart Oglethorpe both translated the original Italian quotations into English and copy-edited the entire manuscript: he did a great job.

Finally, my thanks go to Dr Giuliana Tiripelli, with whom I shared this adventure alongside many others.

CONTENTS

1 Introduction   1

Part I The Italian Communist Party between Socialist Realism and Neorealism (1944–1956)   17

2 Togliatti's *Partito nuovo* and Italian Cinema   19

3 Socialist Realism Italian-Style: PCI Cinematic Propaganda in the Stalin Era   45

Part II Dealing with the Modern (1956–1970)   89

4 Peace and Sputnik, the Boom, and Television (1956–1964)   91

5 The First Years of Unitelefilm and the PCI After Togliatti (1964–1967)   115

6 The Workers, the Students, and the Election Campaign of 1968   139

7 The Lice and the Whale: Filmmakers, Militant Cinema, and the Italian Communist Party   159

viii CONTENTS

Part III	A Decade of Living Dangerously: The Turbulent Peak (and the Seeds of Decline) of the Italian Communist Party (1970–1979)	177
8	The Early 1970s: Unitelefilm, the Fascist Threat, and the 'Historic Compromise'	179
9	Hegemony Within Reach (1974–1976)	203
10	Women's Issues, Feminism, and the PCI	223
11	Hegemony Fades Away (1977–1979)	243
12	Conclusion	265
	Film Index	279
	Subject Index	283

LIST OF IMAGES

Image 3.1	The three Sicilian peasants at Botteghe Oscure	54
Image 3.2	Togliatti in the hospital	57
Image 3.3	Workers on strike	58
Image 3.4	The hammer and sickle symbol	60
Image 3.5	A gymnastics team at the parade	61
Image 3.6	A solid block of Communist workers	62
Image 3.7	The Party intellectual	63
Image 3.8	A child in the crowd	64
Image 3.9	Veiled grandmother	68
Image 3.10	Destitute children in the South	69
Image 4.1	Southern emigrant	104
Image 5.1	Togliatti's portrait alongside that of Gramsci	121
Image 5.2	The new leader Luigi Longo	122
Image 6.1	Lyndon Johnson as a vampire	142
Image 6.2	Southern workers with fashionable haircuts	144
Image 8.1	Vicky talking to Fortunato	185
Image 8.2	Fortunato curses the factory	186
Image 8.3	Demonstration in Brescia after the bombing	190
Image 9.1	Berlinguer delivers a speech in Piazza San Giovanni	212
Image 10.1	The timekeeper and the worker	229

CHAPTER 1

Introduction

The scene takes place in a barbershop. The protagonist Antonio, referred to as '*il ragioniere*' (the accountant), refuses to subscribe to the Italian Communist Party (Partito comunista italiano: PCI) saying that PCI's policy is not for people like him. While having his shave, Antonio falls asleep. Suddenly, he is plunged into a nightmare: the Fascists are back! Blackshirts march along the town's streets, a Jewish citizen is unceremoniously thrown out of a public building, and a group of workers is remorselessly exploited by a boss who mockingly invites them to look for help from the Fascist trade union. In due course Antonio himself is humiliated by a Fascist functionary, who forces him to take off his hat. He wakes up dripping with sweat and realizes that he has just had a nightmare. Out on the street again, he sees with relief some young Communist militants joyfully marching by, and when an army colonel mutters in disapproval he emphatically replies: '*Bello spettacolo, eh?*' ('A lovely sight, don't you think?').

This is the plot of *Chi dorme non piglia pesci* (idiomatically, 'the early bird catches the worm'), a propaganda film produced by PCI-controlled Libertas Film in view of the elections of April 1948. It ran for about twelve minutes and stands out as the first fiction film that the PCI had ever sponsored. It was directed by the professional filmmaker Aldo Vergano, who had just made *Il sole sorge ancora* (*Outcry*) (1946), one of the first films about the Italian Resistance.[1] The leading role was played by the emerging actor Carlo Mazzarella.[2] The film, a sort of moral tale whose narrative structure is very reminiscent of Charles Dickens' *A Christmas Carol* as

© The Author(s), under exclusive license to Springer Nature   1
Switzerland AG 2021
G. Fantoni, *Italy through the Red Lens*, Italian and Italian American
Studies, https://doi.org/10.1007/978-3-030-69197-4_1

well as Frank Capra's film *It's a Wonderful Life* (1946), was a clear attempt to gain the electoral support of the petty bourgeoisie, embodied in the film by the accountant Antonio. Middle-class voters were being reminded that the Italian Communist Party was the one and only real barrier to the return of Fascism. This was precisely why Vergano's film was unanimously banned by the Italian board of censors in November 1947: it made the PCI appear to be the guarantor of Italian democracy, a role that the board's members felt could only be portrayed as the exclusive competence of the democratic state.[3]

Chi dorme non piglia pesci demonstrates the importance the Italian Communist Party gave to cinema as a tool for propaganda, and from the early post-war years. The PCI was the first Italian political party to establish a cinema section, in 1946, and it was the only party that had its own film production company, Unitelefilm (UTF), which operated between 1964 and 1979. Throughout the entire period, the party produced a very respectable number of films, propaganda shorts, newsreels, and documentaries: in all, well over three hundred. Yet, PCI's cinematographic production had been somewhat neglected by historians and film studies scholars.[4]

Not only is this corpus of research on the cinematographic production of the PCI quite modest, but without exception the individual studies only engage with a small number of films over a limited period. This book offers the first comprehensive analysis of the role of cinema in the PCI's communication strategy. It analyses the entire period during which the party had a systematic and organized approach to cinematographic production, starting with the early experiments in 1946 and ending with the closure of Unitelefilm at the end of the 1970s. The book thereby includes the first history of this production company ever written.

From a historiographical perspective, this work belongs to a new era of research, dating from the 1990s, which has addressed social and cultural aspects of the history of the Italian Communist Party, including the motivation behind Communist militancy, the economic, social, and cultural reasons for the PCI's impressive and enduring electoral success in the *'regioni rosse'* (red regions), and the party's propaganda and cultural production, the subject of this book.[5] These trends have injected new approaches into a historiographical tradition that had previously always favoured the ideological and political aspects of PCI history.

The corpus of films produced by the Italian Communist Party in the post-war years represents a last and most sustained attempt made by an

Italian political organization to systematically use the medium of cinema for propaganda purposes. The use of cinema in political struggle, especially in the form of newsreels, was a well-established tradition in Italy. The Fascist regime had made systematic use of the newsreels produced by the Istituto Luce, created in 1924 (Falasca-Zamponi 2000). In the post-war years, the Christian Democrats (DC), the Italian government, and even US-funded agencies such as the ECA (Economic Cooperation Administration) and USIS (United States Information Service) produced documentaries designed to politically influence Italian public opinion by adverting the achievements of DC-led governments, the advantages of market economy and a Western lifestyle.[6] From 1946, the film production company INCOM (Industria Cortometraggi) widely distributed in cinemas its famous newsreels, the 'Weekly INCOM' (Settimana INCOM), which were pro-government and quite openly so (see Chap. 3). However, by the mid-1960s they had ceased all production. The PCI instead continued to produce films until the end of the 1970s. This was due to a fascination with cinema on the part of Communist intellectuals, as discussed in Chap. 2, but especially to the exclusion of the PCI from government-ruled public broadcasting, which forced Communists to resort to the only type of cinematic propaganda that could be produced 'in house' and distributed in a cinema network expressly established for that purpose.

The history of the Italian Communist Party's film production and that of Italian television are indeed intertwined. The PCI decided to resume film production at the end of the 1950s in order to address the challenge posed by the newly born public broadcasting, as discussed in Chap. 4. The demise of Unitelefilm was ultimately the consequence of a boom in independent television broadcasting which occurred in the late 1970s, as discussed in Chap. 11. The corpus of the films produced by the Italian Communist Party from 1946 to 1979 could be described as counter-propaganda; an attempt by the PCI to offer an alternative interpretation of the political, social, and economic development of the country in defiance of the DC- and government-dominated newsreels and radio first, and television later. The attempt was only partially successful, as this book will show (see, in particular, Chaps. 3 and 12), the principal obstacle being the lack of proper avenues of distribution.

When a collection of cinematic texts is to be studied, there is a crucial decision to be made about the structure of the research. Either it can be organized in themes, or a chronological approach can be adopted. In my opinion, the first option is less appropriate for a study of the films produced by the PCI because it leads to the comparison of work produced years apart, which are then evaluated as artistic output without reference to their political and historical context. I would argue that the films produced by the PCI must be considered, first and foremost, as propaganda films, and that their primary aim was to translate issues related to the evolving political struggle into cinematic form.[7] This book therefore adopts a chronological approach, which helps to place the films analysed in their historical context. In order to give each work its proper historical and political context, I have drawn on both the existing literature and the party press, especially *L'Unità*, the PCI's official newspaper, and *Rinascita*, the party's political and cultural review, which converted to weekly publication in April 1962.[8] *Il Quaderno dell'attivista*, an internal publication on the use of propaganda, issued from 1946 to 1958, proved a valuable resource for understanding the management of propaganda films at grassroots level.[9] The inconvenience of a chronological approach is that the same chapter can end up dealing with a variety of topics: all the issues that were 'burning' at a given time and were therefore addressed by party cinematic propaganda. This can make it hard for the reader to follow the chapter's thread. In order to help navigate the quite heterogeneous material discussed, a summary is provided at the beginning and end of most chapters.

Adopting a chronological approach also means losing, at least in part, diachronic concerns, such as thematic and stylistic differences and similarities among the films, or the evolution of the party's outlook on specific issues. In order to address this problem, I have sometimes adopted a diachronic perspective within the chapters. Chapter 4, for example, while dealing with the PCI propaganda productions of the years 1958–1964, discusses PCI policy towards public broadcasting up until 1968. Chapter 5 addresses the production on the issue of the Vietnam War beyond the chapter's temporal boundaries (1964–1967). Most notably, Chap. 10, focused on women's issues in Communist cinema, is organized thematically rather than chronologically. In order to provide a clear and sustained argument throughout, the text contains frequent references to themes and films already discussed in previous chapters, or that will be discussed again in the subsequent ones.

The fact that PCI cinematographic production was principally driven by a political agenda does not mean that Communist films had no artistic value, nor that the party's output was only intended for use as propaganda. Some of the films, especially those directed by famous professionals, are artistically valuable, and a number produced in the 1960s and 1970s were specifically intended for distribution as documentaries. Nonetheless, the content of every PCI film, whether propaganda or documentary, had to be in perfect alignment with the party's political position if it was to be distributed. The films produced by the Italian Communist Party thus cannot be fully understood without reference to the guidelines laid down, and regularly updated, by the PCI's 'Sezione stampa e propaganda' (Press and Propaganda Section), which in turn reflected the policies determined by the 'Segreteria politica' (Central Political Directorate). Alongside my analysis of the films stored at AAMOD (Archivio Audiovisivo del Movimento Operaio e Democratico), I therefore reviewed the material in the Archivio del Partito Comunista Italiano (APCI), conserved at the Fondazione Istituto Gramsci (IG) in Rome, looking in particular at the documents issued by the party's central Press and Propaganda Section.

During a sojourn in Rome, in 2011, I conducted interviews with some of the protagonists of Communist film production, including Carlo Lizzani, Ansano Giannarelli, and Mino Argentieri, partly for their ideas and advice on the direction of my investigation. The involvement of major artists, critics, writers, and professional filmmakers in the production of films for the PCI is in fact one of the most remarkable aspects of this topic. Among the many distinguished cultural figures were also Gillo Pontecorvo, Paolo and Vittorio Taviani, Ettore Scola, Bernardo Bertolucci and Ugo Gregoretti. Work with the party provided valuable experience to many young filmmakers and for several of them it represented the first stage of a successful career in the Italian cinema industry. New questions about the relationship between the PCI and Italian intellectuals are raised by their involvement, which I address in this book: how did these budding artists, soon to be famous, reconcile the need to preserve their artistic freedom with the stringent requirements imposed by cinematographic production that was principally propaganda-driven? What was their contribution to the aesthetic and development of Communist cinematography?

In viewing the films produced by the PCI, I came to realize that they represent a forgotten mine of information on a variety of aspects of the history of the Italian Communist Party, and that they could do much more than simply illustrate the principal motifs of Communist propaganda in post-war Italy. Many of them offer fresh and interesting insights into a range of issues relating to the domestic and international policies of the party, especially when analysed in tandem with other sorts of material.

Furthermore, the power and directness of the filmic images provides invaluable information for investigation of the role of ritual and symbols in Communist militancy. In particular, I will be discussing how cinema was deliberately and effectively used in the construction of the image of party leaders, by means of a highly ritualized filmic documentation of key moments in their political activity: for example, I look at cinematic representation of speeches at election meetings, contributions to party congresses, and, in the case of the most important leaders, even funerals. The book also addresses a number of further questions. What led the PCI to embark on cinematographic propaganda in the first place? What did the party hope to achieve through it, at the various moments when film propaganda was effectively deployed? And why did the PCI leadership decide to abandon this form of propaganda, for the first time at the beginning of the 1950s and then for good at the end of the 1970s?

As already indicated, the PCI produced a relatively high number of films in the period covered by this research, and especially in the years when Unitelefilm was operating. I therefore had to make some difficult choices. For the purposes of this investigation, I only considered films that were fully edited and distributed, thus excluding films that were simply pre-edited and never completed, as well as unedited footage. I then selected films for full analysis on the basis of a number of considerations. Some were chosen because they provided the best illustrations of the recurring themes within Communist propaganda that emerged from investigation of the archival material and party press. Others perfectly captured the party's *Weltanschauung*. Some were by famous directors, while yet others seemed significant from an artistic perspective. In many cases, selection was based on a combination of these factors. One particular group of films omitted from this investigation were those tailored for specific cities or areas of the country with local elections in mind. Some of these are artistically important: by way of illustration, their directors included the young Taviani brothers, who were to become internationally acclaimed filmmakers.[10] Often paid for by the local PCI branches, these films are also interesting politically in that they frequently reflect an issue that recurred regularly within Communist propaganda: the '*buongoverno delle sinistre*', an expression that passed into common usage. According to the party's propaganda, this referred to the manifest excellence of local Communist administrations, especially when compared to their morally questionable and somewhat ineffective counterparts set up by the DC or the centre-left. These latter bodies were commonly referred to by

Communists as the '*malgoverno*' (maladministration) of the DC. However, proper analysis of these films would have required both a thorough investigation of local political issues, which are often very diverse and vary with the historical context, and a much longer book involving far too many digressions from the main theme of each chapter. My view is that Communist cinematographic production relating to local areas is well worth further investigation and a publication in its own right. The only film on local administrations discussed in this book is Carlo Lizzani's *Modena città dell'Emilia rossa* (Modena, a City in Red Emilia, 1950, see Chap. 3), which is a valuable cinematic text both for investigating the influence of Soviet propaganda of the Stalin era on the PCI and for analysing the aesthetic features of early Communist film production.

Antonio Gramsci argued that to write the story of a political party means nothing else than to write the history of a country 'da un punto di vista monografico', that is, from a particular perspective (Gramsci, 1975, 1630). This kind of investigation inevitably brings to the fore cultural, social, and political features of the country in which the political party developed and operated. Furthermore, it seems that cinema can be compared to blotting paper, absorbing ideas, cultural influences, and controversies belonging to the world in which it was produced. Therefore, the book engages with many different topics related to Italian society and politics, and it can be ultimately regarded as a history of post-war Italy from a particular point of view.

The book is divided into three parts, each subdivided into chapters, and as a whole discusses the development of PCI film production against the background of the history of the party and the country. The first part, entitled 'The Italian Communist Party Between Socialist Realism and Neorealism (1944–1956)', in two chapters, deals with the PCI's early cinematographic output, which dried up at the beginning of the 1950s. Chapter 2 offers an overview of PCI history between 1944 and 1956 and focuses on three topics in particular: the relationship between the PCI and Italian intellectuals, the party's policy on cinema, and the view party intellectuals and film critics took on neorealism. The latter is a frequent topic of discussion in scholarly literature, but it is often assumed to be of enthusiastic endorsement. This chapter seeks to rebalance these judgments by showing how most Communist officials and intellectuals did not actually express a particular fondness for neorealist aesthetics but rather recognition of the political worth of certain neorealist films. The category of '*film democratico*' (democratic film, but in the sense of left-leaning film) emerges here as the most relevant analytical tool in order to understand the relationship between Communist intellectuals and Italian cinema. Communist intellectuals based their aesthetic judgement on this interpretative paradigm, which was constructed according to purely political criteria. Chapter 3 discusses Communist film propaganda during this period and analyses the films that best represent it; it investigates what this early production reveals about the PCI's self-constructed political and historical identity in these early years of Italy's post-war democracy. The chapter argues that the films produced in these years offer visual insights into the 'sacralisation of politics' (Gentile 2006) displayed by the PCI in the after-war period. PCI political liturgy seem indeed to possess all of the features that according to some authors are characteristic of politics when it assumes religious form and content: hope for the future after a very difficult period; unity of a political community and subordination of the individual to the collective; sacrifice and cult of martyrdom; the comparison of the leader to a sort of messiah (Augusteijn et al. 2013: 2). The latter in the Communist tradition is known as 'cult of personality'.

Part II, 'Dealing with the Modern (1956–1970)', addresses the resurgence of Communist cinematography at the end of the 1950s and covers the period of Italian post-war economic development; it is covered in four chapters. Chapter 4 shows how the PCI's understanding of film propaganda rapidly evolved between the end of the 1950s and the beginning of the 1960s, due to a range of domestic and international factors: these included the advent of television broadcasting in Italy, new cultural and aesthetic demands created by economic development (the economic miracle), and the new role that the party assigned to propaganda in view of the changing environments of both the international Communist movement and the Italian political landscape. The analysis of the films produced in this period reveals a party that was experiencing a transitional phase: it was halfway between modernity and tradition. Communists embraced the modernity represented by television, but rejected the modernity of the economic boom, and they were almost horrified by the sudden transformation of Italy into an affluent society. They tried to adjust their cultural policy to the new reality, but such a revision turned out to be a long-term and quite laborious endeavour. Chapter 5 discusses the foundation of Unitelefilm and shows how Communist film propaganda dealt with the challenges the Party faced in the wake of the death of its longstanding leader Palmiro Togliatti. In the mid-1960s, modernity came in the shape of thousands of young people getting passionate about the Vietnam War and staging the first occupations of Universities. As a complex and somewhat cumbersome organization, the party reacted slowly to the changes materializing in the society, and it did so in substantial continuity with Togliatti's thought and political strategy. However, the chapter argues that PCI proved that it was, after all, capable of dealing with modernity, even in terms of film propaganda. Chapter 6 addresses the elections of 1968, which were of particular importance as a focus of Communist cinematographic energy. As a year that could make or break the party, 1968 is a watershed. Once again, the party showed that it was capable of coming to term with the modern. As a result of the party's political expansion of that year, and its engagements in the cultural field, including film production, the PCI managed to establish a sort of unofficial political alliance with the student movement. This was one of the reasons for the Communists' electoral successes of the mid-1970s. Chapter 7 examines the years of '*Cinema militante*' (militant cinema) movement, and Unitelfilm's involvement in it. It shows how the PCI and radical left-wing groups engaged a cinematic battle for the soul of the industrial workers. The PCI won, as it was inevitable. The chapter also discusses the part the left-wing filmmakers and intellectual played in this struggle, individually and as a group.

The four chapters of Part III—'A Decade of Living Dangerously: The Turbulent Peak (and the Seeds of Decline) of the Italian Communist Party (1970–1979)'—cover the history of Unitelefilm and cinematographic production between 1970 and 1979. After an initial period in which Communist filmmakers were pressed into action to ward off Italy's potential slide into authoritarianism (Chap. 8), the PCI seemed to be finally and irresistibly on the road to power (Chap. 9). The Communist cultural and political quasi-hegemony was challenged, however, by new phenomena such as the feminist movement (Chap. 10). As the world continued to change rapidly, and adverse forces increased in numbers and strength, in its final phase, Communist cinema reflected the incipient crisis of the party (Chap. 11): a prelude to the political decline that was to become more evident in the 1980s. This part as a whole can be seen as discussing the relationship between the PCI and the incipient post-modernity. Until the middle of the decade, the cultural scenario of the country seemed to favour the PCI. This was especially due to the long-lasting effects of 1968. The desire for change rising impetuously from the society found in the PCI its privileged political interlocutor. Italy was at the culmination of its industrial development, and a socialist outcome seemed actually possible, almost inevitable. It was, however, an optical illusion. Italy soon entered its post-industrial phase. Slowly, but inexorably, the social and cultural habitat changed and became unfavourable for the PCI. This time the party was not as effective in dealing with novelties as it had been in the 1960s. This was due to various reasons, not least of which was that the PCI's leadership could not come up with any new ideas. The most important policy the party engineered and tried to implement in the 1970s, the *compromesso storico*, was substantially a reprisal of Togliatti's *Svolta di Salerno* policy, which dated back to 1944. One could argue, as I do in Chap. 11, that if we judged the *compromesso storico* policy against the background of the political and social reality of 1970s Italy, we would conclude that its implementation was somehow required, and its failure inevitable. Nonetheless, post-modernity called for much bolder and ambitious ideas. However, that was the moment in which the substantial inadequacy and backwardness of Communist ideology and PCI's political culture was revealed.

The ultimate aim of the book is to integrate historical and film studies, developing an original approach that improves our understanding of cinematic texts by placing them in the context of historical research. Obviously, I am not the first scholar to attempt a similar endeavour. The methodology informing this book is based on the literature that has developed as a result of the interest historians have taken in the relationship between cinema and history, whose course of development dates back to the publication in 1947 of Siegfried Kracauer's classic *From Caligari to Hitler: A Psychological History of the German Film*. In an earlier essay (Fantoni 2015), I took stock of the methodological progress that historians have made in the analysis of cinematic texts as sources for historical research, and this has provided the theoretical basis for my research on film and history. This book owes a particular debt to the 'French School'. I have drawn on Marc Ferro's idea that films provide historians with 'a counter-analysis' (1988: 23): they offer opportunities to unearth hidden aspects of a society or, in this case, a sponsoring institution. In Ferro's view, when examining a cinematic text, the historian must look at its every observable feature and, in particular, must look for the clues that uncover its authors' assumptions, leanings, and fundamental beliefs. From this perspective a film, rather than showing, reveals. Ferro has also made several suggestions regarding methodology for the analysis of film, including, famously, the recommendation that we should study both 'the visible and the non-visible' or, in other words, 'the relations between a film and what is extra-filmic' (30). We therefore need to focus on the production background and to research fully the material circumstances in which a cinematographic text was produced and distributed, including its screenplays, production documents, film reviews in the media, and so on. With this in mind I spent time reviewing the PCI's press and archival documents, looking for references to cinematographic propaganda.

Pierre Sorlin's appeal for recognition and appreciation of the specificity of the '*fait filmique*' ('filmic event') has also been taken on board. Sorlin encourages historians not just to utilize cinematographic material as written text, but to investigate the '*effet cinéma*' (cinema impact) on the viewers (1977: 290–97). It is worth stressing, in this regard, that the visual experience of a historian analysing an archival cinematographic text can never be the same as that of its audience at the time of its production. As modern-day viewers, we necessarily have a different perception of film due to the subsequent evolution of cinematographic techniques, narrative styles, and taste. This inevitably affects the analysis: a film can appear obsolete and clichéd, for example, whereas contemporary viewers had no such impression.

This reference to a film's audience of the time leads to another consideration: film does not exist *per se*, but always in relation to its public. This is especially true for propaganda films, which represent a financial investment by a sponsoring institution that wishes to target a specific audience. The film's audience size is therefore a key element of this investigation; whenever available, information on the distribution, number of viewers, and reception of the various films has been provided. Every film conveys its message by means of a series of artistic, cinematographic, cultural, and political codes that its target audience can understand thanks to the cultural and political background shared by the authors of the film and this audience; arguably, this is especially the case for propaganda films. To analyse a particular cinematic text, the historian therefore needs to be equipped with the cultural references and symbols that were shared by its presumed audience. My familiarity with the history, traditions, and parlance of the Italian Communists, which dates back to my time as a student at the University of Florence, was of great help in distinguishing '"unwitting" testimony, the hidden assumptions and attitudes', which are probably more valuable to the historian, from the deliberate and obvious propaganda that can be found in most PCI films.[11] My experience as a filmmaker and video editor also made an important contribution to the analysis of the films discussed in this book; the historian and film studies scholar

12   G. FANTONI

William Hughes has pointed out that a proper interpretation of visual content is reliant on a knowledge of how filmmaking elements, such as camera placement, framing, lighting, and editing technique, 'determine the form, content and meaning of a given length of film' (1976: 51).

NOTES

1. Aldo Vergano began his career under the Fascist regime, directing *Pietro Micca* in 1938. He died in 1957 (Rondolino 1969: 393–94).
2. Carlo Mazzarella subsequently became a character actor and appeared in *Riso Amaro* (Bitter Rice) (1949) and other films; he then moved to the public broadcasting service where he worked as a television reporter (Rondolino 1969: 227).
3. Hence, there are no copies of this film in existence, as no additional copies were printed. The screenplay, however, is available in the AAMOD archive, non catalogato, Faldone *Nulla osta film del PCI non in Archivio*.
4. The published research on Communist cinematographic propaganda is so limited that each contribution can be mentioned in turn. In 1985, the film critic Mino Argentieri, who had been personally involved in Communist film production in the 1970s (see Chap. 9), published a valuable article in the magazine *Cinemasessanta* analysing the most significant films from early PCI production (Argentieri 1985). This was subsequently translated into English and included in an edited collection about propaganda in post-war Italy (Argentieri 2001). The Archivio Audiovisivo del Movimento Operaio e Democratico (AAMOD) of Rome, which preserves the largest collection of films produced by the PCI, published two volumes devoted to the issue of the party and cinema. The first, *Il PCI e il cinema tra cultura e propaganda*, is a collection of documents and interviews with people involved in the production of Communist propaganda, and especially in the activities of Unitelefilm, during the 1960s and 1970s (Medici et al. 2001). The second contains further interviews and some essays, including one by Argentieri that focuses on the cinematographic output of the PCI and the Christian Democrats (Democrazia Cristiana: DC) in the run-up to the national elections of 18 April 1948 (Taviani 2008). Films produced in 1948 by both the PCI and the DC were also the subject of a book edited by Nicola Tranfaglia, *Il 48 in Italia* (1991), which has useful and informative essays by Pierre Sorlin, David Ellwood, Guido Crainz, Nicola Gallerano, Carlo Lizzani and others. A research group at the University of Bologna studied a selection of films produced by the Bologna branch of the PCI, along with a few films produced by the party at national level during the 1960s and 1970s, which are conserved in the Cineteca of Bologna,

Fondo Istituto Gramsci dell'Emilia-Romagna. This research generated a collection of essays, *La vita in rosso* (Nicoletti 2009). Finally, an essay by Mariangela Palmieri on the films produced by the PCI in the years of the economic miracle (see Chap. 4) is included in a collection edited by Pietro Cavallo e Pasquale Iaccio (Palmieri 2016).

5. An interesting analysis of the characteristics of Communist militancy in the late 1940s and early 1950s is provided by Marino (1991); for investigation of the social dimension of the PCI, see Bellassai (2000). For an attempt to start a new phase of research into the PCI at local level, see Battini (2001); see also Forlenza (2010), Fantoni (2011). On PCI propaganda, see Novelli (2000). In regard to Communist culture, authors have focused particularly on the relationship between the PCI and Italian intellectuals (Ajello 1979, 1997) and on how Communist culture developed in response to Italy's modernization and industrialization (Gundle 1995).

6. On the documentaries produced by the Italian government after the war, see Frabotta (2002); on the films produced by US-sponsored agencies, see Bonifazio (2014). On Marshall Plan sponsored films produced in Italy from 1948 to 1955, see Longo (2012).

7. I am adopting the definition of propaganda given by Richard Taylor: 'the attempt to influence the public opinion of an audience through the transmission of ideas and values' (1998: 15).

8. *Rinascita* was edited by the leader of the PCI Palmiro Togliatti until his death in August 1964. On the founding of *Rinascita*, in 1944, see Ajello (1979: 23).

9. The first issue of *Il Quaderno del propagandista* (the publication's original name, changed in September 1946) appeared in February 1946. As *Il Quaderno dell'attivista*, its first series of four issues appeared monthly from September to December 1946. The second series consisted of six numbers (5–11) that came out monthly or bi-monthly until October 1947, and three supplements. The third series consisted of nine issues spread between February 1948 and January 1949, supplemented by frequent special issues. The final series was published on a monthly basis from October 1949. Publication ceased in March 1958, after the release of just two issues that year. On *Il Quaderno dell'attivista*, see Flores (1976).

10. See, for example, *Sicilia all'addritta* ('Sicily on its feet' in Sicilian dialect), produced in 1958 and directed by Paolo e Vittorio Taviani. This film is the only cinematographic account of the PCI's alliance with the Unione Siciliana Cristiano-Sociale (Sicilian Christian Social Union), a political movement that emerged at the end of the 1950s as the result of a split within the Sicilian DC. The film's target audience, the people of Sicily, is made very clear by the on-screen presence of a *cantastorie*: a performer telling stories while referring to a series of images on a large board, a the-

atrical form typical of the Sicilian tradition. Furthermore, Sicilian dialect is used throughout the film, making it unique within Communist cinematographic production.

11. Aldgate and Richards (1983: 1–2) are in turn quoting Arthur Marwick.

Bibliography

Ajello, N. 1979. *Intellettuali e PCI 1944–1958.* Bari: Laterza.

———. 1997. *Il lungo addio. Intellettuali e PCI dal 1958 al 1991.* Bari-Rome: Laterza.

Aldgate, A., and J. Richards. 1983. *Best of British: Cinema and Society from 1930 to Present.* London: I.B.Tauris.

Argentieri, M. 1985. L'immagine del Pci nel film di propaganda. *Cinemasessanta* 26 (5): 27–34.

———. 2001. The Italian Communist Party in Propaganda Films of the Early Post-War Period. In *The Art of Persuasion. Political Communication in Italy from 1945 to the 1990s,* ed. L. Cheles and L. Sponza. Manchester and New York: Manchester University Press.

Augusteijn, J., P. Dassen, and M. Janse. 2013. Politics and Religion. In *Political Religion Beyond Totalitarianism. The Sacralization of Politics in the Age of Democracy,* ed. J. Augusteijn, P. Dassen, and M. Janse, 1–11. Basingstoke, Hampshire: Palgrave Macmillan.

Battini, M. 2001. Per una storia della Toscana rossa. In *Storia della Toscana,* ed. E. Fasano, G. Petralia, and P. Pezzino, 22–43. Bari: Laterza.

Bellassai, S. 2000. *La morale comunista. Pubblico e privato nella rappresentazione del P.C.I. (1947–1956).* Rome: Carocci.

Bonifazio, P. 2014. *Schooling in Modernity: The Politics of Sponsored Films in Postwar Italy.* Toronto: University of Toronto Press.

Falasca-Zamponi, S. 2000. *Fascist Spectacle: The Aesthetics of Power in Mussolini's Italy.* Berkley and Los Angeles: University of California Press.

Fantoni, G. 2011. La Mineraria lavori o lasci lavorare. Myth and Memory of a Struggle in Tuscany. *Modern Italy* 16 (2): 195–208.

———. 2015. A Very Long Engagement: The Use of Cinematic Texts in Historical Research. In *Film, History and Memory,* ed. J.M. Carlsten and F. McGarry, 18–31. Basingstoke: Palgrave Macmillan.

Ferro, M. 1988. *Cinema and History.* Detroit: Wayne State University Press.

Flores, M. 1976. *Il Quaderno dell'attivista. Ideologia, organizzazione, propaganda, nel PCI degli anni cinquanta.* Milan: Mazzotta.

Forlenza, R. 2010. The Italian Communist Party, Local Government and the Cold War. *Modern Italy* 15 (2): 177–196.

Frabotta, M.A. 2002. *Il Governo filma l'Italia.* Città di Castello (PG): Bulzoni.

Gentile, E. 2006. *Politics as Religion.* Princeton: Princeton University Press.

Gramsci, A. 1975. *Quaderni del carcere*. Ed. Valentino Gerratana. Turin: Einaudi.

Gundle, S. 1995. *I comunisti italiani tra Hollywood e Mosca. La sfida della cultura di massa*. Florence: Giunti.

Hughes, W. 1976. The Evaluation of Film as Evidence. In *The Historian and Film*, ed. P. Smith, 49–79. Cambridge: Cambridge University Press.

Kracauer, S. 1974, c1947. *From Calligari to Hitler. A Psychological History of the German Film*. Princeton, NJ: Princeton University Press.

Longo, M. 2012. Between Documentary and Neorealism: Marshall Plan Films in Italy (1948–1955). *California Italian Studies* 3 (2): 1–45.

Marino, G.C. 1991. *Autoritratto del PCI staliniano, 1946–1953*. Rome: Editori Riuniti.

Medici, A., M. Morbidelli, and E. Taviani, eds. 2001. *Il PCI e il cinema tra cultura e propaganda (1959–1979)*. Rome: Aamod.

Nicoletti, C., ed. 2009. *La vita in rosso. Il Centro audiovisivi della Federazione del PCI di Bologna*. Rome: Carocci.

Novelli, E. 2000. *C'era una volta il PCI. Autobiografia di un partito attraverso le immagini della sua propaganda*. Rome: Editori Riuniti.

Palmieri, M. 2016. L'altra faccia del miracolo. Il boom nei filmati di propaganda del PCI. In *Penso che un sogno così non ritoni mai più. L'Italia del miracolo tra storia, cinema, musica e televisione*, ed. P. Camillo and P. Iaccio, 153–168. Naples: Liguori.

Rondolino, G. 1969. *Dizionario del cinema italiano, 1945–1969*. Turin: Einaudi.

Sorlin, P. 1977. *Sociologie du cinéma. Ouverture pour l'histoire de demain*. Paris: Aubier.

Taviani, E., ed. 2008. *Propaganda, cinema e politica 1945–1975*. Rome: Aamod.

Taylor, R. 1998. *Film Propaganda, Soviet Russia and Nazi Germany*. London: Tauris.

PART I

The Italian Communist Party between Socialist Realism and Neorealism (1944–1956)

CHAPTER 2

Togliatti's *Partito nuovo* and Italian Cinema

There are many myths linked to the production and early distribution of Roberto Rossellini's *Rome, open city* (1945) a film widely regarded as the initiator of post-war Italian cinematographic neorealism. One of the most widely known myths is that initially the film was a disaster: its screenings were poorly attended and only a handful of Communist intellectuals liked it. However, according to Ugo Pirro, who has recounted the making of *Rome, open city* in his book *Celluloide*, this is not an entirely accurate account of what happened.[1] *Rome, open city* was generally well received by the public and screened several times between the end of 1945 and the first half of 1946, both in Rome and in other cities. As far as the appreciation of the film by Communist intellectuals is concerned, several authors maintain that it was positive; it is in this context that the review of the film that the leading film critic of *L'Unità* Umberto Barbaro published on 26 November 1945 is often quoted:[2]

> The film reproduces the hardships and injustices of the occupation with an objectivity free of rhetoric and with an implicit political judgment which is judicious and fair and that therefore undoubtedly merits the applause of all honest men.

There is an assumption which seems to be at play here: because the PCI politically backed neorealism in the post-war years, Communist film critics must have liked the first neorealist films. However, Stefano Masi and

© The Author(s), under exclusive license to Springer Nature Switzerland AG 2021
G. Fantoni, *Italy through the Red Lens*, Italian and Italian American Studies, https://doi.org/10.1007/978-3-030-69197-4_2

19

Enrico Lancia are arguably right when they point out that, at a closer look, Barbaro's review was 'mildly favourable' at best (1987, 25). Skilfully combining the inflexible zeal of the professional journalist, and the tactfulness which was required of a Communist when dealing with comrades, Barbaro implicitly suggested that the film written by Communist militant Sergio Amidei, while not having notable cinematic qualities, was nonetheless to be defended and promoted for its political relevance.

In order to appreciate what a positive film review by Umberto Barbaro looked like, it is perhaps instructive to read the one he wrote for Mikheil Chiaureli's *The Vow*:

> We have never seen a work such as this, in which a wide-ranging piece emerges in such perfect harmony: extremely complex and lyrical, vibrant, epic and satirical, born of the very human and tender creative imagination of the great director Chiaureli.[3]

Barbaro had developed an early passion for Soviet cinema, which he had taught at the *Centro Sperimentale di Cinematografia* in the 1930s. During the post-war period, he became an advocate for bombastic socialist realism. This can explain both his enthusiasm for Chiaureli's film, which was almost a cinematic manifesto of socialist realism, and his ambivalence about *Rome, open city*, a film which presented itself as technically poor and mostly inspired by religious motives.

Barbaro's relationship with neorealism and socialist realism is almost paradigmatic of the PCI's cultural approach to cinema in the post-war years: in their quest for realism, Communist officials, intellectuals, and film critics appeared to oscillate between socialist realism and neorealism, that is to say two cinematic styles which are aesthetically antithetic. The PCI promoted socialist realism wholeheartedly because that was the doctrine that informed cultural policy in the Soviet Union in the post-war years and up until the death of Stalin. This doctrine was known as Zhdanovism. Communist's advocacy for neorealism was instead less ardent and always conditional on the political content of each film. It is possible to argue that the PCI truly began to champion neorealism when this was threatened with exaction due to government hostility and the unfavourable conditions of the Italian cinema market (Gundle 1990: 202). The Italian phrase 'i comunisti italiani erano ždanovisti per passione e neorealisti per reazione', that is, supporters of Zhdanovism by political faith and supporters of neorealist by reaction (to the government's attacks on neorealism) nicely sums up PCI's cultural stance on cinema.

At no point, however, did Communist film critics and intellectuals express an appreciation for all the neorealist films without distinction, but only those neorealist films which were also *film democratici* (democratic films). This was an expression Communist officials used in their internal documents to label those Italian films whose content could be easily associated with Communist propaganda issues. In view of the 1946 elections, for example, the PCI planned to use *Rome, Open city* as a propaganda tool. That turned Roberto Rossellini's masterwork into a *film democratico*. The party equipped three vans with cinema-projectors and a copy of the film. According to the Press and Propaganda Section, it was especially important to show the film 'in provincial towns and villages, especially in the South where the film is not well known'.[4] It is quite significant that following this decision by the party's political directorate, Umberto Barbaro offered a positive reassessment of the film, for no Communist militant, not even a famed and quite independent intellectual like Barbaro could disregard the indications originating from the central apparatus of the party.[5]

This chapter deals with the PCI's history during the early post-war years. Its primary aim is to provide the historical context for an analysis of the early PCI propaganda films, which is carried out in Chap. 3. In doing so, the chapter engages with the historiography of the Italian Communist Party. The chapter focuses especially on three issues, which have been the object of extensive scholarly investigations: the relationship between the PCI and Italian intellectuals, the PCI's policy regarding the national cinema industry and, as anticipated above, the PCI's relationship with cinematic neorealism. The chapter argues that the Italian Communist Party's policy towards cinema was insufficient, for the party leadership utterly disregarded the industrial and legislative aspects of cinema. This was ultimately consistent with the PCI leadership's apparent indifference to cinema as a cultural object. Only the propaganda value attributed to cinema was fully appreciated, as proved by the PCI's early interest in propaganda cinema (see Chap. 3). Unlike the political directorate, Communist intellectuals did value cinema as a cultural product and engaged in debate about national cinema. They argued for the importance of neorealism in relation to national cinema. However, as mentioned above, their take on both Italian cinema and neorealism was eminently political. Neorealism, or rather a cluster of films labelled as true neorealism, soon became for the left-wing intelligentsia a sort of paradigm in relation to which every subsequent cinematographic season, and indeed every single film, had to be judged.

The Italian Communist Party that emerged from the cataclysm of the Second World War was very different from the group of Leninists who had stormed out of the Seventeenth Congress of the Italian Socialist Party (PSI) on 21 January 1921, disappointed by the manifest inability of the socialist elite to lead the Italian proletariat to revolution. It was also very different from the small party of professional revolutionaries of the 1930s, which had barely survived in hiding: most of its leaders were in Paris, Moscow, or prison, as was notably the case for Antonio Gramsci, co-founder of the party and the principal Italian Marxist theorist.[6] When compared with its earlier manifestations, the post-war Italian Communist Party was an entirely different entity, even in name.[7] It was a large mass-membership political party, which had expanded from five thousand or so members in July 1943 to 1.7 million by the end of 1945 (reaching two million not long afterwards). Not only was it a legal entity once again, but it also now enjoyed great prestige and credibility.

These achievements were primarily due to three factors. First, the Communist Party had played a major role in the Resistance, the armed movement against Nazi occupation and the Fascist government of the Repubblica Sociale Italiana (RSI) in the period 1943–1945, which had contributed in no small measure to its popularity. Second, with the shift in direction signalled by the '*svolta di Salerno*' (Salerno turn) of April 1944, Palmiro Togliatti, leader of the party from 1930 to 1934 and again from 1938, had accepted the conservative and pro-monarchy Badoglio government in the name of the common struggle against the Nazi and Fascist forces that still occupied central and northern Italy. This act had given the PCI a place in the coalition governments and the opportunity to cast itself as a national and even patriotic political party. Third, the impressive growth in membership had resulted from the adoption of a specific model, the '*partito nuovo*' (new party), by the PCI leadership, and particularly by Togliatti who gave it his strong endorsement. No longer a unit of professional revolutionaries, as expected in the Leninist model of the vanguard party, the *partito nuovo* was instead based on mass participation, intended to encourage the people's involvement in the political life of Italy's fledgling democracy. The '*partito nuovo*' model was certainly a novelty within the Communist tradition, although less so in relation to the political traditions of the Italian Socialist Party, or indeed of the Fascist National Party (PNF).[8]

While presenting these important new features, the PCI was also marked by elements that revealed a political and ideological continuity with its existence over the previous twenty-four years. From the period of exile, in particular, the PCI had retained an unmistakable Stalinist imprint; this particularly characterized the party leadership, beginning with Togliatti himself, who had spent eighteen years in exile in Moscow. The most prominent members of the party's 'old guard' included staunch Stalinists such as Giorgio Amendola, Gian Carlo Pajetta, and Pietro Secchia. This imprint was particularly evident in the way that PCI leaders uncompromisingly defended the interests of the Soviet Union, which they associated with the cause of the international Communist movement and the international proletariat.

The Italian Communist Party was irrevocably bonded to its older brothers, the Communist Party of the Soviet Union (CPSU) and the Soviet Union itself, by the '*legame di ferro*' (iron link), to borrow an expression used by the political scientist and historian Giorgio Galli.[9] According to left-wing historiography, the Stalinist legacy quashed the possibility of a socialist revolution in Italy. From 1944 onwards, Togliatti and the PCI leadership were in fact committed to a relentless effort to contain, moderate, and eventually subdue any revolutionary spirit exhibited by Italian workers, in order to satisfy Stalin's wishes that relations with the United States should not be jeopardized. Right-wing historiography has arrived at very similar conclusions as regards the Communist leadership's subjection to the Soviet Union, although this tends to depict the PCI as a sort of fifth column within the democratic citadel.[10] Most historians with political sympathies towards the PCI, on the other hand, have credited Togliatti with a genuine attempt to establish a democratic system that would safeguard the interests of the working class in particular. For the first time in Italian history, workers would be able to participate, through the mediation of the party, in the government of the country—'*democrazia progressiva*' (progressive democracy) was the term used by Togliatti—while renouncing, in a spirit of realism, the possibility of a revolution, which was deemed unfeasible due to both domestic and international factors.[11] These included the presence in Italy of Allied military forces and the country's location within the Western sphere of influence, as set out by the major powers at the Yalta Conference.

This latter historiographical tradition also regarded Togliatti's post-war policy as a political translation of Gramsci's thinking. This conclusion was based on the particular interpretation of some of the ideas contained in the *Prison Notebooks*: the three thousand or so pages of history and political analysis written by Gramsci during the years of his imprisonment, between

1926 and his death in 1937. Gramsci's well-known theory of 'hegemony', in particular, seemed to support a gradualist political strategy as the best course of action for establishing a socialist regime in Italy. The theory, it was said, suggested that any seizure of power by the working class in a Western country had to be preceded by a period in which the party of the working class succeeded in imposing its vision and ideas on society, establishing them as hegemonic. In Gramsci's words, the working class had to become '*dirigente*' (leading or ruling) before it could be '*dominante*' (dominant) (1975: 41). Other scholarly interpretations of the issue of hegemony, however, have reached different conclusions. Gramsci's theory must first and foremost be analysed against the background of developments in the Russian Revolution from which he had drawn his inspiration. In this light, Gramsci saw the pursuit of cultural hegemony as complementary, rather than preparatory, to political leadership by the working class, otherwise known as the 'dictatorship of the proletariat'.[12]

Whatever the correct interpretation of Gramscian hegemony, Togliatti used Gramsci's writings to provide a theoretical justification for the PCI's '*svolta di Salerno*' policy of collaboration with conservative governments and the King.[13] He personally oversaw the first edition of the *Prison Notebooks*, published by the Einaudi publishing house between 1947 and 1951, making some alterations to the text in line with the political needs of the party (Vacca 1991).[14] In Communist propaganda, Gramsci became the guarantor of the PCI's '*politica nazionale*' (national policy), which meant the party's commitment to Italian national interests; he was presented to the Italian public as a patriot and martyr. According to party mythology, he had prophetically said to the Fascist judge, who had just sentenced him to prison, 'the day will come when you will lead Italy into catastrophe, and then it will be up to us Communists to rescue our country'.[15] The meeting of minds between Gramsci and Stalin and the unshakeable political and personal bond between Gramsci and Togliatti completed the portrayal promoted by the party leadership after the war. This account of Gramsci's opinions was restricted, to say the very least. From 1926 onwards, Gramsci had in fact expressed strong disapproval of both Stalin's leadership and the political outcome of the Russian Revolution, generating serious friction between himself and the PCI leadership.[16]

In the post-war years, the PCI did achieve some significant political victories, including the abolition of the monarchy and the establishment of the Republic, determined by the referendum of 2 June 1946, and the drafting of a relatively progressive constitution that allowed for the possibility of worker participation in the management of factories. However, it could not implement 'progressive democracy'. The actual outcomes of PCI policy were poor, especially with regard to the economy: Italy's reconstruction was instead exclusively led by the capitalist bourgeoisie and geared towards its interests.[17] The main objective of the PCI in this period was to maintain the phase of coalition government for as long as possible, in order to strengthen its political position and stabilize its image as a national party. In this respect we should point out that, arguably, Communist cadres valued *Rome, Open city* because it showcased the Resistance to Nazism and Fascism as a collective effort by both Communists and Catholics, providing a moral and historical justification to the *Governi di unità antifascista*, the permanence of which was essential to Togliatti's post-war strategic design.

The presence of left-wing parties in the Italian government in fact proved untenable in the long run, due to the outbreak of the Cold War. Political pressure from the US government and the Catholic Church led to the expulsion of both the PCI and the PSI in May 1947. That September, the involvement of European Communist Parties in the Cold War was formalized at a conference in Szklarska Poręba, in southwest Poland, where the Communist Information Bureau (Cominform) was established. Andrei Zhdanov, Secretary of the Central Committee of the Soviet Communist Party, presented a report to the conference in which he embraced the idea of the irreversible division of the world into two opposing camps, originally mooted by Winston Churchill in his 'Iron Curtain' speech of March 1946 in Fulton, and imposed a political agenda on the European Communist Parties, particularly the PCI and the French Communist Party (PCF), which had the defence of the Socialist bloc as its focus. In the wake of Szklarska Poręba, the PCI became more markedly Stalinist and highly suspicious of dissidence within its ranks.

In preparation for the Italian Republic's first national elections, scheduled for 18 April 1948, the PCI and PSI formed an alliance, the 'Fronte Democratico Popolare' (Democratic Popular Front). The election results were disappointing for these left-wing parties, which together only won 31.0 per cent of the votes; the DC, meanwhile, won an emphatic 48.5 per cent, which ensured that they had near-complete control over future governments and the bureaucratic apparatus of the state.

The elections of April 1948 marked the beginning of a very difficult period for the PCI and its activists. In subsequent years, the party suffered huge political setbacks, including Italy's adherence to both the Marshall

Plan and the North Atlantic Treaty, which it opposed vehemently. The working-class core, which the party relied on for most of its electoral strength, suffered some devastating defeats as union members; these often resulted in mass redundancies that neither the party nor the Confederazione Generale Italiana del Lavoro (CGIL: the Communist and Socialist trade union federation) was able to resist with any success. Communist militants were persecuted inside and outside the factories, and were even excommunicated en masse by the Catholic Church in July 1949. This happened shortly before the murder attempt on Togliatti's life (14 July) made by a right-wing student, which provoked disorders resulting in the arrest of many Communist militants (see next chapter). PCI members could not feel more under siege.

Despite these setbacks, the PCI survived. In the national elections of June 1953, the left-wing parties successfully countered the drive by the DC and its allies to obtain 50 per cent of the votes, a result that would have automatically guaranteed the winning coalition two thirds of the seats in the Chamber of Deputies, thanks to a law approved the previous March and immediately dubbed the '*Legge truffa*' (swindle law) by the opposition.[18] The DC lost more than 8 per cent of its share of the vote, while the PCI won 22.6 per cent, becoming Italy's second-largest political party by a comfortable margin (the PSI, in third, had 12.7 per cent). The PCI's electoral success was largely due to the vitality of the myth of the USSR and its leader Stalin among Italian workers; the party used this to good effect, and also proved capable of mobilizing the masses on political issues of general interest such as that of peace.[19] The roots that the party had established in some areas of the country during the war of liberation, especially in the *regioni rosse* of central Italy (Tuscany and Emilia-Romagna in particular), proved to be very deep, and were not severed by the political defeats of the post-war period.[20] A further key factor that contributed to the PCI's electoral success was the impressive organizational structure established by party officials and militants at the local level, under the guidance of Pietro Secchia, who oversaw the party's organization until 1954.[21]

For thousands of Italians, being a Communist was much more than a voting choice: it was a lifelong commitment to both a cause and a lifestyle. An exceptionally large number of grass-roots militants were used for political work, propaganda, and extensive distribution of the party press. The PCI's military-style organizational structure pushed militants into constant political activity. Political debate was encouraged at every level, but once a political decision had been taken, any form of public dissent was strictly forbidden: this was the principle of '*centralismo democratico*' (democratic centralism). Internal cohesion was maintained by means of firm discipline and a particular style of organizational culture characterized by factors such as the '*autocritica*' (self-critical statement): every militant and official had to be ready to engage in this whenever their behaviour, public or private, gave rise to criticism from the PCI's higher ranks. The process consisted of an admission of guilt and a prompt account of the reasons for the misdeed; the *autocritica* was one of the purest expressions of the quasi-religious attitude of self-negation that the party required of every good Communist.[22]

Among the political accomplishments of the PCI between 1944 and 1956, the successful establishment of an alliance with Italian intellectuals, resolutely pursued by Togliatti, was certainly one of the most impressive. From 1945 onwards, the party enlisted younger intellectuals in the party's sphere of operations and promoted them to positions of responsibility within its political structure. This was, to quote Stephen Gundle, 'a well-directed strategy aimed at achieving a hegemonic position within national thought and culture' (2000: 12). In creating an atmosphere that welcomed the offspring of the Italian intelligentsia, Togliatti sought to reintroduce Marxism to Italian cultural debate, after twenty years of its near-complete absence, in order to give the PCI cultural legitimacy in Italy's post-war political panorama (Agosti 2008: 158).

The new generation of intellectuals, who had at the same time become influential members of the party, were dubbed '*intellettuali organici*' (organic intellectuals) in reference to a well-known passage in the *Prison Notebooks*.[23] While the Italian Communist Party offered a relatively novel and compelling ideology, its appeal to intellectuals was largely based on the tangible possibilities of a career that it could offer to its recruits. Journalists and writers, for example, could find employment with one of the numerous periodicals that together constituted what Cyrille Guiat, in a perhaps loaded expression, has described as the PCI's 'publishing empire' (2003: 73). Along with the four regional editions of *L'Unità*, its official newspaper, and a few auxiliary newspapers such as *Paese Sera*, founded in January 1948, the PCI promoted a vast range of magazines during the post-war period. Some were specifically aimed at the intellectual and middle-class strata of the population, including first and foremost *Rinascita*, launched in June 1944 (Ajello 1979: 23); others, such as *Vie Nuove*, *Il Calendario del Popolo* and *Noi Donne*, were addressed more to the workers

28 G. FANTONI

and the less well-educated. Finally, the PCI owned two publishing houses, which were to merge within the respected Editori Riuniti in 1953 (Martinelli 1995: 281). The PCI could thus grant someone not only employment, but also the alluring prize, for every artist and intellectual, of a large and growing audience consisting of militants and the wider group of Communist sympathizers.

The golden age of the relationship between the Communist Party and Italy's intellectuals spanned the years between 1945 and 1953, a time that has been described as 'the age of serene certainties' (Valentini 1997: 82). For the Communist militants and party functionaries, 'faith in Communist values was unquestioned and belief in the ultimate triumph of good over evil total' (Gundle 2000: 43). An important moment in the relationship between the PCI and the intellectuals was the PCI's Sixth Congress, in January 1948. In his opening speech, Togliatti delineated the ancillary function that the party assigned to culture in the battle for political hegemony (Bertolissi and Sestan 1985: 337). The eminent classicist and influential party member Concetto Marchesi devoted his speech specifically to culture, and reminded Communist artists of the unwavering need for strict ideological alignment with the party (Bertolissi and Sestan 1985: 375). Such forceful statements demonstrate the strength of Zhdanovism's influence over the PCI during that period. 'Zhdanovism', after Andrei Zhdanov, was the doctrine that informed cultural policy in the Soviet Union in the post-war years and up until the death of Stalin.[24] Alongside the rigorous political and ideological control of culture, Zhdanovism entailed condemnation of formalism and the revival of 'socialist realism' in the arts. At the Sixth Congress, the appointment of Emilio Sereni, a fervent supporter of Zhdanov's doctrine, as head of the PCI's newly created national Cultural Commission provided a tangible demonstration of its adoption by the party.[25]

For many years the issue of realism was central to the Communist critique of all forms of artistic production. The term 'realism', however, had particular and ideologically charged connotations in Communist parlance. It was not used to mean an accurate or true-to-life depiction of reality, but instead referred to an interpretation of reality that took into due consideration the class struggle and the progressive development of class-consciousness inherent in social experience: the phenomena that were seen as lying beneath reality. For this reason, the films of socialist realism, which presented idealized versions of Soviet society and whose plots were schematic and heavy-handed, could nonetheless be regarded as 'realist'.

Although the fascination with Socialist realism in film was to end in the mid-1950s (see Chap. 5), the idea that a work of art without an ideologically correct interpretation of reality was merely impressionistic and superficial, or was even an instrument of ideological corruption, was to persist for some time thereafter. This explains why in 1959, for example, the university professor and prominent Communist intellectual Carlo Salinari could still dismiss Pier Paolo Pasolini's books as morally questionable, formalist, and decadent, and Federico Fellini's *La Strada* (1954) as ideologically misguided and a distortion of reality.[26]

Zhdanovism also had a profound and long-lasting impact on the way that Communist artists and intellectuals viewed their own activities: endorsement of the political line established by the party leadership became for many Communist artists, journalists, writers, and film critics a moral responsibility.[27] A significant number of the young intellectuals who worked for the party in the post-war period had been trained specifically in the field of cinema. The 'Cineguf', cinema sections of the Gruppo Universitari Fascisti (GUF: the Fascist university student organization), for example, proved to be breeding grounds for future Communist militants. The memoirs of several party members, including filmmakers, described the relative freedom of expression and the anti-establishment atmosphere that permeated the cultural life within the GUF. From these accounts, experiences in this organization appeared to have been a sort of apprenticeship in anti-Fascism and almost a preparatory phase for their future Communist militancy (Lizzani 2007: 31–44; Ingrao 2006, 36–46).[28] This interpretation of the role played by the GUF has been challenged by historians (Duranti 2008), while descriptions of its cultural non-conformity by many left-wing politicians and intellectuals who were initially members, and their memoirs of private dissidence, have often been attacked as retrospective justifications for allegiances subsequently deemed shameful (Serri 2005; Battista 2007). The guilty conscience of these intellectuals has been discussed by the historians Aurelio Lepre (1993: 97) and Renzo Martinelli (1995: 289), who both see joining the Italian Communist Party as having been a sort of catharsis for this group: a way of settling the account with their past, and a tangible sign of their intention to break away from their middle-class background in order to share the aspirations and values of the working class.

Many protagonists of the PCI's post-war cinematographic production had shared the experience of the GUF, including Marcello Bollero, head of the party's first 'Sezione Cinematografica' (Cinema Section), and the director Carlo Lizzani. Another forcing house for future Communist cinematographers and politicians had been the Milanese magazine *Cinema*, whose editor from 1938 onwards was the *Duce*'s son Vittorio Mussolini (Caldiron 2002). A certain unorthodox approach among this second set of intellectuals, although not quite open opposition to the regime, seems to be borne out by the collaboration of a group of magazine journalists on the screenplay for *Ossessione*, the first film by the soon-to-be-Communist director Luchino Visconti (Forgacs 1993: 140–43). This group included Aldo Scagnetti, later a film critic of *L'Unità*, Mario Alicata, later head of the party's Cultural Commission, and Giuseppe De Santis, an important Communist film director of the post-war period. *Ossessione* was released in 1943 and provoked outrage from the Church and the Fascist authorities over both its unconventional content and the torrid affair between its protagonists (Argentieri 1974: 57–59).

In view of the number of Communist intellectuals and officials with expertise in cinema, one might expect the party's policy on this medium to have been well conceived and carefully developed. However, that was not the case. As we can see from its early commitment to the production of propaganda films, discussed in the next chapter, the PCI was quick to appreciate the potential of film for disseminating the party message. Its policy towards the Italian cinema industry, however, was inadequate. During the *Governi di unità antifascista*, cinema seems to have been beyond the cultural horizon of the Communist leadership: *Rinascita* did not publish a single article related to cinema before 1949.[29] This happened in spite of the fact that movie-going was probably the most popular cultural activity in post-war Italy, and undoubtedly linked to the dramatic increase of cinemas throughout the country since the end of conflict (Forgacs and Gundle 2007: 207). A cultural prejudice against cinema in the party old guard, and perhaps originating in Togliatti himself, might have played a part here: true intellectuals should not give serious thought to films, which were primarily a form of entertainment. Communists' lack of interest in cinema during the years of the *Governi di unità antifascista* might have been due to the fact that the PCI leadership believed its cultural influence over Italian cinema to be a given. Several factors might have contributed to shaping such an illusion. The results achieved by the PCI in recruiting intellectuals had ensured, at least initially, a Communist hegemony amongst film critics (Ajello 1979: 211). The rise of neorealism might have created the impression that Italian cinema was spontaneously developing along thematic lines which broadly matched the Italian Communist Party's policy.

As a result, the only actions that the PCI took in the field of cinema were of an unofficial nature. The party only tried to influence the new Italian cinema politically by using the personal relationships that some of its *intellettuali organici* had established with emerging film directors. One protagonist of this brief cultural and political phase was Antonello Trombadori, whose friendship with Luchino Visconti and Roberto Rossellini, among others, almost certainly influenced some of the artistic choices made by these prominent directors. Conversely, the PCI underestimated the power of the government to determine the cinema industry's political orientation, and the readiness of producers to follow the government's wishes as to what kinds of film Italians should be watching (Brunetta 2009b: 128–130). In reality, the neorealist period proved to be exceptionally brief, and while some aesthetic traits borrowed from neorealism continued to be trademark features of Italian cinema for quite some time, its left-wing political tone was seldom reflected in the films produced by the national cinema industry. This was principally due to legislative action by the DC and the outbreak of the Cold War.

During the period of anti-Fascist coalition governments, the PCI leadership allowed the cinema sector to remain substantially unregulated. Meanwhile, American films were flooding Italian cinemas, DC politicians had little difficulty in capturing key positions in the unwieldy and extensive bureaucratic machinery inherited from the Fascist regime, and a political restoration was in full swing in the Italian cinema sector.[30] This industry subsequently started to show clear signs of economic distress, and legislation to protect Italian cinema could no longer be deferred.[31] The PCI thus began to cast itself as a champion of the national cinema industry against foreign colonization by American cinematography. It launched a political campaign called *Per la difesa del cinema italiano* (in defence of Italian Cinema).[32] Many professionals in the cinema industry, Communist, and non-Communist, participated in a rally which was organized in the streets of Rome on 20 February 1949.[33] By that time, however, the PCI was no longer in government, and it was relatively easy for the DC to ensure that parliament approved a law granting the government powers to control a cinema industry that was desperately in need of financial aid.[34] The DC consciously used these powers to discourage producers from financing any projects with features that might suggest a left-wing orientation. The picture was completed by a fairly rapid reimposition of cinema censorship.[35]

The law on censorship that was still in operation had been put forward by the Fascist regime in 1923 and provided a variety of reasons for banning a film, among them the inclusion of scenes that might encourage class hatred or were likely to provoke a breach of the peace.[36] In relation to social mores and public order, the PCI leadership wanted to present itself to the moderate public as a conservative political force: a guardian of traditional Italian values and social peace. This was not in fact merely a pose; some fairly strict moral principles, largely modelled on Catholic values, regulated the party's life at the time (Gundle 1995a: 51–52). As a result, the PCI made no attempt to reform film censorship while in government. This proved to be an error that was to have a negative effect not only on Italian cinema, in that in the years ahead countless films were censored to varying degrees and many projects never realized because producers feared censorship, but also on PCI film propaganda. Communist film production was targeted by censorship increasingly often, especially after the outbreak of the Cold War. Eventually, the persecution became so systematic that it accounted for the demise of Communist film production in the early 1950s, as is discussed in Chap. 3.

The most illustrious victim of the Cold War cultural and political climate was, however, neorealist cinema. Neorealism had suddenly pushed Italian cinema forward into the international limelight, reviving a national film industry that had virtually collapsed by the end of the war. Some of the most admired neorealist directors, such as Luchino Visconti and Giuseppe De Santis, were acknowledged fellow travellers of the PCI while others, including the founder of the movement (if neorealism can be so described) Roberto Rossellini, were instead Christian Democrat sympathizers. Despite this, virtually all neorealist films addressed issues that could be associated with Communist propaganda: the central role of the lower classes, the portrayal of social injustice, and the implicit wish for a different and fairer society. On closer inspection, however, the approach to social issues evident in most neorealist films was anything but Marxist, and instead seems to have been generated by a sort of humanism of clearly Christian derivation.[37]

It must be stressed that neither the PCI nor Communist film critics initially engaged in a serious political battle for the promotion of neorealism, diverting energy in a futile effort to boost the diffusion of the bombastic Soviet realist films among militants and workers (see Chap. 3). The party leadership was committed to promote socialist realism over neorealism at least until 1951, when Carlo Salinari replaced Emilio Sereni as the

2 TOGLIATTI'S *PARTITO NUOVO* AND ITALIAN CINEMA   33

head of the Cultural Commission (Brunetta 2009a, 143). There were a variety of positions regarding neorealism among Communist film critics. For example, Guido Aristarco regarded neorealism as a sort of infancy of Italian cinema, a necessary stage in a process hopefully resulting in the allegiance of Italian filmmakers to proper realism (Marcus 1986, 172). However, most Communist intellectuals approached neorealism from a purely political prospective.

As mentioned at the beginning of the chapter, the category of *film democratico*, which was defined according to eminently political parameters, helps a great deal to understand why Communist film critics promoted certain neorealist films in the Communist press, while harshly criticizing other films produced in the same year which also presented the aesthetic features of neorealism. Communist film critic Tommaso Chiaretti made a sort of official partition of neorealist cinematography separating 'true' neorealist films from others which did not deserve the appellation, in an article published in *L'Unità*, in May 1952.[38] According to Chiaretti, the list of films worthy of being remembered and which stood out from the 'plethora of mediocre films' which had inundated the Italian screens over the previous seven years included *Rome, open city*, *Umberto D* (1952), *Shoeshine* (1946) and *Bicycle Thieves* (1948) by Vittorio Sica, *Bellissima* by Luchino Visconti, and *Rome 11 o'clock* (1952) by Giuseppe De Santis. In a couple of articles published shortly after, Chiaretti completed what we could define as the canon of neorealism by adding other films to the list: *Two Cents Worth of Hope* (1952) by Renato Castellani, Visconti's *The Earth Trembles* (La terra trema, 1948), De Sica's *Miracle in Milan* (1951), and *Attention! Bandits!* by the fellow Communist Carlo Lizzani.[39] He claimed that these films were historical evidence of an extraordinary moment in the history of Italian cinema, a phase during which cinema had met ordinary people, and ordinary people, with their problems, dramas, and aspirations had almost physically entered the films. Chiaretti argued for a neorealist film to be regarded as such it had to be politically committed: from *Rome, open city*, which chronicled the 'memorable struggle' of anti-fascism forces during the war, to *Bicycle Thieves*, which depicted the 'drama of unemployment' in post-war Italy, the films of neorealism were, according to Chiaretti, as many indictments against the policy of the Democrazia Cristiana. For this reason, Chiaretti concluded, the DC-led government was trying its best to suffocate neorealism, through a blatantly political use of cinema censorship, as well as by exerting political pressure on authors and producers.

34   G. FANTONI

As can be seen, Chiaretti appreciated just a handful of neorealist films out of the forty-five or so produced between 1945 and 1951 which can be regarded as neorealist, according to Christopher Wagstaff (2007, Appendix 3). Giuseppe De Santis' *Riso Amaro* (Bitter Rice, 1949) was notably but not surprisingly absent.[40] Other films excluded from the neorealist canon included, for example, the film of the so-called *Neorealismo rosa* (pink neorealism)—but Chiaretti did not use this expression—such as the film of the *Bread, Love* and... series, directed by Luigi Comencini. These were films that, while depicting ordinary people and presenting some aesthetic features typical of the neorealism cinematography, were very generic and quite soft as far as the political message they conveyed. This was, sometimes, completely absent.

In an article published in October 1954, another Communist film critic, Aldo Scagnetti polemically attacked the films of the Don Camillo Saga and e Federico Fellini's *La strada* (1954).[41] In the same article, he also lambasted the recent films by Roberto Rossellini, namely those released after the War Trilogy. Scagnetti wondered whether the author of *Rome, open city* was tired or maybe was lacking inspiration, as he could not believe that the man who had given the character of Pina (played by Anna Magnani in *Rome, open city*) to Italian cinema was now palming off female characters 'fading more and more in the fog of a sort of romanticism mixed with implausibility'. As examples of such disappointing characters, the critic of *L'Unità* mentioned Karin of *Stromboli* (1950), Irene of *Europa '51* (1952)—both played by Ingrid Bergman—and 'the idiot of the Amalfi Coast', a phrase which alluded to the character of Nannina, played by Anna Magnani in *L'Amore* (1948). Once again, such strong criticism was purely political in nature. Scagnetti disliked the characters of Rossellini's most recent films because their motivations were not political. They appeared, instead, to be driven by existential impulses, such as the pursuit of personal fulfilment (Karin), or a newly discovered religious ethos (Irene).

As pointed out by Renato Brunetta, the uncompromising and ungenerous attacks against directors such as Rossellini, Fellini, and Michelangelo Antonioni made by Communist film critics in the early 1950s were ultimately a sign of the crisis of both neorealism and socialist realism (Brunetta 2009a, 145). By the time Scagnetti published his reprimand against Rossellini, neorealism was in fact more or less dead, strangled by the political and cultural climate of the mid-1950s. A repudiation of socialist realism by the PCI only occurs in 1956, following de-Stalinization (see Chap. 5).

The eclipse of politically engaged cinema was due to commercial reasons as well as political reasons. Films that simply aimed to entertain had always been more popular with the public than the iconic works of neorealism, which were only part of the total range of Italian cinematographic production (Miccichè 1974: 22–23). At the beginning of the 1950s, the biggest box-office hits had been the melodramas directed by Raffaello Matarazzo and films belonging to the sub-genre of pink neorealism. The subsequent success of Italian-style comedy drove the Italian cinema industry towards the production of escapist films. In order to dispense with a private film industry that was less and less willing to finance films addressing social and political issues, the PCI took a tentative step towards entry into mainstream cinema production by setting up the Cooperativa Cinematografica Spettatori Produttori, a cooperative of cinema-goers intended to organize collective finance for films. However, the complete control of the all-pervading state apparatus that the DC had inherited from the Fascist regime made it easy for them to frustrate this experiment, and bureaucratic obstacles forced the Cooperativa to shut down. Nevertheless, it was responsible for production of two feature films: *Achtung! Banditi!* (*Attention! Bandits!*) (1951) and *Cronache di poveri amanti* (*Chronicle of Poor Lovers*) (1954), both directed by Carlo Lizzani (Petricelli 2004: 153–70; Lizzani 2007: 103–5).

The PCI thus lost the battle for cultural hegemony in cinema, a battle that it joined rather late and fought with limited resources. In the years that followed, the party's Cultural Commission was to defend Italian cinema and demand new legislation to protect the national cinema industry. Communist film critics would recommend politically engaged films to their readers and harshly criticized Hollywood and Italian popular cinema, which they regarded as lowbrow. Above all, for many years they continued to bemoan the end of the neorealist period, seen as the golden age of Italian cinema, and to place their hopes in its revival.[42] An organized attempt by the PCI to enter the film industry, however, or to promote the distribution of a certain type of fictional film, was not to happen.

NOTES

1. Pirro (1995: 224). However, Pirro's book should be regarded as a historical novel rather than a history book. As pointed out by Millicent Marcus, Pirro's recollections are certainly fascinating but not always reliable; see Marcus (2004: 83).

2. See, for example, Bosworth and Dogliani (1999: 106), Shiel (2006: 53) and Brunetta (2009b: 118).
3. See Umberto Barbaro 'Il Regista Sovietico Ciaureli parla ai critici del Festival', *L'Unità*, 18 September 1946, p. 2
4. See the undated 'Piano di propaganda per la Costituente', in IG, APCI, MF 110, p. 566, Stampa e Propaganda, serie 1946.
5. See Umberto Barbaro 'Successo Artistico e Politico di Roma città aperta in America', in *L'Unità* 4 April 1946, front page.
6. For the history of the PCI during the period 1921–1944, see the five-volume *Storia del Partito Comunista Italiano* by Paolo Spriano, published by Einaudi (1967–1976).
7. Initially called the Partito Comunista d'Italia, it became the Partito Comunista Italiano after the dissolution of the Third International in May 1943; see Galli (1977: 235).
8. There have been many analyses of the characteristics of the *partito nuovo* (new party), from political, social and electoral perspectives. For a general analysis, see Martinelli (1995). However, Stalin had endorsed Togliatti's decision to create a mass-based party, believing that there was no viable alternative in a country with a multi-party system; see Gozzini (2007: 298).
9. The first of many editions of Giorgio Galli's *Storia del PCI* was published by Schwarz in 1953, and the most recent by Kaos (1993). For further examples of left-wing historiography that broadly share Galli's view, see Peregalli (1991) and Gallerano and Flores (1992).
10. The forefather of the right-wing reading of PCI history is Bertelli (1980). Right-wing interpretations flourished particularly after the dissolution of the PCI in 1991. For discussion of the PCI leadership's deference to Soviet Communism, see, for example, Aga Rossi and Zaslavsky (1996), Aga Rossi and Quaglieriello (1997) and Aga Rossi and Zaslavsky (1997). For discussion and promotion of the image of the PCI as a threat to democracy, see Pellizzaro (1997), Bertelli and Bigazzi (2001), Donno (2001) and Turi (2004).
11. This interpretation is shared, although in varying degrees, by several authors, including Sassoon (1980), Spriano (1983), Urban (1986), Agosti (1996), Guerra (2005), Gualtieri (2001) and Ventrone (2008).
12. For an example of this interpretation, see Thomas (2010: 159–241).
13. An analysis of the vast literature on Togliatti's development, or arguably exploitation, of Gramsci's thought is beyond the scope of this volume; see Gundle (1995b). On the '*operazione Gramsci*', see the detailed reconstruction by Gozzini and Martinelli (1998: 490–504).
14. According to Aldo Agosti, the effect of Togliatti's involvement in publication of Gramsci's writing should not be exaggerated, as it did not 'notably pervert Gramsci's thought' (2008: 181).

15. See 'Il Partito comunista e la Patria. Intervista con Celeste Carlo Negarville della Direzione del P.C.I.', *L'Unità*, 18 February 1945, p. 2.
16. A detailed reconstruction of the relationship between Gramsci and the party leadership between 1926 and 1937 is provided by Rossi and Vacca (2007).
17. On Italy's economic reconstruction, see Daneo (1975) and Zamagni (2000: 45–49).
18. An analysis of the new electoral law (no. 148 of 31 March 1953) championed by De Gasperi's seventh government is provided by Sassoon (1990: 90–95). For discussion of the catchphrase '*Legge truffa*', see Mariuzzo (2010: 115–17, 154–59).
19. On the campaigns for peace promoted by the PCI in the post-war period, see Giacomini (1984), Guiso (2006) and Mariuzzo (2010: 209–26).
20. On the political and social entrenchment of the PCI in the 'red' regions, see Battini (2001), Forlenza (2010) and Fantoni (2011).
21. On the organizational structure of the PCI, see Martinelli (1995: 177–96) and Marino (1991: 25–31). For a portrait of Pietro Secchia, see Mafai (1984).
22. For further discussion of the *autocritica*, see Marino (1991: 96–100) and Bellassai (2000: 83).
23. The expression '*intellettuali organici*' was in fact being used inappropriately. Antonio Gramsci had used it to describe a new type of intellectual who emerged organically from a specific social class, the proletariat, while it was in the process of achieving political and economic supremacy. These intellectuals were to be entrusted with establishing a new cultural framework that would justify the political power of the new ruling class. By contrast, Togliatti's attempt, and in part achievement, was to co-opt those whom Gramsci would have described as '*intellettuali tradizionali*': the class of intellectuals linked to the pre-existing bourgeois regime. Gramsci discusses this distinction in his notebook number 12, *Appunti e note sparse per un gruppo di saggi sulla storia degli intelletuali* (1975: 1513–51).
24. For discussion of Andrei Zhdanov and his doctrine, see Boterbloem (2004).
25. Emilio Sereni is portrayed by Ajello (1979: 147–51).
26. See Carlo Salinari, 'Problemi del Realismo in Italia, resoconto sommario del dibattito svoltosi a Roma presso l'Istituto Gramsci, dal 3 al 5 gennaio 1959', *Il Contemporaneo* 11 (February–March 1959): 3–15.
27. A large collection of highly ideological statements about cultural issues (including cinema) that appeared in the Communist press between 1944 and 1964 can be found in Guarini and Saltini (1978).
28. In many respects, the prototype for this self-exculpatory literature is Ruggero Zangrandi's *Il lungo viaggio attraverso il fascismo*, first published in 1947, which contains a complete list of participants in the '*Littoriali*

della cultura', the Fascist cultural competitions for university students and the most important national events of this kind organized by the Fascist regime in the 1930s (Zangrandi 1998: 641–713). Many of these, including Zangrandi himself, subsequently joined the PCI.

29. See Virgilio Tosi, 'Sguardi sull'attuale produzione cinematografica', in *Rinascita*, anno V, n. 1, 32.

30. Some statistics effectively illustrate the extent of the American cinematographic invasion: 296 American films were distributed in Italy in 1946, 515 in 1948, and 406 in 1949 (Brunetta 1979: 67). The DC leadership was working to enable the party to challenge the PCI in the near future. This confrontation was also to involve the occupation of strategic positions ensuring control over the propaganda system inherited from the Fascist regime. During De Gasperi's first government, the DC politician Mario Scelba was therefore entrusted with the Ministry of Post and Communications, which controlled the public broadcasting service Radio (RAI, previously EIAR: Ente Italiano Audiofonico Radio), founded during the Fascist regime. An apt example of political restoration in the cinema sector was the appointment (while the PCI was still in government) of Eitel Monaco, the official who had overseen film production during the final years of the Fascist dictatorship, as president of the newly created Associazione nazionale industrie cinematografiche e audiovisive (ANICA), the association of film producers and distributors (Argentieri 1974: 68–69).

31. The crisis of the Italian cinema industry had both financial and political causes. This had its origins in 1945, when legislation protecting the industry, enacted by the Fascist regime in the late 1930s, was repealed under pressure from the Allied Military Government (AMG), which distributed hundreds of films produced by American film studios for both commercial and political purposes. For discussion of AMG policy towards the Italian cinema industry, see Wagstaff (1995: 92–94).

32. See the issue of *Rinascita* largely devoted to said campaign (n. 3, 1949), with contributors such as directors Alessandro Blasetti, Luchino Visconti and Luigi Zampa, the actor Gino Cervi, and the screenplay writer Cesare Zavattini..

33. See the article by Luciano Quaglietti, 'La "gente del cinema" non è più il mito dei quartieri di lusso', in *L'Unità*, 22 February 1949, 3.

34. See, for example, law no. 958 of 29 December 1949. For discussion, see Quaglietti (1980: 50).

35. On censorship in post-war years see Chiarini (1954: 65–89), Argentieri (1974) and Brunetta (2009a: 75–101).

36. *Regio decreto* (Royal decree) no. 3287 of 24 September 1923.

37. The most forthright view on this was offered by Carlo Lizzani, who for many years was an *intellettuale organico* par excellence. He argued (1991:

2 TOGLIATTI'S *PARTITO NUOVO* AND ITALIAN CINEMA   39

97) that no neorealist film, not even Visconti's *La Terra Trema*, could be described as Marxist.

38. Tommaso Chiaretti 'Il volto di Roma nel cinema italiano', *L'Unità*, 9 May 1952, p. 3. Chiaretti worked at *L'Unità* from 1945 to 1956, when he left the PCI. He subsequently worked at *la Repubblica* and was among the founders of cinema magazine *Cinema '60*. See his obituary in *L'Unità*, 26 July 1987, front page and page 25.
39. Tommaso Chiaretti 'Cinema senza liuto', *L'Unità*, 15 May 1952, p. 3; Tommaso Chiaretti 'I migliori film italiani al macero', *L'Unità*, 22 May 1952, p. 3.
40. It is well known as the film was harshly criticized by Communist intellectuals and particularly by Antonello Trombadori, who lashed out at De Santis for having included stylistic features of American movies into a neorealist film. See Liehm (1984: 79); Gundle (1995a: 145).
41. Aldo Scagnetti 'Per la D.C. anche il cinema è divenuto un'"area depressa"', *L'Unità*, 17 October 1954, p. 3.
42. Numerous articles appeared over the years in *L'Unità* in which Communist film critics mourned the end of neorealism, seen as a style of cinema that could combine political commitment and poetic value and could contribute, from a left-wing perspective, to the nation's civic education. Nostalgia for this lost neorealism became even stronger in the 1970s, when the Italian cinema industry was subject to a commercial and creative crisis. See, for example, Tito Ranieri, 'Il cinema della Resistenza. Una lezione da rimeditare', *L'Unità*, 15 August 1973, p. 3.

BIBLIOGRAPHY

Aga Rossi, E., and G. Quaglieriello, eds. 1997. *L'altra faccia della luna. I rapporti tra PCI, PCF e Unione Sovietica*. Bologna: il Mulino.
Aga Rossi, E., and V. Zaslavsky. 1996. The Soviet Union and the Italian Communist Party 1944–48. In *The Soviet Union and Europe in the Cold War 1943–53*, ed. F. Gori and S. Pons, 161–182. New York: St. Martin's Press.
———. 1997. *Togliatti e Stalin. Il PCI e la politica estera staliniana negli archivi di Mosca*. Bologna: il Mulino.
Agosti, A. 1996. *Togliatti*. Turin: UTET.
———. 2008. *Palmiro Togliatti. A Biography*. London: I.B. Tauris.
Ajello, N. 1979. *Intellettuali e PCI 1944–1958*. Bari: Laterza.
Argentieri, M. 1974. *La censura nel cinema italiano*. Rome: Editori Riuniti.
Battini, M. 2001. Per una storia della Toscana rossa. In *Storia della Toscana*, ed. E. Fasano, G. Petralia, and P. Pezzino, 22–43. Bari: Laterza.
Battista, P. 2007. *Cancellare le tracce. Il caso Grass e il silenzio degli intellettuali italiani dopo il fascismo*. Milan: Rizzoli.

40 G. FANTONI

Bellassai, S. 2000. *La morale comunista. Pubblico e privato nella rappresentazione del P.C.I. (1947–1956)*. Rome: Carocci.

Bertelli, S. 1980. *Il gruppo. La formazione del gruppo dirigente del PCI, 1936–1948*. Milan: Rizzoli.

Bertelli, S., and F. Bigazzi, eds. 2001. *PCI: la storia dimenticata*. Milan: Mondadori.

Bertolissi, S., and L. Sestan, eds. 1985. da *Gramsci a Berlinguer. La via italiana al socialismo attraverso i Congressi del Partito Comunista Italiano*, II, 1944–45, Edizioni del Calendario, Vicenza: Marsilio.

Bosworth, R.J.B., and P. Dogliani. 1999. *Italian Fascism: History, Memory and Representation*. London: Palgrave Macmillan.

Boterbloem, K. 2004. *The Life and Time of Andrei Zhdanov, 1896–1948*. Montreal: McGill-Queen's University Press.

Brunetta, G.P. 1979. I cattolici e il cinema. In *Il cinema Italiano degli anni '50*, ed. G. Tinazzi, 305–321. Venice: Marsilio.

———. 2009a. *Il cinema neorealista italiano. Storia economica, politica e culturale*. Bari: Laterza.

———. 2009b. *The History of Italian Cinema: A Guide to Italian Film from Its Origins to the Twenty-First Century*. Princeton: Princeton University Press.

Caldiron, O., ed. 2002. *«Cinema» 1936–1943. Prima del neorealismo*. Rome: Edizioni Scuola Nazionale di Cinema.

Chiarini, L. 1954. *Cinema quinto potere*. Bari: Laterza.

Daneo, C. 1975. *La politica economica della ricostruzione*. Turin: Einaudi.

Donno, G. 2001. *La Gladio Rossa del PCI (1945–1967)*. Soveria Mannelli (Catanzaro): Rubbettino.

Duranti, S. 2008. *Lo spirito Gregario. I gruppi universitari fascisti tra politica e propaganda (1930–1940)*. Rome: Donzelli.

Fantoni, G. 2011. La Mineraria lavori o lasci lavorare. Myth and Memory of a Struggle in Tuscany. *Modern Italy* 16 (2): 195–208.

Forgacs, D. 1993. *L'industrializzazione delle cultura italiana (1880–1990)*. Bologna: il Mulino.

Forgacs, D., and S. Gundle. 2007. *Cultura di massa e società Italiana. 1936–1954*. Bologna: il Mulino.

Forlenza, R. 2010. The Italian Communist Party, Local Government and the Cold War. *Modern Italy* 15 (2): 177–196.

Gallerano, N., and M. Flores. 1992. *Sul PCI. Un'interpretazione storica*. Bologna: il Mulino.

Galli, G. 1977. *Storia del Partito Comunista Italiano*. Milan: Bompiani.

———. 1993. *Storia del Partito Comunista Italiano*. Milan: Kaos Edizioni.

Giacomini, R. 1984. *I partigiani della pace. Il movimento pacifista in Italia e nel mondo negli anni della prima guerra fredda*. Milan: Vangelista.

2 TOGLIATTI'S *PARTITO NUOVO* AND ITALIAN CINEMA   41

Gozzini, G. 2007. La democrazia dei partiti e il "partito nuovo". In *Togliatti nel suo tempo*, ed. R. Gualtieri, C. Spagnolo, and E. Taviani, 277–305. Rome: Carocci.

Gozzini, G., and R. Martinelli. 1998. *Dall'attentato di Togliatti all'VIII Congresso*, Vol. VII of the *Storia del partito comunista italiano*. Turin: Einaudi.

Gramsci, A. 1975. *Quaderni del carcere*. Edited by Valentino Gerratana. Turin: Einaudi.

Gualtieri, R. 2001. *Il PCI nell'Italia repubblicana*. Rome: Carocci.

Guarini, R., and G. Saltini. 1978. *I primi della classe. Il "culturcomunismo" dal 1944 al 1964: un'antologia per ricordare*. Milan: Sugarco.

Guerra, A. 2005. *Comunismi e comunisti: dalle svolte di Togliatti e Stalin del 1944 al crollo del comunismo democratico*. Bari: Dedalo.

Guiat, C. 2003. *The French and Italian Communist Parties: Comrades and Culture*. Portland, OR: Frank Cass Publishers.

Guiso, A. 2006. *La colomba e la spada. "Lotta per la pace" e antiamericanismo nella politica del Partito comunista italiano (1949–1955)*. Soveria Mannelli: Rubbettino.

Gundle, S. 1990. From Neorealism to Luci Rosse: Cinema, Politics, Society 1945–85. In *Culture and Conflict in Postwar Italy: Essays on Mass and Popular Culture*, ed. Zygmunt G. Barański and R. Lumley, 195–224. London: Macmillan.

———. 1995a. *I comunisti italiani tra Hollywood e Mosca. La sfida della cultura di massa*. Florence: Giunti.

———. 1995b. The Legacy of the Prison Notebooks: Gramsci, the PCI and Italian Culture in the Cold War Period. In *Italy in the Cold War. Politics, Culture and Society (1948–1958)*, ed. C. Duggan and C. Wagstaff, 131–147. Oxford: Berg.

———. 2000. *Between Hollywood and Moscow: The Italian Communists and the Challenge of Mass Culture, 1943–1991*. Durham, North Carolina: Duke University Press.

Ingrao, P. 2006. *Volevo la luna*. Turin: Einaudi.

Lepre, A. 1993. *Storia della prima Repubblica*. L'Italia dal 1942 al 1992. Bologna: il Mulino.

Liehm, M. 1984. *Passion and Defiance: Italian Film from 1942 to the Present*. Berkeley: University of California Press.

Lizzani, C. 1991. I film per il "partito nuovo". In *Il 1948 in Italia, la storia e i film*, ed. N. Tranfaglia, 97–103. Scandicci (Florence): La Nuova Italia.

———. 2007. *Il mio lungo viaggio nel secolo breve*. Turin: Einaudi.

Mafai. 1984. *L'uomo che sognava la lotta armata. La storia di Pietro Secchia*. Milan: Rizzoli.

Marcus, M. 1986. *Italian Film in the Light of Neorealism*. Princeton, NJ: Princeton University Press.

42 G. FANTONI

———. 2004. Celluloide and the Palimpsest of Cinematic Memory: Carlo Lizzani's Film of the Story Behind Open City. In *Roberto Rossellini's Rome Open City*, ed. S. Gottlieb. Cambridge: Cambridge University Press.

Marino, G.C. 1991. *Autoritratto del PCI staliniano, 1946–1953*. Rome: Editori Riuniti.

Mariuzzo, A. 2010. *Divergenze parallele. Comunismo e anticomunismo alle origini del linguaggio politico dell'Italia repubblicana (1945–1953)*. Soveria Mannelli: Rubbettino.

Martinelli, R. 1995. *Il "partito nuovo" dalla Liberazione al 18 aprile*, Vol. VI of the *Storia del Partito comunista italiano*. Turin: Einaudi.

Masi, S., and E. Lancia. 1987. *I film di Roberto Rossellini*. Rome: Gremese.

Miccichè, L. 1974. Per una verifica del neorealismo. In *Il neorealismo cinematografico Italiano*, ed. L. Miccichè, 7–28. Venice: Marsilio.

Pellizzaro, G.P. 1997. *Gladio Rossa—Dossier sulla più potente banda armata esistita in Italia*. Rome: Edizioni Settimo Sigillo.

Peregalli, A. 1991. *L'altra Resistenza. Il PCI e le opposizioni di sinistra, 1943–1945*. Genoa: Graphos.

Petricelli, A. 2004. Resistenza tradita. Ombre di un maccartismo all'Italiana sul cinema di Carlo Lizzani. In *Le linee d'ombra dell'identità repubblicana*, ed. P. Cavallo and G. Frezza, 153–170. Naples: Liguori.

Pirro, U. 1995. *Celluloide*. Turin: Einaudi.

Quaglietti, L. 1980. *Storia economico-politica del cinema italiano, 1945–1980*. Rome: Editori Riuniti.

Rossi, A., and G. Vacca. 2007. *Gramsci tra Mussolini e Stalin*. Rome: Fazi.

Sassoon, D. 1980. *Togliatti e la via italiana al socialismo*. Turin: Einaudi.

———. 1990. The Role of the Italian Communist Party in the Consolidation of Parliamentary Democracy in Italy. In *Securing Democracy: Political Parties and Democratic Consolidation in Southern Europe*, ed. G. Pridham, 84–103. London: Routledge.

Serri, M. 2005. *I redenti. Gli intellettuali che vissero due volte. 1938–1948*. Milan: Corbaccio.

Shiel, M. 2006. *Italian Neorealism: Rebuilding the Cinematic City*. London - New York: Wallflower Press.

Spriano, P. 1983. *I comunisti europei e Stalin*. Turin: Einaudi.

Thomas, P.D. 2010. *The Gramscian Moment. Philosophy, Hegemony and Marxism*. Chicago: Haymarket.

Turi, R. 2004. *Gladio Rossa. Una catena di complotti e delitti, dal dopoguerra al caso Moro*. Venice: Marsilio.

Urban, J.B. 1986. *Moscow and the Italian Communist Party, from Togliatti to Berlinguer*. London: I. B. Tauris.

Vacca, G. 1991. Appunti su Togliatti editore delle "Lettere" e dei "Quaderni". *Studi Storici* 22 (3): 639–662.

Valentini, C. 1997. *Berlinguer. L'eredità difficile*. Rome: Editori Riuniti.

Ventrone, A. 2008. *La cittadinanza repubblicana. Come cattolici e comunisti hanno costruito la democrazia italiana (1943–1948)*. Bologna: il Mulino.

Wagstaff, C. 1995. Italy in the Post-war International Cinema Market. In *Italy in the Cold War: Politics, Culture and Society 1948–58*, ed. C. Duggan and C. Wagstaff, 89–115. Oxford: Berg.

———. 2007. *Italian Neorealist Cinema: An Aesthetic Approach*. Toronto; Buffalo, NY: University of Toronto Press.

Zamagni, V. 2000. Evolution of the Economy. In *Italy Since 1945*, ed. P. McCarthy, 42–68. New York: Oxford University Press.

Zangrandi, R. 1998. *Il lungo viaggio attraverso il fascismo. Contributo alla storia di una generazione*. Milan: Mursia.

CHAPTER 3

Socialist Realism Italian-Style: PCI Cinematic Propaganda in the Stalin Era

Having spent seventeen of its twenty-four years in existence as a small and clandestine political organization, at the end of the Second World War the Italian Communist Party was unable to claim a well-established tradition of cinematographic production and distribution, as its French counterpart could (Perron 1998). Nonetheless, the PCI's national Press and Propaganda Section, under the leadership of Gian Carlo Pajetta, showed an early interest in the potential of film propaganda.[1] In this regard, Communist officials had probably learned from both the Italian Fascist and the Soviet regimes in the 1920s and 1930s. The level of literacy in Italy, which was relatively low when compared with that of other Western countries, may also have been one of the factors that convinced the Communist leadership of the need to invest in visual propaganda.[2] More in general, the use of images for persuasive ends was deeply rooted in the Italian tradition; it had been widely deployed by the Catholic Church, particularly since the Counter-Reformation of the sixteenth and seventeenth centuries. However, I would argue that the principal reason for adopting cinematic propaganda resided in the medium itself: it was intuitively felt that, of all the tools available to the propagandist, cinema was the one that could best illustrate and communicate to the militants the charismatic authority underpinning Communist leadership, according to the model set by Soviet dictator Stalin. Besides, film had great power to communicate effectively the political rituals that were central to the life of the party, and it therefore had to be exploited.

© The Author(s), under exclusive license to Springer Nature Switzerland AG 2021
G. Fantoni, *Italy through the Red Lens*, Italian and Italian American Studies, https://doi.org/10.1007/978-3-030-69197-4_3

45

The PCI regarded its own film production as essentially a tool for propaganda, as shown by the rigid division of responsibilities between the *Commissione culturale* (Cultural Commission), which took care of the cultural and legislative problems of national cinema, and the Sezione Stampa e Propaganda, which was entrusted with the supervision of the party's cinematographic production. This was the situation until PCI cinema production ended in 1979.

This chapter concerns the PCI's early production, from 1946 until 1951, when the cinematic effort of the PCI came to a halt. The party resumed the production of films only in 1958, as discussed in Chap. 4. The reasons for the momentary demise of Communist cinematography are discussed at the end of this chapter. Before that, the chapter offers a comprehensive analysis of quite heterogenous a cinematic material. This is very informative, and indeed revealing, of the complex variety of belief, attitudes and even sentiments characterizing at the time Communist militancy and the militants–leadership relationship. I intentionally use the term revealing. The PCI films of this period are more interesting for what they unconsciously disclose than for what they intentionally show, that is, for what was pre-decided in the script.

The two most important films the party produced in this period: *14 luglio* (14 July) and *Togliatti è ritornato* (Togliatti is back), both released in 1948, were allegedly made to, respectively, illustrate the PCI's official interpretation of the events surrounding the murderous attempt on Togliatti (on 14 July 1948), and to celebrate his return to political life after convalescence. However, on closer inspection, they seem to be especially aimed at restoring the confidence of Communist militants in the party's strength and in the inevitable final victory of the Communist ideal. This had been seriously shaken both by the severe electoral defeat on 18 April 1948 and by the disastrous outcome of the unrest in the wake of the attempt to assassinate Togliatti. More importantly to the historian, these two films show 'in the making' some of the political myths that constituted much of the PCI's appeal at grass-roots level, such as the almost supernatural qualities attributed to the leader, known as personality cult. They also offer visual evidence of the rituals and symbols, including cinematic tropes, the Communist leadership used to convey specific ideological narratives to the militants. These films can also contribute to the historiographical debate on the PCI. *Togliatti è ritornato*, in particular, does justice to the true nature of PCI's Stalinism by showing how Stalinism was not much, or not only, a political praxis imposed on the rank and file by the PCI leadership, but also, and perhaps more importantly, the Communist militants' autonomous elaboration nourishing their palingenetic expectations.

Nel mezzogiorno qualcosa è cambiato (Something has changed in the South, 1949) by Carlo Lizzani, was meant to illustrate the PCI's take on the '*questione meridionale*' ('southern question'): the issue of the geographical disparities in Italy's economic development that set apart the poorer South from the richer North. However, it especially shows how, in spite of their best intentions, the PCI leadership was not immune to the racialization of the Southern people, which had informed the Italian ruling elite's political intervention in the South since Unification (Verdicchio 1997, 28–31).

Modena, una città dell'Emilia rossa (Modena, a city in red Emilia), also directed by Carlo Lizzani, and released in 1949, was supposed to rehabilitate the city of Modena, governed by the Communists, in the eyes of the public. In the eyes of the historian, however, the film above all shows the almost pedestrian adherence by the PCI leadership and intellectuals to the themes and style of Stalinist propaganda.

La via della libertà (The Way to Freedom, by Sergio Grieco, 1951), the first historical documentary to be produced by the party, shows the importance of history in the construction of the PCI's identity and demonstrates how the PCI had a deterministic and teleological conception of history.

Pace, lavoro e libertà (Peace, Work and Freedom, by Gillo Pontecorvo, 1951), concerns the Seventh Congress of the PCI. Yet, it says very little about the Congress, but a lot about PCI congressional symbolism and the influence of Catholicism on the political culture of the PCI. References to Christian religion in political discourse were of course not a novelty, especially as far as the socialist tradition was concerned, and not just in Italy. For example, Henk Te Velde has shown how religious metaphors can be found in many autobiographies written by workers coming from different European countries who had 'converted' (the verb seems fitting in this case) to socialism in the nineteenth century (2013: 39–40). This should not come as a surprise: for many centuries, the symbolic universe of the members of the lower class was essentially derived from Christianity, and the new Social–Communist religion had to necessarily negotiate with such a tradition in order to make its way into the hearts and minds of European workers. Bolshevism 'drew heavily on the messianic myths and religious traditions of the Russian people', as argued by Emilio Gentile (2006: 41). *La via della libertà* demonstrates that the PCI specifically drew from

48 G. FANTONI

Catholicism, as can be seen by the overt references to the cult of martyrs depicted in the film.[3]

Before analysing one by one the films produced in this period, this chapter offers some general considerations about the characteristics of early Communist cinematic propaganda, especially in terms of its scope, cinematic features, and deployment, and critically engages with the existing literature on this issue. It also discusses the use the Party made of Soviet cinema for political ends in the late 1940s and early 1950s.

As mentioned above, the interest of the PCI cadres in the medium of cinema as a tool for propaganda was precocious. In February 1946, the PCI established a film division, and a party bulletin invited the local propaganda committees to produce films 'wherever the conditions and the means exist'.[4] While the Communists were quick to show an interest in cinematic propaganda, this interest was also somewhat uncritical. Communist officials particularly liked propaganda films because they looked 'modern'; 'Per una propaganda più moderna' (for more modern propaganda), for example, ran the heading of the first article on the use of cinema in propaganda published in *Il Quaderno dell'attivista*, in the May–June issue of 1947, shortly after the end of De Gasperi's third coalition cabinet and the exclusion of both the PCI and the PSI from the new government.[5] Since the creation of a soundtrack was one of the most technically challenging and expensive aspects of film production at that time, party bulletins suggested that a voice-over commentary could be provided separately by an activist while the images were running. Other aspects of the film's sound such as dialogue, sound effects, and music were not even mentioned: the commentary was seen as the only element essential to the good outcome of a propaganda initiative involving the use of film. This suggests that Communist officials saw cinematic propaganda as simply an alternative to a speech, like a sort of newspaper article in moving pictures, and had not yet become fully aware of the medium's specific characteristics and potential. Moreover, propaganda films were not particularly valued for their own sake, but were seen as a very useful means of attracting people in order to gather an audience that could then by addressed using other and more traditional forms of propaganda: 'taking the film as a starting point, you must immediately have a short meeting', intoned *Il Quaderno dell'attivista*, 'and then party material linked to the film's theme will be distributed'.[6] Any discussion of what features a cinematic text needed in order to be an effective propaganda tool, however, was virtually absent in both *Il Quaderno dell'attivista* and the circulars issued by the national Press and Propaganda Section. Early PCI films appeared on an irregular basis, as they were very often the spontaneous response to a dramatic event or intended as an additional boost to the promotion of an especially important party initiative; archival documents show how production was not planned according to any communications strategy established in advance by the Press and Propaganda Section.

The film critic and historian Mino Argentieri points out how the early Italian Communist propaganda films 'did not inform, and documented little. Their discourse [...] was simple, declarative and lacking in argumentation' (Argentieri 2001, 75). The apparent lack of sophistication of Communist cinematic propaganda during this period is explained by the nature of the audience the PCI films were designed to address: essentially, Communist militants. Technically speaking, the party's propaganda cinema was a 'response reinforcing' form of persuasion, according to the classification of propaganda forms by Jowett and O'Donnell (2006: 31–33). In other words, Communist propaganda films were preaching to the converted; they were not produced in order to enlarge the party's constituency, but rather to give the militants, in a simple fashion, an explanation of the party's political line. Above all, Communist films were supposed to increase the rank and file's reliance on the party leadership.

With the elections of 18 April 1948 approaching, the PCI also made use of Soviet films, and in particular of Mikheil Chiaureli's *Klyatva* (*The Vow*). This is a perfect example of Stalinist cinematic propaganda, depicting the Soviet dictator as a great statesman and beloved leader.[7] The party's national Press and Propaganda Section made great efforts to promote the film, which was given the title *Il Giuramento* for its Italian edition. A four-page pamphlet was distributed with a detailed summary of the plot and a full-page picture of Mikheil Gelovani, a Georgian actor who was regularly cast as Stalin in Soviet realist films.[8]

From the perspective of a modern viewer, it is somewhat surprising that the PCI might have considered a film like *Il Giuramento* to be an effective propaganda tool, as its content is so explicitly propaganda-driven that showing it would seem to have been counterproductive. However, this was not the case, as the director of *Klyatva* himself explained at a press conference following its presentation at the Venice Film Festival in 1946. In response to a hostile question from an Italian journalist about the presence of propaganda in Soviet feature films, Chiaureli argued that every film should be seen as propaganda, as every film, regardless of its national origin, endorsed an ideological vision. However, the viewer whose ideology entirely matched that of the film would not perceive it as propaganda-driven.[9] Soviet films of the Stalin era were viewed by the Italian Communist leadership as an effective propaganda tool because they were specifically used to address the militants, as was generally the case with the party's cinema production.

Soviets films were supposed to counter the deleterious influence of American movies, which very much troubled the PCI apparatus. Although with some delay, Communist film critics and intellectuals had become aware that even escapist films could convey propaganda messages. In August 1948, Antonello Trombadori, in an article published in the *Quaderno dell'attivista* and significantly titled, 'We shall hit the enemy in the cinema field too', alerted readers to the dangerous propaganda contained in American movies, defined as 'the new opium of the people'.[10] However, the only antidote Communist intellectuals seemed to be proposing in order to neutralize 'the venomous American films'[11] was a heightened use of Soviet cinematography which, apparently, was anything but appealing even to Communist militants. On this point, Trombadori invited the readers to a collective *autocritica*:

> How much does each of us spends to see the crimes of Mr. Truman's gangsters? Or the pin-up girls' corrupted and improbable love stories set in New York or Copacabana? And sometimes we are the victims of the class enemy's propaganda and we get to the point of saying that the Soviet film is beautiful, yes, but it is 'heavy', it is 'boring', it is 'difficult'!

No effort was spared by the PCI in its popularization of contemporary Soviet films in the late 1940s and early 1950s. One of its most important endeavours in this respect was the successful attempt to control the movement constituted by the '*circoli del cinema*'. These associations of cinema-lovers were established in many towns and cities at the end of the war; their aim was to promote a wider knowledge of international cinema after the years of cultural censorship by the Fascist authorities. They then came together within a national association, the Federazione Italiana Circoli del Cinema (FICC: Italian Federation of Cinema Clubs).[12] Left-wing members formed the majority in many of these, and the first president of the FICC, the film critic and soon-to-be film director Antonio Pietrangeli, was a candidate for the Democratic Popular Front in the national elections of 18 April 1948.

Despite the effort lavished on the distribution of Soviet films, the PCI was never able to counter the overwhelming power of the American film industry. Soviet cinema only found a niche audience of left-wing intellectuals and film critics, while at the grass-roots level its distribution remained confined to specific areas of the country that were politically dominated by the PCI. It also influenced PCI cinematography during that period, as can be seen in two important films produced shortly after the elections of April 1948, *14 luglio* (14 July) and *Togliatti è ritornato* (Togliatti is back).

14 luglio constituted the PCI's official interpretation of the events that followed the assassination attempt on Togliatti, occurred on 14 July 1948. The news that the leader of the PCI had been shot in the centre of Rome spread rapidly across the country. Many Communist workers and groups of former partisans believed that the shooting marked the outbreak of civil war, and took action accordingly (Gozzini 1998). Historians have debated whether the turmoil that occurred over the period 14–16 July proves the existence of a predetermined Communist plan for insurrection, which was aborted by the party leadership immediately after it had swung into action. Since no conclusive proof of this hypothesis has ever been identified, it is reasonable to interpret the serious clashes that took place on those days both as an expression of repressed frustration, felt by many Communist militants over the electoral defeat of 18 April, and as a clear indication of the revolutionary aspirations of the party's rank and file, although not of its leadership.

At the time, however, the government and the conservative press provided a different interpretation of these events. They claimed that the unrest provided evidence of a Communist plot, the 'Piano K' (Plan K), to overthrow democracy. No measures were taken against the PCI itself, but thousands of Communist workers were arrested over the following days and many faced various criminal charges. Furthermore, the national leadership of the CGIL endorsed the demonstrations up and down the country by declaring a general strike. This was the cause of a bitter rift between the Socialist and Communist trade unionists and the segments of the union federation, principally those with Catholic or Christian Democrat affiliations, that were more pro-government; this was to weaken the Italian labour movement for many years.

14 luglio offers no clue to the historian to conclusively establish whether the quasi-revolution of summer 1948 was somehow the result of a prearranged Communist insurrectional plan. In fact, the film is not particularly informative of what actually happened during those troubled days. As it is the case with other PCI films of the period, *14 luglio* is exclusively concerned with making a number of political points clear to the Communist militants, and two points in particular. First, the general strike had been a spontaneous outburst that had been transformed into a disciplined and peaceful demonstration by the well-timed intervention of the party's national leadership. Second, this strike had resulted in a great victory for the PCI as the Italian working class, guided by the party leadership's wisdom, had shown a sense of responsibility and political maturity that had impressed both their political adversaries and the whole world. Finally, Communist viewers were given reassurance about the degree of agreement within the party leadership. The film's memorable finale showed that the events after 14 July had not given rise to any discord between party leaders; the PCI was instead united under the leadership of Palmiro Togliatti as never before.

14 luglio, which had a running time of thirty minutes, was produced by the PCI's film division and directed by the twenty-nine-year-old Glauco Pellegrini. The script and voice-over were by the Communist writer and journalist Felice Chilanti. These two had both had their cultural education and professional development during the Fascist era.[13] The film credits included a young Rodolfo Sonego, subsequently one of the most important screenplay writers of post-war Italy, and Roberto Natale, who was to have a career in the 1960s and 1970s as a writer of B-movies such as *Cinque tombe per un medium* (Terror-Creatures from the Grave) and *L'isola delle svedesi* (Twisted Girls); both men are listed as '*collaboratori*' (contributors).

According to a statement by Pellegrini, *14 luglio* was produced by order of Gian Carlo Pajetta.[14] Pajetta had pressed Pellegrini to get the film released in time for the first national *Festa dell'Unità*, held in Rome on 26 September 1948. *Togliatti è ritornato* was shot that very day, while the PCI was celebrating the party leader's return to public life after his convalescence. Both films can be seen as cinematic expressions of the Stalinist-style cult of personality that was developed around Togliatti in the late 1940s (Andreucci 2005: 183–186). The assassination attempt itself contributed in no small measure to forming the cult of Togliatti's personality and ultimately reinforced his leadership (Gundle 1995: 93–94; Gozzini and Martinelli 1998: 67–71). As pointed out by Anita Pisch, a personality cult can be regarded as a radical form of charismatic authority (2016: 33–35). Charismatic leaders tend to appear in moments of crisis, when a political community feels threatened. They are entrusted with delivering their followers from danger and restoring hope. The PCI was indeed under political attack, at least since May 1947, as shown in the previous chapter, and Communist militants had suffered varied political and often personal humiliations, particularly as a consequence of the repression which had followed the disturbance provoked by the murder attempt on Togliatti's life. Hence, Communist leadership was increasingly resorting to the construction of a cult of personality surrounding Togliatti, and cinema was consciously employed for that purpose, as proved by both *14 luglio* and *Togliatti è ritornato*.[15]

14 luglio is a sort of docufiction that skilfully blended archival footage and fiction. Its plot was clearly inspired by Chiaureli's *The Vow*; both films have at their centre a message that has to be delivered to the leader of the party so that he will be made aware of a hideous injustice being perpetrated against the workers by the class enemy. Both films offer avuncular images of Communist leaders, Togliatti and Stalin respectively, and suggest that even members at the lowest level within the party could easily meet them in person.

In *14 luglio*, the bearers of the message are three peasants from a village in Sicily: two men, Armando and Giovanni, and a young woman called Franca. They arrive in Rome at dawn on a sunny day in summer; it is 14 July 1948, the day of the attempt on Togliatti's life, but they are not yet aware of this. The three of them make for the headquarters of the Italian Communist Party in Via della Botteghe Oscure (Image 3.1). On their arrival, they are courteously greeted by a doorman. Franca begins to describe the dramatic situation of their fellow agricultural day-labourers in Sicily. Day-labourers are oppressed by their '*gabellotti*' (middlemen in the semi-feudal Sicilian estate system). In a flashback, they are depicted as gangsters: wearing sunglasses, sitting in cafes, drinking beer, and playing cards. The words '*mafia*' and '*mafiosi*' are notably absent from the voice-over that describes these oppressors, although such terms were already in regular use in the Communist press after the massacre of Portella della Ginestra, which took place on 1 May 1947.[16] The peasants' last hope is help from Togliatti; Armando, Giovanni, and Franca had therefore decided to go to Rome.

The doorman reassures the three visitors that they will be able to speak to Togliatti, but not immediately, as the party leader is currently attending parliament. In the meantime, they are offered a tour of the premises of *L'Unità*. When they arrive, another doorman shows them old issues of the newspaper and explains how the history of the party, and of the Italian labour movement, can be traced in its pages. A five-minute digression

54   G. FANTONI

Image 3.1 The three Sicilian peasants at Botteghe Oscure

then presents the history of the PCI. This section features an example of the characteristics typically attributed to the Communist leader in development of the 'cult of personality': his ability to predict the future. This prophetic gift reflects his capacity to interpret historical events correctly. The voice-over quotes the famous (and almost certainly apocryphal) prediction made by Antonio Gramsci to his persecutors on the day he was sentenced to prison, 'the day will come when you will bring Italy to catastrophe and then it will be up to us Communists to save the country'; it then claims that in due course this prediction came true during the Resistance, when Italy was saved 'by the workers, the intellectuals, the young people, and everyone who lives from their own labour'. In the same vein, Togliatti had warned in 1946 that the anti-Communist attitude of the ruling class would inevitably lead to Italy's enslavement by a foreign power. The recent Italian signature of the Marshall Plan, which Togliatti had vehemently opposed in a speech in Parliament only four days before, on 10 July 1948, seems to offer confirmation of the Communist leader's foresight.

The three peasants have just finished browsing the pages of *L'Unità* when a telephone rings, cutting across the background music for this historical digression, which is the Italian national anthem. There are a few seconds of suspense: the camera lingers in a close-up of the ringing telephone and the audience is forced to wait anxiously for someone to pick up the receiver. Eventually, a journalist answers, and the voice-over provides a commentary:

> Gunfire at Palmiro Togliatti, he has been shot four times! The first shot to kill Togliatti, the second against the peace of the people, the third against our freedom, and the fourth was supposed to strike us in the heart, it was to hit our Italian Communist Party.

At the same time, we see five portraits: Marx, Lenin, Stalin, Gramsci, and Togliatti. The symbolism of this scene is crystal clear: after the vile attempt on his life, Palmiro Togliatti has found his place in the hall of fame of the international Communist movement.

Subsequently, the film introduces the viewers to 'the great general strike that the people wanted, which no one will ever be able to forget', using cross-cutting editing that alternates the titles of the special editions of *L'Unità*, archival footage of demonstrations, and footage of empty streets in Italian cities. As the three-quarter light shows, the streets are in fact empty because they were filmed at dawn, probably days after the event, rather than because of the strike. Everything is portrayed as have taken place in an orderly fashion and absolute calm; the impression given is less of a strike and more of an expression of sorrow and dismay on a national scale. The clashes, which occurred in several areas of the country, claimed sixteen deaths and caused over two hundred casualties, are completely glossed over.[17] Noticeably, the role of the CGIL in declaring the general strike is also neglected. Commenting on this part of the film, filmmaker Ansano Giannarelli has concluded that *14 luglio* fails to deliver an accurate depiction of the strike.[18] However, it is also possible that the film's many omissions were intended to emphasize one of the film's central messages, that the PCI, and the PCI alone, maintained firm and undisputed control over a working class that completely identified itself with the Communist Party, and therefore with its leader Togliatti.

56 G. FANTONI

The film's final scene is particularly significant in relation to its political objectives. The viewer is introduced to the serene atmosphere of a beautiful sunlit garden, in fact in the grounds of 'Le Frattocchie', the PCI's political school for its officials in the outskirts of Rome, with Vivaldi's 'Spring' as background music. There, a completely recovered and impeccably dressed Palmiro Togliatti is visited by three of the party's leaders: Luigi Longo, Pietro Secchia, and Edoardo D'Onofrio. 'Perhaps these three dangerous subversives have come to discuss Plan K?' the voice-over ironically suggests. Instead, however, they play chess and talk in a friendly and relaxed manner.

The symbolism is fairly clear: the party's leadership is united and serene. The general aim of this final scene is to mitigate the disappointment of the many militants and cadres who felt that the general strike that had followed the attempt on Togliatti's life had been their best chance of seizing power through a revolutionary uprising, and very probably their last. This end to the film thus suggests that nothing has actually changed, as the party's continuing objective is to fight for the ultimate triumph of the Communist cause. To make this point as clear as possible, the voice-over uses the words of Secchia himself, the powerful deputy leader of the party and champion of the pro-insurrection hard-line tendency within the leadership (although this clash within the Communist leadership had happened beneath the surface and militants were not aware of it):

> The general strike marked the start, not the end, of a great battle. It showed that the forces of democracy are powerful within our country.

As in other PCI films of the early period, the masses are protagonists alongside the leader. We see a crowd of factory workers and peasants, but the voice-over constantly reminds the viewer that two other categories are an integral part of this: intellectuals and young people. Communist members are depicted as living in a symbiotic relationship with the leader: when Togliatti is shot, they inevitably enter a state of unrest; when Togliatti gives a statement from his hospital bed reassuring people about his physical condition, they regain their emotional balance.

14 luglio was shot in different locations, the Piazza della Repubblica and Via delle Botteghe Oscure in Rome, the garden of Le Frattocchie, the Sicilian village, and a few interiors, and therefore must have been a complex production venture. The production team clearly did not have a synchronized audio-recording system at their disposal, and this explains why dialogue between the protagonists is dubbed, out of sync, by the same voice-over. While dubbing and studio sound had long been standard in Italian cinema, lack of synchronicity was not the norm.[19] It should also be pointed out that, in the same period, Incom (Industria Cortometraggi) did use synchronized audio recording in the production of its famous *Settimana Incom* newsreel, which dominated the market thanks to rather blatant support from the government.[20] The cameramen of Incom had shot the only in-sync scene of *14 luglio*, featuring Togliatti's brief speech at the hospital (Image 3.2). The scene was firstly included in the *Settimana Incom* newsreel of 30 July 1948 and only subsequently given to the PCI. The hospital scene in *14 luglio* demonstrates that PCI film production was, at the time, technically inferior to that of a private company like Incom. It would be interesting to determine whether it was the PCI leadership asking the government-backed Incom to record Togliatti's statement or the other way around. The former scenario would prove how the PCI leadership, and Togliatti himself, were doing everything in their

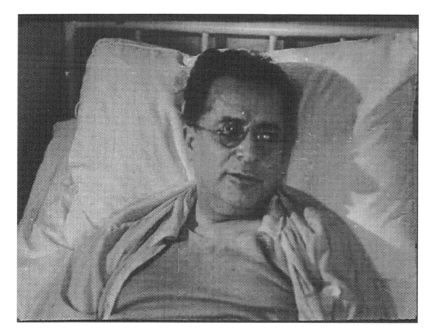

Image 3.2 Togliatti in the hospital

power to blunt the insurrectionary agitation of many of the party's rank and file, the latter that the government was pursuing the very similar objective of placating Communist demonstrators. In all likelihood, they both wanted to diffuse political tension and tacitly collaborated to the same end.

14 luglio is as rich in pictorial and cinematographic references as it is in political messages. Although produced when Zhdanovism was already the official cultural doctrine of the party, the film owes a cinematographic debt to the Russian avant-garde rather than to Socialist realism, as shown by the extensive use of symbolic shots: examples include the fountain whose water stops flowing when Togliatti is injured but restarts when he is declared to be out of danger, and the workers' synchronized folding of their arms to symbolize the beginning of the strike (Image 3.3). The director even echoes a scene in Sergei Eisenstein's *October*, a classic of Soviet formalism, in which a crowd of peasants holds sickles against the sky.

Image 3.3 Workers on strike

The other film produced in the summer of 1948, Carlo Lizzani and Basilio Franchina's *Togliatti è ritornato*, tells us a great deal about a range of political and cultural issues, including the religious ethos that pervaded party life and the characteristics of Italian Communists' Stalinism during that period. *Togliatti è ritornato* is an account of the enormous party organized by the PCI in Rome, on 26 September 1948, in celebration of Togliatti's recovery and return to political life. That same day, in Rome, saw the first celebration of the national *Festa dell'Unità*: the festival that the PCI organized to raise funds for the party press.[21] The film has a running time of thirty-six minutes and is divided into two parts of approximately equal length. The first shows the preparation of the festival site and the impressive parade that took place in the centre of Rome, involving delegates and groups from every area branch of the Italian Communist Party. According to the rather triumphalist account in *L'Unità*, over five hundred thousand people had gathered in Rome that day.[22] The second part is entirely dedicated to the speech given by Togliatti at the Stadio dei Marmi, in the Foro Italico, at the end of the parade. The Board of Censors required a few lines of the commentary and some of the footage to be cut.[23]

From a historical perspective, *Togliatti è ritornato* is a unique visual documentation of the initial stage of the construction of a set of rituals which during the post-war period were to constitute an important part of the PCI's appeal at grass-roots level. In this respect the film's opening scene, showing preparations for the *Festa nazionale dell'Unità*, is particularly interesting, as it shows us many of the features of this social event that had subsequently become traditional: platoons of militants working on the construction of the stands, red flags, and cardboard cut-outs of the hammer and sickle symbol in every corner, kiosks selling roasted pig and watermelon, and numerous posters inviting party sympathizers to subscribe to *L'Unità* (Image 3.4). The *Feste dell'Unità* would assume a crucial importance in the life of the party, in that it was especially at these events that Communists were able to express their camaraderie and mutual trust.

The long section of the film dedicated to the parade documents how the PCI, during a brief period after the end of the war, had become a sort of receptacle for Italy's local community traditions. At the same time, the '*popolo comunista*' (Communist masses) had independently developed a political rituality that combined regional varieties of Italian folklore with elements of scenography borrowed from the Soviet public displays of the Stalin era. *Togliatti è ritornato* allows us to observe the curious result: a procession that mixed together groups of cyclists, girls in traditional

Image 3.4   The hammer and sickle symbol

outfits, community bands, allegorical floats, gymnastics teams, Neapolitan town criers, Tuscan flag-wavers and crossbowmen, and large-scale portraits of Togliatti, Stalin, and Zhdanov made the Communist march seem somewhere between a parade in Moscow's Red Square and a town festival (Image 3.5). Even the background music emphasizes this cultural fusion: traditional Italian music alternated with songs from the historical repertoire of the international Communist movement and, notably, with boogie-woogie themes, which were evidently considered as belonging to Italian folk tradition. The portrayal of the parade is significant, as it is perhaps the only time during this early period when the strictly hierarchical and top-down nature of Communist cinematic propaganda was challenged and subverted. In view of the impressive display organized by the militants, Communist officials had no choice but to devote a large chunk of the film's final edited version to the parade. For the first time in the production of an Italian Communist propaganda film, there was some sort of reciprocity in operation between the party's base (the militants) and its

Image 3.5 A gymnastics team at the parade

higher strata (the officials and intellectuals), with the former imposing some of the content and visual elements on the latter. For those who attended that day, it was in fact the great parade, rather than Togliatti's speech, that remained impressed in their memory. This is illustrated by the recollections of Pietro Ingrao, who at the time was the editor of *L'Unità*:

> In the capital we saw streams of people flowing past … We could see a subject [the Communist masses] that wanted to express an impulse for social change, and at the same time a firm rootedness in their country, even by making an arguably excessive use of folk tradition.

The principal reason why *Togliatti è ritornato* was produced, however, as *Il Quaderno dell'attivista* pointed out, was to record a speech by Togliatti for those many militants who had never had the opportunity to listen to the Communist leader in person.[24] In terms of its propaganda value, the most important part of the film was therefore probably the second half, covering Togliatti's speech at the Stadio dei Marmi sports stadium. This was recorded live but separately from the shooting, due to the aforementioned lack of a synchronized audio- and video-recording system. In all likelihood, the consequent lack of synchronization between the images and soundtrack was not a significant problem for an audience of the late 1940s.

As with *14 luglio*, *Togliatti è ritornato* has two protagonists: the PCI leader and the masses. The people attending his speech fill the stadium to complete capacity, and many spectators are precariously holding onto the white statues that encircle the arena. The camera almost always frames the crowd from a higher position, with the result that they appear to be a compact, and rather indistinct, mass: a solid block of Communist workers (Image 3.6). A few individuals are shown, but when this happens they are framed from below in order to turn them into archetypes: a worker wearing his overalls, an intellectual with a V-neck sweater and horn-rimmed glasses (Image 3.7), a smiling girl sporting the red neckerchief of the

Image 3.6 A solid block of Communist workers

Image 3.7 The Party intellectual

Pioneers.[25] A certain number of children, of course, are also included (Image 3.8). The masses clap almost relentlessly.

The speech by Togliatti demonstrates how at the time the PCI was borrowing heavily from Catholicism for its cultural references. The film consecrated him as a prophet and semi-religious figure, and just like a prophet he addresses his followers calmly and serenely, speaking in parables and even quoting the gospels, including Matthew (3: 10):

> 'Even now the axe is laid to the root of the trees. Every tree therefore that does not bear good fruit is cut down and thrown into the fire'. We can see today [applause from the audience] that the 'tree that does not bear good fruit' is the system that is currently exploiting the workers!

He goes on to promise paradise to believers:

> We battle on with the profound certainty [of final victory] because for twenty, thirty years and more we have been following events in the world

Image 3.8 A child in the crowd

and we have seen a great country, covering one third of the globe, move away from this system of exploitation, start building a new world, and go forward in this construction by adding success to success, victory to victory, for itself, for all of us, and for the workers of the whole world.

Finally, Togliatti blesses the assembly:

Take my greetings right across Italy, take them to the factory workers and to the unemployed from the workshops in Milan, Turin, Genoa and all our industrial centres, take my greetings to the sturdy sharecroppers and day-labourers of the Po valley, to the peasants of southern Italy, take them to the professionals and the office-workers …. Take them greetings that console them in the struggle that they have to face, and that tell them once again that in Italy there is a force, an invincible force exists, the force of the Communist Party.

Togliatti è ritornato undoubtedly offers historians of the PCI insights into the role played by Stalinism in the construction of Communist appeal during the post-war period.[26] At the beginning of the 1990s, there was a proliferation of studies on the Stalinist imprint of Togliatti's *partito nuovo*. Stalinism was said to have fundamentally characterized both Communist leadership and policies.[27] This new historiography was, at least in part, unencumbered by political motivation.[28] By attacking the PCI, right-wing historians aimed to damage the post-Communist PDS (Partito Democratico della Sinistra / Democratic Party of the Left), the only party to have survived the end of the first republic, albeit following a change of the party's name.[29] In the midst of the historiographical quarrel—an historiographical Cold War, as it was defined—historian Maurizio Bertolotti suggested that an anthropological approach could be taken towards the party's Stalinism; he argued that it could be studied as 'an important cultural phenomenon, in which the ways of thinking of millions of peasants and workers are in play', rather than just the personal inclination of a small number of political leaders (1991: XV).[30] A few years before, the historian Paolo Spriano, who lived through that period and like most Communist intellectuals was fascinated by Stalin, had described the feelings held by militants and officials towards the Soviet dictator as a form of filial love (1986: 149–162).

An analysis of *Togliatti è ritornato* confirms the validity of these approaches. By the late 1940s, various symbols, beliefs, and values borrowed from Stalinism, having been absorbed at the grass-roots level, were already embedded in the worldview of many Communist workers. In many respects, the function that Stalinism played in the Communist subculture was not very different from that traditionally played by religion in local Italian communities: a faith that gave hope and acted as a binding force. *Togliatti è ritornato* offers a visual demonstration of this: Stalin, whose face appears for a few seconds while Togliatti is speaking, is presented as a sort of protective divinity, while the USSR, evoked by means of archival footage showing contented Soviet workers, seems to have an eschatological function not unlike that of heaven in Christianity.

To summarize what we have been discussing in this chapter, *14 luglio* and *Togliatti è ritornato* show that their writers and directors held a set of rituals, symbols, and political myths in common with their target audience, the Communist militants. The influence of Stalinism was particularly important, as it pervaded the life of the party. However, the symbolism and cultural references employed by Italian Communists came from the Catholic tradition just as much as from Stalinism. The main cinematographic inspiration for the early PCI films was Soviet cinema, which was also used as a propaganda tool and as a medium for the political education of Communist militants.

Thanks to *Togliatti è ritornato*, the young Carlo Lizzani became a regular director of PCI productions. He was soon sent to southern Italy to shoot another documentary: *Nel mezzogiorno qualcosa è cambiato* (Something has changed in the South). The production of this new film had become a matter of urgency because, in the second half of 1949, a major wave of protest had spread across the southern countryside. In Puglia, Sicily, and Calabria, crowds of impoverished day-labourers occupied the large estates; on several occasions the police opened fire, and many workers died or were injured. These events brought to the fore the '*questione meridionale*' ('southern question'): the issue of the geographical disparities in Italy's economic development that set apart the poorer South from the richer North.

These developments led to the PCI's decision to produce a documentary that would offer the Communist perspective on the matter. The aims of *Nel mezzogiorno qualcosa è cambiato* included showing the workers of northern and central Italy the living conditions of southerners, and explaining the reasons for the endurance of the 'southern question' under democracy. These were not the film's only purposes, however. The PCI leadership was concerned about the radical aims of the day-labourer movement (Gozzini and Martinelli 1998: 96–99), and *Nel mezzogiorno qualcosa è cambiato* was part of a series of initiatives aimed at reining in a protest movement that the party had been unable to control.

The southern branches of the PCI had initially promoted the occupations as part of a campaign for the implementation of land reform. In the party's plan, however, land occupations had been intended as symbolic actions only to be undertaken on a temporary basis. The Communist strategy regarding agricultural workers in fact hinged on widening the social base of the land-reform movement by engineering an alliance between day-labourers and small landowners. The latter could have been scared off by a method of struggle that showed no respect for private property. The day-labourers, on the other hand, believed that the moment had finally come for a long-awaited redistribution of land and attempted to make these occupations permanent. This action implicitly questioned the strategy of the PCI. As well as addressing the workers of the North, *Nel mezzogiorno qualcosa è cambiato* was thus intended for the southern day-labourers who had taken part in the struggles of 1949: it suggested that they would only be able to achieve improvements in their economic and social conditions by embracing the PCI's strategy.

The film is a journey to the South, investigating the economic and social roots of the 'southern question'. According to the voice-over, written by Alicata, the social and economic backwardness of the South is essentially due to the lack of industry and the unfair pattern of land ownership that historically has characterized these regions. How can these problems be solved? There is but one way, says Alicata: southern workers must establish an alliance with the northern working class, under the leadership of the Italian Communist Party.

The PCI's strategy for the South was consistent with Gramsci's reading of the 'southern question' (Gribaudi 1996: 81–82). His influence is evident in the text for the voice-over, which is more or less a summary of his principal theoretical work on this issue, *Alcuni temi della quistione meridionale* (1926).[31] The film suggests that the alliance of northern and southern workers envisaged by Gramsci, the 'change' referred to in the title of the film, is finally possible under the new democratic regime and thanks to the presence of the PCI.

In other respects, however, the film seems to substantially depart from Gramsci's thought. In particular, the film appears to indulge in a racialization of the Southern people. This was the traditional prism through which the elites, both from the north and the south of the country, had often looked to the poorer strata of the southern population. In their eyes, the widespread, visible backwardness of the South proved the cultural and social inferiority of the southern masses. *Nel mezzogiorno qualcosa è cambiato* perpetuated the stereotype of the south as utterly backward and entirely underdeveloped, not least through the omission of features that might have suggested a different reading of the southern environment. The editing deliberately avoids showing tourist sites or city centres inhabited by the southern bourgeoisie, for example; instead, it lingers on the depiction of slums, poor villages, and what the commentary called the '*tragico sasso di Matera*' ('pitiful Matera rockface', in reference to the cave dwellings in Matera). As a result, from watching *Nel mezzogiorno qualcosa è cambiato* one might think that the only inhabitants of southern Italy at the end of the 1940s were destitute children, women wearing tattered clothing, and veiled grandmothers (Images 3.9 and 3.10). The only example of quasi-modernity shown is the steelworks in Bagnoli, near Naples. It is noteworthy that the film devotes far more time to describing the struggles of the southern industrial workers than to covering the land

Image 3.9 Veiled grandmother

occupations by the peasants. It is, however, actually impossible to accurately assess the political significance that the film originally attributed to the land occupation movement, because the censorship board required some of the scenes showing the occupation of the landowners' estates to be cut.[32] The voice-over suggests that the Bagnoli steelworkers had been learning 'discipline and organization' from their northern comrades, to be combined with their innate 'spirit of sacrifice'. It is now time for the southern peasants, the film seems to suggest, exercise patience, and place their trust in the Communist leadership. The film thus establishes a sort of hierarchy: the leadership of the prospective alliance between industrial workers and peasants is assigned to the more politically advanced northern working class. Besides, the authors of *Nel mezzogiorno qualcosa è cambiato* do not seem to be familiar with the Gramscian concept of 'subaltern culture', in the definition by Pasquale Verdicchio, 'an alternative culture that exists within the context of a dominant or official culture' (1997: 137). In Gramsci's writings this expression is anything but derogatory: subaltern

Image 3.10 Destitute children in the South

cultures are proper of non-hegemonic groups, and they should be acknowledged and emphasized. In the film, however, little recognition seems to be given to the southern people's autonomous history and culture. Occasional splashes of local folklore are distributed here and there, like when we see the stereotypical vignette of a worker from Naples playing guitar and singing.

Because of these features, *Nel mezzogiorno qualcosa è cambiato* may seem pervaded by clichés to modern eyes, but at the time it had an impact on its audience due to its portrayal of graphic scenes of poverty. It made such a profound impression on the writer Carlo Levi that he offered Lizzani the opportunity to make a film version of his novel *Cristo si è fermato ad Eboli* (*Christ Stopped at Eboli*) (1945), which had exposed Italian intellectuals to the somewhat disturbing reality of the social and economic backwardness in some parts of southern Italy.[33] In this respect, *Nel mezzogiorno qualcosa è cambiato* contributed to what has been described as 'the discovery of the South' by the left-wing intelligentsia of northern and central Italy (Ajello 1979: 230–232). Lizzani was too young to embark on this project and declined the offer. A dramatized version of Levi's book was made by Francesco Rosi thirty years later.

It seems useful to make one general consideration regarding the cinematographic influences on the films produced by the PCI in these years. In view of the strong support that Communist film critics expressed for neorealism, it might seem surprising that the neorealist aesthetic is scarcely present in the party's productions. Paola Bonifazio has demonstrated how in the late 1940s and early 1950s even the directors working for the government-funded Centro di Documentazione (CdD) resorted to neorealist aesthetics when producing pro-DC and anti-Communist propaganda films. While borrowing stylistic and thematic features from neorealism, these CdD would often reverse the political message of neorealist films, stripping the neorealist aesthetic of the political significance traditionally associated with it (Bonifazio 2014, 25–50). Yet, *Nel mezzogiorno qualcosa è cambiato* is the only Communist film of this period that bears any distinct stylistic resemblance to contemporary neorealist output: it was shot entirely on location, and presented itself as an objective record of actual events and real subjects. However, it is perhaps best described as a sort of iconographic or symbolic neorealism, in that every visual element within the film serves to illustrate the political message contained in the commentary.

The film's topic explains the choice of cinematographic approach: neorealism was the style of choice for portraying backwardness and poverty, and was therefore customarily associated with southern Italy. The association between backwardness and neorealism can arguably be attributed to the model provided by the first post-war film to deal with the problems of southern workers, Visconti's *La terra trema*, which the Communist press had feted as an extraordinary cinematographic achievement.[34] Initial funding for *La terra trema*, first conceived as a propaganda film, came from the PCI; when it subsequently developed into a sort of personal project, the director Visconti had to find other sources of finance.[35]

It can also be argued that the use of neorealism to depict the South of the country was rooted deep in national culture, and it was ultimately a consequence of *verismo* (realism), the literary movement that had had a profound influence on Italian culture and art at the turn of the century. Most of the novels and short stories of the *verismo* were by Southern writers, principally by Giovanni Verga, and portrayed southern Italian life. If Noa Steimatsky is right when she points out that '*verismo* already embedded a photographic modernity, which made it adaptable to the neo-realist project', then the use of neorealism to depict the south must have appeared as an obvious choice to filmmakers—intellectuals of the Italian Communist party (Steimatsky 2008: 101). The link between neorealism and southern realism was established as early as 1941, when Mario Alicata and Giuseppe De Santis published two articles in which they posed the question whether films inspired by Verga's writings could produce a syn-thesis between film documentary and fiction and thus contribute to the stylistic renewal of Italian cinema (Marcus 1986: 14–15). However, Luca Caminati is probably right when he says that the connection between neo-realism and pre-Fascist realism should not be overemphasized as it is to some extent a narrative developed in the post-war years and aimed at mini-mizing the debt neorealism had towards the cinema of the Fascist period, and particularly documentary cinema (Caminati 2012: 55–56). Some of the most characteristic features of neorealism can indeed be found in some films produced during the Fascist Regime. Films shot in the African colo-nies, in particular, were occasions for cameramen, cinematographers, and directors to work with non-professional actors and to shoot on location, sometimes challenging locations (Zinni 2011).

Whatever the role Communist filmmakers attributed to neorealism with respect to the party's propaganda effort, when the task of a film was to depict the achievements of Communism, the only acceptable cinematic aesthetic was the celebrative and pompous Socialist realism; this is per-fectly exemplified by *Modena, una città dell'Emilia rossa*. Produced by Libertas Film in 1949, *Modena città dell'Emilia rossa* was made in order to counter the aggressive campaign mounted by the conservative press against the former Communist partisans, who were accused of having indiscriminately murdered hundreds of Fascists and Fascist sympathizers in the months immediately after the end of the war.[36] Modena lay at the centre of the '*triangolo della morte*' (triangle of death), the area in the region of Emilia-Romagna between the cities of Bologna, Reggio Emilia, and Ferrara where significant numbers of executions of Fascists, whether actual or alleged, had taken place.

The political message of this twenty-eight-minute film was that Modena was not a lawless land—'*il Messico d'Italia*' (Italy's Mexico), to quote the description in the voice-over written by Gianni Rodari—but a city inhab-ited by 'good people, warm-hearted and industrious', who had always been at the forefront of the struggle for liberty.[37] The film thus established a link between the Risorgimento, the nineteenth-century movement for national independence, and the anti-Fascist and anti-Nazi military resistance during the Second World War. A monument to Ciro Menotti, a hero of the Risorgimento originally from Modena, is shown alongside one dedicated to the Resistance, which the voice-over describes as a 'second Risorgimento'. This was the first time that this description was employed in Communist cinema, but certainly not the last, as discussed in Chap. 9. The 'second Risorgimento' was in fact for many years a recurrent topos in PCI discourse and an important propaganda device. It allowed the PCI to present the civil war of the period 1943–1945 as Italy's final war of independence, and to portray the PCI itself as the true heir of Italy's nineteenth-century republican and democratic traditions, and therefore strongly connected to the country's history (Rusconi 1997: 14–15).

Modena città dell'Emilia rossa was the first of a series of films glorifying the social, political and, especially, economic achievements of the cities of Emilia-Romagna governed by the PCI. It can therefore be considered the first visual representation of one of the most enduring leitmotifs of the party's propaganda: the '*buongoverno*' (good government) by Italian Communists at the local level. The parts of the film that extol the achievements of Modena's city council are modelled on Soviet propaganda's exaltation of the accomplishments of socialism; the film thus offers a collection of clichés characteristic of this output in the Stalinist era.[38] These include Communism as a synonym for modernity and efficiency (from the 'trolleybuses shining with modernity' to the new motor racing track); the construction of socialism by means of a titanic struggle against nature (platoons of day-labourers turning wasteland into fertile soil in the city's outskirts); and the progressive childcare policy of socialist systems (the children of Modena's workers enjoying holidays at public summer camps at the seaside).

The film's most visually powerful scenes are those that draw a comparison between working conditions in the new, functional, and modern municipal gasworks built by the Communist administration and those of the less fortunate workers employed in capitalist factories. The latter seem to be living the nightmare portrayed in Fritz Lang's *Metropolis*: dressed in greasy overalls, they operate outdated machinery and inhale toxic fumes. By contrast, in Modena's gasworks the operatives are living the Bolshevik technological dream: clean and modern machinery, efficient working systems, and the natural dominion of man over machine. The voice-over underlines how the man–machine relationship denounced by Marx for its alienation of the worker in capitalist societies has been turned upside down in the factory built and run by Communists. The machine now serves the workers:

> Previously, the factory worker used to serve brutal machines; now, he is the master of perfect devices that are easy to control.

This part seems to be directly addressing Karl Marx's *Grundrisse*, in which Marx says that:

> [t]he worker's activity, reduced to a mere abstraction of activity, is determined and regulated on all sides by the movement of the machinery, and not the opposite. The science which compels the inanimate limbs of the machinery, by their construction, to act purposefully, as an automaton, does not exist in the worker's consciousness, but rather acts upon him through the machine as an alien power, as the power of the machine itself. (1973: 693)

Modena città dell'Emilia rossa must have been the most expensive film produced by the PCI during this period: there is extensive use of camera dollies, and even aerial shots of the city. It was probably a coproduction involving either the city administration itself or the PCI's well-off provincial branches in Emilia-Romagna. Aesthetically, *Modena città dell'Emilia rossa* is as far from neorealism as filmmaking can get, due to its stylistic debt to Soviet realist cinema: the direction faithfully illustrates the ideas expressed in the commentary, and each shot is intended to offer an idealized, exemplary, and impressive vision. The music, by composer Mario Zafred, emphasizes and emotionally enhances the visual images, in a way that is also characteristic of Socialist realist cinema. Mario Zafred was at the time the music critic of *L'Unità* and, according to Ben Earle, 'the most vocal Italian proponent of the Zhadanov line in music criticism' (2013: 159). *L'Unità* regularly praised Zafred's music in the early 1950s because it was free from modernism's 'experimental gimmicks' and as distant as music could be from the abhorred 'formalism'.[39]

The censors imposed some minor cuts to the voice-over.[40]

The year 1951 marked the thirtieth anniversary of the foundation of the party. Accordingly, the PCI produced two significant documentaries dealing with its historical and political identity: *La via della libertà* and *Pace, lavoro e libertà*. The latter concerns the Seventh Congress of the PCI. *La via della libertà* (The Way to Freedom), by contrast, was the first historical documentary to be produced by the party. This twenty-two-minute film was written, directed, and edited by Sergio Grieco; it mixed archival footage with reconstructed action, including depiction of the raids by gangs of Fascist Blackshirts in the period 1920–1922.[41]

The importance of history in the construction of the PCI's identity cannot be overemphasized.[42] During the post-war years, the PCI was, in many respects, a party in search of political legitimacy. The connections with the Soviet Union provided the PCI with a powerful ideological reference point and undoubtedly assured its popularity among the Italian working class. However, the '*partito nuovo*' needed a political identity that was not exclusively based on the international dimension. It had to cast itself as a specifically Italian party in order to counter the allegation that it was a foreign body within the Italian political panorama: an emissary of the Soviet Union with no connections to Italy's political and cultural traditions. The legitimization it required could only be found in history. This determined the need to endorse and promote a specific interpretation of Italian history, particularly among the militants and officials who had only recently joined the party.

La via della libertà is therefore a compendium of modern Italian history told from the perspective of the PCI, and includes many historical myths that defined the party's identity. The first of these myths relates to the party's origins. The rupture at the Congress of Livorno, in January 1921, is presented as a pivotal event marking the definitive victory over the defeatist attitude that had characterized the Italian Socialist Party.[43] At the same time, the PCI is portrayed as the heir to the old PSI's respected values and political traditions. In this interpretation, the PCI had simply taken over leadership of the working class, in the best interests of the Italian people and the international proletariat, when the Socialist Party, paralysed by the action of its reformists, had become incapable of this.

The great event that changed the course of human history was, however, Russia's October Revolution: the myth *par excellence*. The film establishes a parallel between the Italian Communist Party and the Communist Party of the Soviet Union, Togliatti being to Gramsci what Stalin was to Lenin: a comrade, friend, and faithful continuer of his work. The image of two Communist leaders working together in perfect harmony was one of the *topoi* of Communist mythology.[44]

Communist militants are said to be the only ones who resisted the rise of Fascism in Italy and, subsequently, the PCI's opposition to the regime is presented as uncompromising and highly effective thanks to its working-class roots; the film deliberately disregarded the almost total destruction of the party's underground network by Fascist political police in the 1930s, which had in reality caused a dramatic decline in Communist influence on Italian workers (Galli 1977: 168–170). The voice-over also claims that PCI policy was always aimed at achieving unity among the anti-Fascist political parties during the years of the regime. This narrative is pure fabrication. In reality, between 1928 and the mid-1930s, the Italian Communists had accepted the 'social fascism theory' formulated by the Communist Parties at the Sixth Congress of the Comintern, which propounded a similarity between social democracy and Fascism. This was probably the most imprudent and unfortunate decision taken by the Third International in that, by splitting the anti-Fascist forces, it facilitated the spread of Fascism within Europe.

When it comes to the Resistance period, the film notably omits any reference to the political episode that left-wing historiography subsequently used as a basis for the image of the PCI as a national party and pillar of Italian democracy: the '*svolta di Salerno*' (discussed in Chap. 2). It can be argued that the 'Salerno turn' was not an especially alluring topic for the Communist rank and file of the early 1950s, who were far more eager to see episodes that emphasized the party's revolutionary spirit.

In April 1951, the PCI held its Seventh Congress at the Teatro Adriano in Rome. A twenty-seven-minute documentary, *Pace, lavoro e libertà*, was shot to chronicle the five days of the Congress. Gillo Pontecorvo directed the film. Subsequently acclaimed as a film director, he was at the time an official within the FGCI (the Italian Communist Youth Federation), editor of the FGCI magazine *Pattuglia*, and Enrico Berlinguer's roommate in Milan (Fiori 1989: 61). The cinematographers were Carlo Carlini and Giuseppe Rotunno, who both later worked with Fellini on filming several of his masterworks.

The Seventh Congress is especially noteworthy for two reasons. First, Togliatti stated the need to engage in a battle for full implementation of the Constitution, anticipating a political position that was to be more fully developed at the Eighth Congress in December 1956 (Gozzini and Martinelli 1998: 226–228). Second, the congress was largely devoted to the party's organizational issues, with Pietro Secchia making a clear attempt to reshape it, at least partially, along the lines of the Leninist model of a party of professional revolutionaries (Gozzini and Martinelli 1998: 228–235). However, these issues are entirely ignored in Pontecorvo's film, which reduces the political aspects of the Congress to a single and easily understandable concept, as expressed by the commentary:

> The Congress outlined a policy on peace which is already rapidly taking shape.

Even the speech by Togliatti is presented as focused solely on the issue of peace, which certainly was central to the party's policies at the time.[45] However, the decision to avoid any lengthy analysis of the resolutions passed at the congress was especially due to the film's intended purposes. As with other PCI productions on party congresses, the main aim of *Pace, lavoro e libertà* was not to illustrate the political line established during the congress; rather, it was to consolidate, among its largely Communist audience, the perception of the PCI as a mass-based, internationally connected, strong, and united party with its roots deep in Italian society and history. In addition, the film served to depict for its Communist viewers the rituals that constituted the Communist congressional liturgy.

Rituals played a central role in the life of the Italian Communist Party as they bound militants both to the party and to each other, thus providing individuals with a group identity. David Kertzer has described party congresses as 'the holiest of the rites of the PCI' (2001: 104). Precisely for this reason, films of party congresses are of great value to the historian investigating the role of ritual in the construction of Communist identity.

The film accurately depicts the careful choreography of a party congress. The editing, however, enhances the political message of the film by its inclusion of symbolism and use of non-diegetic sound. First of all, the film presents the party leaders. The editing superimposes the Italian national anthem on close-ups of these figures, presented one by one, while the delegates clap enthusiastically. The message is that the Communist masses are solidly united behind their leaders and the PCI is, of course, a national party. The audience warmly welcomes the leader of the PSI, Pietro Nenni, who takes his place next to Palmiro Togliatti, symbolizing the ideological and political proximity of the two parties. Pietro Secchia, giving the opening speech, talks about the party's previous six congresses. The audience is thus reminded that the PCI has a long historical tradition, something Togliatti had famously alluded to in a speech given to the Constituent Assembly: 'We have come a long way, and have a long way yet to go'.[46]

Another crucial moment follows: the procession of delegates bringing offerings up to the podium. This ritual was very reminiscent of the 'offertory' within the Christian service of Eucharist, when bread and wine were brought to the altar, and offers further evidence of the Catholic influence on Communist symbolism and ritual of that period. Workers from Terni donate a portrait of Luigi Trastulli, killed by the police in March 1949 while protesting against Italy's membership of the North Atlantic Treaty Organization (NATO); Trastulli represents the Communist martyr who, like Christ, spilled his blood for the sake of his brothers.[47] Workers from the Officine Meccaniche (engineering works) of Reggio Emilia offer a small-scale model of the 'R60' farm tractor that they themselves had designed and produced during their occupation of the factory; this had lasted over a year and was still ongoing at the time of the congress.[48] This gift symbolized the deep roots that the party had established in Italy's factories. The agricultural labourers of the South are also represented, by the widow of Epifanio Li Puma, the union organizer who 'fell during the heroic struggles of southern agricultural workers'.

The film reaches its climax when one of Antonio Gramsci's fellow prisoners brings a few objects that belonged to the great Communist thinker to the podium. 'A shiver of excitement runs around the hall', says the voice-over, while Togliatti in person receives the gifts, a bowl and a spoon, and holds these quasi-relics up in front of the enthusiastically clapping audience. The congress then turns into a sort of festival of Communist subcultures: '*mondine*' (female day-labourers who worked in the rice fields) singing traditional songs (and not dancing boogie-woogie themes like those depicted in Giuseppe De Santis' *Bitter rice*!), young '*pionieri*' performing a group routine, members of the Resistance and veterans of the Spanish Civil War taking turns at the podium to offer brief greetings. Speeches from the foreign Communist Party delegates, beginning in hierarchical manner with the Communist Party of the Soviet Union, symbolize the PCI's affiliation to the broad international Communist movement. This scene seems to have the particular aim of giving succour to the party's rank and file, reminding them that even in such difficult times they are not alone. The film ends with shots of a speech by Togliatti to a vast crowd in Rome's Piazza San Giovanni a few days after the congress. This conclusion is also weighted with symbolism: it is now time to turn the approach established at the congress into concrete political action and speak to the Italian people as a whole.

Pace, lavoro e libertà marked the end of the first phase of PCI film production. There were various reasons for the national Press and Propaganda Section's decision to stop producing propaganda films at this stage; the most important was the toughening in censorship of Communist cinematography as a result of the build-up of Cold War tension at the beginning of the 1950s.[49] From 1950 onwards, censorship systematically targeted PCI productions. Analysis of the censorship reports demonstrates, in some cases at least, that government officials influenced decisions taken by the board of censors. This was the case, for example, with the banning of the PCI film *I fatti di Celano* (The Celano affair), a ten-minute documentary about the story of two day-labourers killed in the Fucino Basin on 30 April 1950 by private guards employed by a local landowner.[50] As shown in the next chapter, censorship softened at the end of the 1950s (and in fact Communist cinematic propaganda was promptly resumed), but it nonetheless remained a serious problem at least until a new law on censorship was passed, in April 1962.

However, Communist film production also had some intrinsic weaknesses, in particular a lack of proper channels for film distribution. The party could count on a range of venues that had the capacity to show 16 mm films: rooms in the Case del Popolo (Communist community centres), Camere del lavoro (union branch offices), and branches of the Associazione Nazionale Partigiani d'Italia (ANPI: National Association of Italy's Partisans). However, only a few places were equipped with projectors for the standard-gauge 35 mm film. In 1949, the PCI could count on some two hundred halls in total.[51] The PCI's achievements in film distribution had been no match for those of organizations connected to the Catholic Church. The Associazione Cattolica Esercenti Cinema (ACEC: Catholic Association of Cinema Operators), for example, controlled over three thousand cinemas in 1949 (Brunetta 1979: 311). Furthermore, although the distribution network for 16 mm films was well developed in parts of the 'red regions', especially Emilia-Romagna, even this was almost entirely absent in other areas, and in southern Italy in particular.

Figures available for the distribution of *14 luglio* and *Togliatti è ritornato*, the two most successful films produced by the PCI between 1946 and 1956, demonstrate that Communist films enjoyed a rather limited distribution. As regards *14 Luglio*, only twenty-eight copies had been distributed in 35 and nineteen in 16 mm within one year of its release, while the '*partiti comunisti fratelli*' (brother [foreign] Communist Parties) purchased nine copies. As regards *Togliatti è ritornato*, the Press and

Propaganda Section distributed twenty copies in 35 mm and twenty-three in 16 mm to the various branches, while foreign Communist Parties purchased eight copies in 35 mm.[52] These figures would certainly have discouraged the party leadership from investing in a form of propaganda that had been of limited success in terms of audience size and could not be used evenly up and down the country. To a certain extent, distribution was to continue to be a problem during the period when Unitelefilm was in operation, and can therefore be considered the Achilles heel of PCI cinematographic production.

A further serious problem that had to be addressed by officials within the national Press and Propaganda Section was the high cost of film production. The expenditure on Communist films was supposed to be recouped by selling copies to the PCI's regional and provincial branches. This system proved to be scarcely sustainable, as many branches were reluctant to invest their meagre financial resources in this expensive form of propaganda. Severe reprimands were published periodically in *Il Quaderno dell'attivista* criticizing the branches that had failed to acquire the documentaries produced by the party.[53] Sales, however, did not improve.

To summarize, this chapter has made several points about early PCI film production. The Communists saw the Italian South as a sort of leftover from the past: a realm of backwardness that should be represented in accordance with the aesthetic canons of neorealism. Soviet-style socialism, the paradigm for a shining and flawless future, was conceptually its opposite. In the narrative of the PCI, local Communist councillors in northern Italy were already building this resplendent future, which could only be properly depicted by adopting the aesthetic of Socialist realism. In addition, the PCI leadership used cinema to promote a selective and sometimes distorted interpretation of the party's history, seeing an understanding of this history as critical to the party's legitimation among the masses. Cinema was also used to present militants with accounts of Communist congresses, which were theatrical and symbolically charged representations of party unity and strength. The PCI was to resume production of cinematographic propaganda a few years later, in the run-up to the 1958 elections, as is discussed in the next chapter.

NOTES

1. For biographical information on Gian Carlo Pajetta, see Pajetta (1983); Pajetta (1986).
2. In 1951, over 5 million people aged six or more (12.9 per cent of the population) were still illiterate in Italy, with the highest proportions in the South and the islands where those deemed illiterate accounted for 24.0 per cent. See ISTAT (2011: 352).
3. For a theory of the political function of martyrdom, see DeSoucey et al. (2008).
4. IG, APCI, Direzione, MF 110, p. 545, 2 February 1946.
5. *Quaderno dell'attivista*, May–June 1947, 228.
6. See *Quaderno dell'attivista*, special issue for the 1948 electoral campaign, 21.
7. On *The Vow*, see Leyda (1960: 392–394); for the complete cast and crew, see Leyda (1960: 452–453).
8. AAMOD, Faldone *Nulla osta film del PCI non in Archivio*.
9. See Umberto Barbaro, 'Il Regista Sovietico Ciaureli parla ai critici del Festival', *L'Unità*, 4 September 1946: 2.
10. See *Il Quaderno dell'attivista*, August 1948, 29–30.
11. The expression is taken from *Il Quaderno dell'attivista*, March 1949, 31.
12. For a history of the FICC, see Tosi (1979); Tosi (1999).
13. Glauco Pellegrini had started his cinema career under the Repubblica Sociale Italiana, writing the screenplay for *La buona fortuna* directed by Ferdinando Cerchio (Chiti and Lancia 1993: 420). Felice Chilanti had been co-founder, with Vasco Pratolini, of *Domani*, one of the '*riviste di fronda*' (subversive reviews): journals edited by young intellectuals expressing moderate political opposition that was tolerated within the cultural and political framework of the Fascist regime (Zangrandi 1998: 485).
14. See Glauco Pellegrini's obituary in *L'Unità*, 23 July 1991: 21.
15. Marzia Marsili has argued that the cult of Togliatti developed within the context of an institutional charisma, that is to say Togliatti was endowed with superhuman qualities in that, and only because, he was the leader of the party. See Marsili (1998: 249–261).
16. See the headline for the coverage in *L'Unità* on 2 May 1947, the day after the massacre: 'Gli uomini della mafia sono stati gli esecutori materiali' (the men of the mafia were the actual executioners). On the Portella della Ginestra massacre, see Casarrubea (1997); Santino (1997).
17. The best account of the events of 14–16 July 1948 is given by Tobagi (1978).
18. See Giannarelli (1991: 56).
19. On dubbing in Italian cinema and government legislative action on this issue, see Treveri Gennari (2009: 38–61) and Sisto (2017, 393–407).

20. Law no. 379 of 16 May 1947, '*Ordinamento dell'industria cinemato-grafica nazionale*', established the compulsory projection of one newsreel before every film show and guaranteed 3 per cent of the gross income to go towards newsreel production. Incom established an alliance with the Consorzio Esercenti and acquired a dominant position in the market (Quaglietti 1980: 136–137). For an analysis of the Settimana Incom newsreels, see Bernagozzi (1979) and Sainati (2001). In order to counter Incom's insidious pro-government propaganda, the PCI even attempted to produce its own newsreels, the '*Cinegiornali del Popolo*' (Newsreels of the people). In 1949, two of these news bulletins were produced for the Communist film network, but they had trouble with censorship and the experiment was curtailed. Both ran for about ten minutes. Meanwhile, *Il Quaderno dell'attivista* invited militants to disrupt the projection of Incom newsreels in cinemas by shouting loudly from the stalls, in order to 'make heard the indignant protest of democratic citizens against the slanderous lies of Settimana Incom'. See *Il Quaderno dell'attivista*, March 1949, 31.

21. The first local *Feste dell'Unità* had taken place in September 1945 and were based on the French Communist Party's *Feste de L'Humanité*. They soon spread to many towns and cities, and very quickly became one of the most eagerly anticipated annual events for Communist militants and sympathiz-ers. For a history of the *Feste dell'Unità*, see Bernieri (1977). A selection of posters produced for the various *Feste dell'Unità* in the 1940s can be found in Novelli (2000: 52–67). The film by Carlo Lizzani took its title from the poster designed for the *Festa Nazionale dell'Unità*, which showed Togliatti lighting his pipe (Novelli 2000: 62).

22. See Gianni Rodari, 'Oltre mezzo milione di italiani in festa attorno a Togliatti e all'Unità', *L'Unità* (Turin edition), 28 September 1948. This issue also featured an article by Italo Calvino.

23. The complete list of cuts required by the Board of Censors reads as follows:

   (a) The following parts of the captions must be removed:
      (1) an entire people that has decided to forget the other state, that of the police chiefs and the riot police, and to experi-ence all these things … its state, that of liberty;
      (2) there lurk the '*social-traditori*' ['social-betrayers', in ref-erence to the Social Democrats, at the time the PSLI and later the PSDI] and Christian Democrats, newspapers and various agents of foreign imperialism;
      (3) the references to the supposed martyrs of police persecu-tion in Sicily.

82   G. FANTONI

(b)   The following scenes of footage that are extraneous to the documentary and have been inserted in the speech by Parliamentary Deputy Togliatti must be removed:
(1)   riot police vehicles dispersing the crowd;
(2)   the figures of the Prime Minister and the Minister for the Interior;
(3)   headlines from all the newspapers with titles as follows: War—The Atlantic Pact [North Atlantic Treaty] is agreed—Bullets for the Communists—The atomic bomb on Moscow—Italy cannot remain neutral—War.

Presidenza del Consiglio dei Ministri. Direzione generale spettacolo, 12 January 1949, in AAMOD, faldone T, fascicolo *Togliatti è ritornato*.

24. *Il Quaderno dell'attivista*, October–November 1948, 22.
25. The Associazione Pionieri d'Italia (Italian Pioneer Association) was the PCI youth organization, inspired by the Scouts and the Soviet Pioneer movement (Negrello 2000: 99–105). The association had its own magazine, *Il Pioniere* (Franchini 2006).
26. On the 'Soviet myth' in post-war Italy and its exploitation by the PCI leadership, see Galante (1991: 11–75).
27. For an example of the subsequent studies that have promoted the idea of the Stalinist nature of the PCI leadership, see Aga Rossi and Quaglieriello (1997); Aga Rossi and Zaslavsky (1997); Bertelli and Bigazzi (2001).
28. For an analysis of the use of PCI history for political ends in the 1990s, see Fantoni (2014).
29. On the traumatic change of PCI's name, in February 1991, see Kertzer (1998).
30. The expression 'historiographical Cold War' is from Guido Formigoni and appears in Gualtieri (2001: 329).
31. See Gramsci (2007).
32. See Presidenza dal consiglio dei Ministri, Servizi per la cinematografia, nulla osta del film *Nel mezzogiorno qualcosa è cambiato*. In AAMOD, Faldone M, fascicolo *Nel mezzogiorno qualcosa è cambiato*.
33. Intervista a Carlo Lizzani—25 maggio 2006, in AAMOD, codice identificativo IL8700022141, A/BETA/1319.
34. See, for example, Ugo Casiraghi, 'Una giuria di parte ignora un grande film', *L'Unità*, 7 September 1948: 3.
35. For a production history of *La terra trema*, see Semprebene (2009); for a discussion of the film's place within the neorealist movement, see Micciché (1998).

36. See Il *Quaderno dell'attivista*, 1 January 1950, 24. On the trials of former partisans that were taking place in 1949, see Cooke (2011: 40).
37. A member of the Resistance and subsequently a journalist with *L'Unità* and *Paese Sera*, Gianni Rodari achieved fame as a children's author in the 1960s and 1970s; see Argilli (1990).
38. For a discussion of these clichés, see Andreucci (2005: 135–150).
39. See, for example, Fedele D'Amico 'La III sinfonia di Mario Zafred', *L'Unità*, 28 March 1950; 'Il concerto per flauto e orchestra di Zafred', *L'Unità*, 10 April 1951; Diego Carpitella 'Il "Canto della pace" del compagno Zafred si è levato nell'auditorio del Foro Italico', *L'Unità*, 25 November 1951. Zafred also composed the music score of one of Carlo Lizzani's early feature films 'Chronicle of Poor Lovers' (1954), one of the two films produced by Cooperativa Cinematografica Spettatori Produttori (see Chap. 2).
40. The censorship board asked for the following passages to be cut: 'the landless day-labourers, impelled by their poverty, are occupying the hunting reserves. Under their vigorous assault, the privileges that are an obstacle to production give way'; and 'although lacking municipal autonomy'. See *Presidenza del Consiglio dei Ministri, Servizi per la cinematografia, Revisione cinematografica definitiva del 5 giugno 1950*, in AAMOD, faldone M, fascicolo *Modena città dell'Emilia rossa*.
41. Sergio Grieco began his career as an assistant director during the Fascist period and then wrote and directed many B-movies in the subsequent decades, often using the pseudonym 'Terence Hathaway'. Some of the films that he wrote for, such as *Quel maledetto treno blindato* (*The Inglorious Bastards*, 1978), have now acquired the status of cult movies.
42. In this point see, for example, Ballone (1994: 134).
43. See Andreucci (2005: 26–27).
44. See, for example, the article in the Naples edition of *L'Unità*, 21 January 1944, by 'Paolo Tedeschi' (pseudonym of Velio Spano, the edition's editor), celebrating both the twentieth anniversary of the death of Lenin and the twenty-third anniversary of the foundation of the PCI, including this passage: 'the history of the working class is rich with episodes of collaboration between its leaders. Marx and Engels, and, on another level, Luxemburg and Liebknecht in Germany, Gramsci and Ercoli [Togliatti's *nom de guerre*] in Italy, Thorez and Duclos in France: all these constituted, or constitute, formidable working partnerships in which one person's experiences and energies boost and strengthen the experiences and energies of the other. This sort of collaboration has perhaps never been as close and profound, although not at all conspicuous, as in the case of Lenin and Stalin'.
45. The 'Campagna per la pace' (campaign for peace) was a mass initiative on a national scale aimed at defending the Soviet Union against potential mili-

tary attacks by capitalist countries, which seemed a more likely eventuality after the establishment of the North Atlantic Treaty in April 1949. On this peace campaign and the 'Partigiani della Pace' (Partisans for Peace) movement, see Giacomini (1984) and Gozzini and Martinelli (1998: 145–151). The PCI made a seven-minute documentary on the 'Campagna per la pace', with the title '*Gioventù in marcia*' (Youth on the march), covering the event organized in Rome by the Alleanza Giovanile (Youth Alliance), an organization promoted by the PCI, on 10 July 1949. On the Alleanza Giovanile and the July march, see Guiso (2006: 157–161).

46. See the speech by Togliatti published in *L'Unità*, 27 September 1947: front page and p. 3.
47. On the death of Luigi Trastulli, see Portelli (1991: 1–26).
48. On the occupation of the Officine Meccaniche, see the documentary produced by the Archivio Audiovisivo del Movimento Operaio e Democratico, *I giorni dell'R60*, in AAMOD, codice identificativo IL8700012065, A/BETA/580.
49. See, for example, *Verbale di decisioni della riunione del 26/4/1951 della Commissione Elettorale* (minutes of the Election Committee meeting); in IG, APCI, MF 332, pp. 678–679, Stampa e propaganda, 30 April 1951.
50. In AAMOD, Faldone *Nulla osta film del PCI non in Archivio*.
51. *Dati sull'attività di propaganda—Riservato ai membri del comitato centrale*, in IG, APCI, MF 300, p. 358, Stampa e Propaganda, July 1949.
52. See note 51.
53. An example can be found in the March 1949 issue of *Il Quaderno dell'attivista*, p. 30: 'Is their inertia perhaps more effective than censorship by Andreotti?' the writer asks rhetorically.

Bibliography

Aga Rossi, E., and G. Quaglieriello, eds. 1997. *L'altra faccia della luna. I rapporti tra PCI, PCF e Unione Sovietica*. Bologna: il Mulino.
Aga Rossi, E., and V. Zaslavsky. 1997. *Togliatti e Stalin. Il PCI e la politica estera staliniana negli archivi di Mosca*. Bologna: il Mulino.
Ajello, N. 1979. *Intellettuali e PCI 1944–1958*. Bari: Laterza.
Andreucci, F. 2005. *Falce e martello. Identità e linguaggi dei comunisti italiani fra stalinismo e guerra fredda*. Bologna: Bononia University Press.
Argentieri, M. 2001. The Italian Communist Party in Propaganda Films of the Early Post-War Period. In *The Art of Persuasion. Political communication in Italy from 1945 to the 1990s*, ed. L. Cheles and L. Sponza. Manchester and New York: Manchester University Press.

Argilli, M. 1990. *Gianni Rodari. Una biografia.* Torino: Einaudi.

Ballone, A. 1994. Storiografia e storia del PCI. *Passato e Presente* XII (33): 129–146.

Bernagozzi, G. 1979. Le «settimane» del terrore. In *Il cinema Italiano negli anni cinquanta*, ed. G. Tinazzi, 210–234. Venice: Marsilio.

Bernieri, C. 1977. *L'albero in piazza—Storia, cronache e leggende delle Feste dell'Unità.* Milan: Gabriele Mazzotta Editore.

Bertelli, S., and F. Bigazzi, eds. 2001. *PCI: la storia dimenticata.* Milan: Mondadori.

Bertolotti, M. 1991. *Carnevale di Massa. 1950.* Turin: Einaudi.

Bonifazio, P. 2014. *Schooling in Modernity: The Politics of Sponsored Films in Postwar Italy.* Toronto: University of Toronto Press.

Brunetta, G.P. 1979. I cattolici e il cinema. In *Il cinema Italiano degli anni '50,* ed. G. Tinazzi, 305–321. Marsilio: Venice.

Caminati, L. 2012. The Role of Documentary Film in the Formation of the Neorealist Cinema. In *Global Neorealism: The Transnational History of a Film Style,* ed. S. Giovacchini and R. Sklar, 52–67. Jackson: University Press of Mississippi.

Casarrubea, G. 1997. *Portella della Ginestra: microstoria di una strage di Stato.* Milan: Franco Angeli.

Cooke, P. 2011. *The Legacy of the Italian Resistance.* New York: Palgrave Macmillan.

DeSoucey, M., et al. 2008. Memory and Sacrifice: An Embodied Theory of Martyrdom. *Cultural Sociology* 2 (1): 99–121.

Earle, B. 2013. Mario Zafred and Symphonic Neorealism. In *Red Strains. Music and Communism Outside the Communist Bloc,* ed. R. Adlington, 148–171. Oxford: Oxford University Press.

Fantoni, G. 2014. After the Fall: Politics, the Public Use of History and the Historiography of the Italian Communist Party, 1991–2011. *Journal of Contemporary History* 49 (4): 815–836.

Fiori, G. 1989. *Vita di Enrico Berlinguer.* Rome-Bari: Laterza.

Franchini, S. 2006. *Diventare grandi con il "Pioniere" 1950–1962: politica, progetti di vita e identità di genere nella piccola posta di un giornalino di sinistra.* Florence: Florence University Press.

Galante, G. 1991. *L'autonomia possibile. Il Pci del dopoguerra tra politica estera e politica interna.* Florence: Ponte alle Grazie.

Galli, G. 1977. *Storia del Partito Comunista Italiano.* Milan: Bompiani.

Gentile, E. 2006. *Politics as Religion.* Princeton: Princeton University Press.

Giacomini, R. 1984. *I partigiani della pace. Il movimento pacifista in Italia e nel mondo negli anni della prima guerra fredda.* Vangelista: Milan.

Giannarelli, A. 1991. Una lettura dei film del 1948. In *Il 1948 in Italia: la storia e i film,* ed. N. Tranfaglia, 45–63. La Nuova Italia: Scandicci, Florence.

Gozzini, G. 1998. *Hanno sparato a Togliatti. L'Italia del 1948.* Milan: Il Saggiatore.

Gozzini, G., and R. Martinelli. 1998. *Dall'attentato di Togliatti all'VIII Congresso, Vol. VII of the Storia del partito comunista italiano.* Turin: Einaudi.

Gramsci, A. 2007. *La Quistione meridionale.* Ed. Marcello Montanari. Bari: Palomar.

Gribaudi, G. 1996. Images of the South. In *Italian Cultural Studies: An Introduction*, ed. D. Forgacs and R. Lumley, 72–87. Oxford: Oxford University Press.

Gualtieri, R. 2001. *Il PCI nell'Italia repubblicana.* Rome: Carocci.

Guiso, A. 2006. *La colomba e la spada. "Lotta per la pace" e antiamericanismo nellapolitica del Partito comunista italiano (1949–1955).* Soveria Mannelli: Rubbettino.

Gundle, S. 1995. *I comunisti italiani tra Hollywood e Mosca. La sfida della cultura di massa.* Giunti: Florence.

ISTAT. 2011. *L'Italia in 150 anni. Sommario di Statistiche Storiche (1861–2010).* Rome: ISTAT.

Jowett, G.S., and V. O'Donnell. 2006. *Propaganda and Persuasion.* London: SAGE.

Kertzer, D.I. 1998. *Politics and Symbols: The Italian Communist Party and the Fall of Communism.* New Haven: Yale University Press.

———. 2001. Political Rituals. In *The art of persuasion. Political communication in Italy from 1945 to the 1990s*, ed. L. Cheles and L. Sponza, 99–112. Manchester and New York: Manchester University Press.

Leyda, J. 1960. *Kino. A History of the Russian and Soviet Film.* London: Allen & Unwin.

Marcus, M. 1986. *Italian Film in the Light of Neorealism.* Princeton, NJ: Princeton University Press.

Marsili, M. 1998. De Gasperi and Togliatti: Political Leadership and Personality Cults in Post-War Italy. *Modern Italy* 3 (2): 249–261.

Marx, Karl. 1973. *Grundrisse: Foundations of the Critique of Political Economy* (Rough Draft). Trans. Karl Marx [from the German] with a Foreword by Martin Nicolaus. London: Allen Lane: 'New Left Review'.

Miccichē, L. 1998. *Visconti e il neorealismo. Ossessione, La terra trema, Bellissima.* Venice: Marsilio.

Negrello, D. 2000. *A pugno chiuso. Il partito comunista padovano dal biennio rosso alla stagione dei movimenti.* Franco Angeli: Milan.

Novelli, E. 2000. *C'era una volta il PCI. Autobiografia di un partito attraverso le immagini della sua propaganda.* Editori Riuniti: Rome.

Pajetta, G. 1983. *Il ragazzo rosso.* Milan: Mondadori.

———. 1986. *Il ragazzo rosso va alla guerra.* Milan: Mondadori.

Perron, T. 1998. Vie, mort and renouveau du cinema politique. *L'homme et la Société*, 127–128, L'Harmattan, 7–14.

Pisch, A. 2016. *The Personality Cult of Stalin in Soviet Posters, 1929–1953: Archetypes, Inventions and Fabrications.* Acton, Australia: Australian National University Press.

Portelli, A. 1991. *The Death of Luigi Trastulli and Other Stories. Form and Meaning in Oral History*. Albany, NY: State University of New York Press.

Rusconi, G.E. 1997. *Patria e Repubblica*. Bologna: Il Mulino.

Sainati, A., ed. 2001. *La settimana Incom. Cinegiornali e informazione negli anni '50*. Turin: Lindau.

Santino, U. 1997. *La democrazia bloccata. La strage di Portella della Ginestra e l'emarginazione delle sinistre*. Soveria Mannelli: Rubettino.

Semprebene, R. 2009. *La terra trema. Prove tecniche del compromesso storico? Rapporti tra cinema e politica nel secondo dopoguerra*. Turin: Effatà Editrice.

Sisto, A. 2017. The Practice of Dubbing and the Evolution of the Soundtrack in Italian Cinema: A Schizophonic Take. In *A Companion to Italian Cinema*, ed. F. Burke. Chichester, West Sussex; Malden, MA: John Wiley & Sons.

Spriano, P. 1986. *Le passioni di un decennio. 1946–1956*. Milan: Garzanti.

Steimatsky, N. 2008. *Italian Locations: Reinhabiting the Past in Postwar Cinema*. Minneapolis: University of Minnesota Press.

Te Velde, H. 2013. The Religious Side of Democracy: Early Socialism, Twenty-First Century Populism and the Sacralization of Politics. In *Political Religion Beyond Totalitarianism. The Sacralization of Politics in the Age of Democracy*, ed. J. Augusteijn, P. Dassen, and M. Janse, 33–51. Basingstoke, Hampshire: Palgrave Macmillan.

Tobagi, W. 1978. *La rivoluzione impossibile. L'attentato a Togliatti: violenza politica e reazione popolare*. Milan: Il Saggiatore.

Tosi, V. 1979. I circoli del cinema e l'organizzazione del pubblico. In *Il cinema Italiano degli anni '50*, ed. G. Tinazzi, 322–333. Marsilio: Venice.

———. 1999. *Quando il cinema era un circolo: la stagione d'oro dei cineclub: 1945–1956*. Rome-Venice: Marsilio.

Treveri Gennari, D. 2009. *Post-War Italian Cinema: American Intervention, Vatican Interests*. London: Routledge.

Verdicchio, P. 1997. *Bound by Distance: Rethinking Nationalism Through the Italian Diaspora*. Madison: Fairleigh Dickinson University Press.

Zangrandi, R. 1998. *Il lungo viaggio attraverso il fascismo. Contributo alla storia di una generazione*. Mursia: Milan.

Zinni, M. 2011. L'impero sul grande schermo. Il cinema di finzione fascista e la conquista coloniale (1936–1942). *Mondo contemporaneo* 3: 5–38.

PART II

Dealing with the Modern (1956–1970)

CHAPTER 4

Peace and Sputnik, the Boom, and Television (1956–1964)

'Our starting point should be the following: television is not just an enemy which attacks us, no! Television is also something we have to work with. Television unifies information nationally [emphasis in the original]. Propaganda that disregards this fundamental aspect of television is useless propaganda. Any given evening, we know for sure what news millions of Italians have listened to, and therefore we can organize effective counter-measures'.[1] This document written in 1968 by the then person responsible for propaganda, Achille Occhetto, quite effectively illustrates the importance the PCI attributed to television. From the very beginning of a regular television service, on 3 January 1954, this medium had become a central element in the cultural life of the nation: it was principally through television that modern popular culture penetrated Italian society. Furthermore, the RAI (RadioTelevisione Italiana) was a powerful propaganda tool, firmly controlled by the government and therefore by the Christian Democrats (Monteleone 1992: 211–15; Ortoleva 2008: 101–2). Some scholars have argued that the Communists' approach to television showed that they had fundamentally miscalculated its cultural potential. The purely political lens that the PCI adopted in its assessment of the content of television programmes prevented it from appreciating that, despite its rather conservative tone, television represented a powerful vehicle for cultural and social emancipation.[2] In some respects this argument rings true. For the PCI, RAI television broadcasting, in the words of a Press and Propaganda Section bulletin, was 'the great enemy': a medium

© The Author(s), under exclusive license to Springer Nature Switzerland AG 2021
G. Fantoni, *Italy through the Red Lens*, Italian and Italian American Studies, https://doi.org/10.1007/978-3-030-69197-4_4

91

politically dominated by the Christian Democrats that Communist militants had to fight in every possible way.[3] In other respects, however, many intellectuals and leaders of the PCI had a very clear understanding of television's potential and the novelty that it represented. In the contemporary Communist press, statements and observations regularly reveal an awareness of the cultural changes brought by the new medium, including its power to demystify the liturgy of the Church (Bellassai 2000: 130). Furthermore, in its severe criticism of RAI for the biased reporting of its news service and the Church's influence on entertainment programmes, the PCI showed how well it understood the propaganda potential of television and how much it wanted to use this itself. For many years to come, however, Communist access to television would remain rather limited. The only way to compensate for such a disadvantage in visual propaganda was to relaunch film production. This is exactly what the PCI did in 1958.

This chapter deals with Communist propaganda films from 1958, when production was resumed, to 1964, when the PCI decided to establish a proper film production company, Unitelefilm. This decision signalled how, by the end of this period, the Communist leadership had come to regard cinematic propaganda as much more than just a cog in the machine of political communication. As mentioned above, the diffusion of television broadcasting played a major role in this respect. This aspect is discussed further at the end of the chapter. Before that, the chapter deals with quite diverse material in terms of cinematic outputs. In this period, the PCI devoted several films to foreign policy, which appear to have been the most important issue, at least until the end of the 1950s. From 1960 onwards, however, the focus gradually shifted to domestic policy, and more precisely to the impetuous economic development the country was experiencing, the 'economic miracle', as it was termed, or 'the boom'.

As pointed out by Stephen Gundle, Italian cinema was generally critical of the economic miracle.[4] Communist propaganda cinema took a very similar stance on this issue. While the Italian cinema industry satirized materialism, opportunism, and the moral degradation the boom had induced, Communist cinema focused on the unevenly distributed benefits of economic growth, its supposed short-term nature, and the social and personal dramas caused by migration towards the industrial districts of northern Italy. PCI films devoted to this latter issue are of special interest to social historians, in that they represent an extraordinary visual documentation of migratory phenomena of the late 1950s and early 1960s. These films, however, can be misleading. For example, they invariably present emigration as 'men's business'. In PCI's narrative, while men leave their homeland in search of a job (and this is due to the government's ruinous economic policy), women stay behind to take care of the children and the few family assets. However, studies on migration reveal that single girls emigrated in non-negligible numbers in the post-war years, and not just from southern regions, being employed in many sectors, and particularly as servants and in the textile industry (De Clementis 2010: 98–120).

PCI's scant attention to the phenomenon of female migration during the year of the economic boom is perhaps no surprise, if one considers that the first PCI film explicitly devoted to the problem of working women was produced only in 1965 (*Essere donne*, by Cecilia Mangini—discussed in Chap. 10), that is to say when the boom was over. Did a gender bias play a part in this misrepresentation, or partial representation of post-war migrations? Probably. However, I would argue, the problem lay in the fact that the PCI officials were not much interested in illustrating and discussing the actual situation, with all its nuances, but rather in making a political point: the government is failing southern people. A simplified reading of the reality actually helped this endeavour. This is why PCI films—it is worth remembering—should never be taken at face value.

The period between 1956 and 1964 was in many respects a time of crisis for the Italian Communist Party. The shock generated by the publication of Nikita Khrushchev's secret report, in June 1956, forced the party into a partial reassessment of its objectives and, consequently, of its political strategy.[5] Furthermore, the end of the political alliance with the Italian Socialist Party, in the wake of repression of the Hungarian uprising by Warsaw Pact troops, meant the collapse of one of the pillars of the PCI's political strategy. From then onwards, the PCI had to cope with the danger of the political isolation that might result from political rapprochement between the PSI and the Partito Social-Democratico Italiano (PSDI: Italian Social Democratic Party, or 'Social Democrats') and the potential participation of the PSI in a '*centrosinistra*' (centre-left) government coalition with the Christian Democrats.

At the same time, the political crisis of '*luglio '60*' (July 1960) clearly showed that the power of Christian Democracy could not be consolidated by reinforcing the conservative and authoritarian nature of governmental rule.[6] Overall, July 1960 proved that, in spite of the difficult political context of the Cold War, didactic action by the Communist and Socialist parties had borne some fruit: anti-Fascism, in particular, had become one of the pillars of the Italian Republic (Ginsborg 1990: 257). By reinvigorating anti-Fascism, the events of July 1960 also opened the way towards a centre-left alliance, which came into being in 1962 after a long period of political negotiation between the DC and the PSI.[7] However, by that time the PCI had managed to recover from the ideological crisis of 1956; this can be seen in its positive results in the 1963 elections, when it increased its vote by one million. Thanks to its electoral standing, the PCI could once again cast itself as a major protagonist in Italy's political arena, and was able to maintain some space for political manoeuvring.

Above all, the PCI had proven to be strongly and deeply rooted in Italian society, and by strengthening its national character, it was able to mitigate the loss of prestige and credibility that had been suffered by the international Communist movement. The party's Eighth Congress (Rome, 8–14 December 1956), was decisive in this respect; it witnessed the solemn embrace of the '*via italiana al socialismo*' (Italian road to socialism), a strategy that entailed a peaceful and gradual transition to socialism by means of '*riforme di struttura*' (reforms of Italy's political and economic structure) within a democratic political framework. From that moment onwards, any residual aspirations to insurrection were put aside, and the party leadership committed itself to eradicating expectations among the rank and file regarding the delivery of a revolution by the Red Army (Di Loreto 1991: 7).

The Eighth Congress has customarily been presented as a turning point in the history of the PCI. Certainly, the significance of the innovations introduced should not be minimized, particularly as regards the generational change that took place within the party leadership (Gozzini and Martinelli 1998: 628–29). In other respects, however, continuity prevailed, as was demonstrated by the unchanging 'Bolshevik' features of the party's internal organization, such as democratic centralism and self-criticism. Even the policy of the 'Italian road to socialism' was a direct consequence of the fact that the Twentieth Congress of the Communist Party of the Soviet Union (CPSU) had explicitly acknowledged that there might be different ways of achieving socialism (Sassoon 1981: 98).

More in general, a strict ideological and political connection with the Soviet Union still underpinned the PCI's political strategy, and this needs to be taken into consideration when analysing the cinematographic propaganda of this period. The Communist films of this new era present many differences from the party's earlier productions. First of all, they are full-blown propaganda films that address the entire electorate rather than just Communist militants. Second, the films of this period show a better understanding of the medium by party officials within the national Press and Propaganda Section. They are usually shorter and communicate, and then reinforce, a limited number of careful and simple messages, rather than representing a party manifesto in cinematographic form, as had generally been the case with previous output. As a result, they are less enjoyable from a cinematographic perspective, but arguably more effective as propaganda films. The stylistic evolution of Communist cinematography was matched by a general improvement in Communist propaganda during that period. The Press and Propaganda Section experimented with new forms of communication, such as the production of '*fotoromanzi*' (photographic stories), and put increased efforts into the production of propaganda specifically intended for the local elections (Bellassai 2000: 135). This was also the case for cinematic propaganda: the first films geared to specific areas of the country were produced in this period, including *Sicilia all'addritta* (Sicily on its feet) (1958), the first time that Paolo and Vittorio Taviani directed a film for the PCI.

Historian Franco Andreucci maintains that, in the 1950s, 'communists did not laugh', and that their public discourse lacked any sense of irony (Andreucci 2005: 87–88). However, this is not entirely true. The films produced in this period offer a wider range of linguistic registers and make an especially noteworthy use of irony.[8] For example, according to the voice-over for *I Campionissimi* (The super champs, 10 minutes, written by Pietro Ingrao) (1958), the best-known Italian athletes were no match for the DC and other right-wing politicians, who were true champions of competitions such as the 'one hundred tape-cutting ceremonies' (Giuseppe Togni, Minister for Public Works), 'tax raising per second' (Giulio Andreotti, Minister of Finance from 1955) and 'plunging a city into debt' (Achille Lauro, mayor of Naples). The final and most obvious difference is that PCI film production during this period was planned in line with a communication strategy already established by the Press and Propaganda Section.

The record of a meeting held by the party's national Press and Propaganda Section in September 1957 is a particularly important document in relation to any investigation of the cinematographic endeavours of the PCI during this period. A substantial part of contemporary Communist film propaganda, including that produced in preparation for the election of May 1958, seems in fact to have been intended to reflect the political and historical interpretation offered by Pietro Ingrao in his opening address. This concerned the 'capitalist restoration' that had been taking place in Italy ever since the end of the Second World War; according to Ingrao, this restoration had been based on an agreement between the 'large capitalist groups' and the Catholic Church, which together had formed a 'power bloc'.[9] He argued that the vote on 7 June 1953 had been a crucial victory because it had impeded the consolidation of this dangerous alliance, saving what remained of the secular nature of the Italian state and enabling a real prospect of political change. The end to collaboration between the PCI and the PSI, however, had offered the 'monopolistic groups' a fresh chance to establish clear political domination in Italy. In Ingrao's view, the only viable strategy that could be adopted in order to avoid this danger was a revival of '*frontismo*': a new alliance with the PSI that would counter the 'clerical monopoly and the clerical and landowning bloc'. Any possibility of political collaboration between the PSI and the DC therefore had to be energetically opposed. In particular, the PCI needed to be alert to any indication of the PSI's intention to betray the Italian working class; in Ingrao's view, this was the preliminary step that the PSI would have to take in order to join the DC in government. The PSI's criticism of the PCI's Leninist roots and its 'solidarity with the USSR' would have signalled this intention. It should be noted that, from the Communist perspective, Leninism and alignment with the Soviet Union were the two features that fundamentally differentiated true left-wing and pro-worker parties from the much abhorred 'social democracy'; it was feared that the PSI, by breaking with the PCI, would slowly become a social democratic party.

Consequently, Ingrao concluded, PCI propaganda needed to focus on the 'rejection of anti-Communism'. Accordingly, he committed the Press and Propaganda Section to rebuilding a positive image of Communism's homeland, the USSR. The party's propaganda was to divert public attention from the embarrassing legacy of Stalinism by focusing on the issue of peace. There would also be an attempt to capitalize on the achievements of the Soviet space programme.

Two of the films produced for the election of May 1958, *Gli uomini vogliono la pace* (People want peace) and *Gli uomini vogliono vivere* (People want to live), had precisely the purposes discussed.[10] From a narrative point of view, these films might be regarded as paradigmatic of what Bill Nichols calls the 'expository mode' in his classification of documentary styles: a film that makes a strong case, principally by using verbal commentary (2001: 32–33). The Soviet Union is presented as the champion of peace. To paraphrase the voice-over for *Gli uomini vogliono la pace*, the

Western powers, in response to Khrushchev's attempts to promote a new climate of international *détente*, either installed atomic missiles in minor allied countries ═with the complicity of their leaders, as in Italy, or launched military action against their former colonies, as in the attack on Egypt jointly launched by French, British and Israeli forces (the 'Suez Crisis' of October–November 1956). Because of the West's aggressive approach, the world now faced the real danger of a nuclear holocaust: just twelve bombs could wipe Italy off the map. Fortunately, the voice-over makes it clear, the leadership of the USSR is not alone in its efforts to safeguard peace; there is a party, in Italy, which also stands for peace: the Italian Communist Party. The viewer is reminded that the PCI is promoting a campaign to ban nuclear weapons, reiterating a policy that dates back to the late 1940s:

> Once again it's the Communist Party which shows the way with the words of Palmiro Togliatti: billions are being set aside for war between people, whereas we want war on poverty.

Images of poverty follow the commentary. These were to provide visual evidence of the miserable living condition that many Italians still endured at the end of the 1950s, and the desperate need for Italy to channel investment into social programmes rather than wasting money on arms. On closer inspection, however, it can be seen that the shots are mostly archival footage taken from *Nel Mezzogiorno qualcosa è cambiato* (1949); this evidence was therefore some ten years old and proved nothing about contemporary poverty.

The film ends on a note of hope: Italy and the world are not doomed, because a nuclear holocaust can be avoided if countries follow the example set by the Soviet Union. Because it is a socialist country, the USSR places technology at the service of the people, rather than war, and uses science to pursue humanity's progress; this has been demonstrated by a colossal achievement in the field of space exploration, the launch of Sputnik 1 on 4 October 1957. The commentary proudly announces that within a few years, the USSR will have conquered the moon. The achievements of the Soviet space programme were a great boost to the morale of the Italian party faithful, as they seemed to provide incontrovertible proof of the superiority of Soviet science and technology. The special issue of *L'Unità* published on 12 April 1961, the day of Yuri Gagarin's famous flight into outer space, had the triumphant headline 'A man, a Soviet, and a

Communist has achieved the first space flight in the history of humanity'. The Communist use of propaganda campaigns that focused principally on the issue of peace and on the achievements of the Soviet Union reaped dividends. The party held its position in the 1958 elections; at least on the electoral plane, it seemed to have countered the effects of the negative publicity that had followed the publication of Khrushchev's secret report.

The image of the Soviet Union as a champion of peace was developed further in other films produced after the election of 1958. In films such as *Gronchi nell'URSS* (Gronchi in the USSR) (1960), *Tre anni di Storia* (Three years of history) (1960), and *Cinegiornale della Pace* (Peace newsreel) (1963), the issue of peace was always addressed in relation to the principles and interests of Soviet foreign policy. The chancellor of West Germany Konrad Adenauer, in particular, was one of the principal targets of Communist propaganda during that period.[11] Attacks on the West German chancellor were above all an endorsement of Soviet foreign policy, which feared a strong Germany on the western border of the Socialist bloc. In addition, they provided a valuable way of castigating the Italian government for its political alignment with NATO: exposing the spectre of a newly well-armed and aggressive Germany was highly effective in Italy, a country in which memories of Nazi occupation were still fresh.

The PCI also adamantly opposed the Elysée Treaty that Adenauer and French president Charles De Gaulle signed in January 1963. This was essentially seen as the restoration of European capitalism on a new basis, which was how the PCI had viewed all other attempts at European integration within the Western Bloc. Historian Mauro Maggiorani, portrays Palmiro Togliatti as not completely set against European economic integration (1998: 169–82); however, arguably he does not give sufficient weight to the PCI's uncompromising support, under Togliatti, for the Soviet Union's foreign interests. This can be seen from an analysis of the party's propaganda films, for example, the *Cinegiornale delle Pace* (1963). In terms of PCI production, this film broke new ground. It stemmed from a personal initiative by the screenwriter Cesare Zavattini, who published an appeal in *Rinascita* promoting the idea of collaboration with the magazine's readers in the production of newsreels supporting world peace.[12] However, due to the technical difficulties relating to contemporary amateur filmmaking, only a few films, of very poor quality, were ever actually sent to *Rinascita*.[13] The editorial board therefore decided to take the project into its own hands and entrusted the editing of the first *Cinegiornale della Pace*, and the only one ever produced, to a group of intellectuals and professionals who were either members of the PCI or sympathizers.[14] The final product was a one-hour film divided into ten episodes, with an introduction by the writer and film director Mario Soldati.[15]

Cinegiornale della Pace presents itself as politically neutral and motivated solely by genuine concern, especially after the Cuban missile crisis of October 1962, regarding the risk of a nuclear holocaust that would threaten humankind. Some parts of the film display a rather naive attitude towards the issue of peace: for example, Mario Soldati makes a very reasonable but rather banal speech about the consequences of a nuclear war and invites everyone to support peace. Other parts, however, are clearly constructed in order to address, sometimes aggressively, a range of issues related to Italian political and cultural debate, rather than peace; they suggest that *Cinegiornale della Pace* is, essentially, a propaganda film. Zavattini himself privately expressed his discontent over the tendentious tone that the film had assumed by its final cut (Bertozzi 2008: 192).

The first two sections are devoted to a virulent attack on the Elysée Treaty, which is presented as a military alliance between two authoritarian governments likely to endanger peace in Europe. The biggest threat to humankind comes from the 'Paris–Bonn Axis', which Jean-Paul Sartre, in an interview within the first section, compares to the Rome–Berlin Axis, concluding that the French Resistance has been betrayed by De Gaulle.[16] Adenauer is depicted as an opportunist and Nazi sympathizer who wants to rearm West Germany and point 'atomic guns' at both the eastern and western borders of his country. From a cinematographic point of view, this is probably the clumsiest section: it consists almost entirely of archival photographs and the articulation of the message is entrusted solely to the voice-over. Seemingly, it also attempts to manipulate the viewer: the intercutting of images from Germany under Nazism with others from more recent times implies that the country has not really changed since the Nazi period.

The length of the film allows its codirectors to deal with a wide range of issues, and the cinematographic style varies greatly from section to section. 'Marzabotto vent'anni dopo' (Marzabotto twenty years later), by Luigi Di Gianni, solely consists of moving interviews with survivors of the massacre perpetrated by the Nazis in the mountainous area south of Bologna, between 29 September and 5 October 1944. Although there is no voice-over to make the message explicit, the function of this chapter is ultimately political, in that its intention is to remind the audience of the threat represented by a powerful and aggressive Germany. When viewed in its entirety, *Cinegiornale della Pace* is an atypical cinematic text: half authorial documentary, half hackneyed, Soviet-style propaganda film.

The issue of peace offered the PCI opportunities both to influence a range of social and political forces that were not normally reached by Communist propaganda and to attempt to establish some novel alliances. The party tried to exploit these circumstances at the beginning of the 1960s, often at the cost of its customary partisan tone, as can be seen in another film produced during that period: *La Marcia per la pace* (Peace march, 1962). This ten-minute film was directed by Glauco Pellegrini and devoted to the first peace march between Perugia and Assisi, organized by the philosopher and Catholic activist Aldo Capitini, on 24 September 1961. It is quite different from the other films on the issue of peace that the PCI produced during this period. The voice-over commentary, written by Gianni Rodari, is intentionally apolitical, with no mention of either of the two superpowers; it focuses on issues such as the universal brotherhood of man, which must be pursued by 'men of good will' in accordance with the teaching of St Francis of Assisi, 'Umbria's most humble and greatest son'. The PCI was evidently trying to use films like *La marcia per la pace* to broaden the mass base of the peace campaign by drawing in non-Communist groups. Capitini himself was typical of those people who were not politically affiliated and independently developed a political discourse on the issue of peace at the beginning of the 1960s.[17]

One final aspect of the peace debate needs to be taken into consideration if we are to fully understand the Communist approach to this issue: the progressive deterioration of the relationship between the Soviet Union and China. The leadership of the Chinese Communist Party (CCP) had not accepted the principle of 'peaceful coexistence', allowing for the possibility that socialism and capitalism could compete peacefully without a final military confrontation, which had been launched by Khrushchev at the Twentieth Congress of the CPSU. There were both ideological and political reasons behind the CCP's stance. On the one hand, 'peaceful coexistence' was regarded by the Chinese as capitulation in the face of the United States and a betrayal of the anti-imperialist struggles of oppressed colonial populations. On the other, by stabilizing a bi-polar system on a global scale, this approach was likely to frustrate Chinese aspirations to achieving the status of a great power (Benvenuti 1985: LVII–LVIII).

China's antagonistic position had very serious implications for the Italian Communists, because of the threat it posed to the party's internal cohesion. This risk is alluded to in Togliatti's 'Yalta memorandum', the confidential document prepared for Khrushchev by the PCI leader shortly before he died, in the section with the heading 'On the best way of countering the Chinese positions':

> In the party, and at its margins, we have some small groups of comrades and sympathizers who lean towards the Chinese positions and defend these. Some members of the party need to be expelled in view of their responsibility for acts of factionalism and indiscipline.

It should be stressed that the policy of 'peaceful coexistence' was a central element within the PCI's political strategy, because it provided the international frame needed for the national policy of the 'Italian road to socialism'.

At the Tenth Congress of the PCI (Rome, 2–8 December 1962), the tensions that pervaded the international Communist movement broke out. The Chinese delegate, picking up on aspects of Togliatti's opening speech, openly criticized the 'peaceful coexistence' policy.[18] This was just the prelude to events a few days later, when the PCI leader was subjected to fierce ideological attack from the Chinese Communist Party over this policy. On 31 December 1962, the CCP issued a pamphlet with the title. The differences between Comrade Togliatti and Us, in which he was criticized for having abandoned the Leninist just war theory: the war that had to be fought in order to defeat capitalism and enable the socialist revolution. The pamphlet concluded that Togliatti had betrayed Lenin's thought.[19] Although the PCI leadership had made every effort to avoid confrontation with the Chinese, especially wanting to shelter the rank and file from painful and disorientating coverage of the split within the international Communist movement, it was impossible to suppress the news of such a serious attack.

In consequence, the film dedicated to the party's Tenth Congress was forced to address the Chinese criticism with the same rather obsessive attention to narrative and visual details that had typified the PCI's cinematographic output on the party's previous congresses. The film in question is *X congresso nazionale del Pci 1962* (The tenth national Congress of the PCI, by Mario Carbone, 18 minutes).[20] The principal objective of this film was to counter the Chinese positions by presenting them as isolated within the international Communist movement. It begins by showing delegates from the Communist Parties of thirty-six countries arriving at the airport of Rome; this exceptional level of attendance demonstrates the support for PCI policy from the vast majority of the world's Communist Parties. The first part of the film is centred on the speech by the Chinese delegate, which the editing frames within a narrative context that makes it appear erroneous and even preposterous. Before this delegate is shown, the voice-over introduces Frol Kozlov, the Soviet Union representative, who is welcomed by a frantically clapping audience. He criticizes the 'errors of dogmatism', and the editing reveals the Chinese delegate. Kozlov talks about peace, and the other Communist delegates clap. When it comes to the turn of the Chinese representative, however, a hostile silence ensues. The voice-over commentary dismisses his contribution:

> In his speech the delegate expresses the positions of the Chinese Communist Party on a series of issues. The matter of 'peaceful coexistence' and the issue of peace are rephrased in the dogmatic terms that have already been criticized by Togliatti in his opening speech.

After this, celebration of the strength and unity of the Communist Party, so typical of PCI films on party congresses, continues undisturbed.

The period examined in this chapter was also crucial from an economic perspective. During these years, and more precisely between 1958 and 1963, the country experienced the 'boom', as it came to be known: the peak of Italy's post-war economic development (Crainz 2003; Castronovo 2010). The country's economic performance was so phenomenal and unexpected that to many it appeared to be a sort of miracle: a '*miracolo economico*' (economic miracle), as it was described. This was not in fact quite so 'miraculous' as it first appeared; the ground had actually been prepared during the post-war period by numerous factors, not least among them the availability of a large supply of cheap labour from the southern regions.

To start with, the PCI was in denial about the reality of the economic miracle. Italy's economic performance was at odds with the Communist notion of a capitalist system incapable of producing any substantial and enduring economic growth. Moreover, according to the party leadership, Italy was in industrial terms Europe's weakest link. Until the realization of a socialist transformation of its economic structure, Italy was supposedly doomed to remain an agriculture-based economy with a scattering of industrial areas. When the rate of economic growth made it impossible to deny the existence of the *miracolo economico*, the PCI chose to focus on its negative aspects: the unevenly distributed benefits of economic growth, its short-term nature, and the social and personal dramas caused by migration towards the industrial districts of northern Italy. These were recurrent issues in the party's propaganda for the elections of 1963.

In films such as *L'altra faccia del miracolo* (The other side of the miracle), *Il prezzo del miracolo* (The cost of the miracle) and *Il viaggio della speranza* (The journey of hope), Italy's eternally poverty-stricken South once again fulfils the function of stirring the nation's conscience. Symbolic of the failures of DC governments in the 1940s and 1950s, the South is now the living, or perhaps dying, proof that for vast areas of the country, the 'economic miracle' is just an empty expression. As the voice-over for *L'altra faccia del miracolo* claims:

> The expressions 'automation', 'technical progress' and 'wellbeing' have an abstract and offensive sound when declared here!

Cinematographically, *L'altra faccia del miracolo* is probably the most aesthetically sophisticated of this group of films. It includes some particularly noteworthy scenes shot on a train carrying a group of southern peasants to Munich, in Germany, where they hope to find jobs; we see them cutting bread with their typical Italian pocketknives (Image 4.1) and pouring out wine from a plastic container. Everything looks very real, like a piece of television reportage. This is no coincidence, as this fourteen-minute documentary was directed by Sergio Spina, who had worked for the national television broadcaster RAI. This accounts for the film's style, which is clearly influenced by RAI's early documentaries such as *Meridionali a Torino* (Southerners in Turin) (1961), directed by Ugo Zatterin and Brando Giordani. This shows how the improvements in PCI film propaganda between the late 1950s and the early 1960s were in part a consequence of the work by a new generation of professionals. These young filmmakers included the Taviani brothers and directors like Spina; they gave fresh vigour to PCI cinematography, especially from a stylistic perspective.

While *L'altra faccia del miracolo* has a sober and journalistic visual style, the tone of the voice-over is rather melodramatic and less than impartial:

> They leave for foreign lands; tatty suitcases stuffed with so much hope and poor packages are always at the centre of a ritual that is repeated by genera-

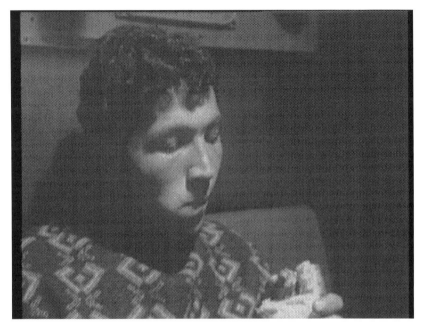

Image 4.1 Southern emigrant

tions and generations; their whole future is at risk, enclosed in the act of a sad and thankless departure, almost a flight from an enemy who besieges their poor home … Goodbye! Come back soon! So goes the muted cry of two million women of the South.

L'altra faccia del miracolo can thus be seen as accommodating two cinematographic sensibilities in coexistence. On the one hand, this film features the rather rhetorical commentary that had characterized previous PCI production, on the other, it has a modern shooting style borrowed from television which was now to be more frequently adopted by the directors who working for the party.

The films produced during this period also show how the Italian Communist Party developed a relatively early critique of consumerism. Various productions make negative references to the new purchasing habits that Italians were rapidly adopting as a consequence of economic growth. In *Torino dopo il miracolo* (Turin after the miracle) (1965), for example, the voice-over lambasts 'the creation of artificial needs' stimulated by the boom while the editing reveals long lines of cars—mostly the typical Fiat 500—swamping the city's streets and pavements. Public transport is said to be in disarray, but the government and businesses such as the Fiat car manufacturer continue to encourage private mobility. Italian economic development had indeed been fairly chaotic, which provided a partial justification for the Communists' caustic statements. Their distaste for consumerism, however, also indicated their fundamental incomprehension of the positive aspects of increased consumption in terms of the social and cultural emancipation of the population's lower strata. Opportunities to spend a Sunday at the lakes or the seaside, or to buy a music record, took people a long way outside the bubble of provincialism, even backwardness, that many Italian had lived inside for generations. Italy had become an 'affluent society', to quote the title of a well-known book first published in the very same year that the Italian economy began its take-off.[21] Consumerism was, all in all, a positive sign; it should have reassured Communist intellectuals and officials about the healthy state of the Italian economy and, consequently, about the stability of Italian democratic institutions, rather than simply prompting some stern and rather moralistic rebukes. It should be noted that most Italians had nothing bad to say about their increased consumption; they enthusiastically welcomed the opportunity to buy a car, regardless of the scarcity of car parks and the sorry state of urban public transport.

Communist intellectuals and officials also harboured suspicions about modern popular culture and the entertainment industry. The nascent youth culture, in particular, was initially seen as a degeneration of Italy's authentic popular traditions, and sometimes even as a tool of American propaganda (Forgacs 1990: 105). At around the time of the economic boom, however, the PCI became aware that nobody, not even the Communist militant, was immune to the influence of modern popular culture. The party therefore tried to adapt its policies to this new situation.

A particular meeting in 1961, attended by members of both the PCI's national Press and Propaganda Section and its Cultural Commission, marked the moment at which the party acknowledged that a reassessment of its cultural policy was needed, notwithstanding its continued condemnation in principle of modern popular culture.[22] The record of the meeting stressed that the party had to prepare in order to fight what was to be a difficult political and ideological struggle against the subtle forms of ideological corruption that were being pursued by the ruling classes with the help of the entertainment industry. At the same time, the document criticized left-wing intellectuals for their aristocratic attitude towards popular culture and hailed the crisis of the cultural dichotomy that had traditionally been characteristic of Italy—one culture exclusively for the lower classes and another for the ruling classes—as a positive development. This statement represented a major change in the Communist approach to the issue of popular culture; until then, the party's cultural policy had specifically required cultural initiatives addressed at intellectuals to differ from those aimed at a wider audience.[23] The short-term goals set were the resumption of a campaign against censorship and a battle for the 'democratization' of the RAI television network, seeking political pluralism in public broadcasting.

It is significant that the PCI mentioned public television broadcasting in its documents. Television was, in fact, the great novelty of this period. Initially, few Italian households owned a television set but most public venues quickly acquired one; as a consequence, the collective viewing of prime-time television shows became a new Italian ritual. The great popularity of some programmes in the early years of television broadcasting can easily be seen to have inspired some of the films produced by the PCI, including, for example, *Carosello elettorale* (Election roundabout). This film, directed by the Taviani brothers in 1960, parodied *Carosello*, a very popular advertising programme broadcast on RAI television from 1957 to 1977 (Lanaro 1992: 256–58; Dorfles 2007). The film presented four fake commercials each of about two and a half minutes (the standard running time of a *Carosello* commercial), parodying characters and situations presented by the original show. A recurring character in *Carosello*, for example, was 'Ispettore Rock', a police detective advertising Linetti brilliantine, a popular brand of hair product. The inspector solved mysterious crimes and concluded every sketch by exhibiting his bald head and claiming that the only mistake he had ever made was not to use Linetti. In the parody version, 'Ispettore Tok', after finding evidence of a theft committed by a DC politician, claimed that his big mistake had been to vote once for Christian Democracy, because in so doing he had become completely bald.

The aggressive campaign waged against television broadcasting did not prevent the PCI's national Press and Propaganda Section officials from negotiating with RAI managers for visibility on every possible occasion. For example, 'after a series of meetings and discussion', they obtained news coverage of the Ninth Congress of the PCI (Rome, 30 January–4 February 1960). The RAI also agreed to broadcast six interviews, each of two minutes, with the Communist leaders Umberto Terracini, Luigi Longo, Gian Carlo Pajetta, Agostino Novella, Mauro Scoccimarro, and Togliatti himself.[24]

A few months later, on 6 July 1960, Italy's Constitutional Court, which passes judgment on the constitutionality of legislation, declared that the state monopoly of television broadcasting could only be considered legitimate if RAI allowed a range of political opinions to be expressed (Monteleone 1992: 329–30). In order to comply with this adjudication, RAI created what was to be one of its most enduring television programmes, *Tribuna Elettorale*, a television news conference for which journalists of varying political orientation interviewed figures from the various parties. Togliatti's momentous first appearance on *Tribuna Elettorale* was scheduled for 14 October 1960, during the run-up to the local elections on 7 November 1960.

The PCI dealt with Togliatti's presence on television as a long-awaited opportunity to address millions of Italian voters at the same time. Detailed instructions on preparation for this event were compiled by the Press and Propaganda Section and issued to the party's local branches, and merit reproducing at length:[25]

> Every branch and [party-affiliated] social venue that has a television should issue open invitations to the public, including using banners and leaflets, to watch the press conference given by Togliatti in our venues.
>
> Any comrade who owns a television set or a radio should invite their neighbours to listen to the press conference at home.
>
> [Local press and propaganda] offices should try, in conformity with the provisions in force, to transmit the press conference outside using loudspeakers, and comrades who have a radio or television at home should place the apparatus by an open window in such a way that the broadcast can be heard in the courtyard.
>
> Branches should attempt to make an audio recording on tape of the press conference, so that this can be used in the following days by means of mobile loudspeakers and at rallies in local wards.
>
> In public venues (and not just in central ones) our qualified '*propagandai*' [propaganda workers] should be on hand to make active contributions to the debates and in the small groups that may form after the press conference.

The *propagandai* were also required to be present in bars and other public venues for the appearances by politicians from other parties, but

108   G. FANTONI

this time in order to 'intervene with forthright interruptions during the broadcast'.

The party also made great efforts to be well prepared for Togliatti's final appearance on national television, which was broadcast on 25 April 1963, only three days before voting in the national elections. Mario Benocci, who was to become the first director of Unitelefilm, prepared a detailed memorandum for the PCI leader with precise instructions on how to behave and what to say during his twelve-minute appeal to the electors. This was put together on the basis of suggestions from 'our comrades who work for RAI':[26]

> The first recommendation made to us is that you should speak in the first person, giving a discursive character to your delivery. In this respect, you are asked to regularly address the listeners directly ('you see'; 'you too will consider'; etc.) … As for the structure of your address, it is believed fruitful to put forward a limited number of issues, emphasizing, repeating, and simplifying. Our comrades in television have confirmed that the greatest effectiveness is achieved by the use of well-organized speeches, divided into parts that also stand up on their own, while still delivering a general picture.

The memorandum also recommended the display of a letter that had been posted to Togliatti, in order to suggest that the leader of the Communist Party received correspondence from ordinary citizens. It would seem that the PCI's communication strategy was slowly but surely adapting to the new medium: even *L'Unità*, the most important source of information for any Communist militant, told its readers about Togliatti's television appearance and published his full speech the following day.[27]

Togliatti conformed faithfully enough to the instructions in the memorandum.[28] He addressed the viewers in a fairly informal style, attempting to look directly at the camera as much as possible and projecting a relaxed manner. His speech was quite emotive, being based on sentiments rather than rational arguments. He described, for example, how the fatigue of his intense election tour had been mitigated by the sympathy that the Italian people had shown him. Finally, he proffered a letter, as the memorandum had suggested, and even spent a few moments describing the tragic situation of the sender, the wife of a worker who had been sacked 'after a lifetime of work' because of an incurable illness.

Communist awareness of the importance of television constantly increased as time passed. In tandem, so did the PCI's frustration over its exclusion from state broadcasting. The few minutes for which Communist politicians could speak to the Italian population, thanks to *Tribuna Elettorale* or *Tribuna Politica* (another well-known political programme broadcast regularly during the year), were little compensation for daily programming that was shaped by the politics, mentality, and religious beliefs of the ruling parties, in particular the Christian Democrats, especially as regarded television news bulletins. For many years to come, however, Communist access to television would remain very limited. The only way of mitigating this disadvantage in visual propaganda was to relaunch film production, which was the principal reason for foundation of the PCI film production company Unitelefilm in 1964.

The election campaign of 1963 also provided significant encouragement for the establishment of Unitelefilm, as the national Press and Propaganda Section was convinced that films had contributed in no small measure to the electoral success of the PCI, which increased the votes cast in its favour by one million:

> Wherever our branches determined that there would be wide use of film showings, the results were excellent. While the propaganda of the DC and the PLI [Italian Liberal Party], both in the normal halls and outside, did not meet with much success, the 182 copies of films that we put into circulation in forty or so branches sometimes garnered a mass audience.

The conclusion of the Section's report reflected on the opportunities:

> Great possibilities have now emerged, which should push us towards a real turning point in the organization of this activity and wider distribution of projectors.

Moreover, the local branches had been asking the national Press and Propaganda Section to produce more films since 1960.[29] The rebirth of Communist cinematography was also aided by a thawing of the Cold War political climate at the end of the 1950s and, most of all, by the new law on censorship introduced in 1962.[30] This legislation, whose enactment was one of the first tangible effects of the involvement of the PSI in government, reformed the composition of censorship boards; it was also much less restrictive than the law of 1923 in terms of the degree of discretion given to the members of these boards, and, most importantly of all,

110   G. FANTONI

determined that films could only be censored when they were offensive to public morality (Argentieri 1974: 195–200).

In conclusion, the years 1956–1964 are fundamental to an understanding of the evolution of the Italian Communist Party's film propaganda. During this period, the party resumed cinema production in response to Italy's cultural modernization, whose most notable sign was the rapid spread of public television broadcasting. Stylistically, Communist cinema evolved significantly, principally because of the model set by television. There was also a major development in the understanding that PCI officials had of the medium as a propaganda tool: many of the films produced in these years were designed with the aim to enlarge the party's constituency; they were shorter and were more straightforwardly propaganda films. In terms of the themes of Communist film, however, continuity with respect to the earlier period prevailed. Deference to the Soviet Union was still central to PCI politics, and in its cinematic form it was presented as an unwavering defence of Soviet foreign policy. The main theme of the PCI films that addressed domestic policy was a critique of the economic miracle, with the Italian South used to expose the shortcomings of the boom. The overcritical attitude the PCI took towards the Italian economic development prevented the party from understanding the crucial social and political transformations which were taking place in the Italian society. It is probably for this reason that the students' political mobilization which occurred at end of the decade caught the party by surprise, as discussed in Chap. 6. Both the encouraging results of propaganda films in the elections of 1963 and, above all, the PCI's determination to compete with the DC-controlled RAI television broadcasting encouraged the party to attempt systematic and large-scale film production by founding Unitelefilm. This is the topic of the next chapter.

NOTES

1. IG, APCI, MF 539, pp. 1169–80, Stampa e Propaganda, *Relazione del Compagno Achille Occhetto alla riunione nazionale dei responsabili provinciali di Propaganda*, Stampa e Propaganda, 26 May 1967.
2. See Crapis (2002: 40); Monteleone (1992: 240).
3. IG, APCI, MF 468, pp. 1475–82, Stampa e Propaganda. *Alle Segreterie delle federazioni*, 1 June 1960.

4 PEACE AND SPUTNIK, THE BOOM, AND TELEVISION (1956–1964)   111

4. Gundle (1990: 214–15). However, he also claims that the satirical comedies did not significantly contribute to the formation of a democratic consciousness in Italy.

5. On the ideological and political consequences for the PCI arising from de-Stalinization and the Hungarian uprising, see Righi (1996).

6. The crisis of '*luglio '60*' was a series of dramatic confrontations between demonstrators and police in several Italian cities in July 1960. The *casus belli* was the decision of the government, led by the DC's Fernando Tambroni, to allow the neo-Fascist Movimento Sociale Italiano (MSI) to hold its national congress in Genoa, a city with strong anti-Fascist traditions. The Tambroni government was in power only thanks to the support from the MSI's parliamentary deputies, which added to the tension. The police used excessive force to quell the initial demonstrations, thus escalating the violence; in Genoa itself, the demonstrations were close to becoming an uprising. Nationally, a small number of protesters were killed and many were injured. Eventually, the government backed down and postponed the MSI congress, and Tambroni resigned shortly afterwards. On July 1960, see Cooke (2000). No PCI films were specifically devoted to these events. The only film to touch on them was *La via sicura* (The safe path) (1964), produced by the Milan branch of the party. Unedited video material on July 1960 is conserved in the AAMOD, Archivio Unitelefilm: eight minutes of silent footage on the funerals of Ovidio Franchi, Lauro Farioli, Emilio Reverberi, Marino Serri and Afro Tondelli, all killed by the police in Reggio Emilia on 7 July 1960 (codice identificativo: IL8300002297), and one minute of silent footage covering the clashes in Genoa, on 30 June, and Rome, on 6 July (codice identificativo: IL8000001303).

7. The first proper centre-left administration, involving the PSI's direct participation in a government coalition with the DC, was formed only in December 1963. From 1962 onwards, however, the government led by Amintore Fanfani was supported by the abstention of the PSI in parliamentary votes. For further discussion, see Ginsborg (1990: 267–73)

8. Irony had been appearing in Communist propaganda since the '*forchettoni*' campaign of 1953, in which caricatures of DC politicians were shown in a series of posters brandishing gigantic forks ('*forchette*' in Italian) for eating Italy's national income (Novelli 2000: 84–86).

9. *Verbale riunione della Sezione Nazionale Stampa e Propaganda*, in IG, APCI, MF 448, Stampa e Propaganda, 5 September 1957. For Ingrao's speech, see pages 1600–36; for the discussion, see pages 1637–63.

10. The two films, lasting twenty and eight minutes respectively, were both produced by the national Press and Propaganda Section. They are entirely made from archival footage, with a voice-over commenting on the images.

No directors are credited. AAMOD, codici identificativi: IL8300001139 and IL8300001167.

11. See, for example, 'Adenauer giuoca la carta del ricatto nucleare', *Rinascita*, 2 March 1963: 11.
12. *Rinascita*, 9 June 1962: 32.
13. Interview of Mino Argentieri by the author, Rome, 16 June 2011.
14. These included Mino Argentieri, Maurizio Ferrara, Antonello Trombadori, the former director of Vie Nuove Maria Antonietta Macciocchi, and the film directors Luigi Di Gianni, Ansano Giannarelli, Massimo Mida and Luciano Viazzi.
15. A DVD of the *Cinegiornale della Pace* was released by the AAMOD in 2005. On Mario Soldati, see Morreale (2006).
16. The expression 'Paris–Bonn Axis' became a *topos* for the Communist press; see, for example, M. A. Macciocchi, 'E' nata l'Asse Parigi–Bonn', *L'Unità*, 23 January 1963: front page. See also Maggiorani (1998: 181).
17. On Aldo Capitini, see Martelli (1993).
18. Togliatti's opening speech and concluding address at the Tenth Congress of the PCI are reproduced in Benvenuti (1985: 315–470).
19. The CCP pamphlet can be seen online at http://www.bibliotecamarxista.org/Mao/libro_19/div_comp_togl.pdf. In February 1963 the CCP published another document with a rather similar title: '*Ancora sulle divergenze tra il compagno Togliatti e noi*' (More on the differences between Comrade Togliatti and ourselves): http://www.bibliotecamarxista.org/Mao/libro_19/anc_div_comp_togl1.pdf.
20. Mario Carbone (born 1924) is a well-known director of documentary films. He subsequently worked on several Unitelefilm productions, and in particular directed films devoted to cities and addressing local issues. For more information, see his online archive: http://www.archiviomariocarbone.com/.
21. See J. K. Galbraith, *The Affluent Society*, first published by Penguin in 1958.
22. IG, APCI, MF 477, pp. 2636–47, Sez. Culturale, serie 1961.
23. See Gundle (1995: 129). The new Communist approach to cultural issues was further developed in Togliatti's speech at the Tenth Congress of the PCI (Rome, 2–8 December 1962), in which he argued that settling disputes in this sphere was no longer the party's duty. See Crapis and Crapis (2016: 29).
24. IG, APCI, MF 468, pp. 1431–32, Stampa e Propaganda, serie 1960.
25. IG, APCI, MF 468, pp. 1544–48, Stampa e Propaganda, *A tutte le Segreterie, a tutti i responsabili propaganda delle Federazioni*, 10 October 1960.
26. IG, APCI MF 489, pp. 1698–99, *Nota per il compagno Togliatti*, 22 April 1963.

27. See *L'Unità*, 26 April 1963: front page and p. 12.
28. The twelve-minute *Appello agli elettori di Palmiro Togliatti* (Appeal to the electors by Palmiro Togliatti), broadcast on 25 April 1963, is conserved in the AAMOD, Archivio Unitelefilm, codice indentificativo: IL8210002232.
29. *Relazione sui convegni regionali di Stampa e Propaganda tenutisi dal 2 al 10 maggio 1960*, in IG, APCI, MF 468, pp. 1461–64, Stampa e Propaganda, 19 May 1960. On the foundation of Unitelefilm, see also the interview with Alessandro Curzi (Medici et al. 2001: 154–55) which highlights the important contribution made by Luciano Romagnoli.
30. Law no. 161 of 21 April 1962, 'Revisione dei film e dei lavori teatrali'.

BIBLIOGRAPHY

Andreucci, F. 2005. *Falce e martello. Identità e linguaggi dei comunisti italiani fra stalinismo e guerra fredda*. Bologna: Bononia University Press.

Argentieri, M. 1974. *La censura nel cinema italiano*. Rome: Editori Riuniti.

Bellassai, S. 2000. *La morale comunista. Pubblico e privato nella rappresentazione del P.C.I. (1947–1956)*. Rome: Carocci.

Benvenuti, F., ed. 1985. *Da Gramsci a Berlinguer. La via Italiana al socialismo attraverso i Congressi del Partito comunista italiano 1921–1984*. III, 1956–1964, Edizioni del Calendario, Vicenza: Marsilio.

Bertozzi, M. 2008. *Storia del documentario italiano. Immagini e culture dell'altro cinema*. Venice: Marsilio.

Castronovo, V. 2010. *L'Italia del miracolo economico*. Bari: Laterza.

Cooke, P. 2000. *Luglio 1960: Tambroni e la repressione fallita*. Milan: Teti.

Crainz, G. 2003. *Storia del miracolo italiano: culture, identità, trasformazioni fra anni cinquanta e sessanta*. Rome: Donzelli.

Crapis, G. 2002. *Il frigorifero del cervello. Il PCI e la televisione da "Lascia o raddoppia?" alla battaglia contro gli spot*. Rome: Editori Riuniti.

Crapis, C., and G. Crapis. 2016. *Umberto Eco e il PCI. Arte, cultura di massa e strutturalismo in un saggio dimenticato del 1963*. Reggio Emilia: Imprimatur.

De Clementis, A. 2010. *Il prezzo delle ricostruzione. L'emigrazione italiana nel secondo dopoguerra*. Bari: Laterza.

Di Loreto, P. 1991. *Togliatti e la "doppiezza". Il PCI tra democrazia e insurrezione (1944–1949)*. Bologna: il Mulino.

Dorfles, P. 2007. *Carosello*. Bologna: il Mulino.

Forgacs, D. 1990. The Italian Communist Party and Culture. In *Culture and Conflict in Postwar Italy. Essays on Mass and Popular Culture*, ed. Zygmunt G. Barański and L. Lumley, 97–114. New York: St. Martin's Press.

Ginsborg, P. 1990. *A History of Contemporary Italy. Society and Politics 1944–1989*. London: Penguin.

Gozzini, G., and R. Martinelli. 1998. *Dall'attentato di Togliatti all'VIII Congresso*, Storia del partito comunista italiano. Vol. VII. Turin: Einaudi.

Gundle, S. 1990. From Neorealism to Luci Rosse: Cinema, Politics, Society 1945–85. In *Culture and Conflict in Postwar Italy: Essays on Mass and Popular Culture*, ed. Zygmunt G. Barański and R. Lumley, 195–224. London: Macmillan.

———. 1995. *I comunisti italiani tra Hollywood e Mosca. La sfida della cultura di massa*. Florence: Giunti.

Lanaro, S. 1992. *Storia dell'Italia repubblicana: dalla fine della guerra agli anni novanta*. Venice: Marsilio.

Maggiorani, M. 1998. *L'Europa degli altri. Comunisti italiani e integrazione europea (1957–1969)*. Rome: Carocci.

Martelli, N. 1993. *Aldo Capitini: profilo di un intellettuale militante*. Bari and Rome: Lacaita.

Medici, A., M. Morbidelli, and E. Taviani, eds. 2001. *Il PCI e il cinema tra cultura e propaganda (1959–1979)*. Rome: Aamod.

Monteleone, F. 1992. *Storia della radio e della televisione in Italia. Società, politica, strategia, programmi 1922–1992*. Venice: Marsilio.

Morreale, E. 2006. *Mario Soldati. Le carriere di un libertino*. Cineteca di Bologna.

Nichols, B. 2001. *Introduction to Documentary*. Bloomington: Indiana University Press.

Novelli, E. 2000. *C'era una volta il PCI. Autobiografia di un partito attraverso le immagini della sua propaganda*. Rome: Editori Riuniti.

Ortoleva, P. 2008. La televisione italiana 1974–2002: dall' "anarchie italienne" al duopolio imperfetto. In *La Stampa italiana nell' età della Tv. Dagli anni settanta ad oggi*, ed. V. Castronovo and N. Tranfaglia. Bari: Laterza.

Righi, M.L., ed. 1996. *Quel Terribile 1956. I verbali della direzione comunista tra il Congresso del PCUS e l'VIII Congresso del PCI*. Rome: Editori Riuniti.

Sassoon, D. 1981. *The Strategy of the Italian Communist Party. From the Resistance to the Historic Compromise*. London: Pinter.

CHAPTER 5

The First Years of Unitelefilm and the PCI After Togliatti (1964–1967)

'In the last decade (and with an increasingly accelerated pace as we approach the present) Marxist research has become more and more articulated, as groups of intellectuals who do not belong to the political parties of the working class have contributed to said research, and also because scholars and artists who do belong, for example, to the Communist Party have initiated their own autonomous elaboration. Hence, we now have a plurality of positions (often antithetical) and we have groups which are born from shared philosophical or artistic views, and not out of a common political militancy'. With these words, in December 1964, Carlo Salinari, Mario Alicata, Antonello Trombadori, Renato Guttuso and the other members of the editorial board of *Il Contemporaneo* communicated to their readers the decision to end publication.[1] The magazine had been created by the PCI ten years earlier. It was supposed to orient the cultural debate within the party and keep Marxist criticism of literature, fine art and cinema on a straight course. Such an endeavour had, however, proved to be increasingly difficult. Party intellectuals had progressively become more independent since de-Stalinization and the PCI could no longer impose its credo on artistic issues. The rise of a modern cultural industry and the advent of television broadcasting had already forced the party to reconsider its cultural policy in the early 1960s, as shown in Chap. 4. In the following years, the PCI showed increasing openness to formal experimentation in art and eventually renounced the impulse of imposing any specific 'poetics' or 'tendency' in art.[2]

© The Author(s), under exclusive license to Springer Nature Switzerland AG 2021
G. Fantoni, *Italy through the Red Lens*, Italian and Italian American Studies, https://doi.org/10.1007/978-3-030-69197-4_5

However, it was not just the party's cultural policy that was showing cracks, but also the party's political unity, as proved by the formation of Maoist fringes within the party (see the Yalta memorandum, discussed in Chap. 4). Things got much worse in the summer of 1964, for the Party had to face one of the most tragic moments in its post-war history. On 21 August 1964, during a visit to the Crimea, Palmiro Togliatti died. This left the Italian Communists bereft of their longstanding leader. Not only had Togliatti steered the PCI's political strategy for many years, but he had also embodied the party's authority and prestige in the eyes of its millions of members and voters. Above all, Togliatti had kept the party leadership in line since the end of the War. Following his death, it was revealed that the members of the political directorate weren't as united as they had always pretended to be, and serious conflicts emerged with respect to the party's strategy. It is in this troubled political environment that Unitelefilm began production.

This chapter concerns Unitelefilm's early production, from 1964 to 1967. It shows how Unitelefilm's documentaries glossed over the struggle occurring within the party leadership after the death of Togliatti, which indirectly demonstrates the gravity of the disagreement. Communist cinema did deal to some extent with the political attacks on the party originated on the left of the political spectrum, but measures were taken from a narrative point of view to de-emphasize their importance.

Cinematic propaganda was widely employed to promote the party's '*politica unitaria*' (unifying policy), which emerged, not without dramatic disagreements, as the party's official political line at its Eleventh Congress, in January 1966. In line with Togliatti's approach, the *politica unitaria* sought a broad inter-class alliance aimed at gradually strengthening the party's electoral base for a long-term political 'war of position'. In order to implement such a policy, the PCI pursued political reconciliation with the Italian Socialist Party and tried to court catholic voters. Unitelefilm contributed to the party's strategy by producing films such as *A Paolo Rossi nostro compagno* (For our comrade Paolo Rossi), which constituted an attempt to bring PCI and PSI together under the common banner of anti-Fascism. Meanwhile, *I comunisti e il paese* (The Communists and the country), a film about the Eleventh Congress includes parts which were aimed at fostering a dialogue between the PCI and left-leaning Christian Democrat voters. The pursuit of PCI's unifying policy also explains the quite impressive number of films on the Vietnam War Unitelefilm produced in these years. That war was turning into a topical issue by the mid-1960s, because large sectors of the population, and most notably youngsters, were publicly and energetically expressing their support for the cause of North Vietnam.

First, however, the chapter briefly illustrates Unitelefilm's management and production context and discusses at length *L'Italia con Togliatti* (Italy with Togliatti), a forty-minute documentary produced by Unitelefilm and covering Togliatti's funeral. This is the first film ever produced by Unitelefilm and one of the most important in terms of productive effort and number of copies sold. It is also one of the most interesting to the researcher. As a faithful recording of the final tribute to Togliatti, the film provides valuable visual documentation of one of the most symbolically charged Communist rites: the funeral of the leader. This was a highly ritualized ceremony, a set of practices and rules meant to honouring and admiring the dead leader. It also served the purpose of easing the militants' sense of loss and of preparing them for the transition to the new leadership.

The Italian Communist Party established Unitelefilm (UTF) in 1964 with two different and to some degree incompatible objectives. First, the party wanted a central unit for the production of propaganda films. Unitelefilm was therefore an integrated part of the PCI structure: it was a branch of the party, financed by the party, and subject to the political control of the national Press and Propaganda Section. Second, the PCI wanted to make UTF profitable in financial terms. Experience had shown that this aim was unlikely to be achieved by selling film copies to the party's branches; UTF was therefore to compete in the market. For this reason, it was legally constituted as a private company and more precisely as a *Società a Responsabilità Limitata* (Srl: Limited Liability Company).

Identifying UTF's core business activity proved difficult. From its very beginning, UTF was entrusted with the release and distribution in Italy of documentaries produced in socialist countries. Another source of revenue was the production of short films with separate audio tracks documenting significant events involving the Italian Communist Party and the Italian labour movement. These were called '*attualità*' (current affairs) and were sold exclusively to Eastern European countries, where they were edited for inclusion in newsreels; this gave UTF a key role in the party's cultural exchanges with the Socialist bloc. Revenue from these two activities, however, was never very substantial, and certainly not sufficient to keep a film production company in activity. A third and potentially more significant source of income was represented by the '*premi di qualità*' (quality awards) for documentaries established by Law no. 1213, passed in November 1965, which not only provided for a monetary prize but also guaranteed that the award-winning films would be shown in cinemas for a certain number of days.[3]

The PCI was in fact always somewhat reluctant to invest in the production of documentaries for the quality awards, since the principal purpose of UTF was supposed to be the production of propaganda films for the party. In the eyes of most of the PCI leadership, moreover, it was not qualified to take initiatives in the cultural field because it reported to the Press and Propaganda Section and not to the 'Sezione Cultura' (Culture Section). In order to produce enough documentaries to submit to the quality awards on an annual basis, the UTF crew had to resort to expedients such as the '*film di recupero*' (recycled films): documentaries put together from edited footage shot for propaganda films that had been fully funded by the party. *Deserto di uomini* (A land with no men) (twelve minutes, 1965), which was the first UTF film to win the quality award, worth seven million lire, was in fact a *film di recupero* extracted from the thirty-seven-minute propaganda film *Vecchio e nuovo nelle campagne* (Old and new in the countryside).

Established on the back of the success achieved by film propaganda for the 1963 elections, UTF struggled to find a clear role in the years when no elections were scheduled, and faced financial uncertainty throughout its history. The *Catalogo generale* that it published in 1979 listed 211 films, of which 163 were UTF productions (Unitelefilm 1979). The rest were Italian editions of foreign documentaries and feature films, mostly produced in socialist countries. Over the period of its existence, from August 1964 to December 1979, UTF in fact had a much larger total output, as neither the propaganda films commissioned by the PCI nor the *attualità* were included in the company's commercial catalogue. The AAMOD conserves a total of 340 films produced by Unitelefilm, and a further 890 films, including the *attualità*, that are classified as '*non finiti*' (unfinished).[4]

The first film the filmmakers working at Unitelefilm were tasked with was one they would have never wanted to shoot: Togliatti's funeral. This film, with contributions from many of the most important professionals within Italian cinema in the 1960s, stands out due to its cinematographic merits.[5] According to Mino Argentieri, the film was conceived by Luciano Malaspina, the first director of Unitelefilm Mario Benocci and Argentieri himself, while the project was coordinated by Glauco Pellegrini. Argentieri recalled its genesis:

> We contacted the directors. We got this team into action within two or three days; the arrival of Togliatti's body was filmed from the airport's viewing terrace, and then everyone got themselves into position so that we could follow the whole route and all the ceremony, ending with the interment which was filmed by Zurlini. It was an extraordinary feat of organization. Then we had a really good idea: to let Mario Serandrei, the film's editor, be named as the director, since he had in fact been the film's real author.[6]

As the historian Franco Andreucci has pointed out, the choreography of Togliatti's funeral was carefully planned (2005: 253), with the aim of conveying a specific image of the party both to its own militants and to the Italian population in general. Because RAI provided a live broadcast of thirty minutes of the funeral, the PCI could not pass up the opportunity for a display of strength and unity for propaganda purposes. It needed to appear simultaneously massive and ordered: a political force made immensely strong by its impressive popular support, and at the same time disciplined and coherent. The film that was actually shot ended up providing a fairly faithful record of the funeral's choreography and its underlying propaganda message. Nevertheless, the careful planning could not prevent real Communist participants from stealing the scene and becoming the film's protagonists. Thanks to this feature, the film offers a poignant and emotional record; it is also a rare and superb portrait of Italy's ordinary Communist militants in the mid-1960s.

L'Italia con Togliatti opens with the PCI leader's body being honoured by young people at the Artek camp for Young Pioneers, in the Crimea, where he had suddenly died; it then moves to Rome, where the funeral took place on 25 August 1964. A long section of the film, about fifteen minutes, is devoted to the final tribute by Communist militants to their beloved leader. Togliatti's sealed coffin is placed on a funerary platform in the entrance hall of the PCI's headquarter in Via delle Botteghe Oscure. In an emotional and rather religious atmosphere, thousands of heartbroken militants slowly file past the coffin for three long days and nights. Lengthy sequences in close-up reveal the Communist masses as they really are, mournful and affecting. We can almost guess their social and regional background: labourers whose faces show the signs of a life of gruelling toil, factory workers who have travelled overnight to be there, young girls from the city's outskirts wearing cheap summer clothes. There is also evidence of the deep religious sentiments held by most Italians of the time, including the Communist voters: while some give the clenched fist salute, most make the sign of the cross and above all, they kiss Togliatti's coffin and make their children kiss it too. Many, men and women alike, weep in despair as if bereft of a close relative or dear friend.

As modern-day viewers we might find it difficult to understand how the death of a politician, however much admired, could have aroused such strong emotions. However, this display was characteristic of the funerals of Communist leaders during that era, in both socialist and non-socialist countries. To understand this behaviour, we need to understand how Communist leaders transcended their status as mere human beings, becoming the living embodiment of the party and thus the embodiment of its members' political faiths, beliefs and hopes. As discussed earlier (e.g. in Chap. 3), Communist propaganda, including film propaganda, deliberately promoted and reinforced this idea. For party militants, the loss of their leader therefore represented the loss of an important part of their own identity, both political and personal.

These ritualized funerals were also intended to address the pain felt by the militants: the deceased leader was to be permanently relegated to a mythical and almost supernatural sphere, helping them to cope with their grief and preparing them for the necessary transition towards a new leadership. In the Communist world, the funerals of leaders seem to be true rites of passage in the sense discussed by ethnographers.[7] The lengthy and carefully staged ritual gave militants enough time to reflect on their leader's history and legacy; this allowed them to close that chapter of their own life in order to be ready to experience a new phase of history, represented by the new leadership. This psychological mechanism is perfectly exemplified by *L'Italia con Togliatti*. In the first part of the film, while people pass by the coffin, we hear Togliatti's voice in excerpts from his speech at the Stadio dei Marmi in 1948 (see Chap. 3). The editing also includes long zoom shots of the portraits of Gramsci and Lenin, hanging on the walls of Togliatti's now empty office. This is the moment to think about the leader and reflect on his legacy to the history of both the Italian and the international Communist movement. Several minutes later, the ritual comes to a conclusion with Togliatti's burial in the Campo Verano cemetery, which the film shows in surreal silence: no music, no commentary, no ambient sound. This is the moment for the final emotional detachment from the deceased leader: the coffin slowly descends into the grave.

Immediately afterwards, the editing reveals Togliatti's portrait alongside that of his old comrade Gramsci: Togliatti himself is now history (Image 5.1). We then see the comrades on the PCI's Central Committee applauding the party's new leader Luigi Longo (Image 5.2). The Italian Communist Party is moving on, and its militants must follow.

If we compare *L'Italia con Togliatti* and *L'addio a Enrico Berlinguer* (Farewell to Enrico Berlinguer), the last film produced by the PCI, devoted to Berlinguer's funeral in Rome on 13 June 1984, we note how the set of rituals marking such a crucial moment in the life of the party had remained unaltered twenty years later. If we set aside the evolution of shooting and narrative techniques, such as the use of colour film and street interviews, *L'Addio a Enrico Berlinguer* presents the same symbolic elements present in *L'Italia con Togliatti*: an endless procession of mourning citizens filing past the leader's coffin, foreign delegations, factory worker representatives complemented by '*uomini della cultura*' (intellectuals) in the guard of honour, the flags of cities under PCI rule, innumerable

Image 5.1 Togliatti's portrait alongside that of Gramsci

Image 5.2 The new leader Luigi Longo

wreaths, and the final assembly in Piazza San Giovanni attended by a vast red-tinged mass. The choreography of the funerals of both Togliatti and Berlinguer in fact drew on the model of the funeral of Stalin in 1953, as seen in *The Great Farewell*, the film produced on that occasion. The most notable difference is that Stalin's body is on public display in the Soviet film, while in the two Italian films all that we see is a coffin.[8] That apart, the three films are very similar, even in relation to the camera angles and editing.

One final observation should be made on the symbolic relevance of Togliatti's funeral within the history of Italian cinema. Images taken from *L'Italia con Togliatti* were incorporated in two films released in the next few years: Pier Paolo Pasolini's *Uccellacci e uccellini* (*The Hawks and the Sparrows*) (1966) and Paolo and Vittorio Taviani's *Sovversivi* (*The Subversives*) (1967). According to Lino Miccichè, both these belong to a group that have been described as '*film della crisi*' (films of the crisis): films addressing the ideological disenchantment of left-wing intellectuals in the mid-1960s (1995: 98–99). In Pasolini's view, Togliatti's death represented a watershed:

> A historical epoch, the epoch of the Resistance, of great hopes for communism, of the class struggle, has finished. What we have now is the economic boom, the welfare state, and industrialization which is using the South as a reserve of cheap manpower and even beginning to industrialize it as well. There has been a real change which coincided more or less with Togliatti's death. It was a pure coincidence chronologically, but it worked symbolically. (Pasolini quoted in Stack 1969: 103–4)

In the Taviani brothers' *Sovversivi*, the funeral of the great Communist leader is a rite of passage for a generation of intellectuals: 'goodbye Togliatti, goodbye to our youth', reads one of the protagonists' diary entries, as the funeral procession passes her house. Reaching adulthood represents both the final renunciation of romantic ideas about revolution and the inescapable decision to pursue calmer and more prosaic routine political activity within a reformist framework. The final scene of the film, in which the Venezuelan character decides to leave his beautiful Italian fiancée and comfortable life in Rome in order to return home and join a revolutionary group, seems to suggest that there is no room left in Europe for revolution and that major political change can only take place in the Third World countries.

This disillusionment might appear surprising and certainly lacking foresight, when we consider that only a few months following the release of *Sovversivi*, during the phase of political mobilization known as the '*contestazione*', a new generation was to assume the task of promoting radical change (discussed in Chap. 6). However, this would be an entirely different group, with few if any links to the generation of intellectuals that included the Taviani brothers and Pasolini; this new generation were young students, without any direct experience of Fascism, who had grown up in the years of the economic boom. This latter generation held a very different and far less legendary image of the PCI, to which they owed neither their successful careers nor a core set of myths, cultural values and political ideas that had served as the foundations of their personal development. In consequence, they could dare to believe that revolution was possible even without the support of the Italian Communist Party, while this idea was regarded as improbable, if not preposterous, by those who were just a few years older.

124   G. FANTONI

L'Italia con Togliatti was by far the greatest commercial success of the early years of Unitelefilm: it sold 135 copies in 16 mm and 91 copies in 35 mm, both in Italy and abroad.[9]

Following Togliatti's death, the PCI entered a period of political and ideological tension. On the one hand, it was subjected to violent ideological attack by radical left-wing groups. On the other, it was shaken by the first split within the party leadership since 1930.[10] In the context of the first issue, criticism from the groups of the '*nuova sinistra*' (new left) had represented a challenge to the PCI leadership since the beginning of the 1960s. The *nuova sinistra*, which encompassed a few small but combative groups of young intellectuals who had gathered around periodicals such as *Quaderni Rossi* and *Quaderni Piacentini*, openly accused the PCI of being a hindrance rather than a help to advancement of the workers' cause. According to an interpretation that had begun to enjoy some popularity, ever since the end of the Second World War, the PCI had been deliberately suppressing the social and political aspirations of Italian workers, gradually becoming a pillar of the bourgeois political system.[11] The theses of the *nuova sinistra*'s will in time inspire fringes of the students movement, which will engage in a cinematic skirmish with the PCI, as showed in Chap. 7.

In 1964, a new political threat arrived in the form of Maoist fringes, both within and outside the party. These aimed to either replace the PCI leadership, which was accused of having betrayed Leninism, or erode the party's grass-roots support through the foundation of a new Communist party. These Maoist groups funded a newspaper, which they gave the tendentious title '*Nuova Unità*' (New Unity) and began to publish anonymous leaflets, the '*Lettera ai compagni*' (Letter to the comrades), welcoming the removal in October 1964 of Khrushchev (ironically described as 'l'uomo del gulasc', a play on words alluding both to 'gulash' and 'gulag'), and describing the PCI leadership as both 'revisionist' and 'reformist'.[12] In October 1966, some Maoists founded a new Communist Party, the 'Partito Comunista d'Italia' (Panvini 2009: 19). To add to all this, the Chinese 'Cultural Revolution', a ruthless civil war mistaken by many for the genesis of a new and more democratic form of socialism, encouraged criticism of the PCI's bureaucratic apparatus. A few intellectuals and, in particular, groups on the fringes of the student movement saw this as an obstacle to socialism (Crainz 2005: 141–42).[13]

The most serious threat to cohesion within the PCI, however, came from the disagreement between two of its senior figures, Giorgio Amendola and Pietro Ingrao, over the significance of the centre-left coalition and its impact on Italian society (Höbel 2010: 129–58). Amendola, along with the party's new General Secretary Luigi Longo and most of the leadership, believed that the coalition between the DC and the PSI had failed in its objectives, as it had achieved very little in relation to the reforms it had promised the electorate. Therefore, there was no reason to change the party's political course. Pietro Ingrao, backed by the FGCI and a few intellectuals including Rossana Rossanda and Luigi Pintor, argued instead that it was thanks to the centre-left coalition that the DC and the ruling classes were on the verge of achieving their major objective: the political and social integration of part of the Italian working class, and the PSI itself, within a social democratic framework (Magri 2009: 190–94). Consequently, Ingrao proposed that the focus should be on the working class and that the party should counter the centre-left by promoting a new wave of struggle in the factories.

This was not the first time that different political visions had clashed at the top of the party. Thanks to Togliatti's unquestioned authority, however, disputes had always been promptly settled and the party leadership had retained its cohesion; the militants had thus never been aware of signs of disagreement at the centre. On this occasion it proved more difficult to find common ground and differences were clearly apparent at the party's Eleventh Congress (Rome, 25–31 January 1966). Moreover, when Ingrao and his supporters, the '*sinistra*' (left), were defeated in the congressional debate, Ingrao argued that the minority had the right to disagree and refused to endorse the majority position. In view of the Communist tradition of democratic centralism, this stance was nothing less than heresy.[14] Although Ingrao's personal standing within the party saved him from any major consequences, his followers did not escape punishment. Rossanda, for example, lost the leadership of the PCI's Cultural Commission; three years later, she and Pintor were expelled from the party, along with others, for having set up an independent Communist magazine, *Il Manifesto*, which was the mouthpiece for a left-wing critique of party policy (Ajello 1997: 94–99; Magri 2009: 252–58).

Unitelefilm produced a twenty-five-minute film about the Eleventh Congress, *I comunisti e il paese* (The Communists and the country), which was directed by Andrea Frezza.[15] Like all previous films devoted to party congresses, *I comunisti e il paese* was principally aimed at presenting the PCI as a strong political party whose leadership stood firmly and unanimously behind its general secretary. This positive message was especially important because the Eleventh Congress was the first without Togliatti, and the militants needed to be reassured about the health of the party and the stability of the new leadership of Luigi Longo. As a result, the film makes no mention at all of the clashes between supporters of Amendola and Ingrao.

After the ritual tribute to the memory of Togliatti, *I comunisti e il paese* does address the Maoist groups' critique of the party's political strategy, but this thorny issue is tackled in a very particular way: the actual existence of the Maoist groups and their criticism is at no point explicitly acknowledged. If viewers are not familiar with the issue, they cannot therefore fully grasp the meaning of some of the statements in the voice-over commentary. This provided a way for the director and the watchful officials within the Press and Propaganda Section, to fulfil dual objectives: the matter was addressed for those militants who were aware of its significance, while the less informed viewers, arguably the majority, were kept in the dark. In order to rebut Maoist comments, the film employs a sort of rhetorical technique: whereas the Maoists saw as mutually exclusive the 'peaceful coexistence' theory and the commitment to combat American imperialism, the voice-over suggests that the two policies are not in contradiction and are instead two sides of the same coin.[16]

Although scarcely informative in terms of the congressional debate, *I comunisti e il paese* is a useful cinematographic text in that it summarizes PCI policy and the themes informing Communist propaganda at the time. The issue of dialogue with the Church and Catholic voters stands out as a central element of the strategy that had emerged victorious at the congress: the *politica unitaria*. The film shows Longo quoting Paul VI, who had invited Catholics to join 'all true peacemakers' in the shared endeavour of freeing mankind from the curse of war. The voice-over goes one step further, arguing that a constructive dialogue between Communists and Catholics on both Italian society's short-term problems and its long-term prospects is essential for Italy's democratic development.

This commentary needs to be viewed as the Communist response to the process of renewal that the Catholic Church had been undertaking since the election of John XXIII as pope in 1958. Various actions and public statements by the new pontiff, especially publication of the first papal encyclical to address not only Catholics but also 'people of good will' (*Pacem in terris*, 1963), had encouraged the PCI leadership's hopes for a softening of the anti-Communist stance that had characterized the papacy of Pius XII.[17] In particular, the Communist Party had followed the

Second Vatican Council ('Vatican II') with keen interest. This had opened under John XXIII on 11 October 1962 and closed under Paul VI on 8 December 1965.[18]

After the conclusion of Vatican II, a report was submitted to Longo by Siro Lombardini, who had been a member of the Sinistra Cristiana (Christian Left) within Lombardy's wartime Committee of National Liberation. Lombardini emphasized that there had been open criticism at the council of the 'principle of the political unity of Catholics' and urged the PCI to create a welcoming environment for potential sympathizers:

> <u>Significant groups</u> (although I believe not numerically very strong) of Italian Catholics who look at our party with true "passion" and feel that the <u>right</u> political place for them is within the PCI.[19]

The PCI thus identified the opportunity for an alliance at the grass-roots level with left-wing groups on the Catholic fringe, potentially enlarging its constituency. This explains the frequent allusions to dialogue between Communists and Catholics in *I comunisti e il paese*, as well as in other films produced by the PCI during the same period. However, the political and ideological links to the Soviet Union remained a central element of Communist identity; the film undertook to remind militants of this, showing the head of the Soviet delegation, Mikhail Suslov, presenting Longo with a bust of Lenin.

In addition to opening some form of dialogue with Catholics, the *politica unitaria* attempted to rebuild an alliance with the Italian Socialist Party in order to preserve the political unity of the working class. This was a particularly pressing issue in 1966, because after a long process of political rapprochement, the PSI and the PSDI were about to merge within the Partito Socialista Unificato (PSU: United Socialist Party), although in the event this was soon to split again. PCI propaganda was therefore assigned the task of countering the increasing distance between the Socialists and Communists, and Unitelefilm made its contribution with the fifteen-minute documentary *A Paolo Rossi nostro compagno* (For our comrade Paolo Rossi), directed by Ennio Lorenzini.[20]

This film deals with the killing of the Socialist student Paolo Rossi by neo-Fascists, which took place at La Sapienza, the university in Rome, on 27 April 1966.[21] This dramatic event was highly relevant to the PCI's aims because it provided an opportunity to bring the established parties of the Italian Left back together in the common cause of anti-Fascism. Although

A Paolo Rossi nostro compagno rather blatantly exploits the death of the young Socialist student for political purposes, it seems to have been made with genuine feeling. The opening scene dealing with Rossi's funeral is especially moving: we see the student's mother and sister, and an endless stream of people and funeral wreaths, while 'We shall overcome', the anthem of the African-American civil rights movement, is played. The voice-over states that Rossi's sacrifice has brought all genuine democrats together, regardless of their social class and political creed. The film then provides unique visual documentation of the occupation of the university's 'Lettere e Filosofia' faculty, which followed the funeral. According to the voice-over, which at various points supposedly voices the students' point of view, the occupation had shown that anti-Fascist values were far more profound than current political divisions:

> Although we were divided on many issues, we found ourselves united in our anti-Fascism and in the defence of the values of democracy. There was thus no other possible response: occupy the faculty.

The student occupation was politically significant, as was shown by visits to the university by major political leaders, including Ferruccio Parri, Luigi Longo and Pietro Ingrao; their presence among the students is duly highlighted in the film. The occupiers targeted *La Sapienza*'s rector Giuseppe Ugo Papi for his alleged tolerance of Fascist violence on the campus, and Papi's eventual resignation was hailed by *L'Unità* as 'the first great victory of anti-Fascist unity at the University of Rome'.[22] It is worth noting that the declaration issued by the students on the last day of the occupation, while expressing satisfaction at Papi's resignation, also emphasized that his departure, far from being the objective of the struggle, should instead be seen as the first step of a long-term endeavour to dispense with 'a university that is grandiose, feudal, and scientifically and morally decrepit'.[23] With the benefit of hindsight this statement seems particularly revealing, as it foreshadows the slogans heard in Italian universities during the clashes of 1968 and thereafter.

It is also significant that this statement, initially present in the screenplay, was eventually deleted in the final version of the film; the officials of the Press and Propaganda Section may well have seen it as superfluous to the documentary's aims.[24] This suggests that the PCI was not particularly interested in the long-term demands of students and was instead keen to exploit the turmoil in the university in order to strengthen the party's *politica unitaria*. Two years later, it was to be caught out by the sudden outbreak of student unrest.

Alongside the issue of anti-Fascism, the PCI saw the Vietnam War as a further opportunity to bolster its *politica unitaria* by fostering cooperation with a wide range of political forces, including members of the PSI and Catholic grass-roots associations. In many respects the conflict in Vietnam was the perfect propaganda issue. On the one hand, it offered the possibility of revitalizing both the campaign for peace and anti-Americanism, two themes that had traditionally been linked together in Communist propaganda. On the other, it was an effective counter to allegations from the Maoist groups and the *nuova sinistra* of the PCI's acquiescence towards American imperialism, because it demonstrated that the PCI was committed to opposing this. Furthermore, this particular conflict elicited a very intense emotional response, especially among young left-wingers and Catholics. The Vietnam War was to shape the political identity of an entire cohort of Italians: the 'generazione del Vietnam' (Vietnam generation), as the secretary of the FGCI Claudio Petruccioli described it in an article for *Rinascita*.[25] Due to the massive media coverage, which for the first time did not spare the audience the graphic details of modern warfare, the response to the war was a global phenomenon (Hallin 1986).

From January 1965 onwards, the PCI urged its branches to organize demonstrations and other initiatives relating to the Vietnam War.[26] These proved very successful in terms of participation, encouraging the party to focus its propaganda on this issue. According to a report for the National Directorate from the Press and Propaganda Section:

> In some areas of the country the movement has such strength and coverage that it can be compared to similar movements that developed in Italy in the period 1949–50: that is, to a movement that saw the greatest mobilization of democratic and worker forces on the issue of the battle for peace.[27]

The national Press and Propaganda Section also created several posters illustrating the atrocities perpetrated by US soldiers.[28] In May 1965, the PCI claimed to have raised funds of 100 million lire in record time for a field hospital to be shipped to the North Vietnamese.[29] At much the same time, Unitelefilm released *Vietnam chiama* (Vietnam calls), the first of a series of propaganda films devoted to the Vietnam War. According to *L'Unità*, this was 'a film that everyone ought to see'.[30]

130 G. FANTONI

Vietnam chiama, which has a running time of twenty-four minutes, was directed by Luciano Malaspina, who had previously directed *Rivoluzione a Cuba* (Revolution in Cuba), one of the first Italian documentaries devoted to the Cuban revolution (Poppi 2000: 259–60). *Vietnam chiama* is put together exclusively from archive pictures and footage. Some of this is somewhat graphic and was clearly intended to generate revulsion among audiences for the crimes committed by both the US Army and the various dictators, puppets of the United States, who took turns to hold power in South Vietnam. Discussion of the historical causes of the war is entrusted to the voice-over commentary, read by the well-known actor Riccardo Cucciolla. This addresses a few forthright messages to both the party militants and the wider public. First, the US government must be regarded as uniquely responsible for the escalation of military conflict in Vietnam. Second, the USSR is actively supporting North Vietnam both politically and militarily; this point aims to counter the allegations of the Maoist fringe groups by stressing that the Soviet Union had not abandoned its commitment to combat imperialism. Third, the PCI is totally fulfilling its fraternal duty to the Communist Party of North Vietnam. On this last point, the voice-over commentary mentions the PCI delegation's official visit to North Vietnam, which had presented the Vietnamese comrades with the combat flag of one of the 'Brigate Garibaldi' (Garibaldi Brigades), as the Communist partisan units of the Resistance had commonly been known.[31] This symbolic gesture established a parallel between the Italian partisans and the People's Army of Vietnam, which was to become a recurrent motif within Communist propaganda.[32] During the election campaign of 1968, for example, the Sunday edition of *L'Unità* published a regular comic strip about the heroic struggle of the Vietnamese. This had the loaded title '*Partigiani nella Giungla*' and was written by the future director of Unitelefilm, Dario Natoli; it ran from 28 January to 21 April 1968. The film ends by making this connection explicit and calling for action to support Vietnam:

> Vietnam is calling. It is an old call, and yet a fresh one. It is the call from Spain, from Cuba, from Algeria, from the Congo, and from San Domingo. It is the call of a people who are fighting for the same ideals that fired up our Resistance, and who want to win liberty, peace, and socialism.

Film production related to the Vietnam War generally met with good commercial success; for example, Unitelefilm sold seventy copies of the

Italian edition of *Le Ciel, la Terre* (The Sky and the Earth), the first film devoted to the Vietnam War by the great Dutch documentary director Ioris Ivens. As for the political impact, a report from the Press and Propaganda Section at the end of 1966 claimed that the campaign on Vietnam had achieved its principal objectives, which were 'bringing Catholic groups closer' and 'taking a firm grip of young people'.[33] UTF had made an important contribution to these achievements: its films on the Vietnam War had been screened more than 2300 times, in a range of cities, and had been seen by an estimated half a million viewers.

UTF continued to produce films on the Vietnam War in the years that followed. One of the most notable was *L'offensiva del Tet* (1968): the 'Tet offensive' had been launched by the People's Army of Vietnam in January 1968 (Schmitz 2005). This twenty-eight-minute film was put together from footage supplied by filmmakers with the North Vietnamese forces, who had made wide use of cinematographic propaganda as a political weapon in the conflict (Barnouw 1974: 268). Experimental composer Luigi Nono wrote the music score. As a cinematic text, *L'offensiva del Tet*, although produced only two years later, reflects a totally different political phase from the 1965 to 1966 UTF production on Vietnam: it belongs to the period of '*contestazione*' (worker and student protest), which is discussed in Chap. 6. This accounts for the belligerent and uncompromising tone of the commentary, intoned in a somewhat triumphalist manner by the actor Gian Maria Volontè. *L'offensiva del Tet*, a piece of explicit pro-North Vietnamese propaganda, is striking for its lack of compassion over the human cost of this bloody campaign; the pacifism previously associated with the topic of the Vietnam War has completely vanished. Only the military aspect is taken into consideration, and the voice-over expresses satisfaction at the losses, actually greatly exaggerated, that had allegedly been suffered by the US army. The film concludes with uncritical and complacent coverage of the arrests of collaborators (who would in reality then have been executed) in the cities temporarily occupied by the People's Army of Vietnam. The final statement of the commentary emphasizes the importance that the Vietnam War has assumed for an entire generation:

> This struggle [of the Vietnamese] makes its appeal to every person, from every corner of the world, and asks everyone for their involvement, because Vietnam has meant something to us all, and its fate is now indissolubly ours as well.

In December 1966, Mario Benocci, the first director of Unitelefilm, pointed out in his annual report that the company could only achieve a balanced budget if it focused on producing documentaries for the quality awards. He also emphasized that any further improvements in UTF production, whether in increased output or in quality, hinged on the guarantee of an annual funding allocation that would allow for long-term production planning.[34] He therefore asked for a commitment to investment in new equipment, including a synchronized sound-recording system for interviews; a new and more spacious central office; an increase in personnel; and 45 million lire for the following year. In the original document, next to Bellocci's requests, a hand-written note, probably either by the head of the Press and Propaganda Section Emanuele Macaluso or by one of the officials in the party's finance office, gives an unequivocal and underlined '*no*'. Given that there were only a few local council elections scheduled for 1967, there was no good reason to increase the party's expenditure on film production.

This lack of financial commitment explains why Unitelefilm produced only a few of its own films in 1967. Instead, it made Italian editions of some classic films from Soviet cinematographic history in order to mount a fitting celebration of the fiftieth anniversary of the October Revolution, an event of paramount symbolic importance for the party.[35] During the 1940s and 1950s, the PCI had notably encouraged its activists to attend showings of the rather bombastic films of post-war Soviet realist cinema; in the mid-1960s, the films offered to PCI branches were those of the pre-war Russian avant-garde. This was surely a by-product of the process of de-Stalinization that had followed the Twentieth Congress of the CPSU in 1956 and also of the debate among left-wing film critics and intellectuals sparked off by publication in the magazine *Cinema Nuovo* in June 1956 of an article by Renzo Renzi, with the telling heading '*Sciolti dal "Giuramento"*' (Released from 'The Vow'), which had led to a rejection of Soviet cinematography of the Stalin era (Aristarco 1981).

Moreover, the films of the Russian avant-garde were enjoying a revival, largely because of the film critics' exaltation of their experimental features, and thus enjoyed some commercial success.[36] The Soviet films of the 1920s acquired canonical status within art-house cinema, and no intellectual could afford to be unaware of films such as Sergei Eisenstein's *Battleship Potemkin* and *October*. In due course, Russian experimental cinema came to symbolize the cultural conformism of Italian intellectuals, which inspired a memorable scene in Lucio Salce's comedy *Il secondo tragico Fantozzi* (The second tragic Fantozzi) (1976). The film's protagonist, the accountant Ugo Fantozzi, an archetypal lower-middle-class white-collar worker, shouts out that '*la corrazzata Kotiomkin è una cagata pazzesca!*' ('Battleship Kotiomkin is a ridiculous piece of shit!': out of respect for Eisenstein, Salce had changed the film title). This line, ever since, has been a popular expression of the ordinary citizen's rejection of the cultural dictates of intellectuals.

In summary, Unitelefilm was from its inception the mouthpiece of the PCI's *politica unitaria*, the political strategy advocating wider unity that had emerged victorious at the party's Eleventh Congress. Central to this approach was a political rapprochement with both the Italian Socialist Party and Catholic voters, and the Vietnam War offered the party an excellent opportunity to follow this through. This explains why the Communist film company produced or edited several films on Vietnam during this period.

The most striking phase of student protest was about to erupt, and this was soon to capture the attention of both the PCI and Unitelefilm. The national elections scheduled for 19 May 1968 were also to represent another important commitment for the party and its film production company in the months ahead. Thanks to the enthusiastic endorsement of cinematographic propaganda by Achille Occhetto, the new head of the Press and Propaganda Section, this was to be the first Communist election campaign in which films played a prominent role. In May 1967, Occhetto had already stressed what an extraordinary effort would be required from UTF as the elections approached. He wanted 'something more than the usual documentaries':

> We need to have a <u>sort of TV from the Communists</u>. By this I mean pieces that contribute to the situation, in which in five minutes party leaders say something and then we have interviews linked to actions and events. We need a rapid output distributed right across Italy on affairs of the moment.[37]

This idea took shape over the following months and developed into a project with the name '*Terzo Canale (quello che la TV non fa vedere)*' (Channel Three: what the TV won't show you).[38] This is the topic of the next chapter.

NOTES

1. 'Saluto ai lettori', *Il Contemporaneo*, n.79, Dec. 1964, 3. The magazine turned into a monthly cultural supplement of *Rinascita*.
2. See, for example, an important article by Giorgio Napolitano, 'Sul problema della direzione culturale', in *Rinascita*, 44, November 1973, 20.
3. For a discussion of Law no. 1213 of 4 November 1965, 'Nuovo ordinamento dei provvedimenti a favore della cinematografia', see De Bernardis (2002). The compulsory showing of award-winning films, however, was largely disregarded by cinema proprietors.
4. At my request, AAMOD staff analysed the archive's database to determine, for the first time, the exact number of films that were produced by Unitelefilm.
5. Those involved included the directors Carlo Lizzani, Elio Petri, Francesco Maselli, Valerio Zurlini, Paolo and Vittorio Taviani, and the cinematographers Carlo Di Palma and Tonino Delli Colli.
6. Interview of Mino Argentieri by the author, Rome, 16 June 2011. Mario Serandrei was one of the most important video editors of Italian cinema. He started his career during the Fascist regime and was the editor of many of Luchino Visconti's films, including *Ossessione* and *La terra trema*. He was a member of the Communist Party. See his obituary in *L'Unità*, 15 May 1966: 19.
7. See Arnold van Gennep's classic *Rites of Passage* (1965: 146–65).
8. The visibility of the body is also a characteristic of Eastern Orthodox funeral traditions: the coffin is kept open in the church while friends and relatives file past in order to pay their last respects to the deceased (Gentile 2006: XVIII). The funeral of the leader French Communist Party's leader Maurice Thorez, who died like Togliatti in summer 1964, was organized according to a very similar choreography. See Cruciani (2008: 103–8).
9. *Produzione dall'agosto 1964 a fine 1964 e nella prima parte del 1965*, in Medici Morbidelli and Taviani (2001: 203–7).
10. For further discussion of the expulsion of the '*gruppo dei tre*' (group of three), namely Pietro Tresso, Alfonso Leonetti and Paolo Ravazzoli, see Galli (1977: 149–60).
11. An analysis of the various groups of the *nuova sinistra* in *Materiali per una nuova sinistra* (1988), and Lumley (1990: 33–41). A list of magazines and journals of the *nuova sinistra* is in Mangano (1979). For a discussion of the work of Renato Panzieri, founder of the *Quaderni Rossi*, see Santarelli (1996: 143–46). A selection of articles from *Quaderni Piacentini* can be found in Fofi and Giacopini (1998). On the PCI reaction to these new magazines, see Ajello (1997: 37–41).

12. A collection of the *Lettere ai compagni* published in 1965 is in IG, APCI, MF 526, pp. 3055–225, Partiti Politici, Gruppi di sinistra extraparlamentare, serie 1965.
13. For an analysis of the influence of the Cultural Revolution on Italian left-wing groups, see Niccolai (1998); Lepre (1993: 230–31).
14. For a detailed account of the debate at the Ninth Congress, see Höbel (2010: 209–20). See also Magri (2009: 195–97).
15. Andrea Frezza was a writer and the prolific director of about forty short films and documentaries. His feature film *Il gatto selvaggio* (The wild cat) (1969) made quite an impression on left-wing circles of the time; the plot revolves around a young anarchist, played by Carlo Cecchi, who decides to begin his own nihilist revolution by going on a killing spree. See Frezza's obituary in *L'Unità*, 30 March 2012: 45.
16. On the issues of 'peaceful coexistence' and imperialism, the PCI's official position was set out in an article by Enrico Berlinguer published a few days before the congress, 'La coesistenza pacifica (tre lettere e una risposta)', *Rinascita*, 1 January 1966: 5.
17. For discussion of the political impact of Pope John's papacy, see Lanaro (1992: 365–76).
18. See the articles published in *Rinascita* by Libero Pierantozzi, who covered the Second Vatican Council for the party, including 'I cattolici italiani dopo il Vaticano II', 18 December 1965: 50; 'Responsabilità dei cattolici', 25 December 1965: 51.
19. *Appunti per il compagno Luigi Longo*, in IG, APCI, MF 527, pp. 835–41, Chiesa e movimenti cattolici, serie 1965. Emphasis in the original.
20. Ennio Lorenzini (1934–1982) was a prolific documentary director known for his political commitment and the experimental features of his films. He also directed a feature film, *Quanto è bello lu murire acciso* (The Expedition, or How Wonderful to Die Assassinated) (1976). See his obituary in *L'Unità*, 17 March 1982: 8.
21. On the death of Paolo Rossi and its consequences for the Italian political climate, see Panvini (2009: 10–17).
22. See *L'Unità*, 3 May 1966: front page.
23. See 'Impegno di lotta democratica e antifascista dell'Università di Roma', *L'Unità*, 4 May 1966: 3.
24. The film's screenplay is archived in the AAMOD, Faldone P, Fascicolo *A Paolo Rossi nostro compagno*. The '*visto di censura*' (censorship certificate) authorizing the film's projection without any cuts is in the same folder.
25. Claudio Petruccioli, 'La generazione del Vietnam', *Rinascita*, 9 July 1966: 2. See also Aldo Tortorella, 'Una politica per la "generazione del Vietnam"', *Rinascita*, 6 December 1968: 13. For discussion, see Crainz (2005: 130–33).

136   G. FANTONI

26. *A tutte le Federazioni*. Bulletin issued by the Press and Propaganda Section, in IG, APCI, MF 523, p. 165, Stampa e Propaganda, 11 January 1965.
27. In IG, APCI, MF 523, p. 192, Stampa e Propaganda, 21 April 1965.
28. These can be found in Novelli (2000: 178–87).
29. See 'Raggiunti i cento milioni per il Vietnam', *L'Unità*, 23 May 1965: front page and p. 15.
30. 'Un crudo racconto della sporca Guerra nel Viet', *L'Unità*, 21 May 1965: 7.
31. On the official visit to Vietnam by a PCI delegation led by Gian Carlo Pajetta, in April–May 1965, see 'Ho Chi Min riceve a colloquio la delegazione del PCI', *L'Unità*, 1 May 1965: front page. See also IG, APCI, MF 528, pp. 774–75, Estero, Vietnam, serie 1965. Another diplomatic mission to North Vietnam, led by Enrico Berlinguer, was organized the following year: see IG, APCI, MF 528, pp. 774–75, Estero, Vietnam, serie 1966.
32. See Cooke (2011: 97).
33. IG, APCI, MF 537, pp. 938–42, Estero, Vietnam, serie 1966.
34. *Nota sulla Uniletelefilm*, in IG, APCI, MF 535, pp. 1243–59, Istituti e Organismi vari, Unitelefilm, 19 December 1966.
35. These films were *La caduta della dinastia Romanov* (The Fall of the Romanov Dynasty, originally released in Russia in 1927), *La fine di San Pietroburgo* (The End of St Petersburg, 1927), Sergei Eisenstein's *Sciopero* (Strike, 1925), and Dziga Vertov's experimental documentary *Tre canti su Lenin* (Three Songs about Lenin, 1934).
36. *Bilancio Unitelefilm al 31/12/1969*, in IG, APCI, MF 70, pp. 276–318, Istituti e organismi vari, Unitelefilm, serie 1970.
37. *Relazione del compagno Achille Occhetto alla riunione nazionale dei responsabili provinciali di propaganda*, in IG, APCI, MF 539, pp. 1169–80, Stampa e Propaganda, 26 May 1967. Emphasis in the original.
38. *Note sul lavoro di propaganda per le elezioni*, in IG, APCI, MF 547, pp. 2229–41, Stampa e Propaganda, 12 January 1968. On Terzo Canale, see Novelli (2006: 89).

Bibliography

Ajello, N. 1997. *Il lungo addio. Intellettuali e PCI dal 1958 al 1991*. Bari and Rome: Laterza.

Andreucci, F. 2005. *Falce e martello. Identità e linguaggi dei comunisti italiani fra stalinismo e guerra fredda*. Bologna: Bononia University Press.

Aristarco, G. 1981. *Sciolti dal Giuramento. Il dibattito critico – ideologico sul cinema negli anni cinquanta*. Bari: Dedalo.

5 THE FIRST YEARS OF UNITELEFILM AND THE PCI AFTER... 137

Barnouw, E. 1974. *Documentary, a History of the Non-fiction Film*. Oxford: Oxford University Press.

Cooke, P. 2011. *The Legacy of the Italian Resistance*. New York: Palgrave Macmillan.

Crainz, G. 2005. *Il paese mancato. Dal miracolo economico agli anni ottanta*. Rome: Donzelli.

Cruciani, S. 2008. Il mito di Palmiro Togliatti e Maurice Thorez nella propaganda politica del comunismo italiano e francese. In *Propaganda, cinema e politica (1945–1975)*, ed. E. Taviani, 77–110. Annali AAMOD: Rome.

De Bernardis, F. 2002. 1965: la legge sul cinema. In *Storia del cinema italiano*, ed. G. Canova, 379–396. Marsilio: XI – 1965/69. Venice.

Fofi, G., and V. Giacopini, eds. 1998. *Prima e dopo il '68. Antologia dei "Quaderni Piacentini"*. Rome: Edizioni Minimum Fax.

Galli, G. 1977. *Storia del Partito Comunista Italiano*. Milan: Bompiani.

Gentile, E. 2006. *Politics as Religion*. Princeton: Princeton University Press.

Hallin, D.C. 1986. *The Uncensored War: The Media and Vietnam*. Berkeley: University of California Press.

Höbel, A. 2010. *Il PCI di Luigi Longo (1964/1969)*. Naples: Edizioni Scientifiche Italiane.

Lanaro, S. 1992. *Storia dell'Italia repubblicana: dalla fine della guerra agli anni novanta*. Venice: Marsilio.

Lepre, A. 1993. *Storia della prima Repubblica. L'Italia dal 1942 al 1992*. Bologna: il Mulino.

Lumley, R. 1990. *States of Emergency. Culture of Revolts in Italy from 1968 to 1978*. London and New York: Verso.

Magri, L. 2009. *Il sarto di Ulm: una possibile storia del Pci*. Milan: Il Saggiatore.

Materiali per una nuova sinistra. 1988. *Il Sessantotto. La stagione dei movimenti (1960–1979)*. Edizioni Associate: Rome.

Micciché, L. 1995. *Cinema italiano: gli anni sessanta e oltre*. Venice: Marsilio.

Niccolai, R. 1998. *Quando la Cina era vicina, la rivoluzione culturale e la sinistra extraparlamentare italiana negli anni '60 e '70*. Pisa: Biblioteca Franco Serantini.

Novelli, E. 2000. *C'era una volta il PCI. Autobiografia di un partito attraverso le immagini della sua propaganda*. Rome: Editori Riuniti.

———. 2006. *La turbopolitica. Sessant'anni di comunicazione politica e di scena pubblica in Italia 1945–2005*. Milan: Rizzoli.

Panvini, G. 2009. *Ordine nero, guerriglia rossa. La violenza politica nell'Italia degli anni Sessanta e Settanta (1966–1975)*. Turin: Einaudi.

Poppi, R., ed. 2000. *Dizionario del cinema Italiano. I registi*. Rome: Gremese.

Santarelli, E. 1996. *Storia critica della repubblica. L'Italia dal 1945 al 1994*. Milan: Feltrinelli.

Schmitz, D. 2005. *The Tet Offensive. Politics, War and Public Opinion.* Lanham: Rowman & Littlefield Publishers.

Stack, O. 1969. *Pasolini on Pasolini: Interviews with Oswald Stack.* London: Thames & Hudson.

Van Gennep, A. 1965. *Rites of Passage.* London: Routledge & Kegan Paul.

CHAPTER 6

The Workers, the Students, and the Election Campaign of 1968

1968. Rossanna Rossanda has called it the 'year of the students' (Rossanda 1968). It was the year university students emerged as an independent political subject. It was not the first time. In 1966, the occupation of La Sapienza by a large front of anti-Fascist students had had quite a significant political impact. The PCI had devoted a film to that event (see Chap. 5). That occupation, however, was entirely consistent with the PCI's *politica unitaria*. Therefore, it made total sense to the party, and the party had effortlessly managed the situation. This time the situation was different. Right from the start of the protests in the autumn of 1967, the PCI was appalled by a student movement that made explicit reference to Marxist–Leninist doctrine, but still seemed to include traditional left-wing parties as targets in its uncompromising criticism of Italian society in its entirety. In particular, fringe groups within the student movement severely criticized the PCI strategy for its lack of revolutionary perspective (Crainz 2005: 144–52).

The PCI's attitude towards the students' movement evolved in the course of 1968 as a reaction to the unfolding events of that memorable year. Initially, the PCI looked down on the students, considering them little more than sons of the bourgeoisie playing at revolution. This stance clearly emerges by an analysis of the minutes of the meetings of the Press and Propaganda Section. Such a negative judgement, however, was soon revised. The party proved to be willing to listen to the students and showed some inclination to welcome at least part of their demands. This is

© The Author(s), under exclusive license to Springer Nature 139
Switzerland AG 2021
G. Fantoni, *Italy through the Red Lens*, Italian and Italian American
Studies, https://doi.org/10.1007/978-3-030-69197-4_6

140   G. FANTONI

demonstrated by an analysis of one of the films produced in that period and dealing with the students' rebellion: *Della Conoscenza* (On knowledge). This is a very original film: a collaborative project involving a group of students and Unitelefilm crew, *Della Conoscenza* was meant to bolster political understanding between the students' movement and the PCI. Eventually, the PCI ended up regarding the students as part of the Italian revolutionary movement and an ally of the working class. This was no small achievement for the Italian Communist Party. It was in fact an important political elaboration, which opened the way to the party's electoral triumphs of the mid-1970s (see Chap. 9).

However, not just students were protagonists in 1968, but also young factory workers. These were among the most committed to the series of strikes and demonstrations initiated in 1968 and culminated in the '*autunno caldo*' (hot Autumn) of 1969. 1968 thus marked the year the PCI cinematography finally turned its attention to the factory workers. Two films, in particular, are analysed here. The first, *La fabbrica parla* (The factory speaks), the first PCI film entirely devoted to the conditions of factory workers, is a remarkable cinematic text offering a portrayal of the industrial workers of northern Italy, and particularly those of FIAT, 'in the age of neocapitalism', as the voice-over describes the late 1960s. The second film, *Contratto* (Contract, 1969), directed by Ugo Gregoretti, is about the hot Autumn, which eventually resulted in a stunning victory for the unions. The merit of Gregoretti's film is its identification of the principal reason for that success: the presence of a new generation of the working class, which was determined to reject the authoritarian hierarchies that had characterized the factory system.

Revolutionary students and rebellious factory workers were not Unitelefilm's only concerns in 1968. General elections were scheduled in May. As mentioned at the end of Chap. 5, Press and Propaganda head Achille Occhetto was positive that propaganda cinema was going to make the difference this time. He staked everything on one card: the Terzo Canale project. This involved the production of fortnightly newsreels, of between twenty and twenty-five minutes each, from January until May 1968. To support this venture, the party granted Unitelefilm what Mario Benocci had been refused the previous year (see Chap. 5): money and equipment. This included a forty-million-lire recording studio made in Czechoslovakia and sent over by the Central Committee of the Czechoslovakian Communist Party along with three technicians to install it.[1] A small number of officials were trained to use the new equipment, including Sergio Zaccagnini, who had previously worked for the PCI's Prague-based and semi-underground radio station 'Oggi in Italia' (Cooke 2007). Other than the funding and equipment, various problems had to be resolved for the Terzo Canale project to function well.

The most serious issue was film distribution. The Press and Propaganda Section took the opportunity presented by Terzo Canale to attempt to develop, once and for all, an effective Communist film distribution network. It was to their advantage that the most successful film format in the history of amateur filmmaking had recently been introduced: 'Super 8', launched by Eastman Kodak in 1965 (Monaco 1981: 505). 'Super 8' films had characteristics similar to those of 16 mm films, but were much less expensive to print. With the elections coming up, the Press and Propaganda Section purchased a thousand 'Super 8' projectors for distribution to the branches (Medici et al. 2001: 152); these were supposed to pay the full cost of the projectors, but were to receive the Terzo Canale output free of charge until the election campaign was over.[2] In December 1967, the Section even organized a three-day training event on the use of films for propaganda, aimed at officials from the various branches.[3]

In the end, seven instalments of Terzo Canale were produced before the elections. Each typically presented a report on international politics, two or three reports on domestic politics, and one final section satirizing the PCI's political adversaries. A good example of the latter was the 'Johnson parade' (Terzo Canale no. 2), an animated clip accompanied by a marching song that showed a cardboard cut-out of the US president Lyndon B. Johnson turning into Adolf Hitler, and then into a tiger, a skull, a vampire, and other characters (Image 6.1).

Each Terzo Canale newsreel was devoted to a specific issue. Terzo Canale number 1, for example, waves the spectre of authoritarianism throughout. The first report is titled 'Athens: the dollar over Greece' and concerns the Greek Regime of the Colonels. In the report, the US government is accused of having inspired the coup d'état of 21 April 1967, which had led to a brutal dictatorship now backed by American corporations as well as by the Orthodox Church hierarchy. The second report offers an interview with the authoritative leader of the Italian Resistance, Ferruccio Parri, who issues a plea for the left-wing political parties' unity in order to safeguard democracy against the peril of right-wing dictatorship. The third report graphically describes the coup d'état that could have happened in Italy in summer 1964 if General Giovanni De Lorenzo had managed to execute the so-called *Piano Solo* as revealed by a scoop in the

Image 6.1 Lyndon Johnson as a vampire

weekly magazine *l'Espresso*, in May 1967. Carabinieri are shown breaking into private houses at night and deporting citizens to the Asinara Prison in Sardinia. The film clarifies who were supposed to be the principal targets of this political persecution by showing one of the victims, abruptly awoken by the night raid, grasping at his glasses placed on a nightstand and on top of a copy of the Communist weekly magazine *Vie Nuove*. Subsequently, the voice-over commentary summarizes the career of General De Lorenzo for the viewers, stressing his close political connections with major DC leaders, especially the Minister of Defence Giulio Andreotti. The section concludes reminding 'taxpayers' that the existence of the *Piano Solo* proves how left-wing political parties' leaders and trade unions organizers are the true champions of democracy.

On average, UTF printed about 850 copies of the Terzo Canale newsreel. The exceptions were the fifth and sixth bulletins—monothematic newsreels devoted exclusively to the 'southern question' and the condition of factory workers respectively—which were printed on a smaller scale.

An analysis of these two single-issue bulletins of Terzo Canale, which are in effect documentaries, allows us to appreciate the stylistic evolution of Communist cinematography since the foundation of Unitelefilm. In these later productions, the voice-over commentary is deployed to connect the various parts of the documentary rather than to communicate the author's point of view. Delivery of the political message is mainly entrusted to the many interviews with workers and peasants, filmed with a hand-held camera. The interviewer is directly involved in each interchange, which unfolds as a dialogue in front of the viewer. This communicates a feeling of reality, which is then reinforced by scenes offering vignettes from the interviewee's life: a walk along the seashore while smoking a cigarette, an appointment with the company doctor, or the distribution of leaflets at a factory entrance. These stylistic features were borrowed from two very influential documentary genres, which in many respects shared the same aesthetic: 'direct cinema' and 'cinéma-vérité', developed in the late 1950s and early 1960s in the United States and France respectively (Barnouw 1974: 236–38; Barsam 1992: 300–10).

PCI cinematography of this period seems to have been particularly influenced by *cinéma-vérité*, as is shown by the presence of the interviewer on screen; in contrast, 'direct cinema' filmmakers tried to minimize the interaction between members of their team and the subjects of the documentary in order to capture 'the reality of life' (Ellis and McLane 2009: 217). The adherence of Communist filmmakers to 'cinéma-vérité' principles, however, was purely formal. Their work shows little evidence of the ethical concerns that had been expressed by Jean Rouch, one of the founders of the approach, which included the need for film authors to place themselves in the frame as a way of making explicit the influence of the medium on the subjects interviewed. The showing of the interviewer in the Communist films is instead aimed at making these PCI documentaries resemble journalistic reporting, thus allowing propaganda messages to acquire a veneer of objectivity.

The fifth Terzo Canale bulletin, *Speciale Sud* (Special bulletin on the South), features street interviews with southern workers; there are complaints about the lack of jobs, infrastructure, and welfare assistance. As in *Nel mezzogiorno qualcosa è cambiato*, the South is presented as poor, desolate, and waiting for redemption. These southern workers, however, do not look as poverty-stricken as those in the earlier film: in fact, they are wearing good clothes with fashionable haircuts (Image 6.2). Terzo Canale's fifth bulletin thus illustrates the PCI's inability to abandon

Image 6.2 Southern workers with fashionable haircuts

outdated interpretations and preconceptions regarding the social and economic reality of southern Italy, in spite of the fact that even its own film directors were documenting a rapidly evolving social and economic situation. At some point, however, the voice-over has to acknowledge that '*qualcosa è cambiato*' (something has changed) and that there has in fact been some degree of economic development since the late 1940s. A few large industrial plants have been built in some areas of southern Italy, for example; these include the car-manufacturing plant recently established by Alfa-Romeo, a company controlled by the state-owned Institute for Industrial Reconstruction (IRI), in Pomigliano, near Naples.

According to the voice-over, however, industrial development initiatives launched by the government have not really come to benefit local communities. They are instead 'industrial islands, detached from the land around them, which only provide employment for small groups of workers. After five years of the centre-left's presence, the only option for the great majority of southern workers therefore remains migration to

6 THE WORKERS, THE STUDENTS, AND THE ELECTION CAMPAIGN OF 1968   145

northern Italy or abroad, just as it had been during the years when Christian Democracy had governed more or less unfettered. The film concludes with a declaration of faith in the contemporary relevance of the Gramscian reading of the 'southern question', although this is a slightly updated version of that offered in Lizzani's *Nel Mezzogiorno qualcosa è cambiato*: rather than the northern working class, 'the young southern working class' is now the natural ally of the southern peasantry against the 'industrial and landowning bloc that has been oppressing the South for a century'.

Terzo Canale's sixth bulletin, *La fabbrica parla* (The factory speaks), begins with an aerial view of the largest FIAT plant, Mirafiori, in Turin. We see workers marching towards the factory gates, and the voice-over offers a description:

> These are the FIAT workers, the protagonists of the […] economic miracle; they are the privileged workers of a modern fairy tale, working with the most advanced machinery; they are the most productive and the best paid in Italy, who in their work have achieved the highest level of human and civil dignity. Sooner or later every Italian worker will live as they do, promises the optimistic fable of the bosses.

The film is intended to question the desirability of this goal by exposing its dark side. The message is that despite the adoption of a more modern organization of labour in the automation of production processes, the essence of capitalism has not really changed at all, even in Italy's largest factory. The features of capitalism remain the exploitation of workers through the endless repetition of alienating tasks, occupational illnesses, and industrial accidents. Neocapitalism and its rational organization of the production process are likely to make workers' lives harder rather than easier. By means of a series of interviews, the viewer is confronted with the harsh reality of a working class that is forced to struggle with exploitation and injustice on a daily basis. It is apparent that almost all the workers interviewed have a southern accent, alluding to the dramatic changes in the social composition of the northern working class over the previous decade.[4]

Far from being confined to the working environment, oppression by the capitalist system affects the workers' quality of life outside the factory gates as well. The effects of exploitation are visible in the spread of modern-day illnesses, such as psychosis and neurosis, on an epidemic scale.[5] The voice-over predicts, with some accuracy, that the anger and frustration generated by the situation in the factories will eventually erupt; the '*autunno caldo*' was in fact not far off. On this theme, the film includes footage of one of the first strikes to be called jointly by the three major unions, shot outside the gates of Mirafiori. The workers seem ready for confrontation and not intimidated by the police. According to the voice-over, the struggle's ultimate objective is 'to bring democracy into the factory'.

Democratization within the factory is also one of the themes of *Contratto* (Contract), which was commissioned by the three main unions for engineering workers (FIOM, FIM, and UILM, affiliated to the CGIL, CISL, and UIL union federations respectively) and directed by Ugo Gregoretti. Unitelefilm coproduced this, investing ten million lire. Although strictly speaking *Contratto* was not a PCI film, it is worth analysing because of its extraordinary visual documentation of the struggle of engineering workers between September and December 1969 for renewal of the national engineering employment contract. This was the first time that industrial action had been jointly led on a national scale by the three principal unions, with their different political affiliations. As mentioned above, *Contratto*'s main protagonists are young factory workers. These are, in the words of the voice-over, 'perhaps the least compliant working class that the history of our country has ever known'. Their problematic assimilation within the factory system was due to the generation gap between them and their older workmates. This new generation of workers belonged to the '*prima generazione*' (first generation), which has been examined by Simonetta Piccone Stella (1993): having grown up during the economic boom, they refused to live and work as their fathers had for the previous twenty years, demanding fulfilment of the promises that the media had made in the optimistic years of the economic miracle.

These young workers look different from their fathers, not least physically: they have long hair and scraggy beards, and stand out from the veterans of the *anni duri* at the factory union meetings.[6] The mere presence of this new generation suggests that the working conditions in Italian factories, social hierarchies, and even trade union ritualism are all irretrievably outdated in relation to Italian society outside the factory gates. Furthermore, the younger workers do not attend meetings just as passive spectators: they grab the microphone and assertively express their radical opinions: 'a new cohort of young trade-unionists has suddenly formed in the heat of the clash', says the favourably surprised voice-over. They have also transformed the mood of union demonstrations, which are now pervaded by a bright and busy creativity: improvised drums, musical instruments, songs, irreverent protest signs, and new slogans such as 'The factory will be our Vietnam!'

Cinematographically, *Contratto* is a lively and perhaps even frenetic production that takes the audience swiftly through a range of events and communicates the unique atmosphere of participation and solidarity that characterized the sustained struggle. It can be considered the most complete film account of an extraordinary and optimistic phase of democratic development both in Italy's factories and in the country as a whole. However, this phase was dramatically short. It is significant that the film ends with a reference to the Piazza Fontana massacre, the terrorist attack in Milan on 12 December 1969, when a bomb exploded at the headquarters of the Banca Nazionale dell'Agricoltura, killing seventeen people and wounding eighty-eight. This event is generally seen as marking the beginning of the long period of severe and violent political confrontation known as the '*anni di piombo*' (years of lead).[7] The identities of those actually responsible for the massacre were unknown for many years. However, many people made an immediate connection between this and the industrial action taken by the engineering workers' unions. The voice-over commentary of *Contratto* is unwavering in its interpretation of the Piazza Fontana bombing as a right-wing response to the victorious struggle of the workers, but claims that this act of violence has strengthened rather than weakened the determination of the Italian working class.

Apart from the Terzo Canale newsreels, the PCI commissioned UTF to produce a number of documentaries addressing Italy's political issues of the day, the most significant of these being the '*contestazione*': the student protests that were spreading through the universities and secondary schools (Lepre 1993: 223–49).

The 1968 youth protest occurred at the same time in many different countries, western and non-western, in the north as well as in southern hemisphere. Marcello Flores and Giovanni Gozzini are therefore arguably right when they say that historians should adopt a global perspective when studying this phenomenon (2018). It would be difficult, however, to welcome this suggestion when analysing the corpus of cinematic texts on the *contestazione* produced by the Italian Communist Party at the end of the 1960s. PCI's angle on this issue was, in fact, eminently national. This was consistent with a film production which was progressively abandoning international politics in order to focus on domestic issues. This trend became even more marked in the following years (see Chap. 8).

The head of the Press and Propaganda Section Achille Occhetto, planning the election campaign at a meeting in January 1968, argued that if the party wanted to appeal to the students, it needed to present itself as the 'party of protest'.[8] His view was that the student protests stemmed from the lack of prospects faced by a generation that had been betrayed by the poor results of the 'economic miracle' and the reformist period of the centre-left; he thought that the student movement would be a short-lived phenomenon, and that in view of its associations with a petit bourgeois environment it had little or nothing to do with the long-term objectives of the working class. Nevertheless, the PCI needed to attract the votes of young people by means of 'a youthful propaganda'; this had been one of the reasons why the party had decided to invest in film production in the first place.

As far as its content was concerned, Occhetto argued that PCI propaganda needed to be different from that of the other parties. Whereas it was expected that these would patronize the students, the PCI would alert them to the fact that significant change could only take place in the longer run, and that they therefore needed to make a lifelong commitment to the party that embodied the very idea of protest. One of the films produced for the election campaign, *Comunisti* (Communists), conveys this message in forceful terms.

Comunisti, which has a running time of twenty-three minutes, was an unconventional piece of cinematographic propaganda. It was neither a documentary nor a feature film, but instead a collection of archival footage; accompanied with a lyrical voice-over written by the poet Alfonso Gatto, its aim was to create an evocative and poignant narrative.[9] Nonetheless, the film carries a straightforward political message: young people should join the Italian Communist Party, because it embodies the myths currently inspiring the new generation and is therefore the only party that can realize the change that they demand. *Comunisti* was intended to be appealing, opening with 'A Whiter Shade of Pale', a very popular song that had been released the previous year by the British rock band Procol Harum. While the music plays, we see apparently random shots of young people walking down the streets, laughing and talking. The voice-over begins with a poetic tribute to the new generation:

The future has already arrived. Boys and girls of all ages, exchanging quick looks and laughter when they say goodbye, 'see you tomorrow!', with light in their eyes. And boutiques, flowers, newspapers, fashions, demonstrations, ignoring things in order to hope, being scared from knowing too much, living just for the experience, being in order to become: all this is in the air.

The film then runs through a gallery of the student movement's political icons: Ho Chi Min and the legendary women soldiers of the People's Army of Vietnam, Che Guevara and Fidel Castro among the bearded revolutionaries, Mao's Red Guards, Patrice Lumumba, and the young Lenin. These are intercut with images from events that had a more established place in PCI mythology, such as the volunteers of the International Brigades in the Spanish Civil War and Red Army soldiers celebrating their victory in Berlin. According to the voice-over, all these characters, and the causes they stood for, can be encompassed by one concept: 'the party'. 'The party' can in fact present itself in forms that vary with the historical moment:

> The party of exile, of underground activity, of the Resistance; the party of protagonists, of the leaders of the armed struggle; the modern-day party of organization.

'The party of organization' alluded to the mass-based party with its necessary structure; by stressing that this was simply the modern incarnation of the same party that had fought against Fascism, the commentary intended to refute the allegations of excessive bureaucratization made by elements within the student movement.

The film then resumes the history of the Italian Communist Party; to be more precise, it constructs a historical narrative of epic dimensions, employing elegiac tones and religious metaphor. First comes Gramsci, 'the victim who won', who had to make the ultimate sacrifice in order to change the course of history for the Italian people: 'in him and with him the people take their place in history'. Togliatti follows, prophetically proclaiming a new era of hope with the policy of the '*svolta di Salerno*':

> Togliatti brought a message of collaboration and moderation: collaboration between all the anti-Fascist parties, and moderation in order to give our destroyed and prostrate Italy a government of national unity that would respond to its needs and aspirations.

The voice-over claims that the PCI's commitment to democracy has been demonstrated many times, especially during the crisis of July 1960—here we are shown archival footage—when it thwarted the attempt to establish a Fascist dictatorship by a 'Christian Democracy without the people and without Christ'. The lyricism reaches its pinnacle when the commentary asserts that whoever fights for justice, 'the Communist [trade unionist Giuseppe] Di Vittorio or the Christian Pope John', need not fear 'the heedlessness of truth and the passion of the gospel meant for the workers', but only 'the caution of liars and the hypocritical coldness of their calculation'.

The film ends by reinforcing its central message:

> Di Vittorio, Che Guevara, [Vietnamese General] Giap, these young people who demand liberty, these Vietcong who are fighting for their independence, negroes, children with the flower of peace: now, in this world, they are all images of the one same word: Communism.

Not long after the meeting of the national Press and Propaganda Section at which Occhetto had set out the guidelines for the election campaign, the PCI leadership started to pay more attention to the student movement. This interest was especially aroused by the 'Battle of Valle Giulia': the clashes between students and the police outside La Sapienza's Faculty of Architecture on 1 March 1968 (Crainz 2005: 260–70). The punitive involvement of the police and, more importantly, the attacks at the university by Fascist groups in the days that followed, prompted the PCI to express its solidarity with the students (Höbel 2010: 453–54). Moreover, several members of the FGCI leadership, including Oreste Scalzone, were personally involved in the movement; this presented an issue of cohesion within the PCI. In addition, the elections were approaching and the party's general secretary Luigi Longo, backed by other senior members such as Pietro Ingrao, did not want to miss the opportunity for a political rapprochement with the students. A meeting was organized at Rome's Istituto Gramsci between Longo and some of the student leaders, including Scalzone, in April 1968. A few days later, Longo published a long article in *Rinascita* that laid out the party's official position on the student movement: he argued that its internal political debate represented an important contribution to the shared endeavour whose objective was to make the PCI the 'collective intellectual of the workers' and people's movement that Gramsci had talked about'. Longo admitted to the PCI's

6 THE WORKERS, THE STUDENTS, AND THE ELECTION CAMPAIGN OF 1968   151

failings in its analysis of crucial events such as China's Cultural Revolution and the Cuban Revolution, acknowledging some of the reasons for this:

> A certain degree of bureaucratic sluggishness and a certain fixed rhythm within our party organizations, both centrally and locally, which often prevents us from noticing quickly the new things that gradually appear in the world, and from including these in our study, propaganda and work activities.

However, he also restated the validity of the *politica unitaria*, a fundamental part of the strategy of 'the Italian road to socialism':

> This is our strategy: by means of a vast and deeply rooted unifying movement making demands, and through great worker and popular struggles, to achieve fundamental social and economic change. This would limit the power of the large capitalist groups, and win better living conditions and new and better vantage points in the workers' struggle, from which we can advance with greater confidence and strength towards the socialist transformation of Italian society.

Longo therefore argued that although the PCI was committed to political and social reforms, its strategy could not be labelled 'reformist' because it had never lost sight of the revolutionary objectives that these reforms were designed to achieve.

The collaborative approach taken by the leader of the PCI was reflected in another film produced in 1968: *Della conoscenza* (On knowledge). This is a unique cinematic text within Unitelefilm's output, as it was written and directed by representatives of Rome's student movement with the production company's technical assistance. *Della conoscenza*, which has a running time of thirty minutes, was directed by Alessandra Bocchetti, who was to become one of the leading figures of Italian feminism. She worked on the film with a group of architecture students who were also later to become well known: Massimiliano Fuksas, Franco Purini and Pierpaolo Balbo. Oreste Scalzone and Paolo Liguori were also involved in the film's production; Liguori subsequently became active within the radical left-wing group Lotta Continua and, later still, a well-known journalist and fervent supporter of Silvio Berlusconi. The content of *Della conoscenza* cannot easily be summarized because it brought together statements, interviews, archival footage, and imagery whose aim was to convey the students' point of view on a range of issues, including revolution, the relationship between culture and politics, the role of education in bourgeois society, the issue of violence, and the Vietnam War.

The historical value of the film lies in its faithful rendering of the broad and sometimes rather confused set of ideas, cultural references, and beliefs that inspired student protest. The voice-over commentary mixes together references to the films of Jean-Luc Godard ('we refuse to see ourselves as the children of Marx and Coca-Cola');[10] statements that drew on the book *Lettera ad una professoressa* (Letter to a teacher), which became one of the student movement's sacred texts ('at school we learn a multitude of useless ideas, we learn the entire French vocabulary without being able to speak the language') (Scuola di Barbiana 1967: 23–24);[11] quotations from *The Communist Manifesto* ('the proletarians have nothing to lose but their chains'); evocative but ultimately superficial statements such as 'you will not know us through established models, we are a new way of being all that is vital and the negation of all that is dead', and 'you don't resolve the issue, you change it'; and moments of honesty, such as 'for us, logic is not a constant concern'. The film is striking for its somewhat casual treatment of violence.[12] In one scene, for example, Scalzone claims that 'we do not have a position that rejects diverse cultural stimuli [a bottle of Coca-Cola appears]; the important thing is to adopt a consistent critical approach towards these stimuli [the bottle turns into a Molotov cocktail]'. In another, a hand draws a gun and then shoots at a picture of Lyndon Johnson.

Arguably, the film's most interesting episode is the portrayal of a meeting at the university between factory workers and students. This scene provides an effective illustration of how difficult it was, at that time, to initiate a debate, or even just begin a dialogue, between people from different social classes. Italy's class-ridden society had been keeping bourgeois students and proletarian workers socially and culturally apart; the consequence, as the commentary concludes, was that they lacked a common language:

> Class society has made the languages that we speak different. It is not through these languages that we will come together; instead, we will meet in the struggle.

According to Bocchetti, interviewed in *Il Manifesto*, the party welcomed the film with muted enthusiasm.[13] At a preview staged at the PCI's

6 THE WORKERS, THE STUDENTS, AND THE ELECTION CAMPAIGN OF 1968   153

headquarters in Rome, a representative of the FGCI complained that the scene in which a student throws a pile of books into the air seemed to suggest that young people were rejecting culture, which, for a Communist, was unthinkable. Nevertheless, Unitelefilm presented *Della conoscenza* at the Oberhausen International Short Film Festival in West Germany, where it won an award.

According to Mario Benocci, who wrote the final report on the PCI's film output for the 1968 electoral campaign, the party's efforts had achieved some success. In particular, Terzo Canale had proved effective as a propaganda tool. In some branches, the wide use of cinema by local activists had made a significant contribution to the political engagement of people previously untouched by Communist propaganda, especially the young. The use of film had also aided development of the party's propaganda methods at grass-roots level:

> Around each projector, teams of 2, 3, or 4 activists have come together, or even more (as is the case in Turin and Genoa), often spontaneously; they have undertaken methodical activity in thoroughgoing propaganda, with the distribution of leaflets and flyers both during and after showings, and have launched discussions on the themes covered by the films.[14]

In some branches, the PCI's film showings had for the first time outnumbered its election meetings. This was the case in Genoa (1900 showings to 907 meetings), Turin (1800 to 1200), Lecce (850 to 450) and Naples (700 to 500). Moreover, local militants had made good use of the relative lightness of the 'Super 8' projection system in finding new and ingenious ways to use film propaganda. Screenings had been arranged outside factories, for example, for workers who had just finished their shift, and near state schools while parents were waiting to collect their children. Finally, the films had been widely shown among Italian workers abroad, and the Terzo Canale experiment had even aroused the interest of the French Communist Party.

Benocci's report clearly intended to emphasize the positive aspects of Terzo Canale in addition to the use of cinema for propaganda. Reading between its lines, however, there were also some causes for concern. First of all, it was based on data provided by the provincial branches in which films had actually been projected, and there were only thirteen of these, just three of them in southern Italy: Bari, Lecce, and Naples. Other branches had made little or no use of cinema during the election campaign; not a single 'Super 8' projector had been shipped to Sicily or Sardinia, for example. While propaganda films were fairly effective in attracting audiences at the grass-roots level, they did not seem to have had much impact in electoral terms: the increase in the Communist vote had been modest. Finally, Benocci's report made it clear that the branches either could not or would not purchase propaganda films: Terzo Canale had been successful because copies of the films were free, and several branches had explicitly stated that they would not pay for future output.

The PCI had invested over 170 million lire in producing seven bulletins of Terzo Canale, the documentaries, and their distribution to the branches; it would not be able to bear the full cost of large-scale and regular film production in future. The history of Unitelefilm over the next ten years is a chronicle of unsuccessful attempts to resolve this dilemma.

With regard to Terzo Canale, the Press and Propaganda Section commissioned Unitelefilm to produce more newsreels in order to continue making use of the established Communist film circuit.[15] However, the rate of production fell: fourteen more bulletins were produced between May 1968 and May 1974, when the last one was released, and the branches were required to pay the cost of the films in full. As a consequence, this new series of Communist newsreels had a more limited distribution than the first seven bulletins.

In conclusion, the years 1968–1970 were among the most prolific for Unitelefilm in terms of the number of films it produced, thanks in particular to the Terzo Canale project, which had the full support of the PCI's Press and Propaganda Section. The cinematic quality of PCI films also improved considerably due to the influence of new foreign filmmaking styles such as 'direct cinema' and '*cinéma-vérité*'. The PCI undertook a cinematic journey into Italian factories; for the first time, Communist cinema did not look at factory workers through the usual ideological lenses, but depicted the workers of the late 1960s for what they actually were. Thus, we don't see on the screen the rational and self-restrained male worker, the vanguard of the socialist revolution, but angry protesters, uprooted southerners, as well as newly urbanized Northern peasants, boys and girls, old and young; all of them have had enough to wait for the radiant, and very distant, socialist future and demand a prompt improvement in their conditions. A principal objective of Communist cinematography seems to have been to open a dialogue and establish an alliance with the student movement, which was making a big impression on the headlines of the period. The action taken by the PCI in this respect was ultimately an attempt to exert a political hegemony on the student movement. This endeavour by the PCI leadership was very successful, and in the medium term was to reap dividends in electoral terms: this is discussed in Chap. 9. In the short term, however, there were new political threats looming on the horizon, and the UTF crew, while in the middle of a difficult internal reorganization, was soon asked to produce more films to tackle these, as discussed in Chap. 8. First, however, we shall discuss Unitelefilm's involvement in the *cinema militante* (militant cinema) movement.

NOTES

1. IG, APCI, MF 547, p. 2243, Stampa e Propaganda, 13 January 1968, document signed by Achille Occhetto.
2. IG, APCI, MF 547, p. 2290, Stampa e Propaganda, 4 February 1968.
3. IG, APCI, MF 539, p. 1237, Stampa e Propaganda, 13 November 1967. A report on the seminar, held at Le Frattocchie and attended by twenty-eight people from sixteen different branches, is conserved in IG, APCI, MF 547, pp. 2229–41, Stampa e Propaganda, 12 January 1968.
4. These southern workers accounted for the largest part of a new social group, the '*operai massa*' (mass workers). For a discussion of the sociological interpretations of the mass workers, see Foot (2001: 27–28).
5. Elio Petri's feature film *La classe operaia va in Paradiso* (*The Working Class Goes to Heaven*, 1971), featuring a memorable performance by Gian Maria Volontè, famously addressed the issue of the psychological condition of the northern working class.
6. The expression '*anni duri*' (hard years) was used to describe the 1950s, a particularly difficult historical moment for trade unionism in Italy due to the very unbalanced power relations in the factories. See Pugno and Garavini (1974).
7. For discussion of the Piazza Fontana bombing, see Franzinelli (2008: 50–81).
8. *Relazione del compagno Achille Occhetto nell'attivo nazionale di Propaganda sulla campagna elettorale 1968*, in IG, APCI, MF 547, pp. 2248–85, Stampa e Propaganda, 26–27 January 1968.

9. A major exponent of Italian hermetic poetry, Alfonso Gatto joined the PCI in 1944 but left in 1951, becoming a sort of independent Communist. However, he still occasionally collaborated with the party. He appeared in various films, including Aldo Vergano's *Outcry* (1946). See his obituary, *L'Unità*, 9 March 1976: front page.
10. 'This film could be called The Children of Marx and Coca-Cola' is one of the intertitles between episodes in Jean-Luc Godard's *Masculin Féminin* (1966).
11. *Lettera ad una professoressa* was written by the Catholic priest Don Lorenzo Milani together with the students of the private and free school he had founded to educate the children of peasants in the Apennine mountains in Tuscany (Lancisi 2007). After its publication, Don Milani became an icon of left-wing counterculture and his book inspired many groups within the 'new Left'.
12. On violence as a crucial element in the construction of the collective identity of Italian students in 1968, see Lumley (1990: 68–70).
13. See *Il Manifesto*, 1 March 2008, p. 10.
14. *Nascita e compiti della Unitelefilm*, in IG, APCI, MF 551, pp. 1356–83, Istituti e Organismi vari, Unitelefilm, 7 July 1968, by Mario Benocci.
15. IG, APCI, MF 547, pp. 2384–88, Stampa e Propaganda, 24 June 1968.

BIBLIOGRAPHY

Barnouw, E. 1974. *Documentary, a History of the Non-fiction Film*. Oxford: Oxford University Press.

Barsam, R.M. 1992. *Nonfiction Film. A Critical History. Revised and Expanded*. Bloomington and Indianapolis: Indiana University Press.

Cooke, P. 2007. Oggi in Italia: The Voice of Truth and Peace in Cold War Italy. *Modern Italy* 12 (2): 251–265.

Crainz, G. 2005. *Il paese mancato. Dal miracolo economico agli anni ottanta*. Rome: Donzelli.

Ellis, J.C., and B.A. McLane. 2009. *A New History of Documentary Film*. New York: Continuum.

Flores, M., and G. Gozzini. 2018. *1968. Un anno spartiacque*. Bologna: Il Mulino.

Foot, J. 2001. *Milan Since the Miracle: City, Culture and Identity*. Oxford: Berg.

Franzinelli, M. 2008. *La sottile linea nera. Neofascismo e servizi segreti da Piazza Fontana a Piazza della Loggia*. Milan: Rizzoli.

Höbel, A. 2010. *Il PCI di Luigi Longo (1964/1969)*. Naples: Edizioni Scientifiche Italiane.

Lancisi, M. (2007). *Don Milani. La vita*, Milan: Piemme.

Lepre, A. 1993. *Storia della prima Repubblica*. L'Italia dal 1942 al 1992. Bologna: il Mulino.

Lumley, R. 1990. *States of Emergency. Culture of Revolts in Italy from 1968 to 1978.* London and New York: Verso.

Medici, A., M. Morbidelli, and E. Taviani, eds. 2001. *Il PCI e il cinema tra cultura e propaganda (1959–1979).* Rome: Aamod.

Monaco, J. 1981. *How to Read a Film. The Art, Technology, Language, History, and Theory of Film and Media.* New York and Oxford: Oxford University Press.

Piccone Stella, S. 1993. *La Prima Generazione. Ragazze e ragazzi nel miracolo economico italiano.* Milan: Franco Angeli.

Pugno, E., and S. Garavini. 1974. *Gli anni duri alla Fiat.* Turin: Einaudi.

Rossanda, R. 1968. *L'anno degli studenti.* Bari: De Donato.

Scuola di Barbiana. 1967. *Lettera ad una professoressa.* Florence: Libreria Editrice Fiorentina.

CHAPTER 7

The Lice and the Whale: Filmmakers, Militant Cinema, and the Italian Communist Party

On 8 September 1967, a small Unitelefilm crew was in Venice Lido hoping to catch some good shots of the final night of the twenty-eighth edition of the Venice Film Festival. In all likelihood, the footage they filmed that night, less than three minutes, was subsequently included in one of the *attualità* that Unitelefilm used to sell in those years to Eastern European countries (see Chap. 5). The mute and unedited footage is stored in the AAMOD Archive in Rome. It shows Italian and foreign celebrities, including Alberto Sordi, Luis Bunuel, and Jean Sorel, posing for the usual photocall. Fans line the streets outside the Festival's venue, in front of very large posters advertising Pier Paolo Pasolini's *Oedipus Rex* and Damiano Damiani's *The Day of the Owl*. Luis Bunuel's *Belle de Jour* won the Golden Lion that night. Two films by politically engaged filmmakers were awarded the Special Jury Prize: *La Chinoise*, by Jean-Luc Godard, and *China is near*, by Marco Bellocchio. The former was an indictment of the capitalist system, and the latter a scathing satire of the bourgeois society. Both films included references to Maoism and China's Cultural Revolution. The political ferment that characterized that historical period would soon come out of the screen to invade the Festival's parterre. The twenty-ninth edition of the Venice Film Festival, in 1968, saw a boycott of the festival by ANAC (Italian filmmakers association), demonstrations by students and intellectuals demanding the direction of the Festival to be entrusted to filmmakers, and even police intervention.

© The Author(s), under exclusive license to Springer Nature Switzerland AG 2021
G. Fantoni, *Italy through the Red Lens*, Italian and Italian American Studies, https://doi.org/10.1007/978-3-030-69197-4_7

This was not the only time that demonstrators disrupted a cinema festival that year: fringes of Left-wing students contested Pesaro Film Festival too, as shown below. Why would left-wing demonstrators target film festivals? Because cinema was gaining new status among left-wingers: a tool to investigate the political and social mechanisms of capitalist society, and, at the same time, an instrument that could effectively contribute to its destruction. Unitelefilm crew largely shared such an enthusiasm for the supposed revolutionary power of cinema, as can be seen by Unitelefilm's involvement in the *Cinema Militante* (militant cinema) movement.

Cinema militante was global rather than exclusively Italian, and had its roots in avant-garde filmmaking movements such as the New American Cinema Group; from the beginning of the 1960s, this group had been developing ideas about the liberation of cinema from the shackles of the film industry in order to develop the social and political relevance of the medium (Lewis 1998: 283–84).

The period 1967–1970 saw a proliferation of manifestos by radical groups calling for the political renewal of Western society through the use of cinema. The French director Jean-Luc Godard was especially influential, making several politically engaged and experimental films with the Dziga Vertov Group, the Marxist film collective that he had founded (Hayward 2005: 238).

This chapter offers an analysis of some of the films that were produced within the Italian *cinema militante* movement, between the late 1960s and the early 1970s, with a particular focus on those produced by Unitelefilm. It argues that the development of militant cinema in Italy should be read in the context of the PCI's struggle to maintain political hegemony of the working class, which resulted in clashes with student groups and radical left-wing intellectuals. The latter were organized in the Collettivi del Cinema militante (Militant cinema groups) and in the Centri Universitari Cinematografici (CUC: University Film Centres) that were set up in some universities in northern Italy. In May 1967, a group of students of the University of Turin founded the film magazine *Ombre Rosse*, which soon became the point of reference for the Cinema militante movement (Della Casa 2002: 358–59). The members of these groups opposed the politics of traditional left-wing parties and especially the politics of the PCI. Their inspiration came instead from the *nuova sinistra* (see Chap. 5). The connections between the *nuova sinistra* and the groups involved in the cinema miltante was strengthened by the involvement of figures such as Goffredo Fofi, who was both a founder of *Ombre Rosse* and a member of the editorial board of the *Quaderni Piacentini*.

The factory constituted the battlefield in this context. The filmmakers and film critics of the *cinema militante* believed that cinema had the task of revealing the intrinsically political nature of the conflicts arising within the factories, and the duty to favour their revolutionary outcome. If it failed to reveal the ultimately political nature of trade unionism and refrained from suggesting revolutionary solutions for industrial actions, cinema betrayed its mission. It thus became merely decorative or, worse still, it ended up advocating political conservatism. This is why the filmmakers and film critics ferociously lambasted the militant films the PCI produced in those years, and particularly Ugo Gregoretti's *Apollon, una fabbrica occupata* (Apollon: an occupied factory, 1969), as I will show further ahead. As far as the PCI is concerned, its involvement in the *cinema militante* movement was consistent with PCI policy, whereby there should be an attempt to engage with, and ideally dominate, any political or cultural initiative that emerged on the left of the political spectrum.

The cinematic war between the PCI and the *nuova sinistra* was asymmetrical. The PCI could rely on its own film production company, and was able to invest considerable sums of money in film productions. The students had nothing of that sort. The publication in *Rinascita* of a call to arms by Cesare Zavattini, on 25 August 1967, presented the PCI with a suitable opportunity to show its might. Zavattini appealed for a 'guerilla war' to be waged by means of films produced at the amateur level. This was an elaboration of the previous idea inspiring the *Cinegiornale della pace* (Peace newsreel, 1963, see Chap. 4), and Zavattini named this new project *Cinegiornali liberi* (Free newsreels).

Given the newly charged political climate, there was an enthusiastic response from many left-wing filmmakers and intellectuals, including the Unitelefilm crew, to Zavattini's call. The head of UTF, Mario Benocci even joined the 'Direttivo Nazionale dei Cinegiornali Liberi'; Zavattini had established this national committee in order to coordinate the initiatives, across various cities (Masoni and Vecchi 2000: 131). Therefore, even though the *Cinema militante* movement was pervaded by the political views of the far Left, the PCI managed to play a relevant part in this brief phase of political mobilization with its very high expectations of the revolutionary power of cinema. Between 1968 and 1970, at least five *cinegiornali liberi* were produced with essential artistic and technical support from Unitelefilm, including the above-mentioned *Apollon*. These were all shot in 16 mm black and white film.

The *Cinegiornali liberi* gave the UTF crew a chance to experiment more freely, from a thematic and stylistic point of view, than they could when producing propaganda films for the Italian Communist Party. This is especially evident in Sicilia: *terremoto anno uno*, a twenty-six-minute documentary directed in 1970 by Beppe Scavuzzo and dealing with the disastrous Belice earthquake that hit western Sicily in January 1968. There is no voice-over, no music, and only ambient sound. Nonetheless, with its choice of dramatic images of destruction, the film manages to communicate its political message perfectly well: the government has been manifestly disorganized in its rescue of the population of Belice. No words are needed to communicate the sense of hopeless abandonment felt by the local population. The protest by the area's people is entrusted to the graffiti on the walls of ruined houses, to brief interviews given in a pure and barely understandable Sicilian dialect, and to the striking final scene in which an old man vents his anger and frustration by gesticulating at the camera, his voice drowned out by the Beatles song 'Because' (1969). Although from a political point of view this film was perfectly in line with the PCI position, it would not have been accepted as a propaganda film by the Press and Propaganda Section because its message was complex and therefore susceptible to differing interpretations. Much stricter control was normally exerted by the PCI over UTF propaganda films, and particularly over the text of the voice-over commentary.[1]

Unlike the PCI, the *cinema militante* groups lacked production facilities and their films were self-financed. Consequently, they could not always afford to shoot in 16 mm and often had to resort to the amateur 8 mm. The *collettivo* that was established in Turin in October 1968 was the most productive of all. It managed to shoot and edit two films: *Lotte alla Rhodiatoce* (Struggle at the Rhodiatoce, 1969, 20 minutes, 16 mm) and *La fabbrica aperta* (The factory revealed, 1970, 25 minutes, 8 mm). *Lotte alla Rhodiatoce*—whose political content I will discuss below—is particularly interesting, because it gave cinematic shape to a theory that was circulating within militant cinema; it postulated that militant cinema, to be truly considered such, had to express the workers' point of view. The only way to achieve this was to hand the camera over to the workers and let them film the struggle as it unfolded. This would keep the film free from the nefarious influence of middle-class professional filmmakers. Although the idea was intriguing, the cinematic results were disappointing. As its authors frankly admitted in an article published in *Ombre Rosse, Lotte alla Rhodiatoce* was technically poor. The film's message is entrusted solely to the voice-over commentary, spoken by a nonprofessional voice actor, presumably a worker of the Rhodiatoce. The commentary is not directly related to the situations or people shown on the screen, which gives the viewer a sense of disorientation. In sum, only the most die-hard militant (or a researcher who is passionate about militant cinema) could watch all the way to the end of the film without feeling bored. This was the only time that such an experiment was attempted. As a 'comrade' of the Rhodiatoce put it: '[C]inema must be done by those who know how to do it'.[2]

Some groups therefore took a more realistic approach to militant cinema and accepted help from professional filmmakers. Aldo Agosti, for example, directed the four bulletins of a *Cinegiornale studentesco* (Student newsreels), produced by the Roman student movement in 1968.[3] Skilfully edited by Agosti mixing footage of the demonstrations and the original audio captured in the streets and in the numerous meetings organized by the movement, the *cinegiornali* are a precious documentation of the *Contestazione*. Some words recur more often than others, in the improvised speeches that the young protesters—usually men, and only rarely women—yelled through the megaphones: *masse, lotta, violenza*, and *operai* (masses, struggle, violence, and factory workers). Indeed, the students hoped to mobilize the masses, beginning with factory workers, and to involve them in a struggle that was necessarily going to be characterized by violent confrontations with the police.

Other independent groups that also engaged with militant cinema in that period include the Centro Cinematografico di Documentazione Proletaria (Center for Proletarian Cinematic Documentation) of Genoa, set up by a few students politically linked to the PSIUP, and the Cinema Teatro Azione (Cinema and Theatre Action), established in the town of Suzzara (in the Lombardy region). They generally produced a small number of films, often shot in 8 mm, of which only a limited number of copies were distributed. Consequently, their films did not circulate much at the time and are now very difficult to find. However, these groups issued a considerable number of documents and articles, in which they analysed their experience and explained their approach to militant cinema.[4] They argued, for example, that cinema had to be used as a tool for counter-information. This reveals the frustration of the young protesters, regarding the way they were depicted by the mainstream press and by government-controlled public broadcasting: as either thugs or dreamers. They demanded, instead, to be taken seriously, and wanted the political motivations of their protests to be known.

Alongside the student movement and informal groups at grass-roots level, small political parties of the Left were also attracted to the potential of cinema, and they could count on the collaboration of internationally famous filmmakers such as Marco Bellocchio and Pier Paolo Pasolini. In order to understand how such collaborations came into being, we need to investigate the complex dynamics developing between the student movement and intellectuals in 1968. The involvement of illustrious left-wing filmmakers in the *cinema militante* was provoked by the political and existential crisis many of them were experiencing at the time. The student movement triggered this crisis when it accused professional filmmakers of being nothing more than servants of the capitalist cinema industry.

It all started during the Pesaro Film Festival, in June 1968. Born in the wake of the *centrosinistra* government, the Pesaro film festival was unanimously recognized as a left-wing event. It was a non-competitive festival—proof of its seriousness and intellectual standing, in the eyes of left-wing film critics—and often showcased documentaries produced in Third World countries. Yet, the festival's fourth edition saw approximately two hundred students of the far Left stage a vociferous protest, the festival's venue being temporarily occupied, and the police intervening in an energetic way.[5] At the end of the festival, the student movement issued a document in which it highlighted the impossibility for cinema to be revolutionary, or even just progressive, within the existing cinema industry.[6] It also theorized the necessity for filmmakers to embrace a sort of new Zhdanovism (see Chap. 2): a cinema made by middle-class professionals and intellectuals, who were to renounce—willingly and enthusiastically—their artistic freedom and subjectivity, and to place themselves at the exclusive service of the workers.

It may be difficult to believe today, but the students' criticism hit left-wing Italian filmmakers quite hard. They felt they had to do something to shake off the accusation of complicity with the capitalist system, which the students had levelled against them. This can be seen in the first *Cinegiornale libero di Roma*, where Cesare Zavattini discusses the *Cinegiornali liberi* project along with a number of professional film directors. The group includes Silvano Agosti, Marco Bellocchio, Liliana Cavani, Giuseppe Ferrara and Gianni Toti. The film was shot in five takes, for a total running time of thirty minutes. Zavattini is appalled because the student movement had refused to participate in the *Cinegiornali* project. It should not have come as a surprise, though; in the concluding document they had issued in Pesaro, the students had specifically targeted Zavattini's idea of a cinematic guerrilla war, branding it as little more than a toy for intellectuals. Zavattini asks the following question: is cinema finished because of the medium's rejection by the student movement? This is just one of the many questions that remain unanswered in the film. At one point, Zavattini says that the ultimate objective of the *cinegiornali liberi* project is to overturn the author-viewer relationship; the viewer should be the film's co-author, or at the very least 'accessory' to the production of the film, but never just a spectator. Marco Bellocchio seems the more ideologically aware of the filmmakers that participate in the debate. He speaks of cinema as the 'organizer of the collective revolutionary conscience', and claims that for militant film to be truly revolutionary, it should be realized in such a way that each film projection has the effect of a revolutionary act. In his opinion, there is one film that possesses such a quality: Octavio Getino and Fernando Solanas' *La Hora de Los Hornos* (The Hour of the Furnaces, 1968). Bellocchio's reference to this film is significant; Solana's film had made quite an impression on the public in Pesaro. A crude exposé of neo-colonialism in Latin America, the film was probably the only thing that everyone agreed upon during that troubled edition of the festival.[7] Solanas and Getino would go on writing the manifesto of the Third Cinema movement, in 1969, proposing a 'cinema of subversion' to be brandished against neocolonial oppression (Solanas and Getino 1970). According to Laura E. Ruberto and Kristi Wilson, Third Cinema proves the long-lasting and international influence of neorealism on international cinema, since Third Cinema postulated a rediscovery/reappropriation of the documentary potential of cinema to capture truth in all its social and economic expressions (2007: 12).

As far as the left-wing Italian filmmakers were concerned, they staged their own small revolution during the 1968 Venice Film Festival (25 August–7 September). The story is well known: the members of ANAC (National Association of Filmmakers), by then an association composed exclusively of left-wing authors (following a split within the association), decided to boycott the twenty-ninth edition of the Festival by withdrawing their films. They also tried to disrupt the projections in various ways. The then director of the Festival, Luigi Chiarini, wrote a book about what happened in Venice, published shortly after the events (Chiarini, 1969), where he vented his deep resentment against ANAC, in particular against

166   G. FANTONI

Zavattini, Gregoretti, and Pasolini. His anger and frustration is understandable: the protest cost him the Festival's direction. In his book, Chiarini defines the protesters as hypocritical, and their motivations as confused. He might be right. It would appear that the principal reason for which the ANAC members boycotted Venice 1968 was that French filmmakers and students had a few months earlier successfully disrupted the Cannes Film Festival, forcing the organizers to curtail it. Also, Italian filmmakers needed to prove themselves to the students who had ridiculed them in Pesaro. Not all the members of ANAC, however, were on the same page. Bernardo Bertolucci and Liliana Cavani eventually presented their films, while Pasolini took an ambiguous and contradictory stance. He first announced his disagreement with ANAC, before changing his mind shortly thereafter. He then retired his film—*Theorem*—from the Festival, though it was eventually screened by order of the producer. Pasolini asked journalists not to attend the press screening, but promptly justified those who had decided to stay. Finally, he tried to meet the local university students, but they soundly—and perhaps understandably—booed him (Della Casa 2002: 353). It was not just the indecision he had shown in Venice, though, that angered the students; they had never forgiven Pasolini for the apparently anti-movement poem he had written after Valle Giulia.

It was perhaps in order to regain his status of left-wing film director that Pasolini later accepted to work with the left-wing group Lotta Continua, in the production of a *film militante*.[8] The film, entitled *12 dicembre* (December 12th, 1971, 100 minutes),[9] took two years to produce and saw the collaboration of Goffredo Fofi. It starts as an investigation into the death of Giuseppe Pinelli, a Milanese anarchist who died while being held in custody by the police under suspicion of involvement in the Piazza Fontana terrorist attack (see Chap. 6). In subsequent years, the never-clarified circumstances of Pinelli's death fuelled harsh polemics, especially by Lotta Continua (Foot 2009, 183–195). The first fifteen minutes of the film thus represent a piece of investigative journalism, featuring interviews with Pinelli's comrades and wife. This part aimed at demonstrating that Pinelli did not commit suicide, and that his death must therefore be ascribed to the police officers of the political section within the Milanese police headquarters. Next, the film embarks on a journey through Italy, documenting social turmoil and strikes taking place around the peninsula, while also featuring interviews with former partisans. *12 dicembre* can be described as an anti-PCI film: the Communist Party is accused of having betrayed the Resistance by not promoting profound social and political changes at the end of the war, of having abandoned the southern masses, and of having suffocated the working class's revolutionary spirit.

Around the time Pasolini started his collaboration with Lotta Continua, Marco Bellocchio joined the Unione dei comunisti Italiani (UCI—Union of the Italian Communists), a small Maoist party that was, *ça va sans dire*, fiercely hostile to the PCI. Bellocchio worked on the production of two documentary films for the UCI: *Paola* (1969, 100 minutes), about an illegal occupation of council houses UCI orchestrated in the town of Paola (in the Calabria region); and *Viva il 1° maggio rosso e proletario* (Long live the Red and Proletarian Labor day, 1969, 26 minutes), about the demonstration UCI organized in Milan to celebrate the 1969 edition of International Workers' Day. These films were made under strict political supervision of the party's propaganda officials.[10] Some of the claims included in the script of *Paola* would nowadays sound a bit outlandish: for example, the fact that the Italian State built highways in the South in order to spare the passing holiday-goers the distressing view of the poverty-stricken, southern villages. The film also accuses the left-wing party leaders—particularly the PCI's leaders—of being mainly responsible for the desolation of the South. Similarly, PCI leaders are vehemently criticized at the very beginning of *Viva il 1° maggio rosso e proletario*.

Another member of ANAC directed a militant film in that period: Ugo Gregoretti, a PCI sympathizer who had worked as a director for the Italian Public Broadcaster (RAI) and in mainstream cinema. He shot what is probably the most interesting and by far the most successful of the films produced by Unitelefilm as a result of its involvement in the *cinema militante* movement: *Apollon, una fabbrica occupata*, a sixty-seven-minute film shot in 16 mm. This chronicles the long struggle by workers at the large Apollon printing works in Rome to save their factory from closure and culminates in its occupation, which lasted thirteen months from the summer of 1968 to the summer of 1969. Rome lacked large industrial plants; the occupation of the medium-size Apollon factory by its three hundred or so workers thus immediately became a focal point for the capital's left-wing students, intellectuals, and aspiring revolutionaries. Many regarded 1968 as the dawn of revolution and were looking for their chance to experience the class struggle at first hand.

Among those to join the workers in their occupation of the factory were the members of a group of filmmakers, funded by Unitelefilm and led by Ugo Gregoretti. Rather than produce a documentary, they took the opportunity to make an experimental film that would perfectly embody the spirit of *Cinema militante*: its style and structure were to be decided in agreement with the Apollon workers. The experiment resulted in a somewhat atypical but fascinating film, which might be described as a sort of docudrama. Its most striking feature was the fact that the workers played themselves, re-enacting the events they had lived through during the long struggle that preceded the actual occupation. Senior members of the PCI were cast in the roles of the factory owners. The shoot lasted eight days and used the factory as its location (Gregoretti 2000: 213). Despite its experimental character, the film still has many features typical of UTF productions, including the voice-over commentary, read by Gian Maria Volontè: this is used to link the various scenes, and makes the authors' perspective explicit by providing a political commentary as the plot unfolds.

The Apollon workers may have just wanted to tell their story, hoping that the film would be a useful mechanism for fundraising; it was in fact subsequently used for this, and was remarkably successful.[11] However, the editing and the rather didactic tone of the voice-over commentary turned the film into a sort of guide for trade union organizers. The aim of *Apollon, una fabbrica occupata* seems to be the depiction of an exemplary industrial dispute that could serve as a model for class warfare. The film shows how the Apollon workers, former peasants who had not been properly union-ized, slowly become politically aware during the first half of the 1960s thanks to the tireless activity of some among them: active members of the PCI like Morelli, or people from the 'socialist left' like Scucchia, 'an old anti-Fascists, one of Gramsci's comrades in prison'. The workers learn to see the injustices perpetrated by the factory boss, despite the veil of obfus-cation introduced by a paternalistic management style. Morelli and Scucchia manage to set up a factory committee and organize the first strike. This is a decisive step on the road to political emancipation:

> Scucchia vanquished the boom, paternalism, and the trepidation of the for-mer peasants. The workers, such as himself, Morelli and a few others, had been dreaming for some time, have finally come out of the sections and stopped in the yard, under the eyes of the boss.

As the years pass, the Apollon workers join the vanguard of Rome's union circles. The factory is sold to another entrepreneur, Borgognoni, who starts to sabotage production on a systematic basis. The factory committee hires a private investigator to lay bare the owner's intentions, and they find out that he is secretly planning to shut down the plant in order to build residential accommodation on the Apollon land. A battle of nerves begins between Borgognoni and the Apollon factory committee; the owner delays the payment of wages, while Morelli and Scucchia urge the workers not to react to management provocation in order to avoid police intervention. Borgognoni eventually discloses his intentions, but the workers, who already know of his plans, rapidly occupy the factory in order to stop the machinery being dismantled. The heat is now on; the Apollon workers are determined to resist 'one more minute of the boss'. Over the months that follow, the occupiers benefit from the solidarity and practical support given by the workers of Rome, as well as from further afield, thanks to the organizational effectiveness of the PCI, which has moved quickly to support their struggle. Many artists, intellectuals, and students also align themselves with the occupiers. The factory courtyard serves as a venue for debates, meetings, theatrical performances and even for the celebration of mass. Within its portrayal of the occupation, the film includes a rare visual record of the use of *Cinema militante*: we see a group of students, on behalf of the occupiers, showing a film about the May 1968 protests in France. One of them can be heard declaiming the Italian dubbing of the French film.

Apollon, una fabbrica occupata was the most widely distributed of all the *Cinema militante* films, thanks in particular to its promotion by the PCI and the Associazione Ricreativa Culturale Italiana (ARCI), a Communist partner organization. Forty-one copies were printed and it was shown more than a thousand times, with an estimated total Italian audience of 240,000. It was also shown in West Germany, Switzerland, and the United States, and was sold to the public broadcasting services of Sweden and Finland (Rosati 1973: 9). *Apollon* had thus been a sound investment for Unitelefilm: it cost three million lire to make, and grossed twelve million.[12]

However, the film had many negative reviews. While the film critic Adriano Aprà lambasted *Apollon* from a cinematographic point of view, questioning the decision to re-enact the Apollon story, severe criticism of a political nature came from parts of the *Cinema militante* movement.[13] Goffredo Fofi, for example, did not mince his words in an article published in *Ombre Rosse*, metaphorically entitled 'The lice and the whale' (the lice being the workers of the Apollon, while the whale was the PCI). For Fofi, the film was 'an ugly shot in the back of the working class', which seemed to attenuate Italy's social and political tensions rather than advancing the class struggle. According to Fofi, this was consistent with the traditions of the PCI, which he described as an 'obstructer of the class struggle'.[14] In particular, he argued that the film misrepresented reality in its omission of many of the tensions and clashes that had arisen among the Apollon workers themselves during the long struggle. Those who had wanted to step up the level of confrontation both inside and outside the factory, a tactic suggested by the student movement, had been deliberately ignored in the film, or dismissed as 'provocateurs paid by the boss'. From this perspective, *Apollon* was in fact a reactionary film that depicted an oversimplified dialectical exchange, 'tolerated and allowed by the PCI apparatus', between the students and the workers.

Today's viewer might be struck by the forthright comments within the voice-over for *Apollon*, and might understandably see Fofi's analysis in *Ombre Rosse* as motivated by pure political partisanship. However, there was arguably some truth to his remarks. The commentary itself, albeit obliquely, hints at the complex relationship that had developed between students, workers, and the PCI during the Apollon occupation:

> Workers and students march together through the streets, debating the modes of struggle but certainly not the watchwords that are always and can only be the same: no to the class state, no to the bourgeois state, no to the bosses' state.

Reading between the lines, we can see this statement as revealing that a minority of the workers, urged on by the student movement, had sought to turn the occupation into an open rebellion against the political system. Most, however, had followed the PCI in seeing the occupation as purely a union dispute. In many respects, *Apollon una fabbrica occupata* endorses the *politica unitaria* of the PCI: the factory workers succeed in foiling the plans of the class enemy by means of an alliance with a wide range of political and social forces, under the leadership of the Italian Communist Party. Ultimately, the film reflects how the PCI generally succeeded in maintaining hegemony over the workers' movement and how, in partnership with the trade unions, it managed to keep that period's substantial current of industrial action within legal boundaries.

The film produced by the *Collettivo cinema militante* of Turin, *Lotte alla Rhodiatoce* (Struggle at the *Rhodiatoce*), can be regarded as the anti-*Apollon*. Its political message is indeed the opposite of Gregoretti's film;

the struggle at the Rhodiatoce is presented as having been conducted independently from, and indeed against, the unions and the PCI. Since the trade unions' activists were passive and prone to a compromise with the factory's owner, the 4200 workers had to take things into their hands: 'It was no longer about the unions leading the workers', the voice-over commentary says, 'but about the workers imposing their will on the unions'. The workers could, however, count on the solidarity of the student movement: 'workers and students, same struggle, same enemy', reads a handwritten board hung up on the factory gates. Thanks to the students—the voice-over goes on to explain—the workers had become aware of the political significance of their struggle. As a consequence, the workers' initial demands have lost most of their relevance in the course of the struggle: the *lotta* is important in its own right, as a moment of the class struggle shaking the country, and as a step towards the revolution.

In the film's last scene, we see a group of workers paying homage to a monument that commemorates a partisan group, the *Volante Cucciolo*. This scene is highly significant, as it is meant to suggest a political continuity between the anti-Fascist and anti-Nazi Resistance fighters of the Second World War and the workers'/student movement. As we have seen above, radical left-wing groups accused the PCI of having betrayed the *Resistenza* by allowing the capitalist structure of Italian economy to survive virtually unreformed after the war. They were thus claiming political ownership of the Resistance's moral legacy. This would grant their political struggle historical justification and meaning. Another political group would do exactly the same, only a few years later, this time with the aim of justifying its terrorist attacks: the Red Brigades (see Chap. 9).

With respect to political violence and the rise of left-wing terrorism in Italy, we should point out that the films of the *cinema militante* offer valuable documentation of the progressive acceptance of violence by the radical Left. We have mentioned—in both the previous and present chapter—that the student movement openly contemplated the possibility, or even theorized the necessity, of moments of violent confrontation with the police. In this respect, a film like *12 dicembre* takes a step forward. This can be seen in the part devoted to the Reggio revolt (July 1970–February 1971), when the post-Fascist *Movimento Sociale Italiano* (MSI) managed to harness a burst of outrage from the citizens of Reggio Calabria against the government's decision to make Catanzaro—and not Reggio—the regional capital of Calabria (Crainz 2005: 470–79). However, *12 dicembre* does not seem to mind the right-wing character of the revolt very much.

The fact that the people of Reggio started a revolt against the government is seen as a positive development, and as a potential prelude to what is hoped might happen across the country. Rebellion and violence are thus valued per se and presented as a legitimate form of political struggle. Again, when asked what he would say 'if you were to meet Agnelli [the FIAT car company owner] face to face', a young factory worker replies: 'Nothing, I would just shoot him'. As pointed out by Giovanni De Luna, such a nonchalant endorsement of violence was the inevitable consequence of the radical Left's rhetoric (De Luna 2009, 70–80). By characterizing the Italian Republic as the continuation of the Fascist regime, the radical Left implicitly justified its violent subversion. This is not to say that there is a direct political correlation between the *nuova sinistra* and the left-wing terrorism of the mid-1970s. Rather, the years of the *Contestazione* produced a political milieu that made it possible for political terrorism to arise. However, terrorism was by no means the *Contestazione*'s inevitable outcome.

At the turn of the 1970s, the season of militant cinemas died out. *Ombre Rosse* ceased its publication at the end of 1969, depriving the movement of an important platform for theoretical and cultural discussion. However, the demise of *cinema militante* was mostly due to the fact that film production was expensive and required much work. Making the films available to a large audience also proved to be quite an expensive and laborious undertaking. Once the initial enthusiasm had passed, many found it more convenient to direct their efforts towards different forms of communication and propaganda. Zavattini's *cinegiornali liberi* also did not progress much further. Unitelefilm, by contrast, was able to capitalize on the notoriety it had acquired during the years of the *cinema militante*, and managed to establish collaborations with well-known filmmakers for quite some time thereafter. This was a propitious moment for this kind of experiment, as several Italian directors seemed eager to prove their revolutionary credentials by working in independent left-wing productions for little or no remuneration (Miccichè1995: 348–349). Thus, in 1971, Bernardo Bertolucci directed a film for Unitelefilm, *La salute è malata* (The health service is unwell, 33 minutes), which addressed the problems of the Italian healthcare system.

What remained at the end of militant cinema was the sense of guilt many Italian left-wing intellectuals felt for the contribution they were making to the country's cultural industry: in other words, to the perpetuation of the capitalist system. Their ideological anguish can be best seen in one of the feature films that were produced in this period, Francesco Maselli's *Lettera aperta a un giornale della sera* (Open Letter to an Evening Newspaper, 1970). The film's plot revolves around a group of middle-aged left-wing intellectuals, members of the PCI, who spend their evenings theorizing revolutionary acts (like a direct participation in the Vietnam War) they are evidently unable and unwilling to carry out. They are wealthy, privileged, and socially integrated. Far away from their stylish living rooms, the police chase and brutally torture those who pose a real threat to the capitalist system: the students. Maselli himself was a member of the PCI, and the film's cast included some of his colleagues and comrades. Open Letter to an Evening Newspaper is thus the merciless self-indictment of an entire generation of intellectuals. Italian left-wing intellectuals would only get rid of their sense of guilt and related ideological concerns in the 1980s, following the *riflusso* (see Chap. 11). As a result, though, they would no longer be the same. Having lost the role of vanguard of Italian progressive thinking, which the PCI had given them after the war, they lost any real purpose as a group, ending up on the Roman terraces, with not much more left to do but to contemplate *The Great Beauty*.

NOTES

1. See the statement by Paola Scarnati, who worked at UTF from 1965 to 1979, in Medici, Morbidelli and Taviani (2001: 190–91).
2. Number 8, December 1969, 65–69.
3. See the screenplay of the *Cinegiornale* number 1 (53 minutes) in Rosati (1973, 20–25). Silvano Agosti was going to film protest movements in Rome for the following ten years. Part of the footage he filmed is now visible in the documentary film *Ora e sempre riprendiamoci la vita* (Now and always let's take back our life), released in 2018.
4. See these collected in Rosati (1973).
5. See Mino Argentieri's recollections of the events which occurred in Pesaro in Medici, Morbidelli and Taviani (2001: 64–87). Argentieri was at the time responsible for the *Commissione Cinema* of the Italian Communist Party and one of the organizers of Pesaro Film festival.
6. See 'Cultura al servizio delle Rivoluzione', in *Ombre Rosse*, number 5, August 1968, 3–9.
7. On the political and cultural impact of *The Hour of the Furnaces* in Italy, see Mestman (2017).
8. On Lotta Continua, see Cazzullo (1998).

174   G. FANTONI

9. Pier Paolo Pasolini's first-hand account of his experience with Lotta Continua is in Faldini and Fofi (1981, 33–34).
10. Marco Bellocchio and others speak of these films in Faldini and Fofi (1981, 26–28).
11. According to Ugo Gregoretti, *Apollon, una fabbrica occupata* made 60 million lire from the donations made at thousands of showings in the venues of the PCI's alternative distribution network (Sircana 2010: 85).
12. IG, APCI, MF 161, pp. 615–38, Istituti e organismi vari, Unitelefilm, serie 1971.
13. Adriano Aprà's review, in *Cinema e Film*, 9, 1969, is quoted by Bertozzi (2008: 195).
14. See Goffredo Fofi, 'I pidocchi e la balena', *Ombre Rosse*, 8, December 1969: 70–71. For reviews from the perspective of the PCI, see 'Gli operai dell'Apollon salgono sullo schermo', *Rinascita*, 14 February 1969: 22; 'L'Apollon protagonista in un film', *L'Unità*, 30 January 1969: 3.

BIBLIOGRAPHY

Bertozzi, M. 2008. *Storia del documentario italiano. Immagini e culture dell'altro cinema*. Venice: Marsilio.

Cazzullo, A. 1998. *I ragazzi che volevano fare la rivoluzione. 1968–1978: storia di Lotta Continua*. Milan: Mondadori.

Chiarini, L. 1969. *Un leone e altri animali. Cinema e contestazione alla Mostra di Venezia 1968*. Milan: Sugar.

Crainz, G. 2005. *Il paese mancato. Dal miracolo economico agli anni ottanta*. Rome: Donzelli.

De Luna, G. 2009. *Le ragioni di un decennio 1969–1979. Militanza, violenza, sconfitta, memoria*. Milan: Feltrinelli.

Della Casa, S. 2002. Il cinema militante'. In *Storia del cinema italiano, XI–1965/69*, ed. G. Canova, 349–365. Venice: Marsilio.

Faldini, F., and G. Fofi. 1981. *L'Avventurosa storia del cinema italiano raccontata dai suoi protagonisti, 1960–1969*. Milan: Feltrinelli.

Foot, J. 2009. *Italy's Divided Memory*. New York: Palgrave Macmillan.

Gregoretti, U. 2000. *Intervento di Ugo Gregoretti. In Archivi audiovisivi europei. Un secolo di storia operaia. Convegno internazionale e rassegna di film inediti*. Rome: 20–21 novembre 1998, Rome: Aamod, 212–217.

Hayward, S. 2005. *French National Cinema*. London and New York: Routledge.

Lewis, J. 1998. *The New American Cinema*. Durham: Duke University Press.

Masoni, T., and P. Vecchi. 2000. *Cinenotizie in poesia e prosa. Zavattini e la non-fiction*. Turin: Lindau.

Medici, A., M. Morbidelli, and E. Taviani, eds. 2001. *Il PCI e il cinema tra cultura e propaganda (1959–1979)*. Rome: Aamod.

Mestman, M. 2017. 'L'ora dei forni e il cinema politico italiano prima e dopo il '68'. *Imago* 15: 37–53.

Miccichè, L. 1995. *Cinema italiano: gli anni sessanta e oltre*. Venice: Marsilio.

Rosati, F. 1973. Esperienze di cinema militante: 1968–1972. *Bianco e Nero* 34 (7–8): 1–173.

Ruberto, L.E., and K.M. Wilson, eds. 2007. *Italian Neorealism and Global Cinema*. Detroit: Wayne University Press.

Sircana, G., ed. 2010. *A partire dall'Apollon. Testimonianze e riflessioni su cultura, cinema e mondo del lavoro a quarant'anni dall'Autunno caldo*. Rome: Ediesse.

Solanas, F., and Getino, O. 1970. Toward a Third Cinema. *Cinéaste* 4 (3), latin american militant cinema (winter 1970–71): 1–10.

PART III

A Decade of Living Dangerously: The Turbulent Peak (and the Seeds of Decline) of the Italian Communist Party (1970–1979)

CHAPTER 8

The Early 1970s: Unitelefilm, the Fascist Threat, and the 'Historic Compromise'

The streets and squares of Milan are covered with corpses. Hundreds of youngsters are lying in gardens, near tram stops or inside subway trains. These are the opening scenes of *I Cannibali* (The Year of the Cannibals), a film by Liliana Cavani, released in 1970. The film is set in a dystopian near future. Italy is under the heel of a Fascist-style dictatorship. The State wants the dead to be left in the spots where they were killed, as a warning and a reminder: this is what happen to those who dare to rebel. No one is allowed to touch them. However, a boy and a girl break the law and give some of the fallen a decent and proper burial. They pay dearly their act of defiance, but trigger a new anti-regime movement. Cavani wanted to make a film resembling a Greek myth, and therefore wrote a story clearly inspired by Sophocles' play Antigone. In her opinion, myths represent a state of things, which might or might not became reality.[1] The possibility of a new dictatorial regime seemed very real at the beginning of the 1970s in Italy. This certainly was the impression of the Italian Communist Party, whose policy was above all aimed at averting the danger of a coup d'etat and a return to Fascism. Cinematic propaganda was also largely geared towards this objective.

This chapter concerns the history of Unitelefilm (UTF) from 1968 to the mid-1970s. It first chronicles the actions undertaken by the professional and party officers managing the company to survive the competitive Italian film market by improving and diversifying the UTF offer. Their efforts were mostly fruitless, and this was due to various reasons, including

© The Author(s), under exclusive license to Springer Nature 179
Switzerland AG 2021
G. Fantoni, *Italy through the Red Lens*, Italian and Italian American
Studies, https://doi.org/10.1007/978-3-030-69197-4_8

180   G. FANTONI

saturation of the market for politically engaged films, serious disagreement within the company's management, and lack of firm political direction.

Nonetheless, a few notable films were produced in this period, including the only feature film ever produced by Unitelefilm: *Trevico—Torino*, by renowned filmmaker Ettore Scola. The film offers an interesting depiction of the life of immigrant workers in the northern city of Turin in the early 1970s. It is also a realistic portrait of a city, Turin, struggling to cope with the massive arrival of immigrants from the south. According to Diego Novelli, who collaborated in the writing of the film, Turin was at the time changing at a rapid pace, and not always for the better. The citizens of Turin, in particular, were losing their traditional sense of humanity and deep-rooted class-consciousness and were at risk of surrendering to individualism and selfishness.[2]

With respect to the propaganda films produced in these years, the chapter focuses on two pivotal moments: the election of 1972, and the launch of the '*compromesso storico*' (historic compromise) policy, namely the proposition of an alliance between DC, PSI and PCI. Following the *Compromesso storico* policy, PCI propaganda cinema became less concerned with foreign policy and ideological issues, but focused instead on advertising the party's reasonable domestic policies, values, and history, as discussed both here and in the next chapter.

The 1960s had ended in the worst possible way: the Piazza Fontana bombing had seen the start of the long period of the '*strategia della tensione*' (strategy of tension), as it came to be known (Cento Bull 2007: 65–66). This was characterized by heightened political tension and an unprecedented series of terrorist attacks, perpetrated at least initially by neo-Fascist groups. The post-Fascist Movimento Sociale Italiano (MSI), led by Giorgio Almirante, fostered the resurgence of a form of '*squadrismo*', the violent action by Fascist groups in the 1920s, in order both to counteract the parties of the Left, which seemed to have the upper hand after the *autunno caldo* (see Chap. 6), and to push the moderate public— the supposed '*maggioranza silenziosa*' (silent majority)—towards the right by inflaming the political climate (Ruzza and Fella 2005: 14–15).[3] The early 1970s were thus characterized by widespread violence unleashed by neo-Fascist groups, and Unitelefilm's production for the election of 1972 was almost exclusively devoted to this issue.

The *compromesso storico* policy was instead a consequence of the preoccupation generated by the subsequent electoral growth of the MSI. The PCI leadership began to regard a coup d'état by neo-Fascist political forces as a real threat. Films produced after the 1972 elections thus addressed moderate public opinion. Their principal message was that neo-Fascism was the sole bringer of violence into the Italian political life and that, conversely, the PCI was the true champion of the democratic regime, as proved, among other things, by the *compromesso storico* policy.

The years 1968 and 1969 had in many respects been very positive for Unitelefilm. It had produced more films per year than ever before, thanks in particular to the Terzo Canale project. Its productive capacity had grown accordingly: twelve people were permanently employed within an organization that was equipped with three Moviola machines, one 35 mm and three 16 mm movie cameras, a recording studio, a small cinema, and a rich video archive.[4] Finally, UTF had achieved a degree of recognition in the left-wing cultural and political sphere thanks to its involvement in the *Cinema militante* movement (see Chap. 7).

However, not everything had gone well. The production of documentaries for the quality awards had been neglected and, as a result, the five films entered in 1968 had all been rejected.[5] Furthermore, from a financial perspective some of the films produced in that period had been complete disasters.[6] Things had gone better in 1969, with awards going to seven of the twelve films presented; nonetheless, UTF had a serious budget deficit by the end of the year. During the same period, the increasing amount of television broadcasting across Europe led to decreasing newsreel production. Because this also involved Eastern European countries, the sale of '*attualità*' behind the Iron Curtain ceased completely, with dire consequences to UTF's financial health.

For these reasons, the UTF administrator Venturo Valentini proposed some drastic measures in a confidential report submitted to the Press and Propaganda Section in December 1969.[7] In his view, the company needed to be shut down, especially for tax reasons, and Unitelefilm turned into an '*associazione degli amici del cinema*' (society of friends of cinema). This cultural association would make the valuable UTF equipment available to directors and artists who wanted to produce politically engaged films and documentaries; films could then be produced for both the *Cinema militante* circuit and the quality awards with little or no investment from the PCI. As for the production of propaganda films, the PCI could entrust this to individual directors on a project-by-project basis.

In September 1970, the PCI made an attempt to relaunch the company by imposing changes to its management structure. Ugo Gregoretti, who had finally joined the party, accepted the role of artistic director. The

182   G. FANTONI

appointment of Maurizio Ferrara, who already had roles within the PCI apparatus, underlined the party's intention to exert closer political control over UTF. Ferrara was also a member of the 'Ufficio cinema' (Film Office) and it may have been intended that his presence would improve the working relationship between the PCI's Cultural Commission and its film production company.[8] Finally, Luciana Finzi was appointed as UTF's new administrator. The new management prepared a detailed production plan outlining the political and financial objectives of Unitelefilm over the years to come.[9]

Gregoretti and his colleagues wanted to achieve economic self-sufficiency for Unitelefilm by producing films described as '*a carattere spettacolare*' (entertainment): films that could be distributed to cinemas or sold to the state and foreign broadcasting corporations, and not shown only within the party's scarcely lucrative alternative network.[10] However, this objective could only be achieved with initial funding from the PCI; Finzi therefore asked for 250 million lire.[11] Somewhat predictably, the party ignored this request. Ongoing funding was never granted and it continued to commission films from UTF on a project-by-project basis.

As can be seen from a confidential report sent to the PCI's *Segreteria politica* (Central Political Directorate) by Ferrara in January 1972, the Unitelefilm management itself was in fact far from unanimous in regard to the aims and objectives of the company.[12] Ferrara claimed that Gregoretti seemed to set excessive store by UTF's autonomy, and suggested assigning the company a full-time director based in the Cultural Commission or Press and Propaganda Section so that there could be stricter political control. The PCI therefore decided to appoint the head of the Cultural Commission Giorgio Napolitano—one day to be President of the Italian Republic—as the president of a management group also including Finzi and Gregoretti. In March 1973, Finzi submitted a rather pessimistic report which included her proposals for a radical reorganization of the structure.[13] First of all, she stressed that Unitelefilm was too large and expensive to be an office for film propaganda, but not remotely large enough to be a film production company. She also acknowledged that the production plan presented the previous year had not proved realistic in relations to the company's commercial prospects. Finzi pointed out that Italian cinema in general had experienced dramatic changes between 1968 and 1973: UTF films were no longer the only representatives of their genre, because the cinema industry was now producing plenty of politically engaged films that challenged the establishment, and with notably

8 THE EARLY 1970S: UNITELEFILM, THE FASCIST THREAT... 183

superior artistic results. She was clearly referring to the new wave of '*cinema civile*' (political cinema) that had been flourishing since 1970; in the words of Lino Miccichè, this represented 'the popular and entertainment face' of the *Cinema militante* period, and, one might add, its commercial outcome (1995: 348).[14]

Unitelefilm's management group did its best to improve film sales; for example, an innovative project involving the sale of videotapes was suggested to the PCI publishing house Editori Riuniti, although this was in fact too innovative to be taken up.[15] However, ventures like this could not resolve the fundamental problems of Unitelefilm, which derived from the lack of firm commitment, at the level of the party leadership, to a rationale for the very existence of the PCI film production company. The tensions between Unitelefilm's management and the party leadership eventually broke out during a stormy meeting in November 1973, at which Gregoretti resigned.[16]

Despite these problems, during this period Unitelefilm still managed to produce some films with more of an 'entertainment' focus that were aimed to appeal outside the PCI's film circuit. The most interesting of these was *Trevico–Torino*, also known as *Trevico–Torino, viaggio nel Fiat-nam* (Trevico–Turin: a journey into Fiat-nam): the only feature film ever produced by UTF, it was directed by Ettore Scola and released in 1972. The genesis of the film was rather different from that of the company's usual productions: neither commissioned by the party nor proposed by Unitelefilm to the party, it was in fact the director's personal project. Scola had wanted to direct an independent feature film outside mainstream cinema, and had just finished shooting the footage when he ran out of money. The PCI agreed to help by shouldering the costs of editing and post-production, which were entrusted to Unitelefilm. Scola was politically close to the party, and in return for its support he agreed to direct a documentary for Unitelefilm on the Festival Nazionale dell'Unità, which was to take place in Rome from 23 September to 1 October 1972.[17] One of the reasons for *Trevico–Torino*'s attractions as a project for the PCI was that Scola had written the film together with Diego Novelli, a member of the party and journalist for *L'Unità* who was to become the mayor of Turin after the elections of 1975.

Trevico–Torino has a running time of one hour and thirty-five minutes and was shot in 16 mm colour film, a semi-professional format widely used at the time by independent filmmakers, with hand-held camera and live audio. Scola also used archival footage. Because of these features, it seems

184   G. FANTONI

to lie somewhere between a feature film and a documentary: a '*documentario drammatizzato*' (dramatized documentary), as Roberto Alemanno described it in *L'Unità*.[18]

The plot revolves around an Italian southerner in his early twenties called Fortunato Santospirito, played by Paolo Turco, and his life as an immigrant in Turin. This has autobiographical elements: like Scola, Fortunato comes from Trevico, a small village in the interior of Campania. However, unlike Scola, who grew up in Rome and started off as a screenwriter, Fortunato moves to Turin because he is chasing a dream job with the FIAT company. The encounter with the great northern industrial city is something of a culture shock for the southern boy: the city is cold, noisy, and grey, and, because of the unfamiliar dialect, Fortunato can barely understand what local people are saying. He makes friends in a bar with a waiter, his first guide to the strange city, who helps him to find a place for the night. When night falls, Fortunato realizes that there is no bed in his improvised shelter, a dirty and miserable coal cellar, and he ends up sleeping in Turin's Central Station among the homeless, prostitutes, mentally ill and drunks. He recognizes that if he fails FIAT's aptitude test, he will soon be one of them. His auspicious name holds good and he manages to pass, becoming a factory worker in the largest of Italian companies, whose neon sign dominates the city like a powerful and remote divinity.

Fortunato discovers how difficult it is to establish personal relationships in a big city. He looks for the waiter, his only friend, but finds out that he has been sacked from the bar and is never to be seen again. Suffering from terrible loneliness, Fortunato starts to spend his Sundays at the Porta Palazzo market, the meeting point for southern migrants, looking for people from his village; there, he befriends Prospero Cerabona, another southerner and secretary of a local branch of the PCI. Cerabona explains to Fortunato that although migration affects the relationships with family and friends who have been left behind, in the long term it can result in improvements at the personal level; in particular, trade unions and the Communist Party can help migrants to develop their class-consciousness.

At a demonstration, Fortunato meets Vicky, a pretty young woman and an activist within the '*sinistra extraparlamentare*' (extraparliamentary left: this term described a range of radical left-wing groups that were competing with the PCI for the workers' trust). Vicky was played by Vittoria Franzinetti, who actually was an activist in Lotta Continua, the largest of the extraparliamentary left-wing groups, and a niece of Ugo Pecchioli, a PCI senator and former secretary of the party's Piedmont branch (Cazzullo

1998: 22). Vicky is from Turin and is quite clearly from the upper middle class; she seems to know a lot, especially about politics, and her apparent confidence fascinates the shy boy from the South (Image 8.1). Fortunato starts to accompany Vicky on propaganda tours of migrant neighbourhoods—what Vicky calls '*lavoro di quartiere*' (district work)—and their relationship soon develops into something more than a friendship, although nothing strictly romantic happens.

As time passes, Fortunato gradually realizes that the social gap between himself and Vicky cannot be bridged. Furthermore, he sees that although Vicky's endless discussions appear meaningful, they are in fact completely abstract and of no actual use in addressing the real problems of the workers. The most telling scene in this respect has Vicky questioning Fortunato's decision to attend the evening classes for workers, whose establishment had been a recent achievement by the trade union movement.[19] In this conversation we see the social and cultural distance between Fortunato, the lower-class boy who wants to improve his situation, and Vicky, the

Image 8.1 Vicky talking to Fortunato

personification of the well-off radicals who can afford to despise what they take for granted. Fortunato eventually ends his friendship with her and rejoins his comrades, finally ready to engage in the struggle for the political and social emancipation of the working class.

In the film's final scene, Fortunato is running fast along a road at the side of the Mirafiori plant when he trips and falls badly. He curses the factory, but picks himself up and continues at a walking pace (Image 8.2). The scene can be read as an endorsement of PCI policy and a criticism of the extraparliamentary left, in that it seems to suggest that workers can only achieve emancipation step by step, in the way that the PCI has always advised, while any attempt to speed up the process, running towards revolution in the way suggested by the extraparliamentary left, will result in painful setbacks.

Initially, *Trevico–Torino* could not find a distributor. In particular, it was twice rejected by Italnoleggio, the state film distribution company which, by law, was supposed to support the distribution of non-commercial

Image 8.2 Fortunato curses the factory

Italian films.[20] The PCI exploited this situation by turning *Trevico–Torino* into a symbol of the party's commitment to independent Italian cinema. It was presented at various Festival dell'Unità and, in particular, at the Festival dell'Unità in Turin where the showing was attended by two thousand spectators.[21] Furthermore, at the Venice Film Festival, where *Trevico–Torino* was presented in the '*Giornate del cinema italiano*' category, Giorgio Napolitano claimed that the PCI was fully committed to backing Italian directors in their struggle 'for the liberation of cinema from the laws of profit'.[22] Eventually, the cooperative Nuova Comunicazione, part of the Associazione Ricreativa Culturale Italiana (ARCI), agreed to distribute the film and guaranteed 150 showings.[23] The film won a FIPRESCI (International Federation of Film Critics) award in 1973.[24] *Trevico–Torino* also secured a degree of television distribution: it was sold to the Hungarian broadcasting service for two thousand dollars in 1973 and subsequently to RAI for 12 million lire, being shown on the Italian state broadcaster's second channel on 3 January 1978.[25]

However, there was no much time for the PCI to worry about cinema as the party was very concerned that the right-wing political forces, and particularly the MSI, were trying to create the conditions for an authoritarian political outcome. Furthermore, they assumed that this plan was backed by right-wing elements within Christian Democracy and the state apparatus, and also had some support from the US administration.[26] In March 1971, revelations published in the newspaper *Paese Sera* about the '*golpe Borghese*', the failed coup d'état involving the former RSI army officer Prince Junio Valerio Borghese, seemed to confirm the PCI leadership's worst fears (Arcuri 2004).

Meanwhile, Almirante's strategy seemed to be paying off: at the local elections in June 1971, the MSI made dramatic advances, especially in southern cities (Panvini 2009: 184–85). Subsequently, he promoted the creation of a right-wing coalition, the 'Destra Nazionale', merging the Monarchist Party and the MSI in the hope of achieving even greater success at the national elections of 1972 (Ruzza and Fella 2005: 16). In consequence, most of the Communist cinematographic propaganda for these elections addressed the alleged Fascist conspiracy against democracy.

La trama nera (The dark conspiracy, 1972), a seventeen-minute film directed by Luigi Perelli, depicts Fascism as a virus that, if not contained, can easily spread and destroy freedom and democracy. This was consistent with the Communist conception of Fascism as a sort of by-product of capitalism. Rather than an autonomous political movement with historically determined characteristics, Fascism was seen as one of the tools available to the bourgeoisie for its management of society. If not impeded by the presence of a strong and combative labour movement, the ruling classes could resort to Fascism at any moment, just as they had done in the past. It should be noted that this idea of bourgeois society as both potentially and implicitly Fascist was widely held across the international Communist movement.[27]

In Perelli's film the recent outbreak of Fascist violence is specifically attributed to Christian Democracy, which is playing a dangerous game in allowing it to grow so that it can cast itself as the defender of democracy from both left-wing and right-wing violence. The 'Borghese coup' has shown that the DC strategy could have serious and unexpected consequences. *La trama nera* also exposed the connections between Italian Fascists and the Greek Regime of the Colonels, and hinted at the US government's complicity with Italian anti-democratic forces: 'and the CIA? Is it really nothing to do with this dark conspiracy?' the voice-over asks rhetorically. Finally, the film addresses the moderate public by claiming that the only threat to public order comes from the Right, as has been shown by the innumerable acts of violence perpetrated by Fascist groups over the last three years, while the PCI and the labour movement are the guarantors of peace and democracy. A similar message is conveyed by another propaganda film produced in 1972, which has the significant title *L'ordine non viene da destra* (Order doesn't come from the right) (16 minutes). Both films were put together exclusively from stock footage, probably because the 1972 elections were the first in the history of the Republic to be held out of the expected electoral cycle, and as a result Unitelefilm had no time to plan any new shooting.

The 1972 elections marked a victory for the MSI: it doubled its share of the vote from the previous national elections of 1968, reaching nearly 9 per cent, while both the PCI and the DC remained at much the same level as before.[28] What was even more alarming for the PCI was that there was no relief after these elections from the strategy of tension, which reached its climax two years later. On 28 May 1974, a bomb targeting an anti-Fascist protest in Brescia's Piazza della Loggia killed eight people and injured over a hundred. On 4 August, another bomb exploded on the 'Italicus', a night train, killing twelve and injuring forty-eight.[29] Unitelefilm produced a twenty-five-minute documentary on the Brescia bombing, *I giorni di Brescia* (The Brescia days), directed by Perelli.

I giorni di Brescia is one of the most poignant films produced by the PCI, very effectively depicting the widespread sorrow and anger triggered across Italy by the bombing. The first part, of about seven minutes, features the original sound recording of the speech by trade union organizer Franco Castrezzati in Piazza della Loggia, which was abruptly interrupted by the bomb blast. We hear people screaming 'una bomba, una bomba, aiuto!' ('a bomb, a bomb, help!'), while the speaker urges the crowd not to panic: '[d]on't move, stay still, comrades and friends, stay still, be calm comrades and friends, stay still'. This part features archival footage of previous violence by Fascists, beginning with Piazza Fontana; from the moment of the explosion onwards, we see some rather graphic pictures of the injured people carried into Piazza della Loggia immediately after the attack. The film then shows spontaneous demonstrations in the city on the very same day as the bombing, which seem to be pervaded by anger rather than grief: protesters shout aggressive slogans such as '*Almirante boia*' (Almirante executioner) and '*A morte, a morte, fascisti assassini*' (Death, death, for the Fascist assassins) (Image 8.3).

A few days later, on 1 June 1974, people from Brescia protested about the presence of members of the government at the funeral for the bombing victims by whistling at the Italian President, the Christian Democrat Giovanni Leone, and shouting 'Via! Via!' (Go away!).[30] Despite the tempting opportunity to castigate a prominent DC politician, the PCI refrained from publicizing this incident; Perelli's film, for example, does not show people protesting against Leone.[31] How can this decision be explained? Unlike the propaganda film produced in the run-up to the 1972 elections, *I giorni di Brescia* was not aimed at attributing moral and political responsibility for Fascist violence to Christian Democracy and the government, but instead at strengthening the anti-Fascist front. This was consistent with the policy of the '*compromesso storico*' (historic compromise), launched by the new PCI leader Enrico Berlinguer in September and October 1973 (Vittoria 2007: 123–28).

The 'historic compromise' policy appealed for an alliance of the '*forze democratiche e popolari*' (democratic and popular forces), reaching out to both the PSI and the DC. The aim of this alliance was to avoid the potential destabilization of democratic arrangements, as had happened in Chile in September 1973, and to create a broad front supporting political and social reform (Barbagallo 2006: 262). Shared adherence to the values of the Resistance was intended to cement this accord. It should be pointed out that from the 1960s onwards the Resistance was increasingly accepted

Image 8.3 Demonstration in Brescia after the bombing

by most Italian political parties, including the DC, as the moral foundation of the Italian democratic system (Cooke 2011: 86–93). This is illustrated by the fact that on 2 June 1974, very soon after the Brescia bombing, the DC government allowed former partisans to march alongside the army for the first time in the traditional military parade celebrating the Festa della Repubblica in Rome.[32] The symbolic significance of this decision cannot be overemphasized: the Italian Republic officially recognized the partisans, including Communists, as veterans of the Second World War.

In this cultural and political context, the Brescia bombing also assumed powerful symbolic significance. It resembled an allegory of the historic compromise, in that the victims included four members of the CGIL (the Communist and Socialist trade union federation), the wife of a prominent DC city councillor and a former partisan. Significantly, Perelli's *I giorni di Brescia* shows the CGIL leader Luciano Lama emphasizing the symbolic relevance of the Piazza della Loggia deaths in his speech on the day of the funeral:

> If history asks us today for a commitment to unity, let's show that we are still capable of fulfilling this, faced with the enemy of times past who is still our enemy today.

Mino Argentieri, reviewing the film in *Rinascita*, argued that *I giorni di Brescia* was 'an example of excellent film journalism', but lamented the lack of 'an in-depth cinematographic investigation into neo-Fascism', which he felt was much needed.[33]

The PCI had already taken on this task by entrusting Unitelefilm with the production of a documentary about neo-Fascism, *Bianco e Nero* (White and Black) (1975). This eighty-five-minute film was written and directed by Paolo Pietrangeli, a songwriter who had composed two of the most famous anthems of the protest era, 'Valle Giulia' and 'Contessa', and was also the son of the director Antonio Pietrangeli. The voice-over is provided by the journalist Paolo Gambescia and the music by singer and songwriter Giovanna Marini. *Bianco e Nero* investigates the social and political causes of neo-Fascism and its historical roots. In spite of its documentary-style features and structure, *Bianco e Nero* is clearly a propaganda film in that from its title onwards it never conceals its underlying thesis: that the return of the black (Fascism) is favoured by the white (Christian Democracy). This political stance was clearly at odds with the 'historic compromise' policy. However, elections were scheduled that year and propaganda took precedence over political coherence.

One of the most interesting features of *Bianco e Nero* is the use of interviews secured under false pretences, notably with prominent MSI and DC politicians by UTF journalists and cameramen pretending to be a French television crew. Thanks to this stratagem, Pietrangeli was able to record some frank and sometimes rather shocking statements. Giorgio Almirante, for example, claims to have always been, purely and simply, a Fascist. Prince Junio Valerio Borghese, interviewed in Spain where he had taken refuge after the discovery of his plot against democracy, says that, if given the chance, he would very happily exterminate all Italian Communists. Pino Rauti, a leading figure within the MSI, lauds the 'spiritual values' of German National Socialism. Finally, Mario Scelba, the former Christian Democrat Minister for the Interior, smugly explains that he managed to expel thousands of formers partisans from the police force in the late 1940s, after the end of the anti-Fascist coalition governments, because he had seen them as a threat to democracy.

The voice-over counters Scelba's statements by reaffirming the 'Communist truth': Communist partisans made a decisive contribution to the struggle against Fascism and loyally supported Italy's nascent democracy. Unfortunately, reactionary forces, backed by the US government, managed to break the 'anti-Fascist unity'. Subsequently, Christian Democracy had no shame in accepting support from Fascists: in the 1950s, as many as twenty-eight of their city and town councils, including that of Rome, remained in power thanks to Fascist votes. *Bianco e Nero*'s critique of the DC is that it had politically legitimated Fascism by its preference for an alliance with the MSI rather than one with democratic and anti-Fascist forces.

The voice-over highlights the events of July 1960 as a turning point:

> In the piazzas of Genoa, Reggio Emilia, Catania, Palermo and Rome, it's the whole plan of conservative consolidation of Italian society, involving isolation of the working class, which is being decisively buried.

After July 1960, the road was finally open for a new governmental configuration: the centre-left. From that moment onwards, however, reactionary forces were trying to destabilize the democratic system, constructing the 'dark conspiracy' in which the strategy of tension played an integral part.

Bianco e Nero was one of the few films produced by the PCI that was distributed in ordinary cinemas, by Nuova Comunicazione. Between March 1975 and April 1980, it was screened fairly evenly across the country, grossing 52,338,797 lire.[34] It was also shown at several film festivals, including Krakow, Grenoble, Leipzig, Moscow, and Volgograd, and in various Italian high schools, particularly in Rome.

After the resignation of Ugo Gregoretti in November 1973, Unitelefilm was completely reorganized. Management of the company was entrusted to Dario Natoli, a PCI member who had been working as a film and television critic for *Paese Sera* and *L'Unità*. The party also established a 'Comitato Direttivo' (management committee) to oversee UTF from a political standpoint; its members included *Rinascita*'s film critic Mino Argentieri and representatives of the party's regional branches. Finally, in order to minimize expenditure, the number of Unitelefilm staff was reduced to six.[35] It was decided that the party would meet the costs of UTF staff and its production of commissioned propaganda films only on a project-by-project basis. The PCI's film production company would need

8 THE EARLY 1970S: UNITELEFILM, THE FASCIST THREAT... 193

to raise money independently in order to produce documentaries for the quality awards.

These new arrangements proved effective; Unitelefilm sought financial partnerships and tried to develop proposals for productions that could be distributed outside the Communist film circuit. The AAMOD has conserved a wide range of project proposals developed during these years, many of which were presented to RAI, the trade unions, local authorities, and to the PCI itself. Although most of these were not realized, some of the films that emerged in this period enjoyed the largest circulation in the history of Unitelefilm. One such film is *Fortezze vuote* (Empty fortresses) (1975), a hundred-minute colour documentary directed by Gianni Serra and financed by the Umbria Region and the Province of Perugia, which were both governed by left-wing administrations consisting of PCI and PSI councillors.[36]

Fortezze vuote deals with the reform of the mental health service, a burning topic at the time, and not just in the Umbria Region. In the mid-1960s, the new therapeutic approach adopted by the psychiatrist Franco Basaglia in the Gorizia city mental hospital in northern Italy had opened up a wide-ranging debate about the social causes of mental illness. It had also questioned both the effectiveness and the ethical legitimacy of some therapies that had traditionally been used to treat mental disorders.[37] It should be stressed that the issue of mental illness had political relevance for the PCI, not least because Basaglia's new therapeutic approach seemed to be inspired by a vision that was politicized and left-leaning. This was particularly evident after the foundation of 'Psichiatria Democratica' (Democratic Psychiatry) by a group of psychiatrists, led by Basaglia, in October 1973. Their programme adopted Marxist terminology and advocated the use of psychiatry as a tool to fight social exclusion 'by analysing and rejecting its source in the social structure (the social relations of production) and in the superstructure (norms and values) of our society'.[38]

The PCI made every effort to support Psichiatria Democratica, as is shown by the way that it encouraged local branches to put pressure on party-sympathizing psychiatrists and nurses to attend the first national meeting of the new organization, to be held in Gorizia on 22 and 23 June 1974.[39] The continuing interest of the PCI in this issue is demonstrated by the production of *Fortezze vuote*. The film endorses the idea that mental illness is a consequence of social injustice and, ultimately, a side-effect of the alienation caused by capitalist development. In particular, it develops the thesis that the dramatic end of the traditional rural way of life, following the unchecked mass migration to cities in the 1960s and the consequent cultural and social dislocation of many former peasants, is one of the principal reasons for the proliferation of mental illness. *Fortezze vuote* was shown at the 1975 Venice Film Festival and was generally given positive reviews.[40] It was distributed in both 35 mm and 16 mm by Nuova Comunicazione and Italnoleggio, and was subsequently sold to RAI as well as to Portuguese television.

Another documentary on social issues that Unitelefilm produced in the same period, this time with the involvement of the PCI's Turin branch, was *Perché droga* (Why drugs?) (1976), a film on the problem of drug addiction directed by Daniele Segre and Franco Berbero.[41] The first part chronicles a debate about this issue at a community meeting in Mirafiori Sud, an area in the outskirts of Turin largely inhabited by the families of FIAT workers. The film then presents some interviews with FIAT workers and young addicts. The argument made in *Perché droga* is that drug addiction is a consequence of the social exclusion experienced by young people living in the city's outlying areas. In an interview published in 1976, Segre made the following claim:

> In some marginalized areas of the city, drugs (like theft and prostitution) constitute a personal and asocial response to a problem that is, instead, collective.[42]

This statement corresponded perfectly to the PCI's rather simplistic analysis of problems affecting Italian society, which were always explained as the side-effects of unbalanced and dehumanizing capitalist development. As a result, the solution to any social problem invariably lay in the promotion of community-based ways of living. The film therefore advocates the construction of cultural centres, cinemas, and public gardens in order to turn the outlying Mirafiori Sud, described as a '*quartiere–ghetto*' (ghetto district), into an environment that could foster social relationships and encourage political participation.

Unitelefilm's output in the 1970s, especially under Natoli's management, was typified by a particular sort of production: the documentary exaggerating the social and economic achievements of Communist regimes, whether longstanding or more recently established. For example, Unitelefilm put together four films devoted to North Korea using archival footage provide by that country's government. The first of these, *La nuova Corea* (The new Korea) (18 minutes), was produced in 1970 and followed in 1974 by the other two: *A nord del 38° parallelo* (North of the 38th parallel) (20 minutes) and *Il nuovo re è l'infanzia* (Childhood is the new king) (16 minutes). A team led by Luigi Perelli visited Bulgaria in the summer of 1975 and shot two documentaries, *Parvenez vuol dire primavera* ('Parvenez' means spring) (60 minutes, 1976) and *L'infanzia in Bulgaria* (Childhood in Bulgaria) (12 minutes, 1977), on the supposed efficiency of the country's agriculture and educational system respectively.[43] Finally, two short films were released in 1977 about the policies of the post-colonial socialist government of Mozambique: *Maputo: Una città che rinasce* (Maputo: a city reborn) and *L'organizzazione di una comune agricola* (The organization of an agricultural commune).

Film productions like these might appear out of step with the PCI's interpretation at that time of the political and social situation within the Communist world, which had become increasingly critical following the invasion of Czechoslovakia in 1968 by armed forces aligned with the Warsaw Pact (Pons 2007: 122). The PCI had endorsed this attempt at democratization and creation of 'socialism with a human face' (Alexander Dubček's famous slogan), although not to the point of questioning the Communist bloc's unity or Soviet hegemony (Bracke 2007: 178–82). The Prague Spring was a prime candidate for PCI propaganda in the run-up to the 1968 elections as it demonstrated that socialism and democracy could go forward hand in hand. As a result, Unitelefilm included a report titled '*Socialismo: la via cecoslovacca*' (Socialism: the Czechoslovakian path) in the seventh instalment of Terzo Canale (see Chap. 6). This shows crowded meetings of young people demanding political reform, and the proclamation of Ludvik Svoboda as President of the Republic on 30 March 1968. The voice-over hails 'socialism's new spring', while a young East German student explains to a delighted UTF interviewer that the socialist world is undergoing an epochal transformation:

> One phase of the history of socialism, the phase of concentration of power, has ended; another phase of its history, the phase of socialist democratization, has begun.

The invasion of Czechoslovakia by Warsaw Pact forces in August 1968 generated deep dismay within the Italian Communist Party.[44] On the cinematographic level, this took the form of a sort of Freudian repression: Czechoslovakia was never mentioned again in PCI films and a planned film about the Prague Spring was quickly shelved, even though the director Gianni Toti had already shot most of the footage.[45]

How can the cinematographic revival of the socialist myth in the mid-1970s thus be explained? We have to consider both commercial and ideological factors. In the first place, this kind of production was relatively inexpensive for Unitelefilm thanks to coproduction agreements established at the beginning of the 1970s.[46] Secondly, a significant proportion of the PCI's party faithful was far from disillusioned with socialist countries, holding on to an almost unshakeable faith in the superiority of the socialist system until the fall of the Berlin Wall (Ignazi 1992: 152). This meant that films presenting these countries in a positive light would always find a large audience among the diehard militants. Finally, the party leadership never perceived socialist societies in an entirely negative light either. Berlinguer himself, while questioning specific aspects of the historical experience of socialism as practised within the Eastern bloc, was still committed to the eclipse of capitalism and Italy's transformation into a socialist society. The dramatic economic crisis experienced by Western countries, and especially Italy, in the mid-1970s contributed in no small measure to reinforcing the belief within the party that in the long term capitalism was doomed. For the PCI, socialism represented the only possible solution to the problems of the global economy. As Berlinguer stated from the podium at the party's Fourteenth Congress (Rome, 18–23 March 1975): 'It's a fact: in the capitalist world there is a crisis, and in the socialist world there isn't'.[47]

Even when we take all these factors into account, the rather uncritical tone of these films about socialist countries remains somewhat surprising. In *A nord del 38° parallelo*, for example, the edited footage shows unmistakable evidence of the personality cult that had been created around the Korean president Kim Il-Sung. The voice-over commentary, however, omits to mention the existence of this cult and explains the construction of gigantic statues of President Kim as evidence of the persistence of 'an element of Confucianism' in North Korean popular culture. Similarly, in *Parvenez vuol dire primavera*, the commentary relates the queues of Bulgarian citizens in front of shops to their passion for freshly baked bread.

In summary, this chapter has shown that the principal target of PCI cinematographic propaganda in the early 1970s was the moderate public. It warned Italians about the perils of electoral success for the MSI and signalled the putative existence of a Fascist plot against the democratic system. These concerns also inspired the strategy that was to underlie political action by the PCI until the end of the decade: the historic compromise. The party also focused its film propaganda on issues of general interest, and, for the first time, social issues such as mental health and drug addiction were addressed. Conversely, foreign policy virtually disappeared from Communist cinematography, with the notable exception of documentaries on socialist countries that were expressly produced for the party's diehard militants. The attempt to win over at least part of the moderate public was successful: the PCI was about to experience a phase of political and electoral success, which is discussed in the next chapter.

NOTES

1. See *I cannibali. Intervista a Liliana Cavani*, available online at https://www.youtube.com/watch?v=lDT2uHFmg3I (Accessed 24 September 2020).
2. Novelli (2002: 117).
3. For a PCI interpretation of this *squadrismo*, see Paolo Bufalini, 'Una svolta politica che spezzi le trame reazionarie', *L'Unità*, 6 February 1971: front page and p. 4; 'Una lotta di massa popolare contro lo squadrismo. Stroncarlo alle radici' (interview with Enrico Berlinguer), *Rinascita*, 12 February 1971: 3–5. Pietro Secchia wrote a book establishing a parallel between the events of 1921–1922 and the contemporary Fascist assault on democratic institutions (1973).
4. IG, APCI, MF 70, pp. 321–23, Istituti e organismi vari, 25 September 1970.
5. IG, APCI, MF 161, pp. 615–38, Istituti e organismi vari, Unitelefilm, serie 1971.
6. Luigi Perelli's *Emigrazione '68* (Emigration 1968) (32 minutes), for example, cost 6 million lire while grossing just 650,000. However, in cinematic terms *Emigrazione '68* is one of the best films produced by Unitelefilm on the issue of emigration. Its approach is anthropological, rather than political, and it conveys the sense of cultural displacement experienced by Italians working in Ruhr coal basin, Belgium and Switzerland with an unusual effectiveness. The voice-over commentary is by the writer Dacia Maraini. After a brief career as a director of documentaries for UTF, Perelli went on to work for RAI, where he directed numerous TV shows, including a few seasons of the well-known *La Piovra*.
7. *Relazione di Valentini su situazione Unitelefilm*, in IG, APCI, MF 307, pp. 2522–31, Istituti e organismi vari, Unitelefilm, Roma, December 1969.
8. The 'Ufficio cinema' was a sort of sub-committee answerable to the PCI's Cultural Commission. Over time, there were different bodies within the PCI that had responsibility for cinema matters. In the 1940s and 1950s, there was a 'sezione cinematografica' (cinema section), while in the 1960s,

as well as the Ufficio cinema, there was a 'Commissione cinema' (Cinema Commission).

9. IG, APCI, MF 161, pp. 615–38, Istituti e organismi vari, Unitelefilm, 30 November 1971, riservato, in lettura a Berlinguer.

10. The description '*a carattere spettacolare*' appears in a Unitelefilm document signed by Gregoretti, Finzi and Mino Argentieri (who was a member of the PCI's Cinema Commission: see n. 7), in IG, APCI, MF 45, pp. 1720–27, Istituti e organismi vari, Unitelefilm, serie 1973.

11. *Appunti per l'Ufficio di Segreteria. A Napolitano e Galluzzi, con preghiera di urgente parere.* In IG, APCI, MF 52, pp. 1291–93, Istituti e organismi vari, Unitelefilm, serie 1972.

12. *Relazione di Maurizio Ferrara. Al compagno Carlo Galluzzi e, per conoscenza, ai compagni Armando Cossutta e Giorgio Napolitano.* In IG, APCI, MF 52, pp. 1286–89, Istituti e organismi vari, Unitelefilm, 22 January 1972. Riservato.

13. *Lettera di Luciana Finzi alla Sez. Amministrazione, alla Segreteria, a Pajetta e Giorgio Napolitano.* In IG, APCI, MF 42, pp. 1560–63, Istituti e organismi vari, Unitelefilm, 16 March 1973.

14. The most representative film of this strand of politically engaged cinema is probably *Investigation of a citizen above suspicion*, directed by Elio Petri and released in 1970, which won both the Academy Award for Best Foreign Language Film and the Grand Prize at the 1970 Cannes Film Festival.

15. IG, APCI, MF 45, pp. 1720–27, Istituti e organismi vari, Unitelefilm, serie 1973.

16. See the letter from Gregoretti to Giorgio Napolitano, in IG, APCI, MF 65, pp. 433–35, Istituti e organismi vari, Unitelefilm, 22 November 1973.

17. The film is titled *Festival nazionale dell'Unità 1972* and is stored at the AAMOD, Archivio Unitelefilm, codice identificativo: IL8600001412. See the programme for the Festival in *L'Unità*, 17 September 1972: 7.

18. See Roberto Alemanno, 'Un cinema al servizio del Movimento Operaio. La produzione 1972 della Unitelefilm', *L'Unità*, 12 October 1972: 7.

19. The implementation of workers' rights to an education, originally set out in Article 34 of the Constitution, was one of the central aims of the Italian labour movement in the 1970s. Law no. 300 of 20 May 1970, 'Statuto dei lavoratori', established workers' entitlement to time off work so that they could attend 150 hours of evening courses whose objective was the award of a degree. In 1974, Unitelefilm made a fifty-five-minute documentary about this issue, *Le 150 ore* (150 hours), directed by Vladimir Tchertkoff and produced in collaboration with the Federazione Lavoratori Metalmeccanici. It is conserved in the AAMOD, Archivio Unitelefilm, codice identificativo: IL8600001490. On the '150 hours', see Lauria (2011).

20. See the article 'Presentato il film bocciato dall'Ente Statale del cinema' *L'Unità*, 28 September 1972: 6, in which Mino Argentieri claimed that *Trevico–Torino* had not been rejected because of its subject, 'but because of its form, because of its language, which concedes absolutely nothing to the "norms" of entertainment nor to the "taste" of the public'. On Italnoleggio, founded in 1966, see Torri (2002).
21. See 'Applausi e tante domande per "Trevico–Torino"', *L'Unità*, 14 September 1972: 7.
22. 'Presentato il film bocciato dall'Ente Statale del cinema', *L'Unità*, 28 Septebmer 1972: 6.
23. AAMOD Archive, faldone T (Tri—Tut), fascicolo Trevico–Torino.
24. Cinquina (2002: 316).
25. See *L'Unità*, 3 January 1978: 9.
26. On the possible involvement of the US secret service in anti-Communist conspiracies, see *Relazione di Sergio Segre alla riunione della prima commissione del Comitato Centrale*, in IG, APCI, MF 158, pp. 661–63, 4 May 1971. See also Barbagallo (2006: 128).
27. This concept of bourgeois society was one of the ideological mainstays of the German Democratic Republic, for example; see Diner and Gundermann (1996: 124–25).
28. For an analysis of the 1972 election results, see Caciagli (2003: 146–47).
29. On the *Strage di Brescia*, see Franzinelli (2008: 284–325).
30. Evidence on film of the protest against President Leone is in Silvano Agosti's eighteen-minute *Brescia 1974.*
31. The same choice was made by *L'Unità* in its reporting of the funeral; see 'L'estremo omaggio di Brescia e dell'Italia alle sei vittime del terrorismo fascista', *L'Unità*, 2 June 1974: 3.
32. See 'Il 28° anniversario della Repubblica celebrato nel nome della Resistenza. L'esigenza dell'unità democratica e antifascista riaffermata nelle manifestazioni del 2 giugno', *L'Unità*, 3 June 1974: front page.
33. Mino Argentieri, 'Le giornate di Brescia rivissute in un film', *Rinascita*, 9 August 1974: 23.
34. AAMOD, Faldone B, fascicolo *Bianco e Nero.*
35. In IG, APCI, MF 75, pp. 648–52, Note alla segreteria, II bimestre 1974.
36. See 'Lo scandalo del manicomio', an article by Gianni Serra about the production of *Fortezze Vuote*, *Rinascita*, 12 December 1975: 32–33. Serra worked for RAI television; he had directed another feature film on the issue of mental illness, *Dedicato ad un medico* (Dedicated to a doctor) (1973), starring Bruno Cirino, shortly before *Fortezze vuote* was released.
37. For portraits of Franco Basaglia, see Colucci and Di Vittorio (2001); Foot (2015).
38. For the programme of *Psichiatria Democratica*, see Donnelly (2005: 119–22).

200 G. FANTONI

39. See instructions issued to the local branches in IG, APCI, MF: 77, p. 991, Circolari, 10 June 1974.
40. A selection of film reviews of *Fortezze vuote* is conserved in AAMOD, faldone F, fascicolo *Fortezze vuote*.
41. *Perché droga* was the first film directed by Daniele Segre (born 1952), who went on to have a successful career as a director of documentaries, later becoming a teacher at the Centro Sperimentale di Cinematografia. Franco Barbero (born 1944) instead became a well-known character actor in the cinema and television industry.
42. See the interview with Daniele Segre in *Novella 2000*, 11 June 1976, in AAMOD, Faldone P (Pe–Pir), fascicolo *Perchè droga*. See also 'Dibattito su un film sulla droga nella periferia di Torino', *L'Unità*, 29 April 1976: 11.
43. See *L'Unità*, 3 July 1975: 9.
44. See the rather astonished bulletin from the PCI's Ufficio Politico (Political Bureau: the party's executive committee) condemning the invasion, published in *Rinascita*, 23 August 1968. *Rinascita* also republished, from four years before, the Yalta Memorandum, described as 'an example of lucid analysis and political courage in addressing the difficulties faced at that point by the whole labour movement and Communist International, and whose validity has been dramatically confirmed by current events'. See also Ajello (1997: 85–89).
45. See the film's screenplay, including the transcription of interviews with students and citizens of Prague, in AAMOD, Faldone Proposte (Cic—E), fascicolo *Chi ha paura della Cecoslovacchia*. Gianni Toti was a former partisan, filmmaker, video artist and writer who worked for many years as a journalist on *L'Unità*, *Vie Nuove* and *Paese Sera*. See his long obituary, *L'Unità*, 9 January 2007: 25.
46. See, for example, the 'Accordo di produzione e scambio' (Agreement on production and exchange) with Bulgaria, signed by Ugo Gregoretti in 1972, in *L'Unità*, 14 December 1972: 7.
47. Berlinguer's speech is quoted in Barbagallo (2006: 224). Berlinguer also claimed that 'in these [socialist] countries there is a superior moral climate, while capitalist societies are being increasingly harmed by a decline in ideals and moral values, and by ever more widespread processes of corruption and breakdown'.

BIBLIOGRAPHY

Ajello, N. 1997. *Il lungo addio. Intellettuali e PCI dal 1958 al 1991*. Bari-Rome: Laterza.

Arcuri, C. 2004. *Il racconto del Golpe Borghese, il caso Mattei e la morte di De Mauro*. Milan: BUR.

8 THE EARLY 1970S: UNITELEFILM, THE FASCIST THREAT... 201

Barbagallo, F. 2006. *Enrico Berlinguer*. Rome: Carocci.

Bracke, M. 2007. *Which Socialism, Whose Détente? West European Communist and the Czechoslovak Crisis, 1968*. Budapest: CEU Press.

Caciagli, M. 2003. Terremoti elettorali e transazione tra i partiti. In *Partiti e organizzazioni di massa*, ed. F. Malgeri and M. Paggi, 143–168. Soveria Mannelli: Rubettino.

Cazzullo, A. 1998. *I ragazzi che volevano fare la rivoluzione. 1968–1978: storia di Lotta Continua*. Milan: Mondadori.

Cento Bull, A. 2007. *Italian Neofascism: The Strategy of Tension and the Politics of Nonreconciliation*. Oxford: Berghahn Books.

Cinquina, R. 2002. Filmografia. In *Trevico-Cinecittà. L'avventuroso viaggio di Ettore Scola*, ed. V. Zagarrio, 303–324. Venice: Marsilio.

Colucci, M., and P. Di Vittorio. 2001. *Franco Basaglia*. Milan: Bruno Mondadori.

Cooke, P. 2011. *The Legacy of the Italian Resistance*. New York: Palgrave Macmillan.

Diner, D., and Gundermann, C. 1996. On the Ideology of Antifascism. *New German Critique*, No. 67, Legacies of Antifascism, 123–132.

Donnelly, M. 2005. *The Politics of Mental Health in Italy*. Routledge, Electronic Book, Originally Published in 1992.

Foot, J. 2015. *The Man who Closed the Asylums: Franco Basaglia and the Revolution in Mental Health Care*. London: Verso.

Franzinelli, M. 2008. *La sottile linea nera. Neofascismo e servizi segreti da Piazza Fontana a Piazza della Loggia*. Milan: Rizzoli.

Ignazi, P. 1992. *Dal PCI al PDS*. Bologna: il Mulino.

Lauria, F. 2011. *Le 150 ore per il diritto allo studio. Analisi, memorie, echi di una straordinaria esperienza sindacale*. Rome: Edizioni Lavoro.

Miccichè, L. 1995. *Cinema italiano: gli anni sessanta e oltre*. Venice: Marsilio.

Novelli, D. 2002. Il Caso "Trevico—Torino". In *Trevico-Cinecittà. L'avventuroso viaggio di Ettore Scola*, ed. V. Zagarrio, 116–119. Venice: Marsilio.

Panvini, G. 2009. *Ordine nero, guerriglia rossa. La violenza politica nell'Italia degli anni Sessanta e Settanta (1966–1975)*. Turin: Einaudi.

Pons, S. 2007. Berlinguer e la politica internazionale. In *Enrico Berlinguer, la politica italiana e la crisi mondiale*, ed. F. Barbagallo and A. Vittoria, 119–133. Rome: Carocci.

Ruzza, C., and S. Fella. 2005. *Re-inventing the Italian Right. Territorial Politics, Populism, and 'Post-Fascism'*. London: Routledge.

Secchia, P. 1973. *Le armi del fascismo 1921–71*. Milan: Feltrinelli.

Torri, B. 2002. La nascita dell'Italnoleggio. In *Storia del cinema italiano, XI—1965/69*, ed. G. Canova, 419–426. Venice: Marsilio.

Vittoria, A. 2007. *Storia del PCI. 1921–1991*. Rome: Carocci.

CHAPTER 9

Hegemony Within Reach (1974–1976)

In the mid-1970s, the Italian Communist Party reached the peak of its electoral popularity, breathing down the neck of Christian Democracy. Its membership also regained the levels of 1961, after years of decline (Galli 1993: 265). These achievements, alongside, for example, victory in the referendum on divorce in May 1974 and the PCI's definitive legitimization as a democratic force through recognition of the values of the Resistance as fundamental to the Italian Republic, suggested that the party was about to achieve the 'hegemony' that Antonio Gramsci had envisioned. The PCI's electoral and political fortunes had also been in part a consequence of the 'era of collective action', Paul Ginsborg's description of the years between 1969 and 1973 (1990: 298–347). This period of extraordinary levels of political mobilization helped to make left-wing principles such as anti-Fascism and anti-authoritarianism almost universally accepted. In addition, the rise of radical political groups to the left of the PCI, the '*sinistra extraparlamentare*' (extraparliamentary left), allowed the Communist Party to present itself to the moderate Italian public as a mainstream, law-abiding and reassuring political party, which embodied 'a bland and unalarming way of being progressive' (Ajello 1997: 109).

Communist cinema supported the PCI's political successes and electoral growth by producing films targeted at non-Communist voters, which principally aimed to reassure them about the PCI's political moderateness. With respect to the PCI's appeal to centrist voters, the rise of far-left terrorism from the early 1970s onward was especially embarrassing for the

© The Author(s), under exclusive license to Springer Nature Switzerland AG 2021
G. Fantoni, *Italy through the Red Lens*, Italian and Italian American Studies, https://doi.org/10.1007/978-3-030-69197-4_9

203

PCI; it suggested that political violence could not be exclusively attributed to a Fascist ideology, and thus undermined the longstanding claims of Communist propaganda (see Chap. 7). PCI propaganda cinema adopted a double strategy when dealing with far-left terrorism. On one hand, Communist films discussed this phenomenon as infrequently as possible. On the other hand, they firmly denied that left-wing terrorism was actually rooted in Communist ideology and history.

A couple of films produced during this period celebrated the PCI's electoral advancements that occurred between 1975 and 1976. These victories were interpreted as the fulfilment of Togliatti's political strategy and somehow the completion of a political destiny. The PCI also systematized once and for all its own history on behalf of Communist militants, and cinema played a prominent part in this respect. Particularly, two historical events were the object of the historiographical reassessment that was undertaken during this period: the *Resistenza* and the *svolta di Salerno* policy (Salerno turn, discussed in Chap. 1). These were presented as a continuum. In Communist readings, the PCI had played a prominent role in the Resistance against Fascism and Nazism, but all the democratic parties participated in it, and overall the struggle was not aimed at establishing a Socialist society in the post-war years, but just establishing a democratic regime. Togliatti's decision to cooperate with the King and the country's conservative elite (the Salerno turn) demonstrated the Communist leader's sense of responsibility and even patriotism. Both the Resistance and the *svolta di Salerno* were thus ultimately presented as proofs of the PCI's long-term adhesion to the principles of Western-style democracy, and were therefore meant to justify historically the PCI's aspiration to participate in the government of the country.

As mentioned above, the PCI used cinema to celebrate the victories it enjoyed in these years, and the first of these was the victory of the pro-divorce coalition in the referendum on divorce law, held on 12 May 1974. This victory contributed in no small measure to boosting the PCI's popularity. The party seemed to benefit from the referendum result despite the fact that Italian Communists had never really been strong champions of the right to divorce, in that they regarded it as a bourgeois issue. It was only in the 1950s that they had cautiously started to favour legislation granting this right, following the example of the Soviet Union (Bellassai 2000: 158–64). However, the Communist leadership was concerned that a referendum might heighten the ideological and religious differences between Italians, irremediably fracturing the anti-Fascist front and jeopardizing the 'historic compromise' policy. The PCI therefore made every effort to prevent a popular vote on this sensitive issue, for example, by proposing amendments to the legislation that had introduced divorce (Law no. 898 of 1 December 1970). These proposals sought to reach a compromise, before any vote took place, with the Catholic groups that had called for the referendum.[1] After these efforts had all proved futile, however, the party threw itself wholeheartedly into the referendum battle.

Luciano Cheles argues that the referendum campaign, which made extensive use of posters, was one of the most visual since the elections of 1948 and 1953 (2001: 145).[2] It was certainly one of the most cinematographic, at least in relation to the PCI's activity. Instead of making documentaries, Unitelefilm was asked by the party to produce five short election broadcasts of two-and-a-half-minutes each; these were intended for showing in cinemas and were therefore to be addressed to an audience much broader than just Communist voters. For this reason, Unitelefilm, showing some familiarity with the principles of marketing, cast well-known figures to appear in four of them: the speakers were singer and actor Gianni Morandi, actor Gigi Proietti, comedian Pino Caruso, and actor Nino Manfredi. The short broadcasts featuring these personalities show how the Communists tried to divest the vote of its ideological and religious aspects and focus the viewer's attention exclusively on the practical issues of the divorce law. The 'no' vote against repeal of the law permitting divorce is presented as the most reasonable choice.

The only exceptions to this communication strategy are the jibes in the script voiced by Nino Manfredi. In response to the interviewer's question about the abolition of divorce, he lashes out at the hypocrisy of the Catholic Church, which, while championing the abolition of civil divorce, still allowed for the possibility that a religious marriage could be dissolved at the discretion of its highest appeal court, the Roman Rota:

> I have two friends who have obtained annulment of their marriage by the Holy Rota; they had to pay a few million, but he's comfortably off, and he got the annulment for '*impotentia coeundi*', and he's had four kids! For an impotent man, he seems to me to be fairly prolific! However, we're entering the area of faith and miracles here. His wife hasn't taken one lira, because ecclesiastical annulment makes no provision for maintenance. Moral and material protection of the children? What are you protecting? They can't really exist! ... But they seem to be eating!

The broadcast featuring the actor, author, and television personality Pino Caruso also employs satire, promoting the idea that divorce is exclusively a matter of freedom of choice:

> Is going to France forbidden? No! But it's not compulsory either! Whoever wants to can go, and whoever doesn't want to doesn't go. I, for example, have no desire to go to France, and if I was arrogant I'd say: since I'm not going there, no one else should! So what ought we to do? Cancel all passports?

The most reassuring, and arguably 'bourgeois', of these short Communist broadcasts on the referendum stars Gianni Morandi and his wife, actress Laura Efrikian. Set in the couple's comfortable living room, the film presents what appears to be, by any standard, a perfect couple: young, famous, and with two lovely children. Morandi confirms the viewers' first impressions: 'It's not just a cliché if I say that ours is a happy family'. Nonetheless, the happy couple is firmly in favour of the right to divorce, in order to help those couples who are not as fortunate:

> Why should we close our eyes to some sad stories? Why should we pretend that in some torn and divided families the children are happy and the husband and wife should stay together for the rest of their lives?

As it happened, Morandi and Efrikian were to divorce a few years later.

The referendum broadcast directed by Ugo Gregoretti, starring Gigi Proietti, has a somewhat experimental nature. The actor is shown watering plants on a terrace while he keeps saying 'no' to the camera with different facial expressions and tones of voice. This links to the concluding slogan, which is 'Say no, no, and no to the referendum'. According to Gregoretti, this broadcast went down very well in cinemas, in particular because of Proietti's popularity. The reception from the PCI leadership, however, was cool: Gian Carlo Pajetta, for example, commented sarcastically that 'the political analysis really persuades me!' (Medici et al. 2001: 172).

A fifth short broadcast made use of child actors. In a primary school, a teacher explains the importance of family as one of the pillars of society. One boy is mercilessly teased by his classmates because his parents are not married and he does not have his father's name. 'How come your mother and father haven't been able to marry?' the sympathetic teacher asks. 'Papà is waiting for his divorce. But they're saying that this will be abolished', the embarrassed child replies. 'They won't abolish it, you'll see, because the reasons for divorce include helping a family like yours, which is more united than many others', the teacher explains, allowing the little boy to smile once again.

The results of the referendum in due course showed that Italy had undergone irreversible changes in regard to moral values: it had become a secular society. Pier Paolo Pasolini may have been right when he argued that this was particularly due to consumerism's 'hedonistic ideology', which was undermining Catholic values. In the longer term, this was also to undermine the collectivist values in which left-wing thought was grounded.[3] In the short term, however, the winning 'no' vote in the referendum put wind in the PCI's sails.

At the subsequent local elections, in June 1975, the Communist vote increased dramatically, reaching a total of eleven million. The PCI took key Italian cities like Milan and Naples, built on its longstanding majority in the 'red regions', and became the largest party in many other small and medium-size towns and cities. The party leadership interpreted the result as a powerful popular endorsement of the 'historic compromise' policy.[4] This was presented as the only solution for Italy's problems, and had been the principal theme of one of the most intriguing films that the PCI had produced during the 1975 local election campaign: Ettore Scola's *Confronto, partecipazione, unità* (Comparison, involvement and unity) (25 minutes).

The first part of *Confronto, partecipazione, unità*, about nine minutes long, features street interviews and deals with the '*questione comunista*' (Communist issue): the PCI's offer to collaborate with the DC in the 'historic compromise'. The journalist asks questions such as 'Do you think that the Communists could help us to solve the country's problems?' and 'What do you think about the historic compromise?' Responses vary, but overall the interviewees seem to agree that there should be some form of cooperation between the DC and the PCI, either because they believe that it would be to the country's benefit ('United we could achieve a specified objective') or because they believe that there are no real alternatives ('otherwise everything will fall apart').

The film then goes on to tackle other issues in the Communists' election campaign, such as the problem of violence and reform of the state broadcasting service. An ingenious narrative device introduces a fictional episode: we see the journalist trying to interview two women, who refuse to answer as they are rushing to pick up their children from school. Instead of continuing with the interviews, the camera follows the two women and eavesdrops on their conversation. They embody two types of voter: one represents the well-informed, emancipated, and left-wing woman, whereas the other is poorly educated, politically undecided, and strongly influenced by her husband's conservative opinions.

The conversation starts with the second woman making clichéd remarks about politicians being all the same and not caring about people's problems. The banality of these comments provokes a reaction from her companion, who points out that the opposition cannot be held to account for Italy's problems; these should instead be ascribed to the DC politicians who have been in power for thirty years. Even the politically disengaged woman has to agree: ever since she was a child, she remembers DC politicians promising schools, hospitals, and houses for workers, but few of these promises have been kept. However, she says that in her opinion the most serious problems are rising crime and violence. The eruption of widespread and violent crime at the beginning of the 1970s was, for Italy, something of a novelty. It had been fuelling people's imagination, as demonstrated by the emergence of a new cinematographic sub-genre, the '*poliziottesco*', a hyper-violent form of crime fiction. The left-wing woman replies by arguing that crime needs to be seen as the consequence of a dearth of social policy, thanks to successive DC governments. As far as political violence is concerned, governmental collusion with Fascist terrorism cannot really be denied. 'What about the *brigate rosse*, where do they fit in?' asks the other woman. This is an important moment, being the first mention in a PCI production of the Red Brigades, the most ruthless and best organized of the left-wing terrorist groups that were to wreak havoc in the later 1970.[5] The answer from the politically aware character merits close analysis:

> Well, are you really sure that they are 'red'? And then what about the people for whom they serve a purpose? Their chief has been at large for years, so who's left him wandering about like that? And when they put him in prison, who let him escape?[6] By chance, right after [DC] Senator Fanfani's statement on the opposing extremisms …

This dialogue is a faithful reflection of the PCI's analysis, from 1971 until well after the kidnapping of Aldo Moro in March 1978, of the '*sedicenti Brigate Rosse*' (self-styled Red Brigades), to use an expression frequently used by the Communist press: they were seen as a group of provocateurs who were being manipulated by reactionary forces.[7] The existence of terrorist groups that drew their inspiration from Marxist–Leninist doctrine risked alienating the moderate voter. This explains why the PCI remained for a long time in a kind of stubborn denial about the left-wing orientation of the Red Brigades, and why the issue of left-wing terrorism was barely mentioned in Communist cinematography.

Four years were in fact to pass between *Confronto, partecipazione, unità*, and the PCI's next attempt to address the issue of Red Brigade terrorism on film. *Guido Rossa*, a twenty-two-minute documentary directed by Ansano Giannarelli in 1979, was devoted to the murder of the eponymous Communist trade unionist by the Red Brigades on 24 January 1979.[8] After Rossa's assassination, the existence of 'red' terrorism could finally be acknowledged and presented to the militants. The PCI now had its own martyr in the struggle against terrorism: no one could doubt that the Red Brigades were against the PCI, nor that the PCI vehemently opposed the Red Brigades. In *Guido Rossa*, the voice-over commentary, which normally represents the party's official position, acknowledges the existence of 'red terrorism' for the first time, but continues to express doubt about the origins of left-wing terrorism, arguing that ultimately this has its roots in capitalism:

> Since 1970, alongside the [neo-Fascist] variety, another type of terrorism has been developing, which presents itself as 'red'. In the titles of their 300 organisations there are often words like 'red', 'communism', 'proletarians', and 'workers'. And some people … use this feature to imply that the so-called 'red' terrorism has its origins in the thinking, tradition and history of the Communist Party, when instead it was born out of the values of capitalist society.

After this parenthesis on the treatment of terrorism, we now return to *Confronto, partecipazione, unità*. This moves on to focus on another concern of Communist propaganda in the run-up to the 1975 elections: the reform of RAI. Since the late 1960s, the PCI had been battling to free the public broadcasting service from total government control and make it more open to the views of the opposition.[9] The results of the divorce referendum had contributed significantly to the crisis of legitimacy for state television: in shamelessly campaigning for the 'yes' vote, RAI had shown itself to be a mere vehicle for government propaganda and, even worse for a public broadcasting service, had grossly misjudged the public mood

(Ortoleva 1995: 67–68). *Confronto, partecipazione, unità* features the actor Bruno Cirino, in a cinema editing room, complaining about the DC's firm hold on the television news service. Using Unitelefilm archival footage, Cirino presents examples of recent events that have been misreported by television news programmes or not reported at all. Cirino, brother of the DC politician Paolo Cirino Pomicino, was just one of many actors and intellectuals who had expressed their support for the PCI on the eve of the 1975 local elections: striking proof of the PCI's renewed appeal to intellectuals and artists in the mid-1970s (Ajello 1997: 110).

The reform of RAI was finally approved in April 1975, shortly before the elections. According to several authors, the 1975 reform resulted in the '*lottizzazione*' (political carve-up) of the public broadcaster rather than its democratization; the PCI was to receive its share of power and jobs within RAI, although this was smaller than those of the DC and the PSI (Monteleone 1992: 396–98; Ortoleva 2008: 132–34). The most caustic cinematographic depiction of the pervasive influence of political parties on the public broadcasting service after the 1975 reform is probably in the scenes in which Serge Reggiani plays 'Dottor Stiller', a left-wing intellectual working for RAI, in Ettore Scola's *La terrazza* (*The Terrace*) (1980).

The PCI celebrated its performance in the 1975 election by producing two films: Antonio Bertini's thirty-one-minute *Per un'Italia diversa* (In a different Italy) and *Oltre 11 milioni* (More than 11 million) (16 minutes), put together from footage shot by various filmmakers. *Per un'Italia diversa* begins by showing the headlines in the most influential European newspapers, reporting the PCI's success. It then cuts immediately to the final part of Togliatti's speech shown in *Togliatti è ritornato* (see Chap. 2). The message is clear: Togliatti's vision has finally been realized, and the hegemony of the Italian Communist Party is a reality. The film follows this with interviews of newly elected Communist politicians. There is also an interview with the PCI treasurer Guido Cappelloni, who invites activists and sympathizers to join the PCI: a party, he says, that is funded exclusively from membership cards, subscriptions to *L'Unità*, and contributions levied on the salaries of parliamentary deputies and local councillors. Cappelloni concludes by claiming that 'these are our revenue, and we don't want anything else'. Although it might seem incidental to the argument of the film, this last interview conformed to the PCI propaganda that had relentlessly asserted Communist moral superiority. The party had coined a new slogan on this issue, '*Il partito dalle mani pulite*' (the party with clean hands), the intention of which was to signal the difference between the PCI and other political parties in terms of honesty and integrity (Galli 1993: 261; Ginsborg 1990: 371). Cappelloni omits to mention, for understandable reasons, one of the most important sources of the party's income: Soviet funding, which was not a secret but was never publicly discussed.[10]

The other film produced after the election and celebrating the PCI victory, *Oltre 11 milioni*, provides a record of the celebrations in Rome, Genoa, Turin, and Milan in the wake of the announcement of the election results. In colour, it shows Communist militants and supporters gathering in front of Botteghe Oscure, the party's central offices, while they wait for news of the election results on Monday 16 June 1975. Endorsing what could be described as a deterministic reading of the PCI's history, the voice-over explains what had drawn people to the party's headquarters:

> The eagerness to know the next stage of the journey that Togliatti had described so well in just a few words: we have come a long way, and we have a long way yet to go.

As dusk approaches, the crowd begins to rhythmically chant for the PCI leader: 'Ber-lin-guer! Ber-lin-guer!' They also sing the Red Flag and the Internationale. The voice-over commentary tells us what we are seeing:

> The authentic and popular Rome, the Rome of Porta San Paolo, of the partisans of 1944, of Don Morosini, shot by the Germans in the name of liberty, the Rome of progress, and of peace among men.

Porta San Paolo is the area of Rome where there had been a last stand of the Italian army against the invading German forces. Father Giuseppe Morosini had been the inspiration for the character of Don Pietro, played by Aldo Fabrizi, in Roberto Rossellini's *Rome, open city*.

It is already night when the PCI leader, welcomed by the cheering crowd, finally appears on the balcony of the party headquarters. This was one of the few times that Berlinguer appeared in a PCI film; it is interesting that the party rarely used cinematographic propaganda in order to construct a positive image of this leader. The great popularity that he enjoyed in the mid-1970s was particularly due to feature films such as *Berlinguer ti voglio bene* (*Berlinguer: I love you*) (1977) and to left-wing— but not Communist—newspapers such as *La Repubblica* (Ajello 1997:

101–6, 118–19). Berlinguer's personality also played a significant part, as it seemed ideally suited to the small screen. Whereas Togliatti had developed a reputation for his incisive but rather clinical intellectual rigour, Berlinguer's human qualities, such as his modesty and mild demeanour, seemed to endear him to the contemporary audience.

The final part of *Oltre 11 milioni* shows the demonstrations that took place in various cities the day after the election results. Pietro Ingrao is in Genoa and Gian Carlo Pajetta in Turin, while Berlinguer delivers an inspiring speech explaining the reasons for Communist success to an immense red-tinged crowd gathered in Piazza San Giovanni in Rome (Image 9.1):

> The Communist Party is moving forward for three particular reasons. Above all, it is the party closest to the needs and feelings of the working people: it defends their interests and interprets their deepest needs. Second, its general political approach is clear and fair. The third reason for the PCI's advance lies in the fact that Italians, through their many experiences, have become more adult and more aware. For all these reasons, the advance of the Italian

Image 9.1 Berlinguer delivers a speech in Piazza San Giovanni

9 HEGEMONY WITHIN REACH (1974–1976)   213

Communist Party should only arouse fear in the corrupt and domineering
people who reside in our country.

At the end of the film, a performance by the famous flautist Severino
Gazzelloni, which is given almost a full minute, reminds the viewer that
the cultural advancement of the Italian working class is one of the PCI's
objectives.[11]

The process by which the Resistance achieved almost universal recognition as a pillar of the Italian Republic had started in the 1960s and concluded by the mid-1970s (Bermani 1997: 49; Santarelli 1996: 179). This
had played a decisive role in strengthening the democratic legitimacy of
the PCI, and made the putative participation of the Communist Party in
an Italian government more acceptable to the moderate public. The
Resistance and its history were, therefore, of paramount importance to the
PCI. Moreover, the history and memory of the Resistance needed to be
safeguarded from appropriation by the Red Brigades, whose members did
indeed tend to present themselves as successors to the partisans, claiming
that they were carrying out the social and political revolution that the
partisans had been unable to complete because of betrayal by the PCI
(Cooke 2011: 118–25). To add to this, the year 1975 marked the thirtieth
anniversary of the end of the Second World War. For all these reasons, the
PCI asked Unitelefilm to produce a historical documentary on the
Resistance. The production process took longer than expected, however,
because of the historical research needed for such a complex and rather
controversial issue. The film was eventually released in 1976 with the title
'*Resistenza, una nazione che risorge*' (Resistance: a nation that rises
up anew).

This film was divided into five parts, with a total running time of three
hours and forty-five minutes, and featured footage from national and
international archives such as the Imperial War Museum of London and
the Istituto Luce. It included interviews with former leaders of the
Resistance who had belonged to the parties within the Committees of
National Liberation. The editors for the most part used footage from feature films that included Gianni Puccini's *I sette fratelli Cervi* (The seven
Cervi brothers) (1968) and Carlo Lizzani's *Achtung! Banditi!* (1951).
Ansano Giannarelli was the director, while Mino Argentieri wrote the
screenplay in conjunction with the historian Paolo Spriano. Seven differ-
ent actors, among them Stefano Satta Flores and Gigi Proietti, provided

the voice-over commentary. The film was particularly intended for showing in schools, which accounts for its rather didactic tone.

According to Argentieri, the style of *Resistenza, una nazione che risorge* was inspired by Sergio Zavoli's *Nascita di una dittatura* (The birth of a dictatorship), a television programme on the rise of the Fascist dictatorship that had been shown by RAI in 1972, and by Marcel Ophüls' *The Sorrow and the Pity* (1969). Argentieri describes how he and the director Giannarelli wanted to avoid a bombastic celebration of the Resistance; their intention was instead to deliver 'a political history of the Resistance that would be neither comforting nor sweetened', which was to shed light on the differences and clashes between the various parties within the CLN as well as the unity of the Resistance movement (2012: 17). This may well have been how the film was received by viewers in 1976, in the middle of what the historian Cesare Bermani has described as 'the beatification of the Resistance': this expression encapsulates the process whereby the Resistance, once recognized by all political parties apart from the neo-Fascist MSI, as the historical foundation of the Italian Republic, was necessarily presented as a non-divisive issue and was thus inevitably celebrated in a rhetorical and apolitical fashion (1997: 49). To the modern viewer, however, *Resistenza, una nazione che risorge* seems to offer a complete endorsement of the Communist interpretation of the Italian Resistance. Specifically, this documentary aims to convey three fundamental messages which were also the three central elements of the Communist interpretation of the period 1943–1945. First, the Resistance had been a popular movement with the exclusive aim of liberating the country from Fascist tyranny and Nazi occupation. As the title of the film suggests, the Resistance was thus a 'second Risorgimento'. This had been a longstanding topos within Communist propaganda, as discussed in Chap. 2. Second, the Resistance was '*unitaria*' (unifying): each and every political force that belonged to the '*arco costituzionale*' (constitutional span)—an expression that linked together all the parties that had played a part in the drafting and approval of the Italian constitution of 1948—had been jointly involved in the Resistance in one way or another. Pursuing this theme, the screenplay sets the film's ecumenical tone from the very beginning: the list of early anti-Fascist martyrs includes the Communist Gramsci, the Socialist Matteotti, and the Catholic Don Minzoni. Third, the crucial event of the period 1943–1945 was Togliatti's *svolta di Salerno*, a strategic shift that had allowed a unified anti-Fascist front to form and had paved the way for the establishment of Italian democracy. During the 1970s, this interpretation of the *svolta di Salerno* became a key issue for Communist propaganda in that it gave historical legitimacy to the PCI's aspiration to be part of a national coalition government by stressing the party's endorsement of parliamentary democracy as early as 1944.[12] It should be noted that the Communist interpretation of the *svolta di Salerno* was, by and large, accepted by historiography until the end of the 1980s—see, for example, Spriano (1975) and Sassoon (1981). After the eclipse of European communism, however, a new current within the literature started to question the traditional interpretation of this strategy, describing it as engineered by Stalin in order to consolidate the anti-Nazi coalition and to dispel any suspicions that the Soviet Union wished to control post-war Italy.[13]

Resistenza, una nazione che risorge presents political collaboration between Catholics, Socialists and Communists as the precondition for the development of the Resistance movement, and the basis for the most fruitful period in Italian political history, the years 1944–1947. The implicit suggestion is that this kind of alliance, promoted by the PCI with its 'historic compromise' policy, could be the key to future social, political, and economic achievements. The PCI's policy also finds endorsement in the part of the film devoted to the 'partisan republics': the short-lived temporary states established in areas of northern Italy that were liberated by the partisans in the summer and autumn of 1944 (Legnani 1968). In the opinion of the film's directors, these were characterized by 'a daily demonstration of balance and judgement'. The interviewees and the voice-over commentary all stress how this unprecedented experiment in popular government, rather than producing a socialist government, resulted in remarkable examples of unity across all the anti-Fascist forces. Umberto Terracini, the Communist politician and former member of the provisional government of the *Repubblica partigiana dell'Ossola*, states that 'in the partisan republics, the issue of the social renewal of our country was not even presented'. The role of women in the Resistance, although mentioned occasionally, is largely neglected, even though Liliana Cavani had directed an important documentary on this issue, *La donna nella Resistenza* (Women in the Resistance), as early as 1965.

Resistenza, una nazione che risorge received mainly positive reviews. In *Paese Sera*, the Communist Gianni Rodari praised the impartiality of the film, which in his opinion had not been dependent on any preconceived notions.[14] In April 1976, *Resistenza, una nazione che risorge* was shown in two high schools in Rome, where it was introduced by Terracini.[15] The following year, the ARCI included the documentary in the programme for its circuit in celebration of the thirty-second anniversary of Italy's liberation.[16] The film had limited distribution, however, and grossed just 410,000 lire at the box office.[17]

In 1976, the production of another film in several parts, *Quattro lezioni su Togliatti* (Four lessons on Togliatti), completed the PCI's reassessment of its own history. The four filmed lessons on Togliatti's thought, as in *Resistenza, una nazione che risorge*, allow the past to articulate the present. The intention, however, was to address party activists rather than students. Each lesson is given by a prominent member of the PCI leadership aided by archival footage, and has a running time of thirty minutes. In the first lesson, '*Togliatti e le grandi componenti della società italiana*' (Togliatti and the major elements of Italian society), Gerardo Chiaromonte addresses the *svolta di Salerno* once again, rebutting the criticisms that radical left-wing groups were putting forward in the 1970s. Supported by some historians, they had accused Togliatti of having conspired to limit the social and political aspirations of Italian workers in the period 1944–1947, while the Italian proletariat had actually been politically ready and strong enough to start a revolution.[18] Chiaromonte laid out his argument on this:

> There has been much discussion of the *svolta di Salerno* across this whole period. Some people have talked about a missed revolutionary opportunity, while others, more charitably, have said that action by the advance guard of [socialist] democracy was held back by the presence of foreign troops in our country.

Chiaromonte rejects these interpretations, arguing that Togliatti's strategic approach had stemmed from careful consideration of Italian history and its principal aim had been to prevent Fascism from prevailing once again, as it had managed to do after the First World War by exploiting the divisions among Italy's democratic forces. He stresses that the pursuit of unity has been inspiring Communist policy ever since. This is demonstrated by, for example, the PCI's vote in 1947 in favour of Article 7, which incorporated the Lateran Pacts (the agreements made in 1929 between the Fascist government and the Vatican) into the Italian constitution. The desire for unity is also the basis for the 'historic compromise' policy:

Now more than ever before, I believe, can we see the validity of the policy that Togliatti suggested. Our country's crisis is profound, economic, political, moral, social, and also cultural. There is no escape from this unless we return to the ideals of the Republic's constitution and the anti-Fascist Resistance: to the ideals that drove Palmiro Togliatti forward in the early years of his activity in Italy.

The second lesson, *Rapporto tra democrazia e socialismo* (The relationship between democracy and socialism), is given by Giorgio Napolitano and has the primary aim of demonstrating that the PCI has democratic credentials. Napolitano says that the Italian Communist Party's endorsement of Western-style democracy is deeply rooted in its history. In particular, the concept of 'progressive democracy' that Togliatti had developed in 1944, in Napolitano's account, resolved the dilemma that socialism faced when it came up against bourgeois democratic institutions. Having finally reconciled socialism and parliamentarism, the PCI is perfectly entitled to take part in a democratic government. The involvement of the Italian Communists in the government would not even be that much of a novelty, given that they had been in government alongside the other anti-Fascist parties between 1944 and 1947. Napolitano presents the process that had led to the party's endorsement of Western democratic values as a perfectly logical development of Italian Communist thought and praxis, although the future president of the Italian Republic acknowledges that there have been 'contradictions and even lulls' along the way. His interpretation notably implies that the fifty-five years that have passed since the founding of the party have been nothing more than a period of preparation for the present moment, in which history is finally fulfilled. This kind of determinism was consistent with the ideas that the Italian Communists had always had about history, which was seen as a linear and logical development towards a specific end (Ballone 1994: 134). This had first been seen as a Communist revolution, then as a peaceful transition to a socialist regime, and now, Napolitano seems to suggest, as the much less ambitious involvement in the government of the country.

The third lesson, *Togliatti e il partito nuovo* (Togliatti and the new party), given by Alessandro Natta, future leader of the PCI, concerns the 'new party'. He argues that the creation of this mass-based party, which Togliatti worked for at the end of the war, is proof of the PCI's endorsement of democracy from 1944 onwards, if not before.

The fourth and final lesson, *Analisi del fascismo e dell'antifascismo in Togliatti* (Togliatti's analysis of Fascism and anti-Fascism), delivered by Gian Carlo Pajetta, reminds the Italian working class, described as 'the national class that bears the responsibility for hegemony', of its fundamental duty to obstruct the return of Fascism. Any other issue, whether we are in 1944 or in 1976, has to be seen as secondary:

> Today, the serious danger, which has already reared its head in recent years, is that conservative forces, reactionary forces, forces of the Catholic Right, or the forces that run Christian Democracy should give way to the Right. We need to realize that this is the fundamental issue, and remember our past experiences [of Fascism's victory].

Collectively, the *Quattro lezioni su Togliatti* were intended to provide the party's militants with an explanation of the policy of historic compromise that rooted it firmly in PCI history. In particular, the aim was to assuage the dismay that had been felt at the party's grass-roots as a result of Berlinguer's proposal of an alliance with the DC, which many militants still struggled to accept.[19]

However, this alliance appeared to be the only practicable solution after the national elections of 20 June 1976, at which the PCI increased its share of the vote to 34.4 per cent, but the DC managed to recover from its electoral decline of the previous years by winning 38.8 per cent of the votes cast. This brought the country to a political impasse: the DC could not form a stable government without some support from the PCI, but on the other hand Communist involvement in the government was out of the question due to the vehement opposition not only of right-wingers within Christian Democracy but also, and perhaps more importantly, of both the United States and the Soviet Union.[20]

While the PCI had reached the peak of its electoral popularity, it was immediately clear to its leadership that this result, far from opening the road towards profound political and social change, had placed the party in a situation of uncertainty: '*in mezzo al guado*' (literally, 'in the middle of the ford', or 'in deep water'), according to an expression coined at about that time. This described the 'catch-22' that the PCI found itself in after the election. It could no longer express strong political opposition to the DC government, as this would make the country ungovernable, but at the same time it could not participate in the government. The party was to pay a high price, both electorally and politically, because of this paradoxical situation. The possibility that the PCI could achieve political hegemony, which had emerged between 1974 and 1976, was destined to fade rapidly in the years that followed. Before discussing how the party's cinematographic output reflected its incipient political crisis during the period 1977–1979, it is important to analyse the films devoted to the feminist issue. By the mid-1970s the feminist movement was in fact becoming an important social and political phenomenon, which presented the PCI with some complex problems. This is the topic of the next chapter.

NOTES

1. See *Appunti su divorzio e referendum*, in IG, APCI, MF 66, pp. 897–907, Divorzio e referendum, 1 December 1973. This classified document summarizes PCI policy on the issue of the referendum, saying that 'the quest for an agreement between all the parties across the political spectrum has always been inspired, and in this case explicitly driven, by democratic and unifying political needs: that is, by the need to overcome opposition and heal wounds, to the heart of the popular masses and to the democratic forces, that are harmful and unnecessary'. In conclusion, according to the unnamed author, the referendum on divorce 'would promote the action of anti-democratic forces'.
2. For a range of PCI posters on divorce, see Novelli (2000: 226–29).
3. See Pier Paolo Pasolini, 'Gli italiani non sono più quelli', *Corriere delle Sera*, 10 June 1974. This is reproduced in Pasolini (2006: 39–44).
4. See the analysis of the vote in 'Dichiarazione di Berlinguer', *L'Unità*, 17 June 1975: 1, 8 and 9.
5. On the Red Brigades, see Lumley (1998: 255–72); Bianconi (2003); Clementi (2007).
6. This is a reference to Renato Curcio's escape from Casale Monferrato prison thanks to a raid by a Red Brigades unit, led by Curcio's wife Mara Cagol, on 18 February 1975. See Zavoli (1992: 201–2).
7. See the early short articles published in *L'Unità* reporting the first activities of this new and unknown terrorist group, 'Due gravi provocazioni, un unico disegno', *L'Unità*, 7 January 1971: 2; 'Provocazione all'ATAC', *L'Unità*, 18 April 1971: 10. As regards 1975, a statement by the PCI leadership, 'Debellare il terrorismo e la violenza Fascista', does not even mention left-wing terrorism. Instead, it discusses 'tendencies, present in extremist groups, to have recourse to physical encounters, violent reprisals, and adventurism'. See *L'Unità*, 24 April 1975: 1 and 14.

8. Ansano Giannarelli was an important documentary director who subsequently worked on several productions for the PCI in the 1970s; see Chaps. 9 and 10. He is also known for his experimental feature film *Sierra Maestra* (1969). On his filmmaking, see Medici (2017).

9. See 'Informazione e potere nella società Italiana', a special issue of *Rinascita*'s monthy supplement *Il Contemporaneo* devoted to the Communist struggle to reform RAI, including articles by PCI television experts Carlo Galluzzi, Ivano Cipriani and Dario Natoli: *Rinascita*, 30 April 1971: 15–22. See also Partito Comunista Italiano (1973). Finally, see a film produced by Unitelefilm after the elections of 1968, Massimo Andrioli's *Le antenne del potere* (Power's aerials) (15 minutes), which uses the narrative device of a fictitious TV bulletin to attack the partisan nature of news broadcasting on Italian television and the lack of courage of RAI's management in regard to cultural choice. This film includes a speech by PCI leader Longo on the reform of RAI.

10. See Cervetti (1993). Enrico Berlinguer gave Gianni Cervetti, a member of the PCI who graduated in Economics at Moscow University, the task of putting an end to Soviet financial support: this stopped completely in 1981. The existence of this funding was revealed by Cervetti himself in 1991; see Vittorio Ragone, 'Enrico mi disse: basta con quei soldi', *L'Unità*, 16 October 1991: 5. This issue was brought up again years later with the aggressive aim of demonstrating the strict dependence of the PCI on the USSR during the Berlinguer era; see Bigazzi and Riva (1999).

11. For an account of the Piazza San Giovanni celebrations, see Fiori (1989: 261–62). See also 'Ha vinto la linea dell'unità delle forze popolari', *L'Unità*, 18 June 1975: 2.

12. See the special issue of *Il Contemporaneo* devoted to the *svolta di Salerno*, with articles by historians Ernesto Ragionieri, Enzo Santarelli and Paolo Spriano, and by prominent PCI figures including Giorgio Amendola, Gian Carlo Pajetta, Gherardo Chiaromente and Alessandro Natta, *Rinascita*, 29 March 1974: 11–36.

13. Gallerano and Flores (1992); Narinskij (1994). For an overview of the historiographical and political debate on the *svolta di Salerno* in the 1990s, see Fantoni (2014).

14. Gianni Rodari, 'Resistenza illustrata per la scuola', *Paese Sera*, 5 March 1976, p. 3.

15. 'Al Liceo Cavour lezioni di Resistenza con film e dibattito', *Corriere della Sera*, 7 May 1976.

16. 'La "Resistenza" ma senza retorica', *La Repubblica*, 14 April 1977.

17. AAMOD, Faldone 'R', fascicolo *Resistenza una nazione che risorge*.

18. See, for example, Galli (1977).

19. For further discussion of this issue, see Barbagli and Corbetta (1979: 54).

20. On US hostility to Communist involvement in government, see the compelling analysis by the RAI United States correspondent Rodolfo Brancoli (1976). For an analysis of the USSR leadership's perspective on this issue, see Barbagallo (2006: 233–40). For a general overview of Berlinguer's policy during this period, see Pons (2007).

BIBLIOGRAPHY

Ajello, N. 1997. *Il lungo addio. Intellettuali e PCI dal 1958 al 1991*. Bari-Rome: Laterza.

Argentieri, M., and A. Giannarelli. 2012. *Resistenza, una nazione che risorge*. Reggio Calabria: Città del sole.

Ballone, A. 1994. Storiografia e storia del PCI. *Passato e Presente*, 12 (33): 129–46.

Barbagallo, F. 2006. *Enrico Berlinguer*. Rome: Carocci.

Barbagli, M., and P. Corbetta. 1979. Una tattica e due strategie. Inchiesta sulla base del PCI. In *Dentro Il Pci*, ed. M. Barbagli, P. Corbetta, and S. Salvatore, 9–60. Bologna: il Mulino.

Bellassai, S. 2000. *La morale comunista. Pubblico e privato nella rappresentazione del P.C.I. (1947–1956)*. Rome: Carocci.

Bermani, C. 1997. *Il nemico interno, guerra civile e lotta di classe in Italia (1943–1976)*. Rome: Odradek.

Bianconi, G. 2003. *Mi dichiaro prigioniero politico: storia delle Brigate Rosse*. Turin: Einaudi.

Bigazzi, F., and V. Riva. 1999. *Oro da Mosca. I finanziamenti sovietici al PCI dalla rivoluzione d'ottobre al crollo dell'URSS*. Milan: Mondadori.

Brancoli, R. 1976. *Gli Usa e il PCI. Le personalità della politica e della cultura americana di fronte al "rischio Italia" dopo il 15 giugno*. Milan: Garzanti.

Cervetti, G. 1993. *L'oro di Mosca*. Milan: Baldini&Castoldi.

Cheles, L. 2001. Picture Battles in the Piazza: the Political Posters. In *The Art of Persuasion. Political Communication in Italy from 1945 to the 1990s*, ed. L. Cheles and L. Sponza, 124–179. Manchester and New York: Manchester University Press.

Clementi, M. 2007. *Storia delle Brigate Rosse*. Rome: Odradek.

Cooke, P. 2011. *The Legacy of the Italian Resistance*. New York: Palgrave Macmillan.

Fantoni, G. 2014. After the fall: politics, the public use of history and the historiography of the Italian Communist Party, 1991–2011. *Journal of Contemporary History* 49 (4): 815–836.

Fiori, G. 1989. *Vita di Enrico Berlinguer*. Rome-Bari: Laterza.

Gallerano, N., and M. Flores. 1992. *Sul PCI. Un'interpretazione storica*. Bologna: il Mulino.

Galli, G. 1977. *Storia del Partito Comunista Italiano*. Milan: Bompiani.
———. 1993. *Storia del Partito Comunista Italiano*. Milan: Kaos Edizioni.
Ginsborg, P. 1990. *A History of Contemporary Italy. Society and Politics 1944 – 1989*. London: Penguin.
Legnani, M. 1968. *Politica e amministrazione nelle repubbliche partigiane*. Milan: Istituto Nazionale per la Storia del Movimento di Liberazione.
Lumley, R. 1998. *Dal '68 agli anni di piombo. Studenti e operai nella crisi italiana*. Florence: Giunti.
Medici, A. 2017. *Il cinema saggistico di Anzano Giannarelli*. Turin: Lindau.
Medici, A., M. Morbidelli, and E. Taviani, eds. 2001. *Il PCI e il cinema tra cultura e propaganda (1959 – 1979)*. Rome: Aamod.
Monteleone, F. 1992. *Storia della radio e della televisione in Italia. Società, politica, strategia, programmi 1922–1992*. Venice: Marsilio.
Narinskij, M.M. 1994. Togliatti, Stalin e la Svolta di Salerno. *Studi Storici* 35 (3): 657–666.
Novelli, E. 2000. *C'era una volta il PCI. Autobiografia di un partito attraverso le immagini della sua propaganda*. Rome: Editori Riuniti.
Ortoleva, P. 1995. *Un Ventennio a colori. Televisione privata e società in Italia (1975 – 95)*. Florence: Giunti.
———. 2008. 'La televisione italiana 1974 - 2002: dall'"anarchie italienne" al duopolio imperfetto'. In *La Stampa italiana nell' età della Tv. Dagli anni settanta ad oggi*, ed. V. Castronovo and N. Tranfaglia. Bari: Laterza.
Pasolini, P.P. 2006. *Scritti Corsari*. Milan: Garzanti.
Pons, S. 2007. Berlinguer e la politica internazionale. In *Enrico Berlinguer, la politica italiana e la crisi mondiale*, ed. F. Barbagallo and A. Vittoria, 119–133. Rome: Carocci.
Santarelli, E. 1996. *Storia critica della repubblica. L'Italia dal 1945 al 1994*. Milan: Feltrinelli.
Sassoon, D. 1981. *The Strategy of the Italian Communist Party. From the Resistance to the Historic Compromise*. London: Pinter.
Spriano. 1975. *La Resistenza, Togliatti e il Partito Nuovo, vol. V of the Storia del Partito comunista italiano*. Turin: Einaudi.
Zavoli, S. 1992. *La notte della repubblica*. Rome: Nuova ERI.

CHAPTER 10

Women's Issues, Feminism, and the PCI

PCI cinematography had only sporadically addressed women's political and social issues prior to the 1970s, and there is a particularly conspicuous absence of films devoted to women in the early production history. This was consistent with the ideology of a party that barely acknowledged the existence of women as a specific social group, and was therefore ill-equipped to analyse the problems that they typically faced in Italian society. Women's issues, in the Communist view, were simply an aspect of the wider and more important struggle to achieve emancipation of the working class, and they would finally be resolved once socialist society had been firmly established. In the course of the 1970s, however, the emergence of feminism (or second-wave feminism as it is often described to distinguish it from that which occurred during the nineteenth and early twentieth century) forced the PCI into a fundamental reconsideration of this stance. Most of its films that address women and their issues were therefore produced in precisely these years.

This chapter traces the party's cinematographic engagement with women from the foundation of Unitelefilm onwards, and draws some conclusions regarding the evolution of the Italian Communist outlook on women's issues. Because it was designed to address Communist, and increasingly from the 1960s non-Communist voters, PCI cinema dealing with the problems of women provides a privileged viewpoint to appreciate how the Communist stance on women issues evolved, at first rather slowly during the 1960s and more markedly after 1973. After that year,

© The Author(s), under exclusive license to Springer Nature Switzerland AG 2021
G. Fantoni, *Italy through the Red Lens*, Italian and Italian American Studies, https://doi.org/10.1007/978-3-030-69197-4_10

223

Communists showed some appreciation of the new themes the feminist movement had introduced in the political debate, such as patriarchy, sexuality as a political issue, and reproductive rights. This is mirrored by films such as *La donna é cambiata, l'Italia deve cambiare* (Women have changed, and Italy has to change, 1976), *Non ci regalano niente* (Nothing comes for free, 1977), and although less explicitly also by earlier films such as Cecilia Mangini's *Essere donne* (Being women, 1965). However, the same films also reveal that, well into the 1970s, fundamental differences continued to exist between what can be generally defined as the Italian feminist movement (which was, however, a collection of groups having different opinions on specific issues) and the PCI's apparatus. The chapter argues that the PCI and feminists principally disagreed on one point: the conceptualization of motherhood as either a matter of social importance, and this was the PCI's view, or a private matter, which was the feminists' take on the problem. The well-known clash between the Communist Party and some of the feminist groups in the issue of abortion ultimately depended on the different notion of motherhood they held. PCI films show how feminists and Communists were engaged in a sort of semantic war: 'feminist movement' as opposed to 'women movement'; 'liberation' versus 'emancipation'; abortion as a 'right' or as a 'social injustice'.

Women belonging to the PCI were at the forefront of this struggle, and some of them, being both Communist and feminist, lived through what must have been an intense but also tormented political season. Carla Ravaioli was one of them. In a book she published in 1976 she claimed that when women thought of political psarties that they sought to involve in the women's and feminist struggle, they could not have thought of conservative parties, for the women movement was a revolutionary movement that aimed to undermine the traditional man–woman relationship. This was 'ultimately functional to the current capitalist mode of production' (p. 11).

This quotation allows a further reflection, which, I would argue, sheds some light on the ultimate reason why an understanding between the PCI and the whole of the feminist movement was problematic. Carla Ravaioli's words seemed to suggest that she saw patriarchy as being instrumental to capitalism. This opinion originated in socialist feminism; a variant of the feminist thought born out of the New-Left (Eisenstein 1978). According to socialist feminists, capitalism had incorporated patriarchy in its system of oppression, perpetuating and reinforcing it. Fighting patriarchy therefore meant weakening capitalism. However, not all the groups of the Italian feminist movement stemmed from socialist feminism and the nexus between capitalism and the oppression of women was not accepted by all the feminists, or not to the same extent. The *Movimento di Liberazione della donna* (MDL, *Woman Liberation Movement*) was an example of this not anti-capitalist feminism. A constructive dialogue between the PCI and fringes of the feminist movement was therefore made difficult by the fact that they did not share the same anti-capitalist views. Besides, the emphasis on women's individual choice, which was more or less common to the whole of the feminist movement, was at odds with the type of society Communists wanted to build. This was supposed to be based on collectivist values. We can therefore argue that, ultimately, the PCI and feminists also differed as far as the primary objective of their political struggle was concerned.

Nonetheless, the PCI and important sections of the feminist movement did forge alliances on specific issues, such as divorce and eventually abortion too. PCI leaders were increasingly willing to make amends for the sluggishness the party had shown in welcoming feminist ideas. Finally, the Unione Donne Italiane (UDI—Union of Italian Women), which had been established by the left-wing parties following the war to organize women voters, was, in the second half of the 1970s, a component of the Italian feminist movement in its own right.[1]

Interestingly, when the PCI produced films devoted to women, it relied for the most part on collaboration with external agencies. *Essere donne* (Being women) (1965, 28 minutes), the second film produced by Unitelefilm after *L'Italia con Togliatti* (see Chap. 4) and the first PCI film specifically devoted to gender issues, is a case in point.[2] According to a statement made by its director Cecilia Mangini, the idea of the film came from the party, and specifically from Luciana Castellina, who wanted to produce a film that addressed the problems of working women.[3] Castellina granted complete freedom with respect to both content and style to Mangini, who was an independent filmmaker working for the party for the first time. The latter asked for the voice-over commentary to be written by Felice Chilanti.[4] Giuliana Dal Pozzo was also involved as project consultant and contributed to writing the voice-over; she had been editor of *Noi Donne*, the magazine of the (UDI), and was subsequently a pioneer within Italian feminism. Although it was not intended for use as a propaganda film and was in fact entered for the quality awards, *Essere donne* has themes

226   G. FANTONI

that were typical of contemporary Communist propaganda: the illusory nature of the economic miracle, the deficiencies of the centre-left governments with regard to social care, and capitalist exploitation in the factories.

Essere donne begins with images from fashion magazines, which present the supposed ideal woman of the early 1960s: elegantly dressed, beautiful and sophisticated. While Bertolt Brecht and Kurt Weill's cheerful 'Alabama Song' plays, colourful photographs of models are intercut with black and white footage of nuclear blasts, probably a tribute to the recently released *Dr Strangelove* (1964). This results in a rather curious reminder of the transient nature of earthly life, echoed in the song by the line 'I tell you we must die'.

The voice-over commentary, however, turns quickly to the political, arguing that the magazines' images of fashionable women serve to hide the grim reality of the exploitation that characterizes capitalism. Moreover, 'who can see themselves in these images?' the voice-over asks rhetorically, going on to give the answer: certainly not any of the six million ordinary Italian women who go out to work every day. The film then goes on a journey to find the real women obscured by the images in the magazines, which provide a smokescreen for 'the contradictions and violence of our society'. We see a fifteen-year-old girl working ten hours a day in a pasta factory in Puglia, and girls using precision machinery in a Philips industrial plant in northern Italy. In both situations the girls are exploited, enduring different but equally tough working conditions. The documentary, however, does not demonize factory work. The voice-over commentary in fact claims that the modern world begins just inside the factory gates: factory work provides higher wages and greater social dignity, and for thousands of girls, especially in the South, offers the only opportunity for emancipation. We see a young peasant woman looking from afar at the Superga shoe factory, which is surrounded by a large agricultural estate where scores of women are working as day-labourers. Life is hard for peasants and factory workers alike, but at least the women in the factories can look forward to improvements, in part because of new legislation. To alleviate the lives of working women, a woman in a northern factory argues, the government should build nurseries and give workers the '*settimana corta*' (short week) with Saturdays off; they would then have a more manageable balance between work and family life.

At no point, however, does the film mention a fair division of domestic chores between men and women as part of the solution to the problem. This was consistent with how the whole matter of the 'woman question' had been framed since 1945 by the PCI and the UDI. Because the Communists had focused exclusively on the '*emancipazione della donna*', by which they meant the social and economic emancipation of Italian women by their gradual entry into labour, they saw the problems that women faced as essentially political and economic; they were thus incapable of acknowledging that the oppression of women also related to cultural factors (Lilli and Valentini 1979: 42–43). Consequently, women's only adversary was the government, which should be enforcing women's right to work through legislative measures.

In *Essere donne*, the voice-over repeatedly stresses that the problems faced by women highlighted in the documentary are fundamentally of a political nature and ultimately due to capitalism, as can be seen in its description of the conditions of the women day-labourers in Puglia:

> They head off towards long hours of working the fields. Their toil will have scarce reward due to the laws of profit, imposed by the central offices of the monopolies, in the North, on even the most distant village in the South.

At other points, however, the voice-over seems to acknowledge that due to the culture and social structure of Italian society, women suffer injustices additional to the economic exploitation that male and female workers both endure:

> And so, for this day too, women day-labourers and factory workers will be paid an unjust wage. Just like the men. But women are still also bearing the weight of their old and traditional subjection.

Later, these injustices are mentioned again:

> In every field of production we see the working woman. Too often, even today, she is given the most unrewarding and monotonous tasks: those that the man either can't do, or doesn't want.

These comments, which probably came from Giuliana dal Pozzo, indicate an awareness of the issues of patriarchy and the cultural subordination of women.

Essere donne also tackles the issue of abortion: a woman, not seen on screen, talks about twice having had an abortion, at that point a crime in Italy, because she could not afford to leave her job to take care of yet another baby.

228   G. FANTONI

The film's final scene offers a message of hope for the future. We see a determined young woman climbing a long flight of stairs, while the voice-over stresses the prominent role that women play in the labour movement and alludes to the socialist society of the future in which women's emancipation will finally be achieved:

> [The woman], alongside the male workers, defends the factories. She fights alongside the male day-labourers to eliminate the backwardness of the South. She has paid in person wherever people struggle for the power to make decisions, and also where they protest against the perils of war; she knows that she cannot expect her liberation other than from herself. In a new society, where each person's free development is a condition for the free development of all.

Women's problems will thus only finally be resolved after the advent of socialism, just like virtually every other problem in the Communist political narrative.

The film is visually arresting and effective in its communication of the sense of alienation experienced by factory workers. This can be attributed to Mangini's style of direction, which focuses on details such as people's eyes, their quick glances and then their hands in motion, and to the film's rapid alternation of images, which emphasizes the rhythm of production that the assembly line imposes on the workers. The most remarkable scene was shot at the Philips factory and shows a timekeeper circling above the workers, mostly young women, while a new component appears in front of them every few seconds (Image 10.1). To obtain permission to film in the factory, Mangini passed herself off as a director working for RAI .[5]

Essere donne was the first film ever submitted by Unitelefilm to the quality awards, in 1965, and it was excluded. The Communist press protested vociferously, citing 'ideological censorship'.[6] It was pointed out that the film's rejection could hardly have been due to lack of the 'minimum technical and artistic requirements' specified in Law no. 1213, as it had just been awarded a prize at the Leipzig Documentary Film Festival by a jury that included renowned directors such as Joris Ivens and John Grierson.[7] In the opinion of the left-wing journalist Bruna Bellonzi, who published a long article in *Noi Donne* that included an interview with Mangini, the exclusion of *Essere donne* was for cultural rather than political reasons:

10 WOMEN'S ISSUES, FEMINISM, AND THE PCI   229

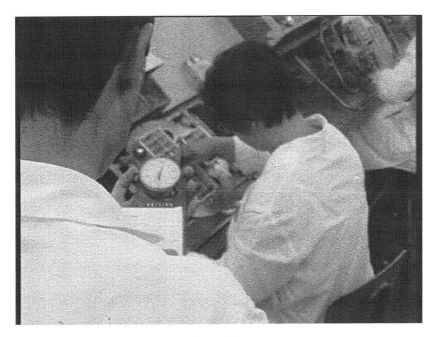

Image 10.1 The timekeeper and the worker

In a world where femininity is seen as sacred, where women's fate is presented as a something to be grateful for, where sacrifice, self-denial and submission are extolled as the desirable qualities of the wife and mother, a frank discussion of the extent to which women's position is misconceived, absurd, unacceptable and unfair was judged to be insufficiently entertaining.

Four years passed before the PCI decided to devote another film entirely to women. *Sabato, domenica, lunedì* (Saturday, Sunday, Monday) was produced by the PCI's Sezione Femminile (Women's Section) as part of the Communist propaganda campaign prior to the 1968 elections, and was directed by Ansano Giannarelli. This twenty-five-minute documentary deals with the quality of life of working women and is in many respects a sequel to *Essere donne*, from where it takes most of its archival footage. The film is presented as a realistic 'slice of life' tale of three women who live in the outskirts of Milan, Caterina, Savina, and Maria, over Saturday, Sunday, and Monday. 'Three ordinary days for three ordinary women.

230 G. FANTONI

Three days like so many others during the year. Three women like so many others in the city', runs the opening line of the voice-over commentary written by the Communist journalist Miriam Mafai. The message of the film is entrusted both to the voice-over, which comments on some of the images and provides information and statistics that demonstrate the exploitation of working women, and to scenes without commentary that capture moments of the three women's lives. These include the meeting of the shop-floor committee at Maria's factory and Sunday lunch at Caterina's house. The film also features street interviews with working women recorded outside the gates of factories in Milan.

Sabato, domenica, lunedì, like *Essere donne*, addresses perennial issues of Communist propaganda such as the government's inadequate provision for industrial workers, the unsustainable cost of living and inadequacy of public transport in big Italian cities, and the incidence of occupational illnesses due to a dehumanizing production system. As in *Essere donne*, the problems women face are presented as ultimately aspects of the more general issue of the emancipation of the working class. However, also as in *Essere donne*, the voice-over in addition maintains that the position of working women is especially difficult. Women suffer discrimination at work ('women are paid less, exploited more, and are the first to be sacked') and shoulder the responsibility for household chores ('Sunday is a day like any other, with a break coming in the form of a different task'). The film highlights the effects of this discrimination by delving into the psychological state of its protagonists: Caterina, Savina, and Maria are constantly plagued by worries, including 'the fear of falling pregnant, the fear of getting the sack, and the fear of not managing'. However, *Sabato, domenica, lunedì* was a Communist propaganda film produced for the election campaign of 1968, and its ultimate aim was to convey a positive message about the workers' determination to fight for a better future. The film's final scenes therefore show Sabina going to Rome for a demonstration demanding legislation for the establishment of state nurseries, and Maria attending a rally on Vietnam.

As mentioned earlier, the rise of the feminist movement forced the PCI to review its policy and stance on women's issues in the second half of the 1970s. According to Donald Sassoon, the economic and social factors that encouraged the development of Italian feminism included women's increased access to education and employment and the reduction in the birth rate during the 1960s (1997: 107–17). The cultural impact of student and worker protest also played a crucial part. At the beginning of the

1970s, a small but significant number of left-wing women, taking much of their inspiration from American feminism, set up groups such as Rivolta Femminile, Lotta Femminista, and the Movimento di Liberazione della Donna.[8] By the middle of the decade, they were creating substantial political and cultural problems for the PCI due to their innovative approach to women's issues. The feminist movement shifted the focus away from the relationship between women and society and towards the relationship between men and women.

Unlike the PCI and its allied organization, the UDI, the feminist movement did not see the oppression of women in contemporary society as simply a by-product of their social exclusion. Instead, it attributed this oppression to cultural factors, and in particular to the patriarchal mentality characteristic of society at all levels, thus pervading the working class just as much as the bourgeoisie. In contrast to the idea of 'emancipation', understood in the Communist sphere as the economic emancipation of women as a group within society, the feminist movement championed 'women's liberation', meaning the personal liberation of every woman from cultural oppression. This approach challenged the strategy that the left-wing parties and the UDI had previously pursued, and had the potential to split the labour movement along gender lines (Rodano 2010: 214). Moreover, since the late 1960s, some fringe feminist groups had been describing Marxism as an ideology pervaded by patriarchal culture, and therefore of no use to women in their quest for liberation.[9] As this view was completely unacceptable to the Communists, it had resulted in numerous severe rebukes for the feminist movement from prominent PCI figures, both male and female, in the early 1970s. For example, Enrico Berlinguer in 1972 claimed: 'the feminists have chosen the wrong battle, men and women cannot be set against each other' (quoted by Valentini 1997: 361). The following year Communist parliamentary deputy Nilde Iotti braded the feminist movement as essentially 'bourgeois': 'I do not depreciate'—she said—'bourgeois feminists, but I doubt the impact of their actions among the masses' (quoted by Bracke 2014: 73). However, public statements by feminists on women's issues did not go unnoticed, and eventually some of the ideas that feminist groups were promoting found their way into Communist discourse, especially influencing UDI members. The ninth national congress of the UDI in 1973, in particular, launched a process of rapprochement with the feminist world; members of feminist collectives were invited and their approach to women's issues was discussed in a critical but constructive fashion.[10] Many UDI members joined feminist groups as a result, starting what has been described as '*doppia militanza*' (dual activism): their simultaneous membership of one of these groups and the PCI. Moreover, while the principal focus of the political debate was the issue of divorce, feminists and women militants within the PCI found themselves on the same side of the barricades.

However, the resounding 'no' vote in the referendum on divorce was followed by a major disagreement between the PCI and part of the feminist movement over repeal of the legislation that criminalized abortion, which was seen as the next fundamental step towards women's liberation. This was a contentious issue within the party itself from 1975 onwards. For example, Nilde Iotti commented that 'for some months now we have not managed to hold a meeting for women at which this issue [the legalization of abortion] is not raised and thrown at us'.[11] It is in this political context that Carla Ravaioli published the book quoted at the beginning of the chapter, and that included interviews on women's issues, and especially abortion, with senior PCI figures such as Enrico Berlinguer, Giorgio Napolitano, and Adriana Seroni.[12]

Although the PCI leadership supported decriminalization, it still favoured legislation that would maintain some restrictions on access to legal abortion with regard to age and circumstances (Rodano 2010: 218). There were both tactical and idealistic reasons for this position. On the one hand, the PCI did not want a clash with the Catholics that would jeopardize the potential alliance with the DC envisaged in the 'historic compromise' policy. On the other, the PCI leadership saw the issue of abortion as not simply a matter of personal choice, but as a social injustice and personal trauma from which Italian women needed to be protected (Barbagallo 2006: 221; Crainz 2005: 515–16). This was consistent with the longstanding Communist conceptualization of motherhood as an issue of social importance rather than a private matter, which had resulted in the battle by the PCI and UDI across the first thirty years of the Republic to establish state nursery provision and support for working mothers by means of legislation.

The purely political approach taken by the PCI on women's issues, and its somewhat conservative stance on abortion, are well illustrated by a propaganda film produced by Unitelefilm for the elections of 1976 and specifically addressed to women voters: *La donna é cambiata, l'Italia deve cambiare* (Women have changed, and Italy has to change), directed by the Italian-Argentinian filmmaker Rosaria Polizzi. In the film, Italian women are said to have developed political awareness through their struggles over the preceding years 'alongside the workers' movement' and thanks to the PCI. They are therefore demanding a different society which would meet their new aspirations, but interviews show women complaining about issues such as the excessive cost of groceries, the lack of nursery provision, inadequate pensions, and the lack of skilled jobs for women. The film thus seems to suggest that the problems women face could be resolved by new legislation, and that what women really need is a change in the government. Furthermore, at no point is abortion presented as a woman's right; the film offers slogans such as '*Consultori per non abortire*' (advice services to avoid abortion) and '*Legge giusta sull'aborto per non morire*' (A good law on abortion to avoid death). New legislation is thus presented as an unfortunate necessity and a last resort in order to avoid the fatalities that result from illegal abortions performed at home, once state-aided family planning has failed to prevent unintended pregnancies. The Communists' rather narrow ideas about abortion set them on an inevitable collision course with the feminist movement.

Although the various feminist groups were far from unanimous over the measures that a new law on abortion should provide for, and even over the actual prospect of new legislation before there had been any real change in Italy's patriarchal culture, a core set of points had been broadly accepted over time. The MDL, in particular, had been arguing since 1971 for new legislation based on two fundamental principles: the right to abortion on demand, and self-determination for women in the decisions over if and when to have an abortion (Bracke 2014: 80–81). These demands inspired one of the best-known Italian feminist slogans: '*Aborto libero, gratuito e assistito*' (freely available, uncharged-for and assisted abortion). In 1971, the MLD manifesto was definitely too progressive for the PCI.[13] By the end of 1976, however, the party's resolve to tackle the issue of abortion had strengthened enough for its parliamentary deputies to present a proposal for a new law. This was fairly radical, and distinctly more progressive than the law that was eventually passed in May 1978; it accommodated most of the MLD's requests including, critically, the point regarding women's self-determination. Although the bill was provisionally approved by the Chamber of Deputies, it was eventually rejected by the Senate, in June 1977, due to fierce opposition from the Christian Democrats. The UDI responded immediately by organizing a march in Rome to protest the bill's rejection and invited feminist groups to join them. This demonstration, on 10 June, provided the setting for an unanticipated attack on the PCI and the UDI by fringe groups within the

234   G. FANTONI

feminist movement. In the view of many feminists, the law had failed to gain approval due to the Communist deputies' lack of resolve, which was in turn due to the priority that the PCI gave to political agreement with the DC in its pursuit of the 'historic compromise' policy. In addition, the UDI was accused of endorsing the PCI's stance of compromise and of being incapable of taking an independent position (Beckwith 1985: 30). The MLD, in particular, abandoned the march and staged a separate demonstration.[14] Political motives were also in play: the MLD had links to the emerging non-Marxist left-wing Partito radicale (Radical Party), which was competing with the PCI for progressive but ideologically non-aligned voters. The non-aligned vote was becoming increasingly important; this is illustrated by the foundation, in January 1976, of a new newspaper, *La Repubblica*, whose aim was to build up a core readership of centre-left and moderately left-wing voters.

It was significant that the first PCI film to deal directly with the feminist movement, *Non ci regalano niente* (Nothing comes for free), began with footage of the demonstration against the Senate's rejection of the legislation on abortion. This sixteen-minute documentary was sponsored by the UDI and directed by Polizzi in 1977; its aim was to defend the image of the UDI and to respond in measured fashion to the charges levelled by the feminist movement against Communist policy on women's issues. The voice-over credits the UDI for the demonstration on 10 June:

> There were thousands of us women, of all ages and from every part of Italy, who came, all together, to shout out our anger and protest against the violence of undercover abortion.

The film goes on to narrate the story of the UDI from its foundation to the present day, focusing on its history of campaigning, including the ten-year struggle for equal pay, the campaign for the legal protection of working mothers, and the 1971 legislation on nursery provision. It includes three interviews with women from different age groups: Evelina, a seventy-nine-year-old housewife, and two working women, thirty-two-year-old Grazia, and twenty-four-year-old Simonetta. These three represent the three phases of the UDI's history: the post-war years, the years of protest and the present day. The voice-over stresses that this history demonstrates that if women want to obtain something, they have to get organized and fight together, otherwise they will achieve nothing: 'nothing comes for free', as the film's title says. The commentary also emphasizes the importance of the referendum campaign on divorce, which for thousands of women was their first personal experience of political involvement. Grazia recalls emotionally the first meeting she attended on the divorce campaign:

> I always remember, an early meeting in the San Lorenzo area [in Rome], with the women, who were talking, or let's say beginning to talk, starting with their families, their own problems, their husbands, their children, and for me this was really new, and lovely, to see that in various ways I identified with these women, that I was no longer alone.

The voice-over goes on to explain that since then the political debate on women's issues has been enhanced by 'the forceful feminist presence'. Credit is given to the feminist movement for having pointed out 'the particular oppression' that women suffer, irrespective of their social class, which is manifest, first and foremost, in family life. However, the commentary also introduces a semantic distinction between '*il movimento femminista*' and '*il movimento femminile*' (the feminist movement as against the women's movement). While the film acknowledges that the former has made a crucial contribution to the latter by exposing the patriarchal and sexist nature of Italian culture and society, it seems to suggest that only the women's movement, which brings together both feminists and non-feminist women, can be the authentic protagonist in the struggle for women's rights. It is the women's movement that the UDI aims to represent and lead. Ultimately, the two movements are natural allies and will fight together for a fair abortion bill and social change. 'Can we find the path of solidarity, to make a difference, as women?' the voice-over dramatically asks. In summary, by acknowledging the importance of feminism in recent Italian history, the film attempts to bridge the gap between the UDI, and therefore the PCI, and the feminist movement. At the same time, it makes it clear that neither the UDI nor the PCI, given their history and electoral strength, are willing to present the feminist movement with the well-earned responsibility for representing Italian women.

Arguably, the UDI and the PCI had scored a point over feminism in the very moment the latter had accepted to put temporarily on hold the struggle to end patriarchy, which is a socio-cultural objective, in order to achieve something very practical such as a law on abortion. Communists knew well the game of parliamentary politics, and had MPs to play it. Feminists did not. Therefore, feminists were now competing on unfamiliar political territory and needed the help of the PCI and other parties in order to succeed. Besides, in this battle the primary enemy was no longer male oppression, but the government, which suited the PCI just fine.

The PCI's outlook on women's problems did not change much in the following films produced by Unitelefilm and dealing with the women's movement. For example, *Madre, ma come?* (Mother, but how?—33 minutes), also directed by Rosaria Polizzi, is an investigation of motherhood from a political and social perspective, which fully endorses its Communist conception as a matter of public interest. Based on scenes from everyday life and interviews, the film tries to show what the struggles of the women's movement have accomplished in relation to safe and informed motherhood, thanks to the support from the PCI and the '*amministrazioni democratiche*' (local councils under the party's control, labelled 'democratic' in Communist propaganda). Among the most important achievements in this regard had been the *Legge sui consultori familiari* (law on family advice services), passed in July 1975, which established advice centres providing psychological and social assistance in preparation for motherhood and responsible parenthood.[15] The film therefore features a meeting at the centre in Cinisello Balsamo, a town within Milan's metropolitan area, attended by many women of different ages and chaired by a woman psychologist. However, much more needs to be done before Italy arrives at a level of maternity support worthy of a 'modern country'. The service provided by state hospitals is particularly unsatisfactory: the film features overcrowded maternity wards and expectant mothers who have been asked to bring their own bed linen and, in some cases, medication. The voice-over informs the viewers that sixty-one women still die for every hundred thousand births in Italy, as against only eighteen in Britain.

Madre, ma come? also provides a valuable visual record of the demonstrations organized by the feminist movement. The slogans on the protesters' placards, which summarize the reasons for the feminist struggles of the period, are particularly revealing: '*La donna è una disoccupata che si chiama casalinga*' (women are unemployed people labelled as housewives), '*Libera nella maternità, autonoma nel lavoro, protagonista nella vita*' (free in motherhood, independent in work, protagonist in life), and the humorous '*Abortiamo la DC*' (let's abort the DC). It is significant that while the film shows a placard reading '*L'aborto è un diritto non un reato*' (abortion is a right, not a crime), the voice-over states that abortion is 'a tragedy and not a crime', neatly illustrating the difference in how abortion was interpreted by the feminist movement and the Italian Communist Party.

From a technical point of view this film stands out, as it is shot in a vivid colour that very effectively conveys the atmosphere of the mid-1970s: the strident and colourful wallpaper of the interiors, the Formica tables and wood-effect furniture, the intense green of a countryside under siege by a concrete-grey invasion of property speculation, and the multicoloured clothes of the many girls and women interviewed by Polizzi's team. The use of music is also noteworthy, with the film's various scenes marked off by a selection of feminist songs of the era that include 'I figli' and 'La nuova lega' by folksinger Anna Identici, 'Il parto' by the Canzoniere Femminista group, and 'Non c'è nessuna differenza' by Ombretta Colli.

With respect to these PCI films directed by women, it is perhaps interesting to try to answer the following question: did the women filmmakers working for the party change the mode of representation of women in Communist documentary? As mentioned before in this book, the presence of women in Communist films is not a frequent occurrence. When women do enter the profilmic, their role is often secondary or even marginal. It is therefore difficult to establish whether Mangini and Polizzi managed to revolutionize the gendered conventions of the PCI, apart from the obvious notation that in their films, women are protagonists and men do not feature much. However, it can certainly be argued that Mangini and Polizzi show a less mediated approach to their subjects, the interviewed women, than male filmmakers do. The most obvious comparison is between Ansano Giannarelli's *Saturday, Sunday, Monday* (discussed above), with its short interviews and prevalence of the voice-over-commentary, and the films on women's issues directed by women filmmakers. In these latter films, the floor is more consistently given to women, who are left free to express their point of view. The mediation by the author is entrusted more to the editing (namely the succession of scenes which ultimately encompasses the film's meaning) than to the voice-over commentary.

One final factor should be noted about films on women's issues sponsored by the PCI or by UDI: they make no mention of the innovative forms of activism developed by the American feminist movement and widely practised by Italian feminist groups in the 1970s, such as, for example, Consciousness-Raising (*autocoscenza*). It is likely that Communists struggled to understand a form of activism rooted in personal experiences rather than political categories and ideological readings of society.

However, it may also suggest that the PCI's officers—who exerted quite a strict control over the documentaries' content—were not particularly interested in knowing more about feminism and their practices. Their primary objective was to channel women's discontent against the government and gain votes as a result.[16]

Despite the fundamental disagreement over an issue as crucial as abortion, the differences between the PCI and the feminist movement never resulted in a political split (Gundle 1995: 346). Feminists felt that the PCI was, for better or worse, their principal point of reference in the political spectrum. The approval of the abortion bill in May 1978, thanks to the decisive contribution of Communist parliamentary deputies, provided definitive conformation of this. The PCI leadership in fact showed itself to be increasingly open to the ideas generated by the feminist movement. A watershed moment was the party's Fifteenth Congress (Rome, 30 March–3 April 1979), at which Enrico Berlinguer demonstrated in his opening speech as leader that he had fully understood the feminist perspective:

> The Italian women's movements go further than the simple demand for equality with men. Through their struggles for the reform of family law, for divorce, for new legislation on cases of pregnancy termination, for advice provision and for welfare services, women have turned matters that once would only have been dealt with in the personal or family sphere into social and political issues. The female masses have thus signalled new areas in which there needs to be profound change: the family sphere, not just the spheres of production and the political institutions; relationships between the sexes, not just class relations.[17]

This new awareness called for a major revision of the long-term political strategy for the working class:

> We need to abandon an old model, whose influence extended to the thoughts and deeds of great revolutionaries of every age, whereby social revolution has to be achieved first and women's issues will be resolved later. It can no longer be like that: the processes of social revolution and women's liberation must go forward in step with each other, and in mutual support.

However, the PCI may have paid a price for its differences with the feminist movement over abortion. In the elections of June 1979, it lost over one and a half million votes: about 4 per cent of the electorate. Research has suggested that these votes either turned into abstentions or were transferred to the Radical Party (Caciagli 2003: 163–64), which had uncompromisingly placed itself at the forefront of the struggle for the right to abortion and had in due course criticized the 1978 law for not being sufficiently progressive. It is therefore very likely that many women voters with feminist leanings, having supported the PCI in 1976, decided not to renew their trust in the party in 1979, despite Berlinguer's last-ditch attempt at the party congress to secure a political rapprochement with the feminist movement. There is some indirect evidence of this in one of the propaganda films that the PCI produced for the 1979 elections; the potential drift in the vote was clearly regarded as a real threat, and the Press and Propaganda Section commissioned the film with the explicit purpose of forestalling this.

The film in question is *Insieme per cambiare* (Together for change) (20 minutes), which like the films of 1977 dealing with women's issues was directed by Rosaria Polizzi. It features interviews with several women, representing different types of potential Communist voter, who tell the viewer why they will be voting for the PCI in the forthcoming elections. One woman who exercised a protest vote for the PCI in the elections of 1976, as a way of showing her dissatisfaction with Christian Democracy, will this time be voting for the Italian Communist Party with conviction and awareness:

> Now it's an informed vote, not least because I have children and so I want them to be able to live in a different society in the future, a society that is equal for all, where there is no discrimination, and I want them to be able to work and live in a world where there is peace.

A young feminist declares that she too is going to vote for the PCI, because she feels that being active in the feminist movement will not on its own resolve women's problems. She also says that the PCI, more than any other, is the party that fights for women's rights. In this regard, the voice-over emphasizes that the abortion bill was only finally approved due to the party's strategy of seeking a compromise with a wide range of social and political forces. This argument was undoubtedly aimed at feminist voters, urging them to avoid radicalism and instead to trust in the gradualism of the Italian Communist Party.

The last street protests seeing mass participation of feminist groups were held in 1981, in order to defend the law on abortion threatened by a referendum promoted by a Catholic association. Voters rejected the proposal, and the 1978 law on abortion was retained. After that, the Italian feminist movement subsided. Its legacy, however, was profound: Italy's

240   G. FANTONI

social mores changed deeply. The 1980s were characterized by what has been termed as 'diffused feminism' whereby feminist ideas continued shaping the attitudes and beliefs of thousands of Italian women, even if many were not fully aware of this and might not style themselves as feminist (Calabrò and Grasso 2004, 27). Feminists' legacy also includes a network of associations, bookshops, and documentation centres on women, some of which still play an important part in the cultural life of many Italian cities. No PCI film, however, recorded the evolution of the feminist movement in the 1980s, for Communist cinema would end in the late 1970s. This is discussed in the next chapter.

NOTES

1. For a history of the UDI, see Rodano (2010).
2. In 1964, the PCI had about 400,000 women members, half of whom were housewives whose husbands were often PCI members (Willson 2007: 139).
3. See the article by Gabriella Gallozzi, '"*Essere donne*": un film, una bandiera. Diretto da Cecilia Mangini, per anni è stato parte del rito dell'8 marzo. È stato restaurato', *L'Unità*, 5 February 2002: 22. Having started as a film critic, Cecilia Mangini (1927–2021) became an important director of documentary films. An overview of Mangini's career is in Piccino (2018: 178–180).
4. See the interview with Mangini at https://www.youtube.com/watch?v=awxFiu5eRxg. Accessed on 26 September 2020. For biographical information about Felice Chilanti, see Chap. 2, note 13.
5. See the interview with Cecilia Mangini (n. 4).
6. 'La Censura c'è e si vede', *L'Unità*, 5 May 1965: 7; 'L'ARCI protesta per la censura a "*Essere donne*"', *L'Unità*, 8 May 1965: 9.
7. '"*Essere donne*". Tema tabù per la supercensura', *L'Unità*, 4 May 1965: 7. Aside from the issue of the loss of prize money, exclusion from the process of mandatory programme scheduling which was granted to fifty documentaries in every three-month period, greatly limited opportunities for the documentary to be seen across the country. In addition, this matter provided ammunition for attacking the PSI: the Minister for Tourism and Entertainment in Moro's second government, from July 1964 to January 1966, was the Socialist Achille Corona, and the Communist press could therefore present the exclusion of *Essere donne* as proof of the PSI's betrayal of left-wing values now that it was involved in centre-left coalition governments.
8. For a fuller list of the feminist groups, see Bono and Kemp (1991: 377–80). For an overview of the feminist movement in Italy, see Lumley (1998: 291–316).

10 WOMEN'S ISSUES, FEMINISM, AND THE PCI   241

9. This position was taken by *Rivolta Femminile*, for example (Bracke 2014: 69–70). On *Rivolta femminile*, see (Calabrò and Grasso 2004: 158–171).
10. Communist women were critical of feminism as they viewed it as pervaded by 'individualism' (Bracke 2014: 79).
11. Quoted by (Barbagallo 2006: 221). See also the *Raccolta di lettere e messaggi sul tema dell'aborto* (collection of letters and messages on the abortion theme) sent to the PCI Women's Section by Communist militants and sympathizers in 1975, in IG, APCI, MF 209, pp. 953–1004, Sezioni di lavoro, VI bimestre 1975.
12. A second book on the relationship between the PCI and the feminist movement came out in 1976: Aida Tiso's summary of the development of Communist thinking on the 'woman question' since Engels, published by Editori Riuniti.
13. The very conventional nature of the Communists' approach to women's issues in 1971 is illustrated by the way that *L'Unità* celebrated 8 March, International Women's Day, that year. 'I Comunisti e la Famiglia' (Communists and the family) read the headline, and the leading article declared that after the approval (in 1970) of the law on divorce, the issues at the forefront of the party's struggle on behalf of Italian women were the attainment of better jobs, houses, schools and social services.
14. See the account of the march on 10 June in *L'Unità*, 11 September 1977: front and back pages. It presented the demonstration as 'generally united', and condemned the presence of 'an isolated extremist march' in reference to the MDL counter-demonstration.
15. Law no. 405 of 29 July 1975, 'Istituzione dei consultori familiari'.
16. A film featuring a meeting of a '*gruppo di autocoscienza*' (consciousness-raising group), is *La lotta non è finita* (The fight is not yet over) (1973), produced by the Rome-based Collettivo femminista di cinema (feminist film collective). The feminist film collective shot a few documentaries and organized festivals that showed films directed by women; it remained active until the early 1980s.
17. Berlinguer's speech, in Pugliese and Pugliese (1985: 5–75); both quotations are on page 62.

BIBLIOGRAPHY

Barbagallo, F. 2006. *Enrico Berlinguer*. Rome: Carocci.
Beckwith, K. 1985. Feminism and Leftist Policy in Italy: the Case of UDI—PCI relations. *West European Politics* VIII (4): 19–37.
Bono, P., and S. Kemp, eds. 1991. *Italian Feminist Thought. A Reader*. Oxford: Basil Blackwell.

Bracke, M. 2014. *Women and the Reinvention of the Political: Feminism in Italy, 1968–1983.* New York: Routledge.

Caciagli, M. 2003. Terremoti elettorali e transazione tra i partiti. In *Partiti e organizzazioni di massa*, ed. F. Malgeri and M. Paggi, 143–168. Soveria Mannelli: Rubettino.

Calabrò, A.R., and L. Grasso. 2004. *Dal movimento femminista al femminismo diffuso: storie e percorsi a Milano dagli anni '60 agli anni '80.* Milano: Fondazione Badaracco, Franco Angeli.

Crainz, G. 2005. *Il paese mancato. Dal miracolo economico agli anni ottanta.* Rome: Donzelli.

Eisenstein, Z., ed. 1978. *Capitalist Patriarchy and the Case for Socialist Feminism.* New York: Monthly Review Press.

Gundle, S. 1995. *I comunisti italiani tra Hollywood e Mosca. La sfida della cultura di massa.* Florence: Giunti.

Lilli, L., and C. Valentini. 1979. *Care compagne: il femminismo nel PCI e nelle organizzazioni di massa.* Rome: Editori Riuniti.

Lumley, R. 1998. *Dal '68 agli anni di piombo. Studenti e operai nella crisi italiana.* Florence: Giunti.

Piccino, C. 2018. Il cinema vissuto. In *We want cinema. Sguardi di donne nel cinema italiano*, ed. L. Buffoni, 166–183. Venice: Marsilio.

Pugliese, D., and O. Pugliese, eds. 1985. *Da Gramsci a Berlinguer. La via italiana al socialismo attraverso i congressi del Partito comunista italiano, IV (1964—1975), Edizioni del Calendario.* Vicenza: Marsilio.

Ravaioli, C. 1976. *La questione femminile. Intervista col PCI.* Milan: Bompiani.

Rodano, M. 2010. *Memorie di una che c'era. Una storia dell'UDI.* Milan: Il Saggiatore.

Sassoon, D. 1997. *Contemporary Italy. Economy Society and Politics since 1945.* London and New York: Longman.

Tiso, A. 1976. *I comunisti e la questione femminile.* Rome: Editori Riuniti.

Valentini, C. 1997. *Berlinguer. L'eredità difficile.* Rome: Editori Riuniti.

Willson, P. 2007. *Women in Twentieth-Century Italy.* Basingstoke: Palgrave Macmillan.

CHAPTER 11

Hegemony Fades Away (1977–1979)

In June 1976, over twelve and a half million voters, 34.4 per cent of the electorate, had put their cross by the symbol of the Italian Communist Party in the elections to the Chamber of Deputies. The difference between this and the votes for the Senate, where the PCI nonetheless secured over ten million votes, clearly showed that the party had galvanized the youth vote. These results were not enough to fully legitimize the PCI as a force in the government—not even outright victory could have done this—but they made it into a partner with whom the Christian Democrats and the new prime minister had to negotiate every piece of legislation. Andreotti's third government was in fact only able to take office thanks to the abstention of Communist parliamentary deputies on 29 July 1976. The period 1977–1979 can therefore be described as the PCI's 'years of triumph'.

However, it can also be argued that these very same years foreshadowed the PCI's political and electoral decline in the 1980s. This chapter analyses a number of propaganda films produced by the Italian Communist Party between 1977 and 1979, and argues that these hitherto under-studied cinematic texts can shed new light on that historical period and, in particular, on the serious difficulties the Party was experiencing in those years. Apparently very strong from an electoral standpoint, the PCI was arguably doomed in the medium term, as emerging social and political factors were progressively undermining the set of ideas and core-values Communist militancy and electoral strength were based on. The films produced by the PCI, discussed along with archival evidence and party press, reveal how

© The Author(s), under exclusive license to Springer Nature Switzerland AG 2021
G. Fantoni, *Italy through the Red Lens*, Italian and Italian American Studies, https://doi.org/10.1007/978-3-030-69197-4_11

243

the party was ideologically ill-suited to deal with the approaching reality of the 1980s, when the crisis of the Party was going to openly manifest itself.

It is possible, however, that the films produced by the Unitelefilm at that time give a particularly negative impression of the situation of the PCI because they reflect the psychological state of those who were involved in producing them: professionals and militants who worked in a structure that the Party had decided to put into liquidation. Unitelefilm was in fact sold at the end of 1979. The reasons why the PCI made such a decision are discussed at the end of the chapter.

The factors eroding Communist consensus at the end of the 1970s include the friction with feminist groups that was discussed in Chap. 10, the serious disagreement both with a segment of Italian youth and with many left-wing intellectuals and the tendency towards political disengagement, which came to be known as the '*riflusso*' (reaction). The latter phenomenon was at least in part an outcome of the electorate's growing disaffection for the Italian party system. In June 1978, in a referendum promoted by the Radical Party, 43.6 per cent of the voters said 'yes' to a repeal of the 1974 law that had established public financing for political parties. This percentage was much larger than the normal constituency of the political groups that were formally supporting the 'yes' vote.[1] Italians were getting tired of their political parties. This affected the others as well as the PCI; the Communists, however, also had to deal with the development of an unfavourable international political environment, which led the public towards increasing scepticism about the particular model of democratic socialism that the Communist Party had been promoting as its ultimate goal. Finally, the PCI was becoming a source of disappointment for many of its own supporters.

Those who had hoped for radical reform after the election results of 1975 and 1976 grew frustrated over the party's policy during the period 1976–1979, when Communist parliamentary deputies offered support to DC-led governments without the PCI's direct involvement in the government itself. Many left-wing voters began to think that the party had accepted subjugation by the DC in exchange for a share of political power. Several historians have also offered an unfavourable assessment of the PCI's politics during the 'years of national solidarity', as the period has been called; it has been described as, for example, a 'compromise without any dignity or outcomes worth recording' (Crainz 2005: 552).[2] Unless the PCI had been prepared to accept the risks of a long phase of political instability, in the context of the most serious economic crisis since 1945, there was no real alternative to Berlinguer's decision to allow the Christian Democrats, led by Giulio Andreotti, to remain in power on their own until 16 January 1978. All things considered, this was in fact consistent with Togliatti's political legacy: the working class should act as a 'national class' and take on Italy's problems.

In order to fulfil this role, in the autumn of 1976 the PCI endorsed the austerity measures put forward by the government. This generated dismay among party militants and resulted in a dramatic split between the PCI and the student movement, which from that moment onwards no longer represented the reservoir of potential votes for the PCI that had been in place since 1968. This became clear in early 1977, when Berlinguer's policy was forcefully challenged by fringe groups of students and young workers. They started a new movement with novel features, subsequently known as the 'Movimento del '77' (movement of 1977) (Lumley 1998: 273–90), which specifically targeted the emerging collaboration between the PCI and the DC, strongly opposed the austerity measures and championed, instead, a reduction in the working week and a hedonistic *joie de vivre*.[3]

To be fair to Berlinguer, he did not simply sanction Andreotti's decision to impose austerity measures. Instead, he sought to exploit the economic crisis and the necessary imposition of austerity measures in order to reshape, at least in part, the country's economic structure. In his view, austerity presented 'an opportunity to transform Italy', which was the title of a speech that the PCI leader made in January 1977 to an audience of left-wing intellectuals (Berlinguer 1977).[4] In Berlinguer's view, austerity could open the door to the construction of a new society based on 'a planned process of economic development whose objective is the elevation of the fundamental individual and social aspects of mankind', 'the overcoming of models of consumption inspired by unrestrained individualism', 'the involvement of workers and citizens in oversight of businesses, the economy and the state', and 'international solidarity and cooperation'.

Although it was no doubt motivated by ethical considerations, including concerns about the destructive impact of industrial production on the environment, Berlinguer's proposal was not widely welcomed. Essentially, it had arrived too late: ever since the years of the boom, consumerism had been increasing its hold on the hearts and minds of the country's citizens, workers, and bourgeois alike. Even the objectives of the Italian labour movement, once the seizure of power had been put aside or indefinitely postponed, had gradually come to include aspirations to higher living standards, and within a framework that was essentially social democratic. This shift had occurred despite the fact that the PCI had always opposed the social democratic model because of its inability to overcome the capitalist system (Gozzini 2001: 119; Lusanna 2007: 155–56).

Berlinguer himself strove to find a new and arguably rather unlikely 'third way' between social democracy and Soviet-style socialism, which came to be known as 'Eurocommunism' (Salvadori 1978; Boggs and Plotke 1980). This approach, developed more or less jointly by the PCI and the Communist Parties of France and Spain, put forward the idea of the gradual introduction into Western societies of a mild form of socialism, without the need for a revolutionary phase and with the retention of Western-style democracy. Berlinguer thought that Eurocommunism would give the PCI the degree of autonomy from Moscow that was necessary for it to be accepted within the government of a capitalist country; he saw it as the only realistic way to advance socialism in Europe.

In this context, Berlinguer's proposal that party members, intellectuals, and the working class should voluntarily embrace austerity was part of a more general plan in which the PCI's revolutionary strategy would be re-engineered in order to peacefully overcome a capitalist system that was regarded, due to a crucial misjudgement, as close to collapse. However, the movement of 1977 did not grasp the complexity of Berlinguer's intentions and interpreted the PCI policy as a surrender to the class enemy. The economic crisis had made young people even more resentful, as it had produced a strong sense of social exclusion: students felt that their degrees would no longer automatically guarantee them well-paid jobs and a good standard of living, while the younger generation of the working class seemed doomed to unemployment or, at best, to unskilled labour. Cultural issues also distanced the PCI from the new movement. In particular, young people's aspirations to material well-being and their strident demands for freedom on all fronts, including the sexual—perhaps the most enduring legacy of the era of student protest—were very far removed from the austere and rather moralistic approach of the Italian Communist Party.

These various issues generated criticism of the PCI, which was accused by the movement of only looking after the interests of the already well-protected workers in the large industrial factories, and of abandoning the lower strata of the population. Initially, the movement of 1977 had a distinctively creative and joyful character. Very soon, however, part of the movement, and in particular a network of radical groups known as the *'autonomia'*, developed a more violent style of protest. A defining moment in the escalation of violence was the confrontation on 17 February 1977, at the university of La Sapienza in Rome, between the *autonomia* and the CGIL's stewards. A few weeks later in Bologna, a city governed by the Italian Communist Party, there were violent clashes between the movement and the police, resulting in the death of Francesco Lorusso, a Lotta Continua activist, on 11 March 1977.

The PCI's reaction to these events was anything but sympathetic to the movement. On 14 March 1977, a meeting of the party's Central Committee was devoted to 'the Communists' duties and initiatives in response to the youth situation in the country's current crisis'.[5] Massimo D'Alema, the leader of the FGCI, argued in his opening report that the events in Bologna marked the beginning of 'a new and more acute phase of the strategy of tension'. In this interpretation, the outbreak of violence was attributed to violent neo-Fascist groups who were exploiting young people's anger over their unemployment in order to attack the PCI and the institutions of the Italian Republic; this would then empower reactionary forces.[6]

Nonetheless, in order to address young people's needs and aspirations, the PCI wanted to subject the movement of 1977 to a more thorough analysis. This was provided, for example, by Ugo Gregoretti's fourteenminute film *I giovani, il lavoro, la crisi* (Young people, work, and the crisis), which offers an effective illustration of the effort that the PCI made to understand the students and to meet the movement halfway. However, it also demonstrates that the party was unwilling to subject its approach to any fundamental scrutiny. The opening statement in the voice-over acknowledges that the student movement has posed questions that the party and the Italian labour movement need to address:

> In 1977, Italy has suddenly rediscovered the existence of a youth issue. The revolt in the universities ... has turned its attack, for the first time, explicitly at the workers' movement and the Communist Party.

Later in the film, Bruno Trentin, the leader of the metalworkers' union FIOM (part of the CGIL), offers a thoughtful analysis of the causes of youth unrest. In his view, this results from the *'scolarizzazione di massa'* (mass education) that the workers' movement has achieved over the previous ten years, producing thousands of educated young people who are no longer content with 'any old wage' and want jobs that match their level of knowledge. The Italian economy, however, is unable to meet these aspirations.

This analysis went beyond the simple criminalization of dissent and its equation with Fascism, which had characterized the PCI's initial response to the unrest; the PCI is now trying to understand the social origins of the movement. However, the voice-over describes the student revolt as motivated by 'a mixture of aspirations to renewal and corporative radicalism': a phrase whose vagueness indicates that the movement of 1977 remained a puzzling phenomenon for the PCI, in that it could not be described using recognized categories and terminology. As a result, the documentary's principal focus is on unemployment, an issue that the party was well acquainted with. The voice-over states that the PCI is determined to tackle the issue of unemployment and to avoid any painful and counterproductive conflict between young unemployed people and industrial workers: 'between those who have a job and may risk losing it, and those who still haven't got a job and aren't finding one'. Young people, the voice-over says, have the right to organize themselves independently but, at the same time, they must find their place 'alongside the workers'.

Meanwhile, footage is provided of that year's protests, showing both peaceful marches by young protesters and members of the *autonomia* wearing helmets and brandishing iron bars. However, as if by a process of Freudian repression, the voice-over never once uses the word '*autonomia*'. Cinematographically, *I giovani, il lavoro, la crisi* is not dissimilar to Gregoretti's *Contratto*, his film of 1969 on the '*autunno caldo*' (see Chap. 6), but in this production he never gives the floor to the protesters and the film's message is entrusted solely to the commentary. It also has no musical accompaniment. These features of the film clearly communicate the PCI's embarrassment and bewilderment in its attempts to deal with the movement of 1977.

The various omissions and the limited political analysis offered by *I giovani, il lavoro, la crisi* also reveal two crucial aspects of Communist policy regarding the movement: the party's stubborn refusal to accept any of the criticisms that had been voiced, and the missed opportunity to revitalize its strategy by taking on board some of the ideas generated by the students and young workers. I would argue that the PCI leadership was fixated on the use of violence by fringe groups within the movement and therefore failed to fully recognize and analyse the profound cultural transformations taking place in society. The party thus missed an opportunity to open a dialogue and establish a new alliance. Its attitude towards the movement of 1968, discussed in Chap. 6, had been very different: on that occasion, the leadership had respectfully agreed to listen to the students and had, at least formally, welcomed their opinions. In electoral terms this approach had paid off over time, as was shown by the PCI's positive results in 1975–1976. In contrast, the deaf ear that the party turned to the movement of 1977 was to damage it in the 1979 elections. It could be said that the PCI's stance towards the movement derived from the impossibility of reconciling its historical role as an intermediary for grass-roots protest with the 'historic compromise' strategy. Ultimately, the problem lay in the inspiration behind this approach. Its fundamental aim was the creation of an ideal society in which political and social conflict would be obviated by a preventative agreement between the democratic parties and a shared management of public affairs (Ignazi 2006: 10–11). Even individual self-interest would be 'systematically fought and defeated at its very roots', so that 'the welfare of the individual will actually correspond to the welfare of all', to quote the Catholic Franco Rodano, a close adviser to Berlinguer and one of the architects of the historic compromise (1975: 40–41). Having adopted this perspective, the PCI leadership saw dissent over the historic compromise as motivated only by a selfish desire to sabotage the efforts to save the nation and create a fairer society. The party was thus unable to mediate between, on the one hand, the urgency of ensuring the stability of a democratic system that seemed seriously threatened by the economic crisis and terrorism and, on the other, the need to reinvigorate its strategy by drawing on the reservoir of ideas generated by the movement. There could have been an open discussion, for example, on how work might evolve in order to be both personally fulfilling and socially equitable, and the constraints of the commitment to austerity could have been abandoned in order to address the growing demand for material goods from a left-wing perspective. Work, consumption habits, and social expectations were all to continue changing in the 1980s, and in many respects the movement of 1977 was just a taste of what was to come; however, the PCI had missed the opportunity to guide and shape these developments, which were to unfold along cultural lines that were ultimately alien to it.[7]

The ambiguous arrangements for the minority government lasted for about eighteen months. At the beginning of 1978, the PCI believed that the time was ripe for it to formally become part of a majority coalition, and asked the DC to jointly form a 'government of solidarity and democratic unity'.[8] However, the anti-Communist stance of part of the DC and strong opposition from the US government proved insurmountable. Negotiations over the potential new government lasted for two months and ended inconclusively. The kidnapping of DC president Aldo Moro by the Red Brigades, on 16 March 1978, forced the PCI into voting in favour of another Andreotti government, which once again excluded the Communists and lasted until January 1979. At the next elections, on 3 June 1979, the PCI lost almost 1.5 million votes. Berlinguer explained the reasons:

> The massive and focused attack, from many different directions, which with an extraordinary wealth of means, and resorting to deceptions of every kind, has been systematically directed at the Communist Party over the last three years and during the election campaign.[9]

In his claim that the attack on the PCI had come 'from different directions', Berlinguer was referring to both the uncompromising criticism expressed by the movement of 1977 and the party's recent ideological and political clashes with the PSI. In an attempt to reverse the progressive political marginalization of the Socialists that had resulted from Berlinguer's 'historic compromise' strategy, their leader Bettino Craxi had mounted a challenge to the PCI on the ideological front, condemning the totalitarian nature of all forms of Communism in their opposition to the libertarian and non-Leninist traditions of the kind of socialism that the PSI represented.[10] The theoretical skirmish that this provoked coincided with a deterioration in political relations between the two enduring parties of the Italian Left (Ajello 1997: 187–92).[11] This protracted dispute had been especially painful for the PCI, which saw the PSI as ideologically close and an essential partner in the 'historic compromise' strategy.

There were, however, a range of cultural and political reasons for the PCI's electoral defeat, which are effectively illustrated by films that the PCI produced in 1979, especially Ansano Giannarelli's *Un film sul PCI* (A film on the PCI). This production has a running time of one hour and chronicles four months in the life of the Italian Communist Party, from December 1978 to March 1979. Fifty hours of colour footage were shot for a film entirely devoted to party militants, featuring interviews with Communist workers, meetings held in local sections of the party branches around Italy and neighbourhood meetings in Bologna and Naples. The only statement by a party leader is an excerpt from Berlinguer's speech to a meeting of the PCI's Livorno branch on 18 February 1978, which alludes to two significant issues: the Sino-Vietnamese War (17 February–16 March 1978) and the party's return to opposition (31 January 1979). The former has profoundly shocked the rank and file, as it seems to deal a further and perhaps fatal blow to socialist internationalism.

A perplexed dockworker in Genoa addresses a question to Giannarelli:

> But aren't both these states socialist? Is there something that's not OK in one of them? It makes me think that here too there's a battle to win the dominant position in the market … what's going to come of the unity of socialist countries?

By the end of the 1970s, the international Communist movement did indeed present a sorry spectacle, not only because of the pervasive political tensions but also because of the many violations of human rights in countries such as Cuba, Vietnam, and Poland. The young activists in the movement of 1977 were disgusted, and by that point had come to view Soviet Communism (or 'Stalinism', as they termed it) as no less evil than American imperialism (Falciola 2015: 85–95). The wrongdoings of Communist regimes also alienated the moderate public from the PCI. To some extent this was not logical, as at the end of the 1970s the distance between the leadership of the Soviet Union and Berlinguer's PCI had never before been so marked (Pons 2003: 85). It can even be said that the PCI was virtually isolated within the international Communist movement; the Eurocommunism project could not alleviate this situation, as it had already lost momentum by that point. However, because the PCI leadership refused to actually break with the Eastern Bloc, and because it tried to minimize coverage of the political differences between the Italian Communists and their Russian comrades, it continued to take the blame for the misdeeds of Communist Parties in power.

In Giannarelli's film, the PCI's ambiguous relationship with the Communist world is reflected in the words of an interviewee who laments the lack of information and analysis by a party leadership that looks increasingly embarrassed when addressing issues related to socialist countries:

> Look, the worker wonders about these things; I'm a dockworker, and I say, what have you not explained to me? Why do things like this [the Sino-Vietnamese War] happen? For instance, I don't know everything that's happened after Mao, how do things work over there? … As a Communist

worker, I ought to be well informed, so that I can manage these discussions among the other workers.

This reticence from the party threatens to undermine the remaining certainties held by militants, including belief in the actual possibility of the democratic form of socialism that the PCI had been committed to realizing. Another dockworker asks:

> Look, what form of socialism should we be thinking about? A socialism that unfortunately still doesn't exist in any country, a new socialism to be built along with all the forces that represent our society, Socialist, Communist, Catholic, as already mentioned, but not just these; we're asking for an alliance with the other classes, the classes that shouldn't be enemies of the working class: the middle classes, small business, the artisan class, and so on. But is it possible, I'm asking, to build a socialism of this type? ... Is what we want to create a utopia?

Subsequently, the film shows how PCI militants generally welcomed the news of the party's return to opposition with relief. As another comrade points out, this seems to be a clear rejection of the 'historic compromise' policy by ordinary militants. Studies conducted during the same period in fact revealed that the policy of collaboration with the DC had not been universally accepted at the grass roots: many militants, while publicly affirming the correctness of Berlinguer's strategy, had nurtured doubts about this ever since its inception (Barbagli and Corbetta 1979: 32–51).

Not only do socialist ideology and national party policy appear to be in crisis, but so too does Communist politics at the local level. In particular, the new left-wing administrations formed after the election of 1975 struggled to meet the high expectations of the people Ginsborg (1990, 395–400). A significant scene shows a public meeting attended by the Communist mayor of Naples Maurizio Valenzi, who seems to be besieged by citizens' demands and complaints. Eventually, he comes to the end of his tether and has a public and rather telling outburst:

> Last summer, I was so frustrated that at night I would get up and couldn't breathe. ... They were sending to my room people with children having tantrums, who wouldn't go away unless I gave them a job. The children who came were peeing in the corridor, and were sick and wanted us to look after them. They tried everything to make my life impossible. But we didn't quit. So let's talk about what you want, but let's start from here, good God!

Otherwise, it's over. Otherwise, we're playing the game of our enemies, who are now trying to blame us for their misdeeds. And lots of us crumble.

Even in Bologna, a city ruled for decades by the PCI following a seemingly invincible model based on class alliances, things are not going as smoothly as in previous years. The wounds of March 1977, in particular, have not yet healed, and the administration is trying to repair its relationship with the student movement. Bologna's mayor Renato Zangheri, in particular, had been one of the targets of the movement of 1977 because of his public support for their repression by the police in March 1977 during the clashes in the city that he governed. The young militants within the movement had come to see him as an embodiment of Berlinguer's pro-state and pro-government PCI (Falciola 2015: 161–62). At the meeting of a neighbourhood committee involving students, the city's mayor presents the measures he has taken in order to support young people and address the issue of their marginalization. A student, however, replies that the statements from the PCI about socially marginalized youth are 'just a nice speech, an abstract position of principle', and argues that marginalization is due not only to unemployment but also to a philosophy of government that left-wing council administrations share with others.

From today's perspective, *Un film sul PCI* seems to have been a fairly honest and even unflinching portrait of the difficulties that the party was struggling with at the end of the 1970s, which were a prelude to its subsequent political crisis. It is also the 'last picture show' for Italy's industrial workers: the last film to give them the floor before the dramatic defeat of the trade unions at FIAT, in September 1980, marked the definitive end of the decade of '*centralità operaia*' (workers centre stage), pushing them into cultural oblivion (Carotti 1992: 60). *Un film sul PCI* was given a favourable review by Mino Argentieri in *Rinascita*.[12] Gian Carlo Pajetta, on the other hand, strongly disliked the film's pessimistic tone and asked for major changes, which Giannarelli refused to make.[13] As a result, *Un film sul PCI* achieved very limited distribution.[14] Some of the issues that it had addressed were further developed in two other productions of that same year. Luigi Perelli made a thirty-minute film devoted to *L'Unità* with the title *Dai comunisti un quotidiano popolare* (A newspaper for the people from the Communists), while Giannarelli himself, using the footage shot for *Un film sul PCI*, put together a nineteen-minute colour documentary, *Giovani* (Young people), on youth marginalization.

The aim of *Dai comunisti un quotidiano popolare* was to restate the importance of *L'Unità* for Communist politics and propaganda, at a moment when the party's official newspaper was slowly losing readers. It is described as not just 'the organ of a party', but rather 'a great newspaper of the people and the masses'. In an interview shown in the film, the paper's editor Alfredo Reichlin quotes Togliatti's description of *L'Unità* as 'the *Corriere della Sera* of the Left', meaning that it was responsible for moulding left-wing opinion.

The first part of the film is devoted to the glorious history of the newspaper, which was founded by Antonio Gramsci and courageously published for the first time on 12 February 1924, when the Fascists were already in power. A shining example of steadfast determination, the Communist newspaper never ceases publication, not even during the Fascist dictatorship. Two days after the liberation of Rome by Allied forces, *L'Unità* is back on the newsstands and 'asserts itself as an essential weapon in the battles for the defence and development of democracy, and for the emancipation of the working classes'. The voice-over claims that the newspaper played a prominent role in the PCI's great victories in the era of the Italian Republic: the struggle against the 'swindle law', July 1960, and the trade union victories in 1968 and 1969.

The tone of the documentary becomes less triumphant as it approaches 1979, however. The crisis experienced by the Communist press emerges strongly from an interview with a group of volunteer newspaper sellers in Tuscany. Door-to-door selling is increasingly hard, because people have become less interested in the party's message; fewer people are attending debates in the local sections of the party branches, and there is a noticeable absence of the younger generation.[15] One of the vendors talks about a 'decline in ideals'. Reichlin, *L'Unità*'s editor, argues that 'the world has changed', because of the expansion of higher education and increase in television-watching; *L'Unità* must change too, 'rethinking and renewing', he says. The newspaper has in fact already undergone some changes, including technological modernization: the documentary proudly shows off the new equipment, including computers, which the Communist newspaper has recently acquired. Technology, however, is not the only issue. The truth, Reichlin claims, is that the PCI's political enemies are constantly trying to demoralize Communist voters. As they can no longer claim, as they used to, that the Communists 'eat children', they are spreading new and more sophisticated lies aimed at demolishing 'the democratic consciousness of the workers', including the ideas that political parties are all the same and that the dichotomy between the exploiters and the exploited no longer exists. In order to counter this political and ideological offensive, in Reichlin's view, the party must formulate what he rather vaguely calls 'big ideas that can support the mass movement and the battle for renewal'. In earlier times he would perhaps have said 'ideology', but he seems to have felt that this was no longer an appropriate term to use when addressing militants and voters; this provides a telling illustration of how the party had changed over time, and how the public was slowly starting to see ideologies, including Communism, in a negative light.

The final part of the film, featuring footage taken from *Togliatti è ritornato* (1948) and Ettore Scola's *Festival dell'Unità* (1972) is very revealing as regards the psychological state of the party. It resembles an attempt to enthuse the audience, presumed to consist of party militants, by recalling the halcyon days of yesteryear: the period of Togliatti's leadership, when militants and officials held an unshakeable faith in the final victory of Communism, and the PCI's ascendancy in the early 1970s, when it was still possible to enjoy the Red Army Choir without embarrassment and to sing the Red Flag with folksinger Giovanna Marini, with gusto, at the Festival dell'Unità.

The second documentary produced in 1979 that sheds light on the crisis of Communist politics at the end of the 1970s is Giannarelli's *Giovani* (19 minutes).[16] The principal aim of this film was the exorcism of two ghosts that were haunting the PCI: the *autonomia* and the '*riflusso*' ('reaction' or 'decline'), which refers to the general tendency towards political disengagement that was increasingly apparent at the end of the 1970s. The *riflusso*, which took the form of a general retreat into the private sphere, essentially resulted from the awareness that politics had somehow failed: it could not solve every problem, as had been widely believed during the long phase of collective political engagement that began in 1968, and it certainly could not resolve issues of personal fulfilment (Ajello 1997: 213–19; Crainz 2005: 560–61). *Giovani* intends to dispel the myth that young people are no longer interested in politics, or that when they practise politics they are only 'adherents to the *autonomia* brandishing guns', by showing them getting organized and fighting alongside the workers under the guidance of the Communist Party. The film includes footage of young members of a farming cooperative near Palermo, a demonstration by unemployed young people in Naples, people protesting against violence and terrorism in Genoa and several interviews. The younger generation is portrayed as still wanting to fight for a better society, despite being affected by serious problems such as unemployment, the lack of affordable housing and the risk of social marginalization: 'this is certainly not decline, individualistic choice, or retreat to the private sphere', says the voice-over, and nor is it 'the ideology of despair, the practice of violence, or pseudo-revolutionary verbosity'.

When we watch the film now, however, it is hard to avoid the impression that it actually manages to demonstrate the existence of what it hopes to deny: the decline in political energy and the consequent crisis in the relationship between the PCI and young people. The narrative structure of the voice-over, based on a set of denials ('young people are not ...', 'they are not ...'), is telling, as is the very fact that the PCI felt that it needed to produce this sort of film. Moreover, there are some revealing admissions. A young militant who joined the PCI after the dissolution of Lotta Continua, in 1976, states that 'there's been a drop in tension compared with a few years ago'; he says that anti-imperialism, in particular, is no longer an issue that energizes young people in the way that it did. This seems to be especially due to the end of the Vietnam War.

The film ends by showing more demonstrations, and the voice-over makes a triumphant closing statement that sounds more like some pipedream:

> Are these exceptional cases? Are they a minority? No, they are examples of hundreds of thousands, millions of young people who, alongside the Communist Party, want to emerge from the crisis, find work, strive together to build new ways of living, develop new values, change society, making it fairer and more human, develop democracy, and fight for the realization of socialism.

However, the neoliberalism of the 1980s and the new ideas that came with it, such as individualism and self-reliance, were soon to undermine people's political commitment; many people withdrew into the private sphere in order to satisfy their personal needs, in the safe environment of their individual living space.

The climate of political disenchantment provided the context for a noticeable drop in PCI film production. In the summer of 1977, Dario Natoli left Unitelefilm to become the deputy director of RAI 3, the public broadcasting service's new third channel, plunging the production company into a crisis that proved to be terminal. The reason for this lay not just in the lack of management—the new director Francesco Maselli was only appointed in 1978—but in a dramatic shift in the PCI's communication strategy. The party in fact decided to focus on television, for two main reasons. First, it had managed to become much more influential within the public broadcasting service than ever before following RAI's reform in April 1975 (see Chap. 9). The non-Communist press saw Natoli's appointment to RAI 3 as a sign that the PCI was finally taking part in the '*lottizzazione*' of the public broadcasting network: the sharing out of power and jobs that the ruling parties had been practising for years.[17] Second, the unchecked proliferation of independent television stations at the end of the 1970s encouraged the PCI to try its hand at private broadcasting.

The topic of Communist involvement in independent television broadcasting has not yet been addressed by historians. Research conducted in both the Archivio Gramsci and the AAMOD has shown that there were about twenty local television stations controlled by the PCI at the beginning of the 1980s. This number is not as impressive as it might seem when we consider that there were 676 independent television stations and no less than 3353 radio stations broadcasting in Italy at the end of 1979, according to the official figures (Ballini 2002: 30). This striking expansion, which had no parallel in other European countries, resulted from the absence of formal regulation of the private broadcasting sector for over a decade. There was in fact a sort of tacit agreement between the principal corporations investing in private broadcasting and the leading political parties, particularly the DC and the PSI, which entailed electoral support for the government in return for a deregulation that would allow business and profit to grow exponentially. The absence of constraints on the sale of advertising space was to be exploited very effectively by the future media mogul Silvio Berlusconi, who was laying the foundations of his empire; notoriously, his political patron was the leader of the PSI Bettino Craxi (Monteleone 1992: 443; Ortoleva 2008: 145). In this context, independent television broadcasting became pivotal to the communication strategy of the DC and the PSI.

As the 1979 election approached, many local television stations, which were constantly on the lookout for low-cost programming to fill their schedules, broadcast shows that were very much like the '*tribune elettorali*' (party political news conferences); politicians would pay to appear, and the programmes were generally characterized by a blatant pro-government stance. The following year, in the run-up to the local council elections, Italians saw for the first time on their local television stations a range of short party political broadcasts (Novelli 1995: 256–57).

Communist interest in independent broadcasting was thus driven by the need to keep pace with other political parties over propaganda, especially at the local level. Most of the Communist television stations were in fact set up at the initiative of the PCI's regional and provincial branches. Many quickly went bankrupt because of their lack of funding, but some, such as Video Uno of Rome, Teleradio Milano 2, TeleReggio and TeleVenezia, survived the breaking-in phase and became well known at the local level. The PCI therefore decided to fund the establishment and development of local television stations and to invest in the production of television programmes, which would be syndicated to the various broadcasters with links to the party by the newly created Nuova Emittenza Televisiva (NET: New Television Broadcasting).[18] In 1980, the PCI spent 840 million lire just on television equipment.[19] A year later, however, the NET experiment had already failed, leaving the PCI with a huge debt. There were various reasons for this failure, including the fact that the relationship between the PCI's centre and its outlying branches had profoundly changed over the years. The branches had become increasingly independent and rejected the intrusion of the centre in the management of 'their' television; they did not, for example, accept having to purchase NET production, which they deemed too expensive.[20] This was further proof of the crisis of the PCI in that the party's traditional organizational model did not seem to be standing the test of time.

The money to finance NET and the PCI network had to be diverted from other types of propaganda. The consequent scarcity of funding made Unitelefilm's final two years especially difficult. Its catalogue lists only eight films produced in 1979, for example, including *Dai Comunisti un quotidiano popolare* and *Un film sul PCI*, discussed earlier, and *Guido Rossa* (see Chap. 9).

The end of the PCI's ownership of Unitelefilm came with the appointment of Adalberto Minucci, a strong supporter of the commitment to television, as the new head of the party's national Press and Propaganda Section. The company was bought out by one of Unitelefilm's employees, Luciano Vanni, at the end of 1979. In that November, the Archivio Audiovisivo del Movimento Operaio e Democratico (AAMOD) was established with the aim of preserving the large collection of films and footage produced and collected by Unitelefilm over fifteen years of activity.[21]

Unitelefilm might have remained active for longer if it had played a more central role in the PCI's cultural policy. This, however, had never been the case. Unitelefilm's appearance as redundant and outdated was underlined by the emergence of a new cultural initiative in Rome, the famous '*Estate romana*' (Roman summer), a sort of festival of leisure and culture dreamt up by Renato Nicolini, the city councillor with responsibility for Rome's culture, and sponsored by the city's left-wing administration. During the first of these festivals, in 1977, Rome's residents enjoyed a variety of cultural events, such as poetry readings, plays, and film shows, scattered around the capital's streets and archaeological sites (Gundle 1995: 479–86; Nicolini 2011). Since the festival was aimed at entertaining Romans who were keen to forget the economic crisis, terrorism, and the widespread violence plaguing the country, its programme listed escapist feature films rather than the politically engaged documentaries that were Unitelefilm's customary output. This seemed to suggest that Communist film production was not suitable for the general public. However, the problem was less that Unitelefilm films were not sufficiently entertaining for the current public mood and more that the *Estate romana* marked a complete reversal in the PCI's approach to culture.

Communist cultural policy had previously been based on the principle that initiatives had to be developed with the aim of promoting the cultural elevation of the Italian masses, regardless of the breadth of their appeal. With the *Estate romana*, a new approach was adopted by Communist intellectuals and party leaders: initiatives needed to be evaluated in terms of quantifiable measures, such as the number of people attending events, rather than by their supposed and unquantifiable educational value. This approach led to the reassessment of areas of cultural production such as Hollywood movies and Italian popular cinema, which previously, at least in public, had been disparaged by Communist intellectuals. Moreover, profit became paramount. Within this new cultural environment, the very existence of a production facility in permanent financial deficit made no sense. Significantly, Unitelefilm's production crew and new director Maselli were among those within the party who opposed its new approach (Medici, Morbidelli and Taviani 2001: 102–3).

Film production by the PCI did not come to a complete end with the sale of Unitelefilm; a few more films were in fact produced in the 1980s. In the run-up to the local council elections of 1980 and 1981, for example, the party commissioned a group of left-wing directors to make four documentaries about the achievements of left-wing council administrations in the cities that the PCI had won as part of its successes in the mid-1970s. Ugo Gregoretti shot *Comunisti quotidiani* (Everyday

Communists) (80 minutes), about Rome; Ettore Scola was entrusted with a film on Turin, *Vorrei che volo* (I wish I could fly) (66 minutes); Aldo and Antonio Vergine made *Un'eredità difficile* (A difficult legacy) (66 minutes), about Naples; and Giuseppe Bertolucci filmed *Panni sporchi* (Dirty laundry) (95 minutes), which was supposed to depict the left-wing administration of Milan, but actually became a documentary on social marginalization entirely shot in the city's Central Station.[22] These four documentaries each cost about a hundred million lire, but from a propaganda perspective were less than effective; their length made them unsuitable for propaganda purposes, and the editing process was concluded too close to the elections (Novelli 1995: 218).

Although the final film produced by the PCI has already been discussed in Chap. 4, it merits further mention in the context of Unitelefilm's demise. *L'addio a Enrico Berlinguer*, chronicling Berlinguer's funeral in June 1984, was a collective project that somewhat symbolically involved many of the directors who had worked on films produced by the Italian Communist Party from the early years onwards. These included Carlo Lizzani, Gillo Pontecorvo, Paolo and Vittorio Taviani, Rosaria Polizzi, Carlo di Palma, Ansano Giannarelli, Luigi Perelli, Riccardo Napolitano, Ugo Gregoretti, Bernardo Bertolucci, Giuseppe Bertolucci, Paolo Pietrangeli, and Ettore Scola. *L'addio a Enrico Berlinguer* can thus truly be regarded as a final homage not only to a much-loved Communist leader, but also to Communist cinema, to a certain concept of culture that, for better or worse, had played a crucial role in Italy, and finally to the Italian Communist Party itself, which just a few years later, on 3 February 1991, was to be dissolved.

NOTES

1. For an analysis of the referendum of June 1978, see Bonini (2003: 19).
2. For a very similar interpretation, see Lanaro (1992: 412–18).
3. For a comprehensive analysis of the Movimento del '77, see Falciola (2015).
4. For an overview of the interpretations of Berlinguer's *austerità* in the historiography, see Soddu (2007: 69–71).
5. See *L'Unità*, 14 March 1977: front page.
6. D'Alema's report is in *L'Unità*, 15 March 1977: front page and p. 6.
7. A similar interpretation is offered by Edwards (2009: 196, 204); see also Falciola (2015: 157).

8. See 'Domani le dimissioni di Andreotti', *L'Unità*, 15 January 1978: front page.
9. See 'Dichiarazione di Berlinguer', *L'Unità*, 5 June 1979: front page.
10. On the publication of the 'Vangelo socialista', attributed to Craxi but actually written by Luciano Pellicani, in the magazine *L'Espresso* in 1978, see Musella (2007: 155–66).
11. For a general overview of the PCI–PSI quarrel in the 1980s, see Colarizzi (2007).
12. See *Rinascita*, 27 April 1979: 36.
13. Interview of Ansano Giannarelli by the author, Rome, 30 June 2011.
14. *L'Unità* reported a showing organized by the PCI's Rome branch at the city's *Teatro Centrale* on 11 April 1979. See 'Sarà presentato oggi "Un film sul PCI"', *L'Unità*, 11 April 1979: 10.
15. On the decline of grass-roots militancy, not just among the Communists, which was to become marked in the 1980s, see Pombeni (2014: 318–19).
16. Ninety-five copies of *Giovani* were distributed to PCI branches. See AAMOD, Unitelefilm Archive, Faldone "G", fascicolo "Giovani".
17. 'Siamo lottizzati ma anche bravi. La parola ai dirigenti messi sotto accusa', *La Repubblica*, 12 August 1977, p. 13.
18. 'Tv locali? Si, ma intelligenti. I progetti della neonata NET', *L'Unità*, 23 May 1980: 8.
19. *Informazioni e proposte sulla nostra rete televisiva*, in IG, APCI, MF 488, pp. 1348–59, December 1980.
20. Interview of Luciano Vanni by the author, recorded on July 15, 2010; Vanni worked at both NET and Teleconsorzio, the subsequent syndicated service which was also sponsored by the PCI.
21. IG, APCI, MF 439, p. 2458, Istituti e Organismi vari, Archivio Storico audiovisivo del Movimento operaio, VI bim. 1979.
22. See Ettore Scola, Ugo Gregoretti and Giuseppe Bertolucci, 'Un film una città. Cinque cineprese puntate sulle nostre città', *L'Unitá*, 11 May 1980: 11.

BIBLIOGRAPHY

Ajello, N. 1997. *Il lungo addio. Intellettuali e PCI dal 1958 al 1991*. Bari-Rome: Laterza.

Ballini, P.L. 2002. Le regole del gioco: dai banchetti elettorali alle campagne disciplinate. In *Storia delle campagne elettorali in Italia*, ed. P.L. Ballini and M. Ridolfi, 1–57. Milan: Bruno Mondadori.

Barbagli, M., and P. Corbetta. 1979. Una tattica e due strategie. Inchiesta sulla base del PCI. In *Dentro Il Pci*, ed. M. Barbagli, P. Corbetta, and S. Salvatore, 9–60. Bologna: il Mulino.

Berlinguer, E. 1977. *Austerità, occasione per trasformare l'Italia*. Rome: Editori Riuniti.

Boggs, C., and D. Plotke, eds. 1980. *The Politics of Eurocommunism: Socialism in Transition*. Montreal: Black Rose Books.

Bonini, F. 2003. Apogeo e crisi dell'istituzione partito. In *L'Italia repubblicana nella crisi degli anni settanta, Vol III, Partiti ed Organizzazioni di massa*, ed. F. Malgeri and L. Paggi, 17–36. Soveria Mannelli: Rubettino.

Carotti, C. 1992. *Alla ricerca del paradiso. L'operaio nel cinema italiano: (1945-1990)*. Genoa: Graphos.

Colarizzi, S. 2007. I duellanti. La rottura tra il PCI di Berlinguer e il PSI di Craxi alla svolta degli anni ottanta. In *Enrico Berlinguer, la politica Italia e la crisi mondiale*, ed. F. Barbagallo and A. Vittoria, 105–118. Rome: Carocci.

Crainz, G. 2005. *Il paese mancato. Dal miracolo economico agli anni ottanta*. Rome: Donzelli.

Edwards, P. 2009. *More Work, Less Pay. Rebellion and repression in Italy 1972–7*. Manchester: Manchester University Press.

Falciola, L. 2015. *Il Movimento del 1977 in Italia*. Rome: Carocci.

Ginsborg, P. 1990. *A History of Contemporary Italy. Society and Politics (1944–1989)*. London: Penguin.

Gozzini, G. 2001. Il PCI nel sistema politico della Repubblica. In *Il PCI nell'Italia repubblicana*, ed. R. Gualtieri, 103–141. Rome: Carocci.

Gundle, S. 1995. I *comunisti italiani tra Hollywood e Mosca. La sfida della cultura di massa*. Florence: Giunti.

Ignazi, P. 2006. Italy in the 1970s between Self -Expression and Organicism. In *Speaking out and Silencing. Culture, Society and Politics in Italy in the 1970s*, ed. A. Cento Bull and A. Giorgio, 10–29. London: Legenda.

Lanaro, S. 1992. *Storia dell'Italia repubblicana: dalla fine della guerra agli anni novanta*. Venice: Marsilio.

Lumley, R. 1998. *Dal '68 agli anni di piombo. Studenti e operai nella crisi italiana*. Florence: Giunti.

Lusanna, F. 2007. Il confronto con le socialdemocrazie europee. In *Enrico Berlinguer, la politica Italia e la crisi mondiale*, ed. F. Barbagallo and A. Vittoria, 147–172. Rome: Carocci.

Medici, A., M. Morbidelli, and E. Taviani, eds. 2001. *Il PCI e il cinema tra cultura e propaganda (1959 – 1979)*. Rome: Aamod.

Monteleone, F. 1992. *Storia della radio e della televisione in Italia. Società, politica, strategia, programmi 1922 – 1992*. Venice: Marsilio.

Musella, L. 2007. *Craxi*. Rome: Salerno Editrice.

Nicolini, R. 2011. *Estate Romana, un effimero lungo nove anni*. Reggio Calabria: Città del Sole.

Novelli, E. 1995. *Dalla TV di partito al partito della TV. Televisione e politica in Italia*. Florence: La Nuova Italia.

Ortoleva, P. 2008. La televisione italiana 1974 - 2002: dall' "anarchie italienne" al duopolio imperfetto. In *La Stampa italiana nell' età della Tv. Dagli anni settanta ad oggi*, ed. V. Castronovo and N. Tranfaglia. Bari: Laterza.

Pombeni, P. 2014. Il sistema dei partiti dalla prima alla seconda repubblica. In *L'Italia Contemporanea dagli anni Ottanta ad oggi*, ed. S. Colarizi, A. Giovagnoli, and P. Pombeni, vol. III, 318–319. Roma, Carocci: Istituzioni e Politica.

Pons, S. 2003. L'Italia e Il PCI nella politica estera dell'URSS di Brežnev. In *L'Italia Repubblicana nella crisi degli anni settanta. Tra guerra fredda e distensione, vol. I, Atti del ciclo di convegni, Roma, novembre e dicembre 2001*, ed. Agostino Giovagnoli and Silvio Pons, 63–88. Soveria Mannelli: Rubettino.

Rodano, F. 1975. *Sulla politica dei comunisti*. Turin: Boringhieri.

Salvadori, M. 1978. *Eurocomunismo e socialismo sovietico: problemi attuali del PCI e del movimento operaio*. Turin: Einaudi.

Soddu, P. 2007. Berlinguer e l'austerità: un'ipotesi di riforma. In *Enrico Berlinguer, la politica italiana e la crisi mondiale*, ed. F. Barbagallo and A. Vittoria, 37–76. Rome: Carocci.

CHAPTER 12

Conclusion

> We need to understand that there are millions and millions of Italians who know nothing about our programme and are still poisoned by Fascism's twenty years of anti-Communist propaganda. To win over these electors a nice poster or an incisive pamphlet will not be enough, nor will a rally, however well planned and carefully managed. Propaganda bears fruit wherever it finds fertile ground, but is discarded with disdain and disbelief by anyone who does not know what the PCI's policies really are. We therefore need to get close to the electors, go from house to house and farm to farm, to explain how to vote and who they ought to vote for.

These comments by Togliatti's personal secretary Mario Spinella were published in *L'Unità* on 12 April 1946. They exemplify the crucial role that the PCI leadership assigned to propaganda in the post-war period; they also provide an interpretative key for understanding the function assigned to films, as well as to other media, in the party's communication strategy. Propaganda tools were not supposed to plough the ground, but rather to plant seeds in ground already prepared by the work of persuasive militants across the country.

With this task in mind, film was just one of the many tools available to the propagandist. This explains why the officials in the PCI's national Press and Propaganda Section did not spend time developing their thinking on the specificities of film as a tool for propaganda. Moreover, they shared a misconception, widespread at the time, that films were 'a

© The Author(s), under exclusive license to Springer Nature Switzerland AG 2021
G. Fantoni, *Italy through the Red Lens*, Italian and Italian American Studies, https://doi.org/10.1007/978-3-030-69197-4_12

265

singularly powerful medium for propaganda' (Pronay and Spring 1982: 16), and as a result a decision was made in 1946 to invest in cinematographic propaganda. This was also a matter of prestige for the PCI: it was a visible indication that it could match the state-owned film company Istituto Luce in effectiveness (Lizzani 1991: 102). This aspiration explains the tendency to imitate the style of the newsreels produced under the Fascist regime, especially the stentorian voice-over that is heard in the film *Togliatti è ritornato*, for example.

My analysis of early Communist propaganda films illustrates how both Stalinism and Catholicism deeply influenced party culture. In order to communicate the cultural values, political perspectives, and specific imagery of the PCI, its leadership deployed to great effect various symbolic elements borrowed from these two cultural traditions. Films were also made in order to bolster the image of the leader, who was endowed with charismatic and even mythical traits. The research has also shown that the early PCI films were unsuitable, for these reasons, for addressing non-Communist voters.

Over the decades that followed, the approach of party leaders and officials in the Press and Propaganda Section to film propaganda did not evolve significantly. It was in fact very often rather narrow, being based on the assumption that propaganda messages, especially those conveyed in the voice-over commentary, had to be both straightforward and explicitly consistent with the party's policies. The production of propaganda films and documentaries, entrusted to the PCI's Press and Propaganda Section, was kept separate from the thinking on cinema being developed by the party's Cultural Commission. Nevertheless, PCI cinematography did improve with respect to narrative devices, as well as to shooting and editing technique, and by the later 1950s Communist propaganda films had become much more effective. These improvements owed much to the work of numerous top-flight filmmakers and intellectuals who became involved in the party's cinematographic production.

Until the crisis of 1956, those who worked on the PCI's films were the party's 'organic intellectuals', and generally considered themselves as such. Soldiers in an epic battle of ideas and ideologies whose outcome was already determined by the immutable laws of history, heralds of the cause of the proletariat, which was also the cause of justice on this earth, they felt no pressure, or at most very little, from the officials in the Press and Propaganda Section, whose views were to a great extent their own. After the death of Stalin in March 1953, the struggle for power in the Soviet

Union, culminating in execution of the deputy premier Lavrentiy Beria, challenged the myth of harmonious unity among the Soviet leaders. Three years or so later, the Twentieth Congress of the Communist Party of the Soviet Union and the subsequent denunciation of Stalin's crimes, followed by the Soviet army's repression of the Hungarian uprising in November 1956, provoked dismay at the grass-roots level in Italy and the disenchantment of many intellectuals (Ajello 1979: 429–52). The shock drove a substantial number of the latter away from the party. However, others remained and new ones were recruited; these included the Taviani brothers, who played their part in the PCI's renewed ventures in film production in the second half of the 1950s. This was possible because the Italian Communist Party, in a country that was dominated culturally by the Catholic Church and Christian Democracy, had come to be seen by many intellectuals of the new generation, rightly or wrongly, as an oasis of secularism and the provider and enabler of an alternative perspective. Togliatti's personal charm and influence over many intellectuals were also significant factors: they saw him as the politician who knew the most, saw the furthest, and embodied a particular and intellectually attractive image of the Communist Party.

The change of strategic direction in the PCI's film propaganda represented by the foundation of Unitelefilm in 1964 coincided with the death of Togliatti. From the outset, the Communist film production company was plagued by an inherent problem: it was an uncomfortable hybrid, being both a party organ and a private company. Too expensive to be financed exclusively by the party, Unitelefilm was both underfunded to the extent that it could not compete efficiently in the market and too concerned with ideological and political issues to function effectively as a private company. Within this new entity, the relationship between the party and those involved in Communist cinematographic production became less ideological and to some extent more professional. In consequence, the directors, cinematographers, screenwriters, and others generally demanded a greater degree of autonomy. Officials from the party's national Press and Propaganda Section would usually check the film after the pre-editing phase, and if necessary demanded modifications with respect to form and content. Sometimes, as was the case for Ansano Giannarelli's *Un film sul PCI*, disagreement between the Section and the director meant that the film was not distributed. It was rare, however, for disputes to have such a dramatic outcome; after all, the people who worked on Unitelefilm productions were left-wingers, and as they were also very often either PCI members or sympathizers, they were generally willing to sacrifice some of their artistic freedom for the sake of the party. In the late 1960s, at least while the attraction of *Cinema militante* lasted, working for the PCI was fashionable among filmmakers in general. Subsequently, the Communist production company was able to find new contributors both because of the working opportunities that it offered many young filmmakers and because of the attraction for intellectuals and artists of a Communist Party whose march to power seemed unstoppable. A part was played in this by Enrico Berlinguer, who was perceived as an earnest and honest politician whose integrity could be 'doubted only by those who had none' (Sassoon 1996: 590).

Was the PCI's cinematographic propaganda effective? Nicholas Reeves has demonstrated how difficult it is to make successful and appealing propaganda films, and his research has shown that the assumption that cinema was necessarily a powerful propaganda tool, able to radically affect viewers and profoundly influence the population's attitudes and ideology, was ill-founded (1999). If even Nazi and Soviet endeavours obtained results that have been deemed slight in relation to their levels of investment in cinematographic propaganda, what could reasonably have been expected from the much smaller and somewhat ill-equipped Italian Communist Party? My research has in fact shown how the absence of a well-organized film distribution network represented the most serious obstacle to the development of Communist cinematography in the 1960s and 1970s, while in the earlier period of the late 1940s and early 1950s, the primary difficulty had been censorship.

Communist film propaganda had its moment of glory in the run-up to the 1968 elections, when the PCI put an unprecedented level of investment into film production and distribution because it wanted to reach younger voters. After these polls, whose results demonstrated that the power of cinematographic propaganda to sway voters was far from overwhelming, Unitelefilm's fundamental problems became chronic and it struggled to find an effective organizational and management structure. Despite this, the company made its contribution to PCI propaganda over the next ten years and even produced some important films intended for distribution outside the Communist cinema network.

In the late 1950s and throughout the 1960s, the PCI produced several films on international issues. In the 1950s, these were invariably aimed at advocating the objectives of Soviet foreign policy. In the mid-1960s, the focus shifted decisively to the Vietnam War, and the films produced on this topic essentially represented anti-American propaganda. From the late 1960s onwards, however, foreign policy was almost abandoned. In the 1970s, Unitelefilm produced and sold documentaries depicting everyday life in socialist countries in a rather positive light, but very few of its films directly engaged with global issues such as the development of the Cold War. This was arguably due to the bewilderment caused by the crushing of the 'Prague Spring', the process of political and economic reform that the First Secretary of the Communist Party of Czechoslovakia Alexander Dubček undertook from January 1968 onwards (see Chap. 8).

The damage for the Italian Communist Party was great, not so much at the electoral level, but more at a moral, even psychological level. In the following two decades, the PCI leadership and thousands of militants had to live with an incurable contradiction: hoping for the democratization of the Communist system while receiving continuous proofs of the fact that Soviet-style communism could not be reformed and was fundamentally incompatible with Western-style democracy. Following the repression of the Prague Spring, the PCI leadership began a process of political detachment from the Soviet Union. Initially, this was a very cautious one, but it subsequently gained some momentum under Enrico Berlinguer's leadership (Pons 2003: 85). This reverberated at grass-roots level, taking the shape of a growing disillusionment regarding the consistency and viability of communism, as demonstrated by one of the films discussed in Chap. 11: Ansano Giannarelli's *Un film sul PCI*.

As this book has shown, the films produced by the PCI provide a particular record of the party's history and development by addressing many of its principal policies and concerns. It is also interesting to consider what issues PCI films failed to tackle. In relation to its early output, for example, it is striking that although Communist cinema often served to praise the achievements of the USSR, it was never used to explain the basis of Communist ideology, such as the thought of Marx and Lenin, to the party's militants. It could be argued that this ideology played a marginal role in the relationship between the party's leadership and its grass-roots activists. In this there were similarities between the Italian Communist Party and the Catholic Church or, to be more precise, the Church prior to the Second Vatican Council: the rank and file were required to believe in the party and its leadership rather than in the sacred texts. The study of the latter by non-experts could actually be dangerous, as it might result in interpretations that were at odds with official party doctrine.

It is also surprising that not a single film about Antonio Gramsci was distributed. To be fair to the crew of Unitelefilm, it did put forward a project for a documentary on Gramscian thought, aimed at marking the fortieth anniversary (in 1977) of the death of the Communist thinker and politician.[1] It was intended that the film would be divided into three parts, each entrusted to a director paired with an eminent scholar. Ansano Giannarelli and the historian Franco De Felice were to cover the section on Taylorism and Fordism, director Riccardo Napolitano (brother of Giorgio Napolitano) and Pasquale Villani were supposed to deal with Gramsci's interpretation of the 'southern question', and Carlo Lizzani and Corrado Vivanti were to tackle the Gramscian reading of the Risorgimento. The project secured financial support from the prestigious Einaudi publishing house, which had recently issued the critical edition of Gramsci's *Prison Notebooks*. In spite of this promising start, the project foundered because all attempts to give cinematic form to the abstract concepts in the preliminary scripts from the three scholars proved hopeless.

It should be emphasized that the year 1977 marked both the height of Gramsci's popularity in Italy's cultural debate and the widest distribution of his writings among Italian Communist militants and sympathizers, not least because of the new edition of the *Prison Notebooks*. On closer scrutiny, this was a surprising phenomenon. Despite the constant and almost ritual reference to Gramsci's thought by the Communist leadership, the policy of the historic compromise, which put forward the idea of an alliance between the workers and the middle class (represented by the DC), constituted a blatant disavowal of the thinking at the heart of Gramsci's political strategy, which had instead focused on the potential alliance between industrial workers and peasants. More in general, it can be argued that Gramsci's legacy had in reality been of limited political relevance to the PCI, especially after 1956. The main inspiration for the party's policies had in fact always been Togliatti's strategy of progressive enlargement of its social and electoral base. The only serious attempt to develop a policy at least in part inspired by Gramsci's thinking had been in the late 1940s, specifically regarding the problems of agriculture and land ownership afflicting the Italian South (discussed in Chap. 3). The DC-sponsored land reform of the early 1950s marked the ultimate failure of this policy. Nonetheless, as discussed in Chap. 6, the Gramscian interpretation remained an indispensable cultural reference for every PCI public discussion of the 'southern question'. During the 1980s Gramsci's fame in Italy was to slowly fade, while the global crisis of Communist ideology was to become increasingly acute (Gundle 1995: 459–60). Looking back, both the PCI's desire to produce a film about the Sardinian thinker and the failure of this project appear symbolic.

Another point of interest is that until the late 1960s, PCI cinematography virtually ignored industrial workers, devoting only a handful of films to the social class that supplied the largest share of Communist militants and was supposedly entrusted with Italy's future political direction.[2] It should be noted that the same could be said for Italian cinema in general; relatively few Italian films released in the post-war years have industrial workers as protagonists (Carotti 1992: 11; Ben-Ghiat 2001: 36). PCI cinematic propaganda also ignored the work of left-wing intellectuals such as Renato Panzieri and Mario Tronti, who focused their attention on the industrial working class and laid the foundation for '*operaismo*' (workerism) (Grandi 2003: 8–16), which was then developed by Toni Negri and others in the 1970s.[3] As a result, the Communist films of that period offered an image of Italian society as composed almost exclusively of southern peasants, middle-class students, and generic 'democratic citizens' peacefully marching for North Vietnam. This was certainly consistent with the strategy of the '*politica unitaria*' (unifying policy) that had initially been developed by Togliatti and was subsequently endorsed by the PCI leadership in the wake of the party's Eleventh Congress, in 1966. It was argued that the PCI's links with the industrial workers should not be emphasized, so that the party could be portrayed as safeguarding the interests of a wider range of social groups. This approach certainly made its contribution to the PCI's electoral endurance.

PCI cinematography only became more attentive to the industrial working class after 1968, and in particular after the 'hot autumn' had opened up the decade of '*centralità operaia*' (workers centre stage). Unitelefilm then produced films such as *Sabato, domenica e lunedi* (discussed in Chap. 10), *La fabbrica parla* (the sixth film in the Terzo Canale series, discussed in Chap. 6) and *Un film sul PCI* (Chap. 11). However, the most important documentary on the Italian working class, *Contratto* (Chap. 6), was produced not by the PCI but by CGIL, while the party's most interesting film of that period, *Apollon, una fabbrica occupata* (Chap. 7), was a rather atypical product born in the cultural climate of *cinema militante*. Whereas the early PCI propaganda films were addressed directly at the party's militants, Unitelefilm's productions seem to have principally been aimed at petit bourgeois and middle-class voters such as professionals, students, shopkeepers, and small landowners.

As argued in Chap. 10, Communist cinema also disregarded women, in particular working women. Although there were exceptions, like Ansano Giannarelli's *Sabato, Domenica e Lunedi* (1968), in PCI films the male factory worker was the sole representative of the Italian working class during the years of the boom.[4] *Essere donne*, the first PCI film about women's working conditions, was released only in 1965, and its production was due to a rather extraordinary circumstance: the unprecedented collaboration between an unorthodox Communist like Luciana Castellina (later expelled from the party) and Cecilia Mangini, one of the most unconventional documentary filmmakers ever to work in post-war Italian cinema, as well as a proto-feminist.[5] The subsequent eruption of second-wave feminism forced the party to pay more attention to women's problems, but again it wasn't the world of work that became the setting of the Communists' cinematic investigation of women, but rather family life, as proved by films like *Essere madre* (1977).

This book has discussed the use of music in Communist cinematography, in relation to specific films (see, e.g. Chaps. 3, 6 and 10). A conclusive reflection on this important aspect of film production may be of interest to the reader. Music had a prominent role in early PCI production. It was sometimes deployed to enhance the film's political message in a highly calibrated fashion (see, e.g. the 1951 film *Pace, lavoro e libertà*, discussed in Chap. 3). More often, though, its function was decorative; music added emotional intensity to the film, and it was therefore meant to help extol the strength of the party and the wisdom of its leaders. The inspiration for such a use of music came from Fascist newsreels as well as from Soviet cinema.

Music in Communist films became less intrusive in the 1960s, due to the example set by *Cinéma-vérité*, which greatly inspired the filmmakers who were working for the party (see Chap. 6). Within the new aesthetic, the musical score was refused altogether, as it seemed to make documentary films lose in realism. However, it was not just the way music was used in Communist film productions that changed dramatically between the 1950s and the 1960s; the musical taste of Communist intellectuals also changed. At the end of the 1950s, a new generation of music critics—some of whom were also composers, like Giacomo Manzoni—took over the cultural pages of *L'Unità* and began to vigorously promote experimentalism. The hitherto celebrated Mario Zafred, who—throughout the 1950s—had been the principal proponent, in Italy, of the adoption of models from socialist realism in music writing, was

12 CONCLUSION   273

unceremoniously put aside, becoming almost an object of derision (Manzoni 2013: 26). *L'Unità* now sponsored neo-modernist composers such as Bruno Maderna and Luigi Nono.[6] The latter was contracted by Unitelefilm in the 1960s and wrote the musical score for several films, including *L'offensiva del Tet* (1968), discussed in Chap. 5. Nono was also a party member, and in 1975 he was appointed to the PCI's Central Committee.[7]

The music produced by *cantautori* (singers and songwriters) also played an important part in Communist film production. The encounter between the PCI's cinema and the first generation of *cantautori* was in part the result of political affinity. In the early 1960s, songwriters advocated pacifism, social justice, and, just like the PCI, they were generally critical of the economic miracle and its deleterious social effects (Carusi 2018: 25–30). Their songs were employed only occasionally in the 1960s, but with remarkable results. An effective use of the *cantautori's* repertoire can be seen in *Il viaggio della speranza* (The Journey of hope—1963), directed by Gianfranco Bertacco. The film is part of a series of films produced in the early 1960s and presenting emigration from the south (in this film, specifically from Sicily) as a negative effect of the economic boom. The film begins by showing a train running along the coast. We hear Piero Ciampi's *Lungo treno del sud* (Long train of the south), a poetic song about lovers being separated due to emigration. The combination of images and music communicates a soft, melancholy emotion. This vanishes, however, as soon as the train enters the Turin station, when jazz music takes over; jazz was often associated with the city in Communist cinematography. The editing gets faster, and the viewer is overwhelmed by images depicting what the voice-over commentary defines 'the spurious euphoria of the Miracolo Economico': traffic jams and neon signs of the venues attended by the urban middle class, as they go shopping in the city centre.

In the 1970s, a growing number of Italian *cantautori* were writing politically engaged songs. As a result, they were welcomed in the party's Festival dell'Unità. For example, the documentary on the Festival Nazionale dell'Unità, directed by Ettore Scola in 1972, features performances by folksingers Anna Identici, Paolo Pietrangeli, Giovanna Marini, and *Il nuovo canzoniere italiano* group.[8] The *cantautori's* songs were included in the Unitelfilm productions, for example, in *Essere madre* (1977—see Chap. 10). Whereas jazz, protest songs, and folk music are strongly present in Communist cinema, rock music is virtually absent.

Rock, and particularly progressive rock, was culturally and politically linked to the 'youth proletariat' and to the radical left-wing groups. These were the protagonists of the 1977 movement, which is discussed in Chap. 11 (Borio 2013: 182).

At the end of the 1970s, in the face of a boom in independent television broadcasting, cinema suddenly appeared to be an outdated and ineffective propaganda tool. Consequently, the PCI decided to end its involvement in Unitelefilm. Cinema was about to change anyway. As noted by Laura Mulvey, the 1970s 'would be the last decade in which films could only be viewed by the public, collectively, projected and in a darkened theatre' (2015: 18). Due to the broadcasting of a large number of films by public and private televisions and, shortly thereafter, the diffusion of VHS, the spectator–film relationship increasingly became a fragmented and private experience.[9] In this new fruition context, no political mediation by party officers (such as the classic, and often ridiculed, post-projection debate) was possible.

The history of Communist engagement in independent broadcasting merits future research in view of the insights it could provide into the propaganda activity, decision-making processes and culture of the Italian Communist Party, at both national and local level, from the early 1980s onwards. The PCI's involvement in public broadcasting also deserves attention, given that one of its principal objectives during the 1980s was to ensure control over one of the RAI television channels. The fact that the PCI decided to renounce cinema, a twentieth-century means of communication like few others, in order to bet its money on television, showed that the PCI was still reactive as a political body, willing to adapt to a rapidly evolving environment. At the same time, however, the spectacular failure of what was supposed to be a revolution in the PCI's communication strategy showed that it lacked the cultural equipment—starting with an entrepreneurial capacity—to inhabit the world that was taking shape.

The advent of multi-channel independent broadcasting can now be seen as a sign that a particular phase of Italian history was inexorably coming to an end: Italy was entering its post-industrial age. The reassuring and fundamentally unchanging world that had nurtured the growth of the Italian Communist Party, a world ordered in relation to well-defined ideologies and social classes, was crumbling with increasing speed, to be replaced by a very different society. This would appear, to Communist eyes, shapeless, confused and unreasonably optimistic. The new Italy was faithfully reflected by the world of independent broadcasting: a mixture of anarchism, exaggerated localism, smug ignorance, and bright entrepreneurial intuition. This was the age of '*neotelevisione*' ('Neo-Television'), as Umberto Eco famously first described it in 1983, which built a new relationship with the viewer through its unbroken, chaotic, and vaguely insane stream of television shows and commercials, ultimately shaping a new kind of citizen (Eco 1990). The Communists experienced a gradual cultural marginalization that episodes such as the huge gathering at the funeral of Berlinguer, or victory in the 1984 elections for the European Parliament, might hide but could not reverse.

When the last leader of the PCI Achille Occhetto burst into tears—very unusual behaviour for a Communist leader—at the party's Nineteenth Congress (Bologna, 7–11 March 1990), after the decision had been made to change the party's name, there were no Communist filmmakers in attendance to record this historic moment for Communist militants. That same night, however, an anonymous mass of television viewers saw the scene on the evening news.

NOTES

1. See the folder on this project in AAMOD, Faldone *Progetti non realizzati*, fascicolo *Einaudi – 3 doc. Su Gramsci*.
2. Industrial workers accounted for 39.5 per cent of the total PCI membership in 1962, by far the largest social group, and still the same percentage ten years later (when the total membership was 1,584,147). See Lanaro (1992: 404), Partito Comunista Italiano (1973: 19). The Unitelefilm crew did film various events involving Italy's industrial workers, including strikes, demonstrations and union meetings, but the footage was very rarely edited. There are several examples of unfinished films on Italian workers conserved in the AAMOD.
3. '*Operaismo*' (workerism) was a school of thought that saw industrial disputes as the key events driving progress forward, and believed that socialist revolution in the Western world could only be achieved by the actions of industrial workers, rather than by the established Communist Parties.
4. On this point, see Palmieri (2016).
5. On feminist militant discourse in Cecilia Mangini's documentaries, see Missero (2016).
6. On the work of Luigi Nono, see Nielinger-Vakil (2015).
7. See *L'Unità*, 24 March 1974, 7.

8. On *Il nuovo canzoniere italiano* (founded in 1962) and the role it played in the promotion of folk and protest songs, as well as in the development of ethnomusicology, see Portelli (2001: 265–66).
9. A negative criticism of how local televisions used feature films in their daily programming can be found in Miccichè (1997: 8–9): '[private televisions] turned feature films into "television shows", inundating the small screens of the whole of Italy with hundreds and hundreds of films, every given day, thousands of films per month. And they would place shoulder to shoulder (actually one after the other) [...] movie stars and genre films, art films found in film archives, or sold off by impoverished film collectors and American film studio's lowbrow productions. And because these were no longer films but TV shows, it was OK to cut, alter, redub with impossible dialogues or re-edit them with improbable music, and, it goes without saying, to interrupt the vision of these films with an explosive number of commercials'.

BIBLIOGRAPHY

Ajello, N. 1979. *Intellettuali e PCI 1944–1958*. Bari: Laterza.

Ben-Ghiat, R. 2001. The Italian Cinema and the Italian Working Class. *International Labor and Working Class History* 59: 36–51.

Borio, G. 2013. Key Questions of Antagonist Music-Making: A View from Italy. In *Red Strains. Music and Communism Outside the Communist Bloc*, ed. R. Adlington, 175–191. Oxford: Oxford University Press.

Carotti, C. 1992. *Alla ricerca del paradiso. L'operaio nel cinema italiano: (1945–1990)*. Genoa: Graphos.

Carusi, P. 2018. *Viva L'Italia. Narrazioni e rappresentazioni della storia repubblicana nei versi dei cantautori «impegnati»*. Milan: Le Monnier.

Eco, U. 1990. A Guide to the Neo-Television of the 1980s. In *Culture and Conflict in Postwar Italy. Essays on Mass and Popular Culture*, ed. Z.G. Barański and R. Lumley, 245–255. New York: St. Martin's Press.

Grandi, A. 2003. *La generazione degli anni perduti. Storia di Potere Operaio*. Turin: Einaudi.

Gundle, S. 1995. *I comunisti italiani tra Hollywood e Mosca. La sfida della cultura di massa*. Florence: Giunti.

Lanaro, S. 1992. *Storia dell'Italia repubblicana: dalla fine della guerra agli anni novanta*. Venice: Marsilio.

Lizzani, C. 1991. I film per il "partito nuovo". In *Il 1948 in Italia, la storia e i film*, ed. N. Tranfaglia, 97–103. Scandicci (Florence): La Nuova Italia.

Manzoni, G. 2013. Towards Political and Musical Renewal: The Other Idea of Communism. In *Red Strains. Music and Communism Outside the Communist Bloc*, ed. R. Adlington, 23–29. Oxford: Oxford University Press.

Miccichè, L. 1997. Un decennio di transizione. In *Il cinema del riflusso. Film e cineasti degli anni '70*, ed. L. Miccichè, 3–15. Venice: Marsilio.

Missero, D. 2016. Cecilia Mangini: A Counterhegemonic Experience of Cinema. *Feminist Media Histories* 2 (3): 54–72.

Mulvey, L. 2015. 1970s Feminist Film Theory and the Obsolescent Object. In *Feminisms*, ed. L. Mulvey and A. Backman Rogers, 17–26. Amsterdam: Amsterdam University Press.

Nielinger-Vakil, C. 2015. *Luigi Nono: A Composer in Context*. Cambridge: Cambridge University Press.

Palmieri, M. 2016. L'altra faccia del miracolo. Il boom nei filmati di propaganda del PCI. In *Penso che un sogno così non ritoni mai più. L'Italia del miracolo tra storia, cinema, musica e televisione*, ed. P. Camillo and P. Iaccio, 153–168. Naples: Liguori.

Partito Comunista Italiano. 1973. *PCI '73. Almanacco del Partito Comunista Italiano*.

Pons, S. 2003. L'Italia e Il PCI nella politica estera dell'URSS di Brežnev. In *L'Italia Repubblicana nella crisi degli anni settanta. Tra guerra fredda e distensione*, ed. A. Giovagnoli and S. Pons, 63–88. Soveria Mannelli: Rubettino.

Portelli, A. 2001. The Centre Cannot Hold: Music as Political Communication in Post-War Italy. In *The Art of Persuasion. Political Communication in Italy from 1945 to the 1990s*, ed. L. Cheles and L. Sponza, 258–276. Manchester and New York: Manchester University Press.

Pronay, N., and D.W. Spring, eds. 1982. *Propaganda, Politics and Film (1918–1945)*. Hong Kong: Macmillan Press.

Reeves, N. 1999. *The Power of Film Propaganda. Myth of Reality?* London: Cassell.

Sassoon, D. 1996. *One Hundred Years of Socialism: The West European Left in the Twentieth Century*. London: I. B. Tauris.

Film Index[1]

A

Apollon, una fabbrica occupata (Apollon, an occupied factory, 1969), 161, 167–169, 174n12, 271

B

Bianco e Nero (White and Black, 1975), 191, 192

C

Carosello elettorale (Election roundabout, 1960), 106

Chi dorme non piglia pesci (The early bird catches the worm, 1948), 1, 2

Cinegiornale della Pace (Peace newsreel, 1963), 98–100, 112n15, 161

Cinegiornali del Popolo (Newsreels of the people, 1949), 81n20

Comunisti quotidiani (Everyday Communists, 1980), 260

Confronto, partecipazione, unità (Comparison, involvement and unity, 1975), 207, 209, 210

D

Dai comunisti un quotidiano popolare (A newspaper for the people from the Communists, 1979), 253, 254, 258

Della Conoscenza (On knowledge, 1968), 140, 151, 153

Deserto di uomini (A land with no men, 1965), 118

E

Emigrazione '68 (Emigration '68, 1968), 197n6

Essere donne (Being women, 1965), 93, 224–230, 240n3, 240n7, 272

---

[1] Note: Page numbers followed by 'n' refer to notes.

© The Author(s), under exclusive license to Springer Nature Switzerland AG 2021
G. Fantoni, *Italy through the Red Lens*, Italian and Italian American Studies, https://doi.org/10.1007/978-3-030-69197-4

280 FILM INDEX

F

Festival nazionale dell'Unità 1972
(1972), 183, 198n17, 273
Fortezze vuote (Empty fortresses,
1975), 193, 194,
199n36, 200n40
14 luglio (14 July, 1948), 46, 51–53,
55–58, 62, 65, 78

G

Giovani (Young people, 1979), 253,
255, 261n16
Gli uomini vogliono la pace (People
want peace, 1958), 96
Gli uomini vogliono vivere (People
want to leave, 1958), 96
Gronchi nell'URSS (Gronchi in the
USSR, 1960), 98
Guido Rossa (1979), 209, 258

I

I Campionissimi (The super champs
1958), 95
I comunisti e il paese (The Communists
and the country, 1966),
116, 125–127
I fatti di Celano (The Celano affair ,
1950), 78
I giorni di Brescia (The Brescia days,
1974), 188–191
I giovani, il lavoro, la crisi (Young
people, work and the crisis,
1977), 247, 248
Il nuovo re è l'infanzia (Childhood is
the new king, 1974), 195
Il prezzo del miracolo (The cost of the
miracle, 1963), 103
Il viaggio della speranza (The journey
of hope–1963), 103, 273
Insieme per cambiare (Together for
change, 1979), 239

L

L'addio a Enrico Berlinguer (Farewell
to Enrico Berlinguer, 1984),
121, 260
*La donna é cambiata, l'Italia deve
cambiare* (Women have changed,
and Italy has to change, 1976),
224, 232
La fabbrica aperta (The factory
revealed, 1970), 162
La fabbrica parla (The factory speaks,
1968), 140, 145, 271
L'altra faccia del miracolo (The other
side of the miracle, 1963),
103, 104
La Marcia per la pace (Peace march,
1962), 100
La nuova Corea (The new Korea,
1970), 194
La salute è malata (The health service
is unwell, 1971), 172
La trama nera (The dark conspiracy,
1972), 187, 188
La via della libertà (The Way to
Freedom, 1951), 47, 73, 74
La via sicura (The safe path,
1964), 111n6
Le antenne del potere (Power's aerials,
1968), 220n9
Le 150 ore (150 hours, 1974), 198n19
L'infanzia in Bulgaria (Childhood in
Bulgaria, 1977), 195
L'Italia con Togliatti (Italy with
Togliatti, 1964), 117, 119–122,
124, 225
L'offensiva del Tet (Tet offensive,
1968), 131, 273
L'ordine non viene da destra (Order
doesn't come from the right,
1972), 188
*L'organizzazione di una comune
agricola* (The organization of an
agricultural commune, 1977), 195

FILM INDEX   281

M
Madre, ma come? (Mother, but how? 1977), 236
Maputo: Una città che rinasce (Maputo: a city reborn, 1977), 195
Modena città dell'Emilia rossa (Modena, a City in Red Emilia, 1950), 7, 71–73, 83n40

N
Nel mezzogiorno qualcosa è cambiato (Something has changed in the South, 1949), 47, 66–70, 82n32, 97, 143, 145
Non ci regalano niente (Nothing comes for free, 1977), 224, 234
A nord del 38° parallelo (North of the 38th parallel, 1974), 195, 196

O
Oltre 11 milioni (More than 11 million, 1975), 210–212

P
Pace, lavoro e libertà (Peace, Work and Freedom, 1951), 47, 73, 75–77, 272
Panni sporchi (Dirty laundry, 1980), 260
A Paolo Rossi nostro compagno (For our comrade Paolo Rossi, 1967), 116, 127, 128
Parvenez vuol dire primavera ('Parvenez' means spring, 1976), 195, 196
Perché droga (Why drugs?, 1976), 194, 200n41
Per un'Italia diversa (In a different Italy, 1975), 210

Q
Quattro lezioni su Togliatti (Four lessons on Togliatti, 1976), 216, 218

R
Resistenza, una nazione che risorge' (Resistance: a nation that rises up anew, 1976), 213–216

S
Sabato, domenica, lunedi (Saturday, Sunday, Monday, 1968), 229, 230
Sicilia all'addritta (Sicily on its feet, 1958), 13n10, 95
Sicilia: terremoto anno uno (Sicily, earthquake year one, 1970), 162
Socialismo: la via cecoslovacca (Socialism: the Czechoslovakian path, 1968), 195
Speciale Sud (Special bulletin on the South, 1968), 143

T
Togliatti è ritornato (Togliatti is back, 1948), 46, 51–53, 59, 61, 62, 65, 66, 78, 82n23, 210, 255, 266
Torino dopo il miracolo (Turin after the miracle, 1965), 104
Tre anni di Storia (Three years of history, 1960), 98
Trevico–Torino, viaggio nel Fiat-nam (Trevico–Turin: a journey into Fiat-nam, 1972), 183

U
Un'eredità difficile (A difficult legacy, 1980), 260

282 FILM INDEX

Un film sul PCI (A film on the PCI, 1979), 250, 253, 258, 267, 269, 271

Vietnam chiama (Vietnam calls, 1965), 129, 130
Vorrei che volo (I wish I could fly, 1980), 260

V

Vecchio e nuovo nelle campagne (Old and new in the countryside, 1964), 118

X

X congresso nazionale del Pci (The tenth national Congress of the PCI, 1962), 101

Subject Index[1]

NUMBERS AND SYMBOLS
8 mm (film format), 162, 163
12 dicembre (December 12th 1971), 166, 171
16 mm film format, 78, 141
35 mm film format, 78

A
Abortion, 224, 225, 227, 232–239
Achtung! Banditi (1951), 35
Adenauer, Konrad, 98, 99
Agosti, Silvano, 164, 173n3, 199n30
Alicata, Mario, 30, 67, 71, 115
Almirante, Giorgio, 180, 187, 191
Amendola, Giorgio, 23, 124–126, 220n12
American movies/films/cinematography, 31, 38n30, 38n31, 39n40, 50, 51, 276n9
Andreotti, Giulio, 84n53, 95, 142, 243, 245, 250

Andrioli, Massimo, 220n9
Anni di piombo (years of lead), 147
Anti-Fascism, 29, 33, 93, 94, 116, 127–129, 203, 218
Archivio Audiovisivo del Movimento Operaio e Democratico (AAMOD), 5, 12n3, 12n4, 84n48, 111n6, 112n10, 112n15, 113n28, 118, 134n4, 135n24, 159, 193, 198n17, 198n19, 200n40, 200n45, 257, 258, 275n2
Argentieri, Mino, 5, 12n4, 30, 38n30, 49, 110, 118, 119, 173n5, 191, 192, 198n10, 199n20, 213, 214, 253
Aristarco, Guido, 33, 132
Associazione Cattolica Esercenti Cinema (ACEC, Catholic Association of Cinema Operators), 78

---

[1] Note: Page numbers followed by 'n' refer to notes.

© The Author(s), under exclusive license to Springer Nature Switzerland AG 2021
G. Fantoni, *Italy through the Red Lens*, Italian and Italian American Studies, https://doi.org/10.1007/978-3-030-69197-4

284 SUBJECT INDEX

Associazione Nazionale Autori Cinematografici (ANAC, National Association of Filmmakers), 159, 165–167
Associazione Nazionale Partigiani d'Italia (ANPI, National Association of Italy's Partisans), 78
Associazione Ricreativa Culturale Italiana (ARCI), 169, 187, 216
Austerity, 245, 246, 249
Autocoscenza, 237, 241n16
Autocritica (self-criticism), 27, 50, 94
Autonomia, 247, 248, 255
Autunno caldo (hot autumn), 140, 146, 180, 248, 271

B
Balbo, Pierpaolo, 151
Barbaro, Umberto, 19–21
Barbero, Franco, 200n41
Basaglia, Franco, 193
Belice (earthquake), 162
Bellocchio, Marco, 159, 164, 165, 167, 174n10
Bellonzi, Bruna, 228
Benocci, Mario, 108, 118, 132, 140, 153, 154, 161
Beria, Lavrentiy, 267
Berlinguer, Enrico, 75, 121, 122, 135n16, 136n31, 189, 196, 200n47, 211, 212, 218, 220n10, 221n20, 231, 232, 238, 239, 245, 246, 249–253, 260, 260n4, 268, 269, 275
Berlinguer ti voglio bene (Berlinguer: I love you, 1977), 211
Berlusconi, Silvio, 151, 257
Bertacco, Gianfranco, 273
Bertolucci, Bernardo, 5, 166, 172, 260

Bertolucci, Giuseppe, 260
Bicycle Thieves (1948), 33
Bocchetti, Alessandra, 151, 152
Bollero, Marcello, 29
Bolshevism/Bolshevik, 47, 72, 94
Borghese, Junio Valerio, 187, 191
Brescia (bombing), 188, 190
Brescia 1974 (film), 199n30
Brigate Rosse, *see* Red Brigades
Bunuel, Luis, 159
Buongoverno delle sinistre, 6

C
Calendario del Popolo (Magazine), 27
Camera del lavoro, 78
Cannes (Film Festival), 166, 198n14
Cantautori, 273
Canzoniere Femminista, 237
Capitini, Aldo, 100
Cappelloni, Guido, 210, 211
Carbone, Mario, 101, 112n20
Carlini, Carlo, 75
Caruso, Pino, 205, 206
Castellina, Luciana, 225, 272
Castro, Fidel, 149
Catholic Church/Catholicism/ Christian religion/Christianity, 25, 26, 45, 47, 48, 63, 65, 78, 96, 126, 205, 266, 267, 269
Cavani, Liliana, 164, 166, 179, 215
Cecchi, Carlo, 135n15
Censorship/censors/Board of Censors, 2, 31–33, 38n35, 50, 59, 68, 73, 78, 81n20, 81n23, 83n40, 84n53, 106, 109, 228, 268
Centralismo democratico (democratic centralism), 27, 94, 125
Centri Universitari Cinematografici (CUC, University Film Centres), 160

SUBJECT INDEX 285

Centro Cinematografico di
Documentazione Proletaria
(Center for Proletarian Cinematic
Documentation), 163
Centro di Documentazione (CdD), 70
Centrosinistra/centre-left alliance,
93, 94, 164
Che Guevara, Ernesto, 149, 150
Chiaretti, Tommaso, 33, 34, 39n38
Chiarini, Luigi, 165, 166
Chiaromonte, Gerardo, 216
Chiaureli, Mikheil, 20, 49, 53
Chilanti, Felice, 52, 80n13,
225, 240n4
Chinese Communist Party (CCP),
100–102, 112n19
Ciampi, Piero, 273
Cinegiornale studentesco (Student
newsreels), 163
Cinegiornali liberi (Free newsreels),
161, 162, 164, 165, 172
Cinema civile (political cinema), 183
Cinema militante/militant cinema, 9,
155, 159–173, 181, 183,
268, 271
Cinema Nuovo (magazine), 132
Cinema Teatro Azione (Cinema and
Theatre Action), 163
Cinéma-vérité, 143, 154, 272
Circoli del cinema, 50
Cirino, Bruno, 199n36, 210
Cirino, Pomicino, 210
Cold War, 25, 31, 32, 65, 78, 82n30,
93, 109, 269
Collettivi del Cinema militante, 160
Collettivo femminista di cinema
(feminist film collective), 241n16
Colli, Ombretta, 237
Comencini, Luigi, 34
Comintern, 75
Communist Party of the Soviet Union
(CPSU), 23, 74, 77, 94, 100,
132, 267

Compromesso storico (historic
compromise policy),
10, 179–197, 205, 207,
215, 216, 218, 232, 234,
252, 270
Comunisti (Communists, 1968), 148
Confederazione Generale Italiana del
Lavoro (CGIL), 26, 51, 55, 146,
190, 247, 271
Consciousness-Raising, *see*
Autocoscienza
Contestazione, 123, 131, 147,
163, 172
Contratto (Contract, 1969), 140, 146,
147, 248, 271
Cooperativa Cinematografica
Spettatori Produttori, 35, 83n39
Craxi, Bettino, 250, 257, 261n10
Cristo si è fermato ad Eboli (Christ
Stopped at Eboli, novel), 69
Cronache di poveri amanti (1954), 35
Cuban missile crisis, 99
Cuban Revolution, 130, 151
Cucciolla, Riccardo, 130
Cult of personality/personality cult,
8, 46, 52–54, 196
Cultural Commission (Commissione
culturale), 28, 30, 33, 35, 105,
125, 182, 197n8, 266
Cultural Revolution, 124, 135n13,
151, 159

D

D'Alema, Massimo, 247
Dal Pozzo, Giuliana, 225, 227
De Gasperi, Alcide, 37n18,
38n30, 48
De Gaulle, Charles, 98, 99
De Lorenzo, Giovanni, 141, 142
De Santis, Giuseppe, 30, 32–34,
39n40, 71, 77
Delli Colli, Tonino, 134n5

286 SUBJECT INDEX

Democrazia Cristiana (DC)/Christian
Democrat(s), 3, 6, 7, 12n4,
13n10, 25, 26, 31–33, 35,
38n30, 51, 81n23, 91–96, 103,
106, 109, 111n6, 111n7, 111n8,
116, 125, 142, 180, 188–192,
207, 208, 210, 218, 232–234,
236, 243–245, 249, 250, 252,
257, 270
Democrazia progressiva (progressive
democracy), 23, 25, 217
De-Stalinization, 34, 111n5, 115, 132
Di Gianni, Luigi, 99, 112n14
Di Vittorio, Giuseppe, 150
Direct cinema, 143, 154
Divorce/divorzio, 203–207, 209,
219n1, 225, 232, 235, 238
D'Onofrio, Edoardo, 56
Dubbing, 57, 80n19, 169

E

The Earth Trembles/La terra trema
(1948), 33, 39n37, 70,
82n35, 134n6
Economic Cooperation Administration
(ECA), 3
Economic miracle/boom, 8, 13n4,
92, 93, 102, 103, 105, 110, 123,
145, 146, 148, 226, 273
Editori Riuniti, 28, 183
Eisenstein, Sergei, 58, 132, 133
Emigration/migratory phenomena/
migration, 92, 93, 103, 144, 184,
194, 197n6, 273
Estate romana (Roman summer), 259
Eurocommunism, 246, 251
Europa '51 (1952), 34

F

Fanfani, Amintore, 111n7, 208

Fascism/Fascists/Fascist National
Party (PNF), 1–3, 12n1, 22, 24,
25, 29–32, 35, 38n28, 38n30,
38n31, 50, 52, 71, 74, 75,
80n13, 83n41, 111n6, 123, 128,
134n6, 149, 150, 172, 179–197,
197n3, 204, 208, 214, 216, 218,
248, 254, 265, 266, 272
Fellini, Federico, 29, 34, 75
Feminism/feminist movement, 9, 151,
219, 223–240, 240n8, 241n10,
241n12, 272
Ferrara, Gianni, 71
Ferrara, Maurizio, 112n14, 182
Festa/e (Nazionale) dell'Unità, 52,
59, 81n21, 187
FGCI (the Italian Communist Youth
Federation), 75, 125, 150,
153, 247
FICC (Federazione Italiana Circoli del
Cinema/Italian Federation of
Cinema Clubs), 50
Film democratico, 7, 21, 33
Finzi, Luciana, 182
Fofi, Goffredo, 134n11, 161, 166,
169, 170, 174n9, 174n10
Forchettoni (campaign), 111n8
Franchina, Basilio, 59, 82n25
Franzinetti, Vittoria, 184
Frezza, Andrea, 125, 135n15
Fronte Democratico Popolare
(Democratic Popular
Front), 25, 50
Fuksas, Massimiliano, 151

G

Gagarin, Yuri, 97
Gambescia, Paolo, 191
Gatto, Alfonso, 148, 156n9
Gazzelloni, Severino, 213
Gelovani, Mikheil, 49

Giannarelli, Ansano, 5, 55, 112n14, 209, 213, 214, 220n8, 229, 237, 250, 251, 253, 255, 260, 267, 270, 272
Giap (Vietnamese General), 150
Godard, Jean-Luc, 152, 159, 160
Golpe Borghese, 187
Governi di unità antifascista, 25, 30
Gramsci, Antonio, 7, 22–24, 36n14, 37n16, 37n23, 54, 55, 67, 68, 74, 77, 83n44, 120, 121, 149, 150, 168, 203, 254, 257, 270
Gramscian reading of the 'southern question, 145
The Great Farewell (1953), 122
Gregoretti, Ugo, 5, 140, 146, 161, 166–168, 170, 181–183, 192, 198n10, 206, 247, 259, 260
Grieco, Sergio, 47, 74, 83n41
Grierson, John, 228
GUF/Cineguf, 29
Guttuso, Renato, 115

H
Hegemony (Gramscian theory of), 24, 28, 30, 35, 155, 160, 170, 195, 203–219, 243–260
Ho Chi Min, 149

I
I cannibali (The Year of the Cannibals, 1970), 179
Identici, Anna, 237, 273
Il Contemporaneo (magazine), 115, 220n9, 220n12
Il Giuramento (Klyatva, The Vow), 49
Il nuovo canzoniere italiano, 273, 276n8
Il secondo tragico Fantozzi (The second tragic Fantozzi, 1976), 133

Il sole sorge ancora (Outcry, 1946), 1, 156n9
INCOM/Settimana INCOM, 3, 81n20
Ingrao, Pietro, 29, 61, 95, 96, 111n9, 125, 126, 128, 150, 212
Intellettuali organici (organic intellectuals), 27, 31
Iotti, Nilde, 231, 232
Iron Curtain, 25, 181
I sette fratelli Cervi (The seven Cervi brothers) (1968), 213
Istituto Luce, 3, 213, 266
Italian road to socialism, 94, 101, 151
Italnoleggio, 186, 194
It's a Wonderful Life (1946), 2
Ivens, Ioris, 131

J
Jazz, 273
John XXIII (Pope), 126, 127
Johnson, Lyndon, 141, 152

K
Khrushchev, Nikita, 93, 97, 98, 100, 101, 124
Kozlov, Frol, 102

L
La classe operaia va in Paradiso (The Working Class Goes to Heaven, 1971), 155n5
La Hora de Los Hornos (The Hour of the Furnaces, 1968), 165
La lotta non è finita (The fight is not yet over, 1973), 241n16
Lama, Luciano, 190
L'amore (1948), 34
La Repubblica (newspaper), 39n38, 211, 234
La strada (1954), 29, 34

288 SUBJECT INDEX

La terrazza (The Terrace, 1980), 210
Le Ciel, la Terre (The Sky and the
Earth, 1965), 131
Legame di Ferro (iron link), 23
Legge truffa (swindle law), 26, 37n18
Lenin/Leninism/Leninist, 22, 55, 74,
75, 83n44, 96, 101, 120, 124,
127, 149, 269
Leone, Giovanni, 189, 199n30, 210
Lettera ad una professoressa,
152, 156n11
Lettera aperta a un giornale della sera
(Open Letter to an Evening
Newspaper, 1970), 173
Levi, Carlo, 69, 70
Li Puma, Epifanio, 77
Libertas Film, 1, 71
Liguori, Paolo, 151
Lizzani, Carlo, 5, 7, 12n4, 29, 30, 33,
35, 38n37, 47, 59, 66, 69, 70,
81n21, 83n39, 134n5, 145, 213,
260, 266, 270
Lombardini, Sirio, 127
Longo, Luigi, 56, 107, 121, 125–128,
150, 151, 220n9
Lorenzini, Ennio, 127, 135n20
Lorusso, Francesco, 247
Lotta Continua, 151, 166, 167, 184,
247, 256
Lotta Femminista, 231
Lotte alla Rhodiatoce (Struggle at the
Rhodiatoce, 1969), 162,
163, 170
Luglio '60/July 1960, 93, 111n6
Lumumba, Patrice, 149
L'Unità (newspaper), 4, 19, 27,
30, 33, 34, 39n42, 53, 55, 59,
61, 73, 83n44, 97, 108,
128–130, 183, 184, 192,
200n45, 210, 219n7, 220n10,
220n11, 240n7, 241n13, 253,
254, 265, 272, 273

M
Macaluso, Emanuele, 132
Macciocchi, Maria Antonietta, 112n14
Maderna, Bruno, 273
Mafai, Miriam, 230
Mafia, 53, 80n16
Malaspina, Luciano, 118, 130
Manfredi, Nino, 205
Mangini, Cecilia, 93, 224, 225, 228,
237, 240n3, 272, 275n5
Maoism/Maoist tendency within the
PCI, 159
Maraini, Dacia, 197n6
Marchesi, Concetto, 28
Marini, Giovanna, 191, 255, 273
Marshall Plan, 13n6, 25, 54
Marx, Karl, 55, 72, 73, 83n44,
152, 269
Marzabotto, 99
Maselli, Francesco, 134n5, 173,
256, 259
Matteotti, Giacomo, 214
Mazzarella, Carlo, 1, 12n2
MDL (Movimento di Liberazione
della donna/Woman Liberation
Movement), 225, 231,
233, 241n14
Mida, Massimo, 112n14
Milani, Lorenzo (Don
Milani), 156n11
Militant cinema, *see* Cinema militante
Minucci, Adalberto, 258
Minzoni, Giovanni (Don
Minzoni), 214
Miracle in Milan (1951), 33
Mondine, 77
Morandi, Gianni, 205, 206
Moro, Aldo, 208, 240n7, 250
Morosini, Giuseppe (Don
Morosini), 211
Movimento del '77 (Movement of
1977), 245–251, 253

SUBJECT INDEX   289

MSI (Movimento Sociale Italiano), 111n6, 171, 180, 187, 188, 191, 192, 196, 214
Mussolini, Vittorio, 30

N

Napolitano, Giorgio, 182, 187, 217, 232
Napolitano, Riccardo, 260, 270
Natale, Roberto, 52
Natoli, Dario, 130, 192, 194, 220n9, 256, 257
Natta, Alessandro, 217, 220n12
Negri, Antonio, 271
Nenni, Pietro, 76
Neorealismo/neorealism, 7, 19–21, 30–35, 39n42, 70, 71, 73, 79, 165
Neorealismo Rosa (pink neorealism), 34, 35
Neotelevisione, 275
NET (Nuova Emittenza Televisiva/ New Television Broadcasting), 258, 261n20
New American Cinema Group, 160
Nicolini, Renato, 259
Noi Donne (magazine), 27, 225, 228
Nono, Luigi, 131, 273
Novelli, Diego, 81n21, 111n8, 180, 183, 258, 260
Nuova sinistra, 124, 129, 134n11, 160, 161, 172

O

Occhetto, Achille, 110n1, 133, 148, 150, 155n8, 275
October Revolution, 74, 132
Ombre Rosse (magazine), 160, 161, 163, 169, 170, 172
Ophüls, Marcel, 214
Ossessione (1943), 30, 134n6

P

Paese sera (newspaper), 27, 83n37, 187, 192, 200n45, 215
Pajetta, Gian Carlo, 23, 45, 52, 80n1, 107, 136n31, 206, 212, 218, 220n12, 253
Paola (1969), 167
Papi, Ugo, 128
Parri, Ferruccio, 128, 141
Partigiani della Pace (Partisans for Peace), 84n45
Partito nuovo, 19–35, 65, 74
Partito radicale, 234
Partito Social-Democratico Italiano/ Italian Social Democratic Party/ Social Democrats (PSDI), 81n23, 93, 127
Partito Socialista Italiano, *see* PSI (Italian Socialist Party)
Pasolini, Pier Paolo, 29, 122, 123, 159, 164, 166, 167, 174n9, 207
Paul VI (Pope), 126, 127
PCF (French Communist Party), 25, 81n21, 134n8
PDS (Partito Democratico della Sinistra/Democratic Party of the Left), 65
Peaceful coexistence (policy), 100–102, 126, 135n16
Pecchioli, Ugo, 184
Pellegrini, Glauco, 52, 80n13, 100, 119
Perelli, Luigi, 187–190, 195, 197n6, 253, 260
Pesaro Film Festival, 160, 164, 173n5
Petri, Elio, 134n5, 198n14
Petruccioli, Claudio, 129
Piano Solo, 141, 142
Piazza Fontana (massacre), 147, 155n7, 166, 180, 189

290 SUBJECT INDEX

Pietrangeli, Antonio, 50, 191
Pietrangeli, Paolo, 191, 260, 273
Pinelli, Giuseppe, 166
Pintor, Luigi, 125
Pionieri/pioneers, 63, 77, 225
Pius XII (Pope), 126
Politica unitaria (unifying policy),
    116, 126, 127, 129, 133, 139,
    151, 170, 271
Polizzi, Rosaria, 232, 234, 236, 237,
    239, 260
Pontecorvo, Gillo, 5, 47, 75, 260
Prague Spring, 195, 269
Pratolini, Vasco, 80n13
Press and Propaganda Section/Sezione
    stampa e propaganda, 5, 21,
    45, 49, 77–79, 91, 95, 96,
    105–107, 109, 111n10, 117,
    118, 126, 128, 129, 131–133,
    139, 141, 148, 150, 154, 162,
    181, 182, 239, 258,
    265–267
Prison Notebooks, 23, 24, 27, 270
Proietti, Gigi, 205, 206, 213
PSI (Italian Socialist Party),
    22, 25, 26, 48, 74, 76, 93,
    94, 96, 109, 111n7, 116,
    125, 127, 129, 133, 180,
    189, 193, 210, 240n7,
    250, 257
Psichiatria Democratica (Democratic
    Psychiatry), 193
Purini, Franco, 151

Q

Quaderni Piacentini, 124, 134n11
Quaderni Rossi, 124, 134n11
*Quaderno del propagandista/
    dell'attivista* (magazine), 13n9
Questione meridionale/southern
    question, 47, 66

R

RAI (Radiotelevisione Italiana),
    38n30, 91, 92, 103, 106–108,
    110, 119, 167, 187, 193, 194,
    197n6, 199n36, 209, 210, 214,
    220n9, 221n20, 228, 256,
    257, 274
Rauti, Pino, 191
Ravaioli, Carla, 224, 232
Red Brigades, 208, 209, 213, 219n5,
    219n6, 250
Reggio revolt, 171
Regioni rosse, 2, 26
Reichlin, Alfredo, 254, 255
Renzi, Renzo, 132
Resistenza/Resistance, 22, 25, 54, 72,
    75, 77, 83n37, 99, 123, 130,
    141, 149, 167, 171, 189, 203,
    204, 213–217
Riflusso, 173, 244, 255
Rinascita (magazine), 4, 13n8, 27,
    30, 38n29, 38n32, 98, 112n11,
    129, 150, 161, 191, 192,
    200n44, 220n9, 220n12, 253
Riso Amaro (1949), 12n2, 34
Rivolta Femminile, 231
Rock (music), 273, 274
Rodari, Gianni, 71, 81n22, 83n37,
    100, 215
Romagnoli, Luciano, 113n29
Rome 11 o'clock (1952), 33
Rome, open city (1945), 19–21, 25,
    33, 34, 211
Rossanda, Rossana, 125, 139
Rossellini, Roberto, 19, 21, 31,
    32, 34, 211
Rotunno, Giuseppe, 75
Rouch, Jean, 143
RSI (Repubblica Sociale Italiana), 22,
    80n13, 187
Russian avant-garde/Soviet
    formalism, 58, 132

S

Salinari, Carlo, 29, 32, 37n26, 115
Sartre, Jean-Paul, 99
Satta Flores, Stefano, 213
Scagnetti, Aldo, 30, 34, 39n41
Scalzone, Oreste, 150–152
Scavuzzo, Beppe, 162
Scelba, Mario, 38n30, 191, 192
Scola, Ettore, 5, 180, 183, 184, 207, 210, 255, 260, 273
Secchia, Pietro, 23, 26, 37n21, 56, 75, 76, 197n3
Segre, Daniele, 194, 200n41
Serandrei, Mario, 119, 134n6
Sereni, Emilio, 28, 32, 37n25
Seroni, Adriana, 232
Serra, Gianni, 193, 199n36
Sezione Stampa e Propaganda, *see* Press and Propaganda Section/ Sezione stampa e propaganda
Shoeshine (1946), 33
Sinistra extraparlamentare (extraparliamentary left), 184, 203
Sino-Vietnamese War, 251
Socialist realism, 20, 28, 29, 32, 34, 45–79, 272
Soldati, Mario, 99, 112n15
Sonego, Rodofo, 52
Sordi, Alberto, 159
Sorel, Jean, 159
Soviet cinema/films/cinematography, 20, 48–51, 66, 122, 132, 272
Soviet Union/URSS, 20, 23, 28, 74, 77, 83n45, 94, 96–98, 100, 102, 110, 127, 130, 204, 215, 218, 251, 267, 269
Sovversivi (1967), 122, 123
Spano, Velio, 83n44
Spina, Sergio, 103
Spinella, Mario, 265

Spriano, Paolo, 36n6, 36n11, 65, 213, 215, 220n12
Sputnik, 91–110
Squadrismo, 180, 197n3
Stalin, 7, 20, 23, 24, 26, 28, 36n8, 45–79, 122, 132, 215, 266, 267
Stalinism/Stalinist(s), 23, 25, 46, 47, 49, 59, 65, 72, 82n27, 96, 251, 266
Strategia della tensione (strategy of tension), 180, 188, 192, 247
Stromboli (1950), 34
Student movement, 9, 124, 139, 148–152, 155, 163–165, 170, 171, 245, 247, 253
Suez Crisis, 97
Super 8 (film format), 141, 153, 154
Suslov, Mikhail, 127
Svolta di Salerno (Salerno Turn), 10, 22, 24, 75, 149, 204, 214–216, 220n12
Szklarska Poręba (conference), 25

T

Tambroni, Fernando, 111n6
Taviani, Paolo e Vittorio (Taviani brothers), 5, 6, 12n4, 13n10, 103, 106, 113n29, 122, 123, 134n5, 134n9, 141, 206, 259, 260, 267
Tchertkoff, Vladimir, 198n19
Television/television broadcasting, 3, 8, 12n2, 91–110, 115, 181, 187, 191, 192, 194, 199n36, 200n41, 206, 209, 210, 214, 220n9, 257, 258, 274, 275, 276n9
Terracini, Umberto, 107, 215
Terzo Canale, 133, 140–143, 145, 147, 153, 154, 181, 195, 271
Third Cinema (movement), 165

292 SUBJECT INDEX

Third International, 36n7, 75
Thorez, Maurice, 83n44, 134n8
Togliatti, Palmiro, 8–10, 13n8, 19–35, 36n8, 36n13, 36n14, 37n23, 46, 51–65, 74–77, 80n15, 81n21, 81n22, 82n23, 83n44, 84n46, 97, 98, 100–102, 107, 108, 112n18, 112n19, 112n23, 113n28, 115–133, 149, 204, 210–212, 214, 216–218, 245, 254, 255, 265, 267, 270, 271
Toti, Gianni, 164, 195, 200n45
Trastulli, Luigi, 77, 84n47
Trentin, Bruno, 247
Tribuna elettorale, 107, 109
Trombadori, Antonello, 31, 39n40, 50, 112n14, 115
Two Cents Worth of Hope (1952), 33

U

Uccellacci e uccellini (The Hawks and the Sparrows, 1966), 122
Ufficio cinema (Film office), 182, 197–198n8
Umberto D (1952), 33
Unione dei comunisti Italiani / Union of the Italian Communists(UCI), 167
Unione Donne Italiane/Union of Italian Women(UDI), 225, 227, 231–235, 237
United States (US), 23, 25, 100, 129–131, 141, 143, 169, 187, 188, 192, 199n26, 218, 221n20, 250
United States Information Service (USIS), 3

Unitelefilm (UTF), 2, 3, 6, 8, 9, 12n4, 79, 92, 108–110, 111n6, 112n20, 113n29, 115–133, 140, 142, 143, 146, 147, 151, 153–155, 159–162, 167–169, 172, 179–197, 197n6, 205, 210, 213, 220n9, 223, 225, 228, 232, 236, 244, 256, 258–260, 267–271, 273, 274, 275n2

V

Valentini, Venturo, 181
Valenzi, Maurizio, 252
Vanni, Luciano, 258, 261n20
Venice Film Festival, 49, 159, 165, 187, 194
Verga, Giovanni, 70, 71
Vergano, Aldo, 1, 2, 12n1, 156n9
Verismo, 70
Via delle Botteghe Oscure, 56, 119
Via italiana al socialismo, *see* Italian road to socialism
Viazzi, Luciano, 112n14
Vie nuove (magazine), 27, 142, 200n45
Vietnam/Vietnam War, 4, 8, 116, 129–131, 133, 136n31, 147, 149, 152, 173, 230, 251, 256, 268, 271
Visconti, Luchino, 30–33, 38n32, 39n37, 70, 134n6
Viva il 1° maggio rosso e proletario (Long live the Red and Proletarian Labor day, 1969), 167
Volontè, Gian Maria, 131, 155n5, 168

Y

Yalta memorandum, 100, 116, 200n44

Z

Zaccagnini, Sergio, 141
Zafred, Mario, 73, 83n39, 272
Zangheri, Renato, 253
Zavattini, Cesare, 38n32, 98, 99, 161, 164–166, 172
Zavoli, Sergio, 214, 219n6
Zhdanov, Andrei, 25, 28, 37n24, 60
Zhdanovism, 20, 28, 29, 58, 164
Zurlini, Valerio, 119, 134n5

Printed in the United States
by Baker & Taylor Publisher Services